QUIXOTE'S SOLDIERS

For my colleague Beth —

Let's keep the dream alive!

abrazos

David Montejano

Sept 2010

NUMBER TWENTY-SIX

*Jack and Doris Smothers Series in
Texas History, Life, and Culture*

QUIXOTE'S

A LOCAL HISTORY OF THE
CHICANO MOVEMENT,
1966–1981

SOLDIERS

DAVID MONTEJANO

UNIVERSITY OF TEXAS PRESS ⤣ AUSTIN

Publication of this work was made possible in part by support from the J. E. Smothers, Sr., Memorial Foundation and the National Endowment for the Humanities.

Requests for permission to reproduce
material from this work should be sent to:
    Permissions
    University of Texas Press
    P.O. Box 7819
    Austin, TX 78713-7819
    www.utexas.edu/utpress/about/bpermission.html

∞ The paper used in this book meets the minimum
requirements of ANSI/NISO Z39.48-1992 (R1997)
(Permanence of Paper).

Library of Congress Cataloging-in-Publication Data

Montejano, David, 1948–
    Quixote's soldiers : a local history of the Chicano movement,
1966–1981 / David Montejano. — 1st ed.
       p.   cm. — (Jack and Doris Smothers series in Texas history,
life, and culture ; no. 26)
    Includes bibliographical references and index.
    ISBN 978-0-292-72124-1 (cloth : alk. paper) —
    ISBN 978-0-292-72290-3 (pbk. : alk. paper)
    1. Mexican Americans—Texas—San Antonio—History—20th
century. 2. Mexican Americans—Texas—San Antonio—Politics and
government—20th century. 3. Chicano movement—Texas—San Antonio. 4. San Antonio (Tex.)—Race relations—History—20th century.
5. San Antonio (Tex.)—Politics and government—20th century. I. Title.
    F394.S21 19M51736 2010
    305.8968'720730764351—dc22
                                           2010000793

Pa' mi hermana Diana y las mujeres en lucha.

[H]istorians must and ought to be exact, truthful, and absolutely free of passions, for neither interest, fear, rancor, nor affection should make them deviate from the path of the truth.

MIGUEL DE CERVANTES, *Don Quixote,* First Part, Chapter IX

CONTENTS

ACKNOWLEDGMENTS

FOR A PROJECT THAT HAS LINGERED for some three decades, there are many people to thank. A few follow. I ask forgiveness from those I may have overlooked.

In San Antonio, Diana Montejano, Rodolfo Rosales, Mario Compean, Willie Velásquez, George Velásquez, and Rosie Castro, all of them participants in one way or another in the Chicano movement, were critical for capturing the San Antonio story. Diana introduced me to the Brown Berets and provided feedback on the writing. In some ways, this history is also her story. Rodolfo not only gave me feedback, but he passed along copies of movimiento newspapers and interviews he had collected for his own work. At different points, Mario, George or Rosie kept me informed and also kept me "straight" about what I was doing. Willie just kept encouraging me to finish. Naturally I salute the Beret leadership—Juan Guajardo, Ben Guajardo, Jerry Arispe, Lalo Martínez, "L.A." Dave Martínez, José Morales, Victor San Miguel, Frank San Miguel, Paul Hernández, Ernesto Fraga, and Susana Almanza—who admitted me into their confidence. And the twenty or so other batos who let me hang around with them obviously deserve my warmest thanks. Without them, there would have been no story. I also wish to thank the social workers—Mike Bustamante, Eduardo Villarreal, Ernesto Gómez, Jesse Sauceda, and Tomás Atencio—who provided the context for the story.

Although my professors then at Yale University—Wendell Bell, Kai Erikson, Stanley Greenberg, John Kendrick, and Rodolfo Alvarez—never saw much of this project, I thank them for their encouragement and support way back then in the mid-seventies. A residential fellowship from the School of American Research (SAR) in Santa Fe, New Mexico, in the late eighties renewed my faith in the project. Jonathan Haas of SAR, Richard Fox, David Noble, and the other SAR fellows and associates provided important feedback on my initial thinking about the research I had carried out. A faculty grant from the University of New Mexico allowed me to employ graduate students Angélica Luna and Elena Gallegos of Albuquerque for transcription work. Tobías Durán, professor and director of the Center for Regional Studies, University of New Mexico, provided moral support over a number of years, as well as a summer grant. Armando Villarreal was a good sounding board.

A second sabbatical in the mid-nineties at the Center for Advanced Studies in the Behavioral Sciences (CASBS) in Stanford, California, gave me the time to write and rewrite chapter drafts, and to consider the prospects of actual publication. CASBS editor Robert Scott, fellow resident Carlos Vélez-Ibáñez, and, on the Stanford campus below, Renato Rosaldo, Mary Pratt, and Ben Olguín provided a very supportive environment. A generous grant from CASBS and the University of Texas at Austin Faculty Development Program made my year at Stanford possible. Several modest faculty research grants from the University of California, Berkeley, provided the support to bring this project to a conclusion.

A number of resource individuals provided critical support for this project. Regarding the Henry B. Gonzalez Collection, Christopher Anglim, then the Government Documents librarian at St. Mary's University in San Antonio, and Patrick Cox, associate director of the Center for American History, University of Texas at Austin, were extremely generous with their assistance. Clarissa Chavira of the Texana department of the San Antonio Public Library provided much needed juvenile delinquency reports at the request of a stranger emailing from California. Tom Shelton and Patrick Lemelle of the Institute of Texan Cultures at the University of Texas at San Antonio were an important resource for historical photographs. Ricardo Romo, César Martínez, Gregg Barrios, and George and Andrea Velásquez shared their collection of documents and photographs with me. Emiliano Calderon did yeoman service as my research assistant in San Antonio. Margo Gutierrez of the Benson Latin American Collection, University of Texas at Austin, and Lily Castillo-Speed of the Ethnic Studies Library at UC Berkeley helped me recover some priceless images. Analisa Xavier, Marcella Garcia, and Sonia Montejano prepared the maps, charts, diagrams, and images. I also wish to acknowledge Ignacio García, Armando Navarro, and Rodolfo Rosales, whose scholarship on the Raza Unida Party, MAYO, and San Antonio politics (respectively) served as critical reference points for this history. Rosales and I continue our dialogue on the meaning of "inclusion." Gracias a todos!

I am especially indebted to the readers of early drafts of the book. Emilio Zamora, David Montgomery, Martín Sánchez-Jankowski, David Matza, Philip Gonzales, Andrés Jiménez, and Roberto Hernández read various incarnations of the entire manuscript and offered important recommendations. Ed Garcia, Toni Nelson-Herrera, Juan Esteva, Pablo González, Jaime Mejía, Sonia Montejano, and Christine Trost also provided welcome feedback on various chapters. Finally, for her support during the "final push" of this long-overdue book project, Veronica Garcia has my everlasting gratitude. None of the above, of course, is responsible for the following interpretation.

Brown Berets from San Antonio, Dallas, and Austin lead a protest to the Texas State Capitol, Austin, October 11, 1974. Photo by Alan Pogue.

QUIXOTE'S SOLDIERS

INTRODUCTION

THIS IS A LOCAL HISTORY with national pretensions. The geographical scope of the narrative is largely limited to San Antonio, Texas, and to nearby areas. Change the names of people and neighborhoods, however, and we see a similar storyline of social and political change playing out in the late sixties and early seventies in Albuquerque, Denver, Los Angeles, and other southwestern cities. A reference to the South is not unseemly: in the sixties, San Antonio was considered a "moderate" city, similar in race relations and segregationist practices to Little Rock, St. Louis, Cincinnati, Baltimore, and other urban areas of the southern fringe—with the exception that its restive "minority" community consisted of Mexican Americans. The best comparative case is arguably Atlanta, a similarly sized city with a similarly complex race-class order, and one that experienced similar political convulsions during the sixties and seventies. Indeed, change the accents and skin color of the political actors, and the following history becomes one of the many movement narratives of social change that shook nearly all the major urban areas of the country during that time. In the South and Southwest, these movements basically took down the last legal-political vestiges of Jim Crow segregation.[1] This local history was part of that national political transformation.

Except for those who lived in the Southwest, Mexican Americans were a somewhat invisible "minority" in the sixties. Unlike the national presence of African Americans, Mexican Americans at that time had a smaller population and were regionally concentrated in the southwestern margins of the country. Not surprisingly, then, the post–World War II history of protest against segregation and discrimination waged by the "second race" is not generally known. That history has remained somewhat isolated from the main civil rights narrative.

The Chicano movement of the mid-sixties was fueled by essentially the same provocations that had fueled the Black civil rights movement since the early fifties: segregation, poverty, and racism. Most Mexican Americans lived in poor urban neighborhoods. In Los Angeles, police brutality and urban renewal added to the anxieties of barrio residents. In Denver, police brutality and lack of political representation loomed as key community issues. What worried those in San Antonio were the annual floods and the biennial gang wars, along with police brutality. Throughout the region, most Mexican American youths attended ill-equipped schools and faced limited vocational career paths. Not surprisingly, then, the winds of change generated by the Black civil rights movement, then already a decade old, found favorable ground among barrio youths and helped ignite a parallel race-ethnic movement.[2]

The specific spark was set off by the California and Texas farmworker strikes of 1965–1966. These strikes—known as "la causa," or "the cause"—struck a resonant chord among urban Mexican American college students, most of whom were only a generation removed from the fields. They joined the support committees, acquired experience, and elaborated ideas about equality and justice. In a short time, these politicized students left the farmworker cause and created new organizations focused on other issues facing Mexican American communities. They recruited others and broadened the message of "la causa" beyond its farmworker meaning to refer to a general race-ethnic struggle for civil rights.[3]

The intensity of these efforts created a social movement that transformed the pejorative lower-class labels of "Chicano" and "Chicana" into positive identities. These new identities, based on the notions of "la raza unida" (the united people) and "carnalismo" (brotherhood and sisterhood), came to signify solidarity among activists and believers. As cultural nationalists, most activists and intellectuals drew on Mexican and Mexican American history and culture for their motivating lessons. Some established mythological connections with the Aztecs and rechristened the Southwest "Aztlán," the name of an ancient northern Aztec homeland. The Cuban Revolution, like the Mexican Revolution, also became an iconic reference for social change. Chicano art, music, drama, and literature emerged to give vivid expression to the nationalist sentiment. Within a few short years of the initial farmworker strikes, "la causa" had inspired a political and cultural renaissance among Mexican American youths of the Southwest.[4]

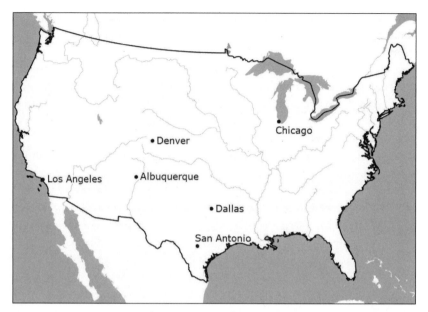

Major urban hubs of the Chicano movement.

Not surprisingly, these Chicano youths soon ran afoul of their conservative elders, not to mention the Anglo authorities. The more militant youths were causing trouble in high schools and on college campuses, and insulting and directly challenging the police and the political establishment. Young twenty-somethings were running for political office and, in Texas, were organizing a third political party whose gubernatorial candidate was just twenty-nine years old. These impatient youths were rejecting their parents' gradualist posture and calling for the downfall of "gringo supremacy."[5]

The following history takes a major urban area impacted by the Chicano movement and subjects it to close examination. The narrative looks at the barrios of San Antonio and describes the generational and class conflicts that erupted, the collective identities that shifted, and the political changes that took place as a result. The case of San Antonio is especially important because it is the one major urban area where the Chicano movement can arguably claim a victory. In fact, the organizing energies generated by that singular success have had, and continue to have, regional and national repercussions.

As I detail in the following chapters, the militant challenge of the movement activists would be blunted by internal divisions within the Mexican

American community, but such activism, nonetheless, greatly enhanced the organizational capacity of the working-class barrios. This kind of pressure "from below" proved to be a critical factor in the downfall of the long-standing Anglo political elite in the mid-seventies. Facing a seemingly radical movement, a reluctant elite proved receptive to Mexican American middle-class and working-class demands for political entry.[6] By the late seventies, a new political order, more inclusive and responsive to the needs of barrio neighborhoods, had been established.

The following narrative offers a thick description of these events. But it is also guided by a series of questions about social movements. Just exactly how did the movement impact the barrios? How can one measure this impact? How did such rapid mobilization happen? And what did "becoming political" mean for barrio youths? For the gang members? For the women? Moreover, how could such pressure bring down the entrenched political establishment? A close-up examination offers some answers to these questions.

Because this history is guided by these sociological concerns, I at times refer to my text as a "narrative explanation." Several arguments and sub-arguments are embedded in the following narrative explanation. As a form of preview, let me make explicit the main points.

Organization of the Narrative

The narrative is divided into three parts that follow a rough chronological order. Part 1 deals with 1966–1971, Part 2 with 1971–1975, and Part 3 with 1974–1981.

Part 1, "The Conflict Within," describes the bitter clash that erupted within the Mexican American community over the aggressive nationalism of movement activists. Ironically, such discord surfaced as movement organizing and experimenting brought an end to the gang warfare that had periodically paralyzed the working-class barrios. A singular if little noticed achievement of the Chicano movement in San Antonio—and undoubtedly elsewhere—took place when neighborhood cliques transcended their local identities and assumed an overarching race-ethnic Chicano identity. For a few years, the message of unity and brotherhood interrupted the cycle of barrio warfare.

Part 2, "Marching Together Separately," takes a close look at the dynamic evolution of a movement and identifies an organizational "structuring" along gender and class lines. The movement message of equality and justice for the Chicano community was interpreted and honed through group-specific experiences and interests, giving rise to group-specific organizations. Using the language of the movement, women activists questioned machismo and the double standard, and began to form their own organizations. Using the language of "la causa" and "carnalismo," the politicized barrio youths, concerned about gang warfare and police harassment, created paramilitary organizations and set out to establish neighborhood peace. Women created space to press for respect and equity, while former gang members sought legitimacy for the organizational space they already had.

Part 3, "After the Fury," steps back from a focus on barrio youths to address the larger picture of political change in San Antonio. I consider the question of leadership as it appeared to the Mexican American community in the mid-seventies. I draw on a handful of biographies to illustrate the role of individual agency in the demise and transformation of the Chicano movement, and I make a distinction between "unrealized" and "realized" leadership, resting the distinction on whether or not "organizational capacity" had been created.

Despite formidable opposition from authorities and many "wrong turns" in the area of leadership, the Chicano movement can lay claim to a worthy legacy: a virtual overhaul of the Mexican American organizational field and of San Antonio's political system. These changes were brought about by movement-influenced organizations, or by what I call "second-generation" movement organizations. These played a critical part in securing the election of Henry Cisneros as mayor in 1981. As the first mayor of Mexican descent since Juan Seguín of the Texas Republic days, Cisneros symbolized a new inclusive political order. An equally visible break occurred with the increasingly prominent presence of Mexican American women in the political arena, signaling a significant change in gender roles. The training of much of this leadership had come from the second-generation movement organizations.

One commentator has suggested that San Antonio is too unique a case to serve as a template for other towns and cities in the Southwest. It would be more accurate to say, in the words of movement activist Juan Maldonado of the Rio Grande Valley, that "San Antonio sets the pace. As San Antonio goes, so goes the rest of South Texas."[7] By the 1980s, these second-generation movement organizations, having consolidated their San Antonio base, had begun exporting their organizing models throughout the Southwest and Midwest. Over time, related projects began springing up in urban centers across the country, from the Pacific Northwest to the East Coast. Even today, some thirty years after the movement, a notable share of the political organizing in Latino communities in the United States can trace a lineage to the Chicano organizations and activists of San Antonio in the seventies.[8] The transformation of San Antonio, in short, had wide-ranging, long-term consequences for Latino politics in the United States.

Being a Native

As a San Antonio native, my narrative explanation has a certain autobiographical quality to it. Hardly anyone living in a San Antonio barrio in the 1950s and 1960s could ignore the gang youths known as "pachucos." I grew up in a West Side subdivision built in the early 1950s, in the Edgewood School District, one of the poorest in the state and later made famous for its successful challenge of the state's educational financing schema. My neighborhood was a poor, working-class neighborhood surrounded by poorer neighborhoods on three sides. The Menchaca Courts, a public housing project, was only a few blocks away. As adolescents, my brother and sister and I had a few run-ins, consisting of rock throwing and verbal insults, with the young pachucos of Menchaca Courts. This kind of conflict reinforced parental admonitions to stay away from pachucos, and it reinforced our sense of caution whenever we walked by "los courts." On the fourth side of the neighborhood, across a wide thoroughfare, was the beginning of the middle-class Anglo North Side. The name of the avenue was Culebra, meaning "snake," a seemingly appropriate name for the line of separation between Anglo and Mexican at the time. I recall sensing as much tension when crossing Culebra and walking through the Anglo neighborhood as when walking by Menchaca Courts.

My working-class neighborhood was not like the very poor communities of the "sal si puedes" (get out if you can) sort, like the Menchaca Courts seemed to be, but it had poverty, and many families struggled to make ends meet. The contrast was evident in the vastly different paths into adulthood that the adolescents from my barrio followed. Some made it into the middle class, others maintained the working-class status of their parents, and still others slid into greater poverty. Tony, our local grocer and owner of Tony's Family Market, kept a mental inventory of the life trajectories of the neighborhood kids. "You and Diana did fine," he once told me. "Your neighbors didn't turn out so well—drugs and murder. Willie and George [Velásquez] on Laurel [Street] did fine, but Fulano down the block died of an overdose. His sister, on the other hand, went to business college."[9] In that sense the neighborhood was a crossroads—a hit-or-miss, up-or-down, out-or-further-in sort of place.

In a curious way, then, my working-class neighborhood afforded views of great economic contrast: a checkered pattern within the neighborhood, obvious poverty close by on three sides, and across the wide asphalt boundary of Culebra Avenue, what seemed like affluence at the time. In my previous work, *Anglos and Mexicans in the Making of Texas*, I addressed the racial boundary represented by Culebra Avenue.[10] In this work, I turn my gaze back toward the barrios.

This account is based on newspaper articles; biographies; organizational papers; congressional documents and papers; reports from police, the FBI, and social work agencies; and interviews with key participants—ample material, in short, for reconstructing and interpreting the events of the period with some confidence. I carried out much of the research in the mid-seventies with the intention of using the material for a dissertation. For a number of reasons, I was unable to complete the project at that time. Since then, several primary and secondary sources have become available to provide a solid foundation for this narrative of social change.[11] The passage of time, and the perspective and documentation that time has provided, makes the writing of this history possible now.

This local history provides a microscopic look at the civil rights movement and the social change it engendered. It provides a sustained look at the agency and consciousness of "those from below." By focusing on young barrio men and women, I describe groups not usually considered in discussions of social movements. Generally the lower classes are presumed to live silently, misleading political observers into thinking that they have no distinctive agency. But then, in times of turmoil, they surface, surprising everyone with their voice and perspective. This is a narrative explanation about such a moment.

PART ONE

Valley marchers arrive in San Antonio, August 27, 1966. *San Antonio Express & News* Collection, University of Texas at San Antonio Institute of Texan Cultures, E-0012-187e-4.

THE CONFLICT WITHIN

IN EARLY 1966, the San Antonio newspapers were filled with front-page items that highlighted the protests and troubles taking place across the country. In mid-March (March 16–18), a flare-up involving "600 Negroes" had taken place in Watts, California. The disturbances, which had spread to Pacoima and involved Black and Mexican youths, were considered "minor" compared to the riot of the previous August, when thirty-four people had been killed and $30 million of damage inflicted. The following week, on March 27, thousands marched in anti–Vietnam War protests throughout the country. On April 11, striking grape pickers, led by César Chávez, completed a 300-mile march to Sacramento. And in mid-May, racial tensions in Los Angeles erupted again in "the Negro section," prompting Floyd McKissick, director of the Congress on Racial Equality (CORE), to warn of possible race violence in forty cities.[1] Against this backdrop, San Antonio appeared to be a bucolic oasis—with the exception of its Mexican barrios.

While the Black civil rights movement and the farmworker strikes were beginning to stir Mexican American communities throughout the Southwest, San Antonio was in the midst of juvenile gang warfare. Drive-by shootings in the Mexican "West Side" had become a regular occurrence and the subject of considerable public discussion. Six months of violence had left one dead and more than a dozen wounded. The death had occurred in front of the Good Samaritan Center after, in the words of a newspaper account, a "poor boy" dance. The settlement houses, established to serve the poor neighborhoods, ironically seemed to serve as sites for conflict; they seemed inadequate for the task of maintaining peace. Sgt. Dave Flores, speaking of the month of May, said, "We have been having a shooting in the area almost nightly for the past month."[2]

Later that summer, in August, a ragtag procession of one hundred striking farmworkers and supporters from the lower Rio Grande Valley marched through San Antonio, singing "We Shall Overcome." They were on their way to Austin to meet with the governor, John Connally. It was the first sign of a brewing political storm for San Antonio and South Texas. When Governor

Connally refused to meet with the marchers, the rebuff merely strengthened the resolve of the farmworkers and their youthful supporters. The farmworker cause gathered still more momentum when the Texas Rangers roughed up and arrested some strikers and supporters in a highly publicized confrontation a few months later. Through such high-profile conflict, the farmworker strikes in the lower Rio Grande Valley and in California became the catalyst for the first stirrings of a Chicano movement in San Antonio and throughout Texas.

In the mid-sixties, San Antonio was a paternalistic, segregated society ruled by a handful of old Anglo families. A sizable fraction of the population (four out of ten residents) lived in impoverished Mexican American barrios. The recognized Mexican American leadership was divided over how to respond to these conditions, on whether to stay to its gradualist approach to politics or to adopt a more aggressive stance. Into this discussion ventured some impatient college students who, inspired by César Chávez and the farmworker cause, began to challenge the established leadership. They recruited not just other students, but also the street youths into an emerging movement organization, the Mexican American Youth Organization (MAYO). One controversial MAYO project was a "freedom school" where college students and barrio youths could discuss and learn about "la causa" (the cause), "carnalismo" (brotherhood and sisterhood), and a "raza unida" (united people).

Through such deliberate efforts, the demand for equality and justice, framed within an ideology of Chicano cultural nationalism, touched all sections of the Mexican American community, including the "gang" youths of the impoverished barrios. School walkouts, protest rallies, and the emergence of a Chicano political party were consciousness-raising events for barrio youths. The formation of the Brown Berets was an organic expression of this political consciousness. As a result, the Chicano movement, with its emphases on la raza unida and carnalismo, introduced a semblance of peace and unity to the West and South sides of town.

The politicization of barrio youths would become a controversial matter in the late 1960s and early 1970s, commanding as much media attention as the gang wars of earlier years. The mobilization of angry working- and lower-class youths startled the established leadership of both the Anglo and Mexican American communities. Against a national backdrop of urban riots and increasing Black militancy, they worried about the signs of restlessness in the barrios. In the fifties and through the mid-sixties, the Anglo and Mexican American elites had guided San Antonio through a peaceful and gradual desegregation of city facilities and schools. A paternalistic arrangement had provided for some representation of Mexican Americans and African Americans on the city council and the school board. In 1961, San Antonio had elected Henry B. Gonzalez to Congress, another sign of the city's moderate outlook on race and ethnic relations. Nonetheless, the Chicano movement, by drawing attention to the rather obvious class and race inequities in the city and state, posed a strong challenge to this paternalistic arrangement. In defense of this status quo stepped Congressman Gonzalez, the old "radical" of the desegregation battles of the 1950s. The political climate became ugly.

The controversy reflected an internal disagreement within the Mexican American community over how to advance politically, a disagreement that surfaced mainly along social class and generational lines. Middle-class Mexican Americans were alarmed by the threatening rhetoric of the youthful Chicanos. The "old guard" leadership feared that these radical college and barrio youths would introduce the polarizing dynamics of racial violence that had already spread from Watts in California to the northern cities. For their part, some young Chicanos fanned this fear at every opportunity, calling for the elimination of racist "blue-eyed gringos" by any means necessary.

This internal community conflict surfaced publicly in several dramatic incidents involving fisticuffs, public denunciations, death threats, police surveillance, congressional inquiries, college expulsions, arrests, and prison sentences. For the Mexican American community of San Antonio and South Texas, the six-year period from 1968 to 1973 was not one of marching together, but of "vitriolic divisions of charge and counter-charge, bite and bite back, physical walk-outs and emotional blow-outs."[3] As a result of this political drama, some common Mexican insults referring to *machismo* (manhood) or lack thereof, *pendejos* (idiots), and *vendidos* (sellouts) became regular breakfast fare for the English-reading public of South Texas. Newspaper coverage, particularly that of Paul Thompson, gadfly columnist for the *San Antonio Express & News*, provided regular interpretations of the unfolding conflict.

In the following chapters of Part One, I describe the Chicano movement, the manner in which the so-called gang youths became part of it, and the reactions that all of this provoked.

THE LEAKING CASTE SYSTEM

1 IN THE MID-SIXTIES, San Antonio was, in the words of one insightful observer, "a city of deference and racial differences; it was still a southern center." San Antonio was "southern" in its segregation, even though the main racial divide was between Anglo and Mexican. The city's population (587,718 in 1960) was 51 percent Anglo, 41 percent Mexican American, and 7 percent African American. By 1965, due in part to Anglo migration to outlying suburbs, San Antonio was well on its way to becoming a Mexican American majority city.[1]

The city's racial neighborhood zones were plainly evident. The East Side was the Black side of town; the North Side was the Anglo side; and the West and South sides were considered the Mexican side of town. Despite some breeching of the walls, the boundaries of the Mexican side were clear in the mid-sixties: Culebra Street from Loop 410 across San Pedro Park to San Pedro Street formed the northernmost boundary; San Pedro Street through downtown, to its connection with Roosevelt, and Roosevelt as far as the Loop formed the eastern boundary; Loop 410 marked the western and southern boundaries of the Mexican side of town, nearly one-third of the city in the mid-sixties.

The stark segregation of this period was regularly commented on by outside observers. According to Leo Grebler, Joan Moore, and Ralph Guzman, a visiting social science team from UCLA, San Antonio appeared caste-like. However, because the rise of a new middle class among Mexican Americans had made the segregated order "somewhat less rigid," they qualified their description and called it a "leaking" caste system. Sociologist Buford Farris likewise described the social relations between Anglos and Mexican Americans in the mid-sixties as a "model of two almost separate systems." San Antonio, according to Farris, was a conflictual situation of "assimilation with resistance." Anglos perceived "a separate political unity" of Mexican Americans to be the "largest threat" to San Antonio. Speaking Spanish was also considered a threat. Mexican Americans, on the other hand, expressed support for ethnic political unity and saw Spanish as "an emotional language."[2]

Segregation was not just a question of separate systems, but of hierarchy and authority as well. Generally the only Anglos who entered the barrios were police officers, teachers, social workers, and bill collectors. Anglos were essentially individuals with authority. This was the gist of the testimony that seventeen-year-old Edgar Lozano, then a junior at Lanier High School, gave in 1968 when asked about the effects of segregated schooling on Mexican American students:

> Well, that is the only people you know. I mean, if you have only known Mexican American people, as far as you are concerned, that is the whole world right there.
>
> And then let's say you move out of that part of town, or you go to another city, then you meet nothing but Anglos. I mean, you know, that is strange to you. You have never met this type of people, maybe only as your teacher or your boss, or something else. So, consequently you have an idea that they're always—that they're always your boss, your supervisor and they always dress better, nicer, and they always tell you what to do.[3]

Segregation, in other words, embodied a hierarchy of both race and class.

The hierarchy built on segregation also made itself felt on the Anglo side of town. At the very top, a "stodgy old guard," as one observer described the city's elite, kept firm reins on the citizenry and on any new economic developments. "Twenty families," according to a former city manager, "ran San Antonio." A developer who moved to San Antonio from Dallas in 1963 described San Antonio of that time as "a little kingdom run by a small group of people who controlled all commerce and development."[4] At the head of this "little kingdom" was Walter McAllister—businessman, founder of the oldest and largest savings and loan, longtime civic leader, and mayor from 1961 to 1971. McAllister was the "moving force" behind the Good Government League (GGL), organized in the early fifties to promote business interests as well as efficiency in government. As the instrument of the business-political elite, the GGL dominated San Antonio politics for nearly two decades. The at-large elections for nine city council seats favored the GGL, which had the resources to recruit and finance full electoral slates. From 1955 to 1975, seventy-seven of eighty races for city council were won by members of the GGL. As aptly described by Kemper Diehl and Jan Jarboe, it was an "elitist" arrangement:

> San Antonio was a town ruled by a small group of businessmen who worked in downtown banks and law firms, played tennis, golf, and poker at the San Antonio Country Club, and were well-organized politically under the auspices of the GGL. Yes, it was elitist.[5]

Despite segregation, San Antonio was considered a "moderate" southern city because the GGL had included token representation from the Mexican and Black communities on its city council slates since the mid-fifties. Selected by a secret nominating committee of the Anglo business elite, these "minority" representatives rarely lived in the Mexican or Black neighborhoods.[6] Yet such token representation was a progressive step from the Jim Crow system of the 1940s, and it was emblematic of the paternalistic rule of San Antonio's Anglo business-political elite.

Much pressure for change had come from the activism of the World War II and Korean War veterans and the rising middle class of the Mexican American community. Although the GGL had extended its influence through a "West Side" branch, the Mexican American community occasionally elected a few mavericks—Albert Peña, Joe Bernal, Pete Torres, and early in his career, Henry B. Gonzalez—and these individuals kept the city moving forward in improving race relations. Prodded by Gonzalez, then a city councilman, the city had officially desegregated its schools and public facilities in the mid-fifties. In 1963 San Antonio began a voluntary desegregation of privately owned but publicly used facilities. As Mayor McAllister would later testify (in 1968), of the 655 hotels, motels, and restaurants that were impacted, "all but two motels and one restaurant voluntarily agreed to integrate." According to the mayor, a "spirit of tolerance in human relations" characterized the city of San Antonio.[7]

Paternalism rather than tolerance was a better description of the way the Anglo elite related to Mexican Americans at this time. County commissioner Albert Peña, a bitter critic of San Antonio's political and social structure, described the top as "a very, very small group of San Antonians, old families, with wealth and position." Below these few, at a second level, was a group several times as large, climbing their own ladders . . . in business, at the bar, and in the other professions. These are the men who take care of political strategy and governmental details, and they point out the civic direction. . . . They make their living as errand boys for those at the top—and a nice living it is.[8]

The third level down included the officeholders—those on the city council; the water, public service, and transit boards; the San Antonio Housing Authority; and some school boards. These individuals did "what they [were] expected to most of the time without question." In Peña's opinion, they were "little more than puppets."[9]

Perhaps nothing better symbolized the paternalistic relations of San Antonio than the annual public celebrations of "Fiesta Week." This weeklong commemoration of the defeat of Santa Anna in 1836 provided a festive occasion for entertaining the citizenry. A major sponsor of the events was the mounted Texas Cavaliers, whose appearance in "resplendent uniforms complete with swords" was meant to commemorate the fallen heroes of the Alamo. Each year the group would crown one of its members as "King

San Antonio City Council, 1966: *front, left to right*, Lila Cockrell, Mayor Walter McAllister, and John Gatti; *back, left to right*, Herbert Calderón, Robert Jones, S. H. James, Felix Treviño, Gerald Parker, and Ronald Bremer. Zintgraff Collection, University of Texas at San Antonio Institute of Texan Cultures, Z-2154-54849, courtesy of John and Dela White.

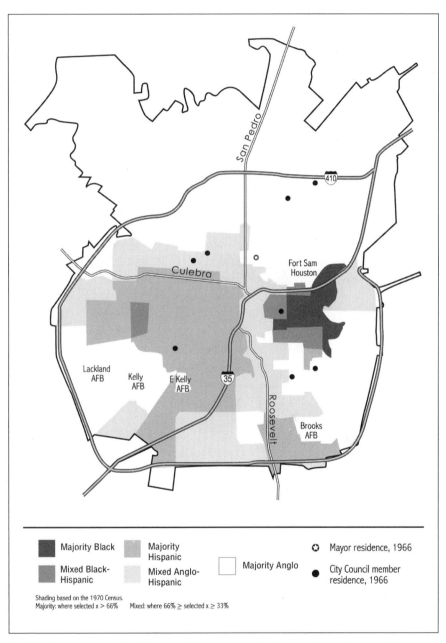

■	Majority Black	▨	Majority Hispanic	❂	Mayor residence, 1966
■	Mixed Black-Hispanic	▨	Mixed Anglo-Hispanic	●	City Council member residence, 1966
		□	Majority Anglo		

Shading based on the 1970 Census.
Majority: where selected x > 66%   Mixed: where 66% ≥ selected x ≥ 33%

Residential patterns and residences of the mayor and city council members, 1966.

Antonio" to head up the festival. The debutantes who comprised the Fiesta Court were likewise drawn from the upper ranks of San Antonio society.[10] Every April these festive displays of Anglo influence and beauty were paraded before a largely Mexican American spectator audience. But aside from the cheers and applause they gave the carriages, floats, and bands, the Mexicans of San Antonio expressed little love toward the city's leadership. In a satirical swipe at "King Antonio," the League of United Latin American Citizens (LULAC) created an alternative Rey Feo—the Ugly King—who quickly became a popular figure among the Mexican American population.

In the mid-sixties, outside influences were clearly threatening to upset the paternalistic and peaceful order of San Antonio. The Watts riot of August 1965 had signaled the beginning of many summers of urban race riots in the country, and "Black Power" signaled a new mood, an angry turn, in

LEFT: King Antonio, 1966 Fiesta, San Antonio. *San Antonio Express & News* Collection, University of Texas at San Antonio Institute of Texan Cultures, E-0012-0127-29A.

FACING: San Antonio Cavaliers, Battle of Flowers Parade, 1970. *San Antonio Light* Collection, University of Texas at San Antonio Institute of Texan Cultures, L-6474-A, courtesy of the Hearst Corporation.

a civil rights movement that was then more than a decade old. Indications suggested that this was beginning to influence the Mexican American communities of the Southwest.

Which Way for the Middle Class?

In the mid-sixties, middle-class Mexican Americans constituted perhaps as much as 20 percent of the Mexican American presence in San Antonio.[11] The social base for the middle class before World War II consisted of the exiled elite families who had fled Mexico during the 1910s and 1920s, on the one hand, and of small business families serving the Mexican community— the grocery store owners, the funeral parlor owners, the labor contractors, and so on—on the other. After the war, the veterans who used the GI Bill to receive college educations and secure federal jobs added a third prominent layer to middle-class ranks. In post–World War II San Antonio, federal employment at the city's five military bases anchored the growth of the Mexican American middle class.

The old middle-class families lived in modest barrio enclaves (in Prospect Hill on the West Side or in Riverside near downtown); members of the new middle class were buying homes in new subdivisions (Loma Park) or breaking into the previously race-restricted areas of Jefferson, Harlendale, Olmos Park, and even Alamo Heights.

The returning veterans and their families, emboldened by their proven loyalty, began to press openly for first-class citizenship and began a campaign against Jim Crow segregation. They organized poll tax drives, registered voters, and began to run for political office. Blatant instances of discrimination, such as the refusal of a funeral home to handle a soldier's body because he was Mexican, galvanized organizing efforts, especially by the American GI Forum, founded by Dr. Hector P. Garcia of Corpus Christi. Political activity increased in San Antonio as a result of efforts by LULAC, the American GI Forum, the Pan American Political Association (PAPA), and a host of other organizations.[12] These efforts resulted in important victories in desegregating the city's public facilities and buildings, schools, and in securing representation on the city council and school board. The political accomplishments of the World War II generation were personified in the pioneering career of Henry B. Gonzalez, who in the 1950s became "the first Mexican American" in memory to win a seat on San Antonio's city council, the first in memory to serve in the Texas Senate, the first to run for governor, and later (in 1961) the first from Texas to win a seat in Congress. While segregation and poverty remained the reality for most Mexican Americans, race relations in the 1950s and 1960s seemed qualitatively different from those of the 1930s and 1940s. Token representation on the city council and school board was seen as representing progress.[13]

In his excellent study of San Antonio, historian Richard García describes the new middle class of San Antonio and throughout the Southwest as "ideologically pragmatic, Americanist in its patriotism, and acutely conscious of its civic obligations to all Mexican Americans regardless of class and status." Reflecting Cold War anxieties, the new leadership was staunchly and reflexively anti-Communist, and constantly stressed their patriotism. The shift to Americanism, as educator and civil rights activist George I. Sanchez suggested in 1951, was a pragmatic way to continue political organizing and developing a civil rights movement given the "red scare" climate of the times. Nonetheless, middle-class reformers continued to emphasize the ethnic consciousness of Mexican Americans in using the concept of "la raza" as a rallying cry. This emerging group was intent on developing a mass political power base in order to secure more educational, legal, and economic opportunities for Mexican Americans.[14]

Although aggressive in challenging Jim Crow restrictions, the middle-class Mexican American leadership was basically conservative on the question of social change. It rejected anything that suggested "political radicalization from labor or the Communist party." In the 1950s, in the midst of the Cold War with the Soviet Union, Mexican Americans, like other Americans of that time, accepted the political consensus, "with its fear of communism and its adherence to McCarthyism." For this generation of Mexican Americans, as noted by García, "communism personified the anti-Christ."[15]

Nonetheless, the pressing poverty of "la raza" was a reality that Mexican American leaders could not ignore. Housing, education, sanitation, and drainage, for example, were all matters of community concern that called for some plan of action. Each flood that inundated the West and South sides of town reminded residents of their living conditions. Even the anointed Mexican American representatives of the GGL soon lost favor.

Consequently, sharp disagreements over what constituted "progress" and over the proper course of future action often surfaced among the Mexican American middle class. Nothing better illustrates the emotional import of this question than an exchange that took place in 1966 between "maverick" county commissioner Albert Peña and GGL city councilman Herbert Calderón in the pages of the *Texas Observer*. Peña, in calling for a "Marshall Plan" to alleviate the widespread poverty of Mexican Americans, excoriated the San Antonio "power structure." Peña had especially harsh words for the Mexican Americans who were part of this power structure:

The Mexican-American who by economic and social success should offer leadership instead lives in the affluent Northside and seeks acceptance and recognition by the Anglo power structure. These should-be leaders do serve on city boards and committees and are even allowed to run with the Anglo power structure-dominated city council. But San Antonio's power structure is no friend of the Mexican-American.[16]

Peña cited the explanation of Ed Idar, Jr., former chair and executive director of the national American GI Forum, that Mexican Americans did not complain about poverty, discrimination, and lack of opportunity because they "suffered from lack of leadership."[17]

Dr. Calderón—a dentist as well as city councilman, and thus one of those at the base of the power structure—responded in a blistering letter to Peña's analysis. Peña had the gall of accusing the "power structure" of exploiting the Mexican-American, noted Calderón, when Peña was "its greatest offender." Peña had "so effectively overplayed the theme of discrimination in San Antonio" that many people had lost confidence in their own resourcefulness, "thus remaining in economic and social isolation." Calderón acknowledged that "a certain amount of discrimination still exists" and that "positive measures must constantly be exerted" to eliminate it.

> But we cannot and should not blame anything and everything on discrimination. The Mexican-American has an obligation to himself and to society to make an honest effort to break out of the poverty cycle.[18]

Finally, noted Calderón, Peña had distorted the facts by complaining about the economic and social isolation of Mexican-Americans,

> while at the same time objecting to the tens of thousands who succeeded in breaking the poverty cycle and who have thus moved into other sections of the city. Mr. Peña objects to this geographic move because every person moving out of the West Side means one less vote that he can control.

Calderón ended his retort by noting that there were several individuals interesting in helping the poor, including those involved with the United Fund, the March of Dimes, Goodwill Industries, the Community Welfare Council, Boy Scouts of America, "and many other worthy organizations."[19]

Besides being labeled as uncaring about the poor, the only other action that could set off such emotional reaction among the middle-class leadership was any aggressive public display on the part of the lower classes themselves. The emerging middle class, best represented by LULAC and the GI Forum, espoused assimilationist strategies such as speaking English, dressing well, and being respectful in race relations.[20] Against this assimilationist model stood the pachuco, in what appeared to be a lower-class rejection of middle-class lifestyles. "Pachucos" were essentially Mexican American youths who had fashioned a distinctive "outlaw" look and lingo.

Along with the soldier and war veteran, the pachuco was a central figure in the barrios of the Southwest in the 1940s. The origins of pachuquismo remain shrouded in mystery, but a consensus of opinion holds that the subculture was influenced by the drug underworld of El Paso. Pachuco youths developed a distinctive linguistic argot, flaunted a colorful dress style, and were aggressive in defending their neighborhoods. In showing off their barrio fashion, much of it influenced by African American styles, they triggered "a socio-cultural panic" that antagonized Anglos as well as the higher classes of Mexicans and Mexican Americans.[21] The 1943 zoot suit riot of Los Angeles, in which Anglo sailors and marines decided to cleanse the city of its pachucos, may have been the most dramatic example, but many other such incidents occurred in the Southwest throughout the fifties.

Mexican intellectual Octavio Paz, on a visit to Los Angeles in the late fifties, was struck by the "tangle of contradictions" that the pachuco represented. Paz called pachucos "instinctive rebels" and recognized that North American racism had "vented its wrath on them more than once." Yet the pachuco had no answer to this hostility except an "angry affirmation of his personality." Paz's view was one likely shared by many older, middle-class Mexican Americans:

> . . . the pachuco is an impassive and sinister clown whose purpose is to cause terror instead of laughter. His sadistic attitude is allied with a desire for self-abasement which . . . constitutes the very foundation of his character: he knows that it is dangerous to stand out and that his behavior irritates society, but nevertheless he seeks and attracts persecution and scandal.[22]

The defiant pachuco, in other words, invited hostility and harassment.

This community disagreement among Mexican Americans—basically over whether to assimilate or to assert difference—surfaced openly during the Chicano movement of the late sixties. It surfaced mainly along class and generational lines as the established middle-class Mexican American leadership sought to contain the organizing efforts of angry working- and lower-class youth. The elements most upsetting to them—lower-class pachuquismo and radical Communist influences—were seen as combined in the growing Chicano movement.

Los Barrios Desunidos

Although the Mexican American middle class spoke in the name of the entire community, it was dwarfed in size by the working and lower classes. In the late sixties San Antonio was the poorest city in the nation, with more than half of its population living below the government's "poverty line" of $3,000 in annual income for a family of four. The poverty core lay in the West and Southwest sides of San Antonio, an eighteen-square-mile area with nearly 300,000 people. Set off from downtown by major freeways, the area had for many years been a community harboring drug addiction, unemployment, alcoholism, and overcrowded and underfinanced schools; business opportunities were almost nonexistent.[23]

In the late 1960s, unemployment in the west and south side barrios was 12.9 percent, compared to 4.2 percent for the city and 3.7 percent for the nation. Underemployment was a staggering 47 percent. Of those employed full-time, nearly half (48.4 percent) worked in unskilled or semiskilled service or labor jobs, earning less than $60.00 a week, or the equivalent of the annual $3,000 poverty level. Hunger was an issue. Not surprisingly, nearly 80 percent of the heads of households had less than a high school diploma, and slightly more than half (54 percent) were functionally illiterate.[24]

Neighborhood conditions matched these human features. Until 1957, the city had no ordinance governing housing. In the 1960s, "shacks" were commonplace. One-third of the West Side houses were considered "blighted," with dirt floors, walls constructed from old Coca-Cola signs, pit privies, and no running water. One could still find barracks or "shotgun houses" arranged around a courtyard with a single faucet and outdoor privy. Floods were regular occurrences during the rainy seasons.[25]

Political scientist Charles Cotrell, in a provocative study of the mid-seventies, described these conditions as "internal colonial." Fifteen percent of the homes were "dilapidated structures beyond rehabilitation," and another 65 percent required rehabilitation. Only 20 percent, or one of every five homes, complied with the San Antonio Building Code.[26] Cotrell traced these conditions, on one hand, to the legacy of racial deed restrictions prior to 1950 (declared unconstitutional in 1948) and, on the other, to the fact that the zoning commission had not been aggressive in protecting the residential quality of life in the South Side quadrants as compared to those on the North Side. Indeed, city administrative practice had been to spend bond monies for improvements on the expanding North Side of San Antonio at the expense of the other sides of town.[27]

Annual flood, West Side of San Antonio, January 30, 1964. University of Texas at San Antonio Institute of Texan Cultures, E-0010-28-A.

Despite the apparent sameness of poverty in the West and South Side barrios, the people who lived there drew important internal distinctions, as two social science teams working with San Antonio youths in the late 1950s and early 1960s quickly discovered. One team, under the direction of sociologist Buford Farris, was connected with the Wesley Community Centers. According to its 1965 study of the Colima Street, Riverside, and Columbia Heights neighborhoods—the service areas of the Wesley Centers—there were important variations in economic status. Three basic types of families lived in these neighborhoods: the upwardly "mobile" working class, the "stable" working class, and the "action-oriented maladapted families."[28]

The upwardly mobile working class consisted of stable, two-parent families working at Kelly Air Force Base or running small businesses, whose children generally graduated from high school and might go to college. The stable working class consisted of stable, usually father-dominated, extended families, with the head of household working in construction or a semi-skilled job. Boys in this group might get involved in gangs. The action-oriented maladapted families consisted of an unstable female-headed family setting with either a weak adult male figure or a "male figure in and out of the house." "Boys in this group usually are involved in gangs and may move into addiction problems. Girls may move into prostitution." The "more adequate" families were on public assistance.[29]

Not surprisingly, the Wesley Center researchers noted that there were tensions between these groups. The upwardly mobile families were seen as "agringado" (Americanized) and arrogant, whereas the maladapted were generally despised by everyone, including the stable working poor. Wesley Center workers faced hostility because of their interest in the neighborhood "hoodlums," who were to a large extent from "multi-problem hardcore families." Neighborhood residents and people who worked for social agencies and the schools blamed these families for their problems:

> These people don't want to help themselves. The only way you can get
> along with them is to coddle them and what you will probably do is
> teach them they can get away with anything. However, I don't want anything to do with them, you can be helpful by keeping them out my hair.[30]

School officials generally described the upwardly mobile as "very nice," the stable working class as "passive," and the maladapted group as "trouble."[31]

The other social science team working in San Antonio consisted of Muzafer and Carolyn Sherif, social psychologists from the University of Oklahoma who were interested in studying youth interaction and self-esteem along class and racial lines.[32] But they were moved to an ecological analysis by the especially strong neighborhood attachments of "low-rank Latin" youths. The Sherifs concluded that these neighborhood attachments stemmed from a lack of transportation and from vigilant police practices that had restricted these young people to certain spaces. Put another way, police monitoring and harassment had been effective in confining Mexican youths to "their" side of town. Thus the "ecology of the immediate neighborhood" was a significant matter for low-rank Latin boys.[33]

The observations of the Sherifs were echoed and extended by Farris and Hale of the Wesley Community Center. In their estimation, the Mexican American barrio constituted "a somewhat isolated social system" that was divided not just by the relative economic status of its residents, but by its "extremely neighborhood oriented" activities and perspectives. Barrio residents restricted their daily lives "to the immediate neighborhood in which they live." "Very seldom," observed Farris and Hale, "do the lower-class Mexican-Americans move outside of their neighborhood."[34]

The Best- and Worst-Case Scenarios

In the mid-sixties, some upward and outward mobility for minority youths was possible in the "leaking" caste system of San Antonio. One notable factor in this regard—but one that remains curiously understudied—was a pathway offered by the local Catholic parish church and school. Many identified their neighborhood by reference to their Catholic parish. To say "I'm from Sacred Heart" or "I'm from St. James's" immediately located one's neighborhood while at the same time identifying one as a likely church parishioner. In addition to subclass and geographic distinctions, barrio residents were further differentiated by their degree of involvement with the local Catholic parish.

The salvation offered was a rather secular one. The Catholic church provided resources for its congregation, and perhaps the most important of these was an educational alternative to the segregated and underfunded public school system. For those families who could afford tuition, the Catholic school system offered religiously motivated teachers who could provide a solid secular education. By the early sixties, the system was so elaborate that it was possible to attend Catholic school from kindergarten through college without venturing far from the West or South Side of town. (Until 1973, when the University of Texas at San Antonio was founded, the only four-year institutions of higher learning in the city were four private universities.)

By the mid-sixties, some post–World War II barrio "baby boomers" were graduating from Catholic high schools and entering local Catholic colleges and universities. These first-generation college students would constitute an important pool of leaders and supporters for the emerging Chicano movement. The Catholic school system proved to be one of the "leaks" that eroded San Antonio's caste structure.[35]

Involvement in the parish-based school system further differentiated the fortunes of barrio youths. The vast majority of them attended extremely segregated public schools that suffered from dropout rates of more than 50 percent and offered those who graduated vocational degrees. In the worst-case scenario, the schools were seen by many barrio youths as loci of conflict and tension. Conflicts arose from contact between students from different neighborhoods and from confrontations with Anglo teachers and authority figures. The estrangement of barrio youths from the school system was suggested by its close association with juvenile delinquency: in 1960, almost half of the "Latin" delinquents were "out of school," while the other half were behind in their "proper grade."[36]

For those who had dropped out or were in danger of doing so, local schools were not a basis for loyal identification. Unlike the church parish youths, those who were organized in "clicas," or gangs, used secular terms to identify their neighborhoods. Most of the gang names were place-names, mainly references to neighborhoods, housing projects, or simply street corners. Alazan, Cassiano, and Mirasol, for example, all referred to housing projects where clica members lived. A few names, such as "Chicago," suggested familial or migratory connections to a city, but some, as we shall see shortly in the case of "Detroit," were apparently picked in reaction to an existing rival group. Another handful of names were cultural, historical, or mythical references, such as La India, Los Apaches, El Gaucho, and El Gray Eagle. The Ghost Town drew its identity from the large cemeteries in its neighborhood. Likewise, the Tripa gang owed its name to its neighborhood packinghouses. La Piedrera, or "The Rocks," which claimed the corner of El Paso and Nineteenth streets, drew its identity from the large number of laborers in the neighborhood who worked at a North Side quarry. And El Con, also on El Paso Street, identified its space by the grocery story with the huge ice cream cone sign.[37] Barrio residents only had to read the graffiti to learn which gang held their turf.

In short, out of the material conditions of poverty, the people of the West and South Sides had created neighborhoods with distinct boundaries and identities. A neighborhood's boundaries were generally set off or identified by natural features, such as streams or marshes, or, more likely, by major thoroughfares, housing projects, churches, and other manmade constructions. The social life within these boundaries formed the basis for neighborhood identity. Given names by parishioners, given names by youth gangs, the various neighborhood identities suggest a complexity glossed over by stock views of a poor ethnic community. Although the vast barrio slums of San Antonio's West and South sides appeared to form one homogeneous lower class, differences based on subclass distinctions, geographic distinctions, and even on degrees of local parish involvement often distinguished barrio residents from one another.

In a similarly superficial fashion, residents of these distinct neighbor-hoods were often described, because of their apparent political passivity, as "a sleeping giant." It would have been more accurate to say that the working and lower classes were preoccupied with economic survival and numerous internal divisions. Frequent flare-ups of gang conflict were signs of the tension and disunity.

2 ALTHOUGH THE GREAT majority of barrio youths were not in "conflict gangs," the notoriety of the latter dominated the image of young Mexican Americans. From the mid-fifties through the mid-sixties, gang warfare had broken out on the Mexican side of town every few years. "Outbreaks" of gang violence occurred in 1956, 1958, 1960, 1962, 1963, and 1966—nearly every two years over an eleven-year period.[1] "The main battles were territorial," as one investigative reporter put it:

> The Dot and Circle gangs fought over Concepción Swimming Pool near the missions; second-generation Alto and Ghost Town gang members fought for control of Cassiano Park, and half a dozen gangs vied for the Elmendorf Lake turf. Playgrounds and school dances became battle-grounds.[2]

The periodic conflicts had a serious impact on the quality of life. Street lights were continually being knocked out, and neighborhood residents were afraid to go out at night. No one seemed able to control the gang members. Older barrio residents, public housing authorities, school authorities, and the settlement house centers all pointed fingers of blame at one another.[3] Moreover, the cyclical history of conflict, apparently based on the "coming of age" of youth cohorts, suggested an enduring structure to gang identity. There seemed to be no end in sight for gang violence.

As mentioned earlier, in the late 1950s and early 1960s, two social science teams were conducting research on San Antonio's barrio youths. Both had to confront the obvious social problem of gang violence. One team, led by the social psychologists Muzafer and Carolyn Sherif of the University of Oklahoma, had entered the field with an interest in understanding how youth self-esteem varied by class and race. The incidence of gang conflict led them to develop an ecological explanation of neighborhood-based competition. Missing from their analysis, however, was a recognition of the diversity of youth relationships. The Sherifs had caught a glimpse of such divisions within their "Low Rank Latin" youth sample. When members of this group had been asked to list people whom they would not want to have as friends, the Sherifs were surprised that non-ethnic referents—"gang boys," "gangs," "pachucos," "hoods"—surfaced among 15 percent of their sample. Carolyn Sherif observed, without a hint of irony, that since the low-rank group under study was already regarded as a gang, these findings indicated "more complex cleavages in their intergroup relationships than those faced by groups in the middle and high rank areas."[4] The Sherifs, like many outside observers, had assumed that lower-class youths were all gang members—an assumption widely held by the police and school authorities as well.

The other team consisted of sociologists from the University of Texas at Austin, who along with some social workers were involved in the Wesley Community Center Youth Project. This gang delinquency project commenced in 1960 and lasted for nearly eight years under the direction of sociologist Buford Farris. Other sociologists and social workers involved included William Hale, Richard Brymer, Gideon Sjoberg, and Gil Murillo. This team recognized the complexity of youth relationships. In summing up research collected over five years (1960–1965), they concluded that the idea of the gang as "a well organized group never did fit the picture" of their field observations. Gang identity, they felt, was "a type of latent group identity connected with a certain geographic area" that only became meaningful under certain circumstances. "[O]nly very seldom does conflict break out," said the sociologists, although they acknowledged that when it did, "it tends to be very dangerous."[5]

At first sight, the two research teams seemed to have offered contradictory assessments about gang activity in San Antonio's barrios. Before the reality of periodic gang warfare, a history that the ecological explanation of the Sherifs could easily accommodate, the argument about "latent group identity" offered by the Wesley Center sociologists appeared quite weak, if not completely mistaken. Assuming that the methodology of both research teams was sound, how does one reconcile a seeming contradiction in their explanations or emphases? Or, more to the point, what was the *complex* gang reality that barrio youths—and the rest of San Antonio—faced in the sixties?

This chapter describes the gang problem and provides explanations of this problem from three expert parties: social scientists, social workers, and ex–gang members. After this review, I propose an explanation that reconciles the notion of "latent group identities" with a cyclical history of gang violence. The key to such an explanation lies in the fractured and atomistic nature of barrio youth society.

Cartoon depicting gang activity by Bob Dale, *San Antonio Express & News*, circa June 1966. Courtesy of Eduardo Villarreal.

A History of Conflict

In 1967, in response to the latest "outbreak" of gang violence, the staff of the Good Samaritan Center compiled a listing of twenty-eight identifiable "fighting gangs" in San Antonio that had been involved in more than a thousand shootings and knifings between 1959 and 1967. Ten of the twenty-eight had been fighting gangs for eight years or more. Some rivalries went back further, to the early fifties.[6]

The Ghost Town gang, perhaps the most notorious of the West Side, had been a fighting gang for at least fifteen years. Most of its activity was directed at its neighbors. To the east was the El Alto gang (also known as "Los Altos"), with whom the Ghost Town had been enemies for ten years; during that time, there were reports of 200 incidents of shootings and knifings, eighteen woundings, one killing—and two bombings! To the north was the Lake gang, with whom the Ghost Town had been fighting for fifteen years, marked by 200 shootings and knifings, twelve woundings, and two killings. On the northwestern flank of the Ghost Town was El Detroit gang, enemies for eight years, with one hundred shootings and knifings, eight woundings, and one killing, and the Mirasol and Las Palmas gangs, also enemies for eight years, with ninety shootings and knifings and twelve woundings. Finally, to the south of Ghost Town was the Tigers gang, enemies for four years, with eighty shootings and knifings, and fourteen woundings. Four other gangs, peripheral to Ghost Town territory—Alazan, Apache, Cassiano, and La India—had been enemies with the Ghost Town gang for at least eight years.[7]

Most gang territories extended only a few blocks, and some were simply identified with a strategic street corner. Every housing project had its own gang—Alazan-Apache, the Alazan gang; Villa Veramendi, the Detroits; Cassiano Homes, the Cassiano and El Alto gangs; Mirasol Courts, the Mirasol; and San Juan Courts, La Blanca gang. Mike Bustamante, a former gang worker with Buford Farris in the early sixties, observed that the neighborhoods were smaller and denser in the West Side than in the South Side: "The West Side is much older than the South Side. Also more assimilated. Remember that the South Side just developed in the last twenty years [in the mid-fifties]." Thus the gangs in the West Side had smaller "turfs" compared to those in the South Side.[8]

A sketch of a "gang map" showing approximate territories in the mid-1960s suggests the compactness of the West Side (see Map 2.1). Within a three-square-mile radius, there were some twenty known gangs. Nineteenth Street was a central axis, crossing into Lake gang territory at West Commerce Street, passing the "street corner" gangs of La Piedrera at El Paso Street and the "Hot Corner" at Tampico, and roughly dividing, from Guadalupe Street to Merida Street, Ghost Town territory on the west from that of El Alto to the east.

Not surprisingly, then, during the first six months of 1966, Nineteenth Street was at the epicenter of what police and social workers characterized

APPENDIX E

Gang Activity Known to Staff of
Good Samaritan Center (1959-1967)

Gang Names	Shooting & Knifings (approx.)	Woundings	*Killings	Enemies for:	Others:
Ghost Town Versus -					
1. Alazan	4	4		8 yrs.	
2. Alto	200	18	1 Ghost Town	10 yrs.	2 bombings
3. Apache	4	2		8 yrs.	
4. La Blanca	14	6		5 yrs.	
5. Brady	6	3		3 yrs.	
6. Cassiano	25	10		10 yrs.	
7. Los Changos (Circle)	2	1		2 yrs.	
8. El Charco	3	8		3 yrs.	
9. Chicago	14	8		5 yrs.	
10. Circle	40	5		5 yrs.	
11. El Con	4	4		4 yrs.	
12. Detroit	100	8	1 Detroit	8 yrs. (off & on)	
13. El Dot	4	7		4 yrs.	
14. Los De La Calle Flores (Dot)	10	3		3 yrs.	
15. El Gaucho	4	5		4 yrs.	
16. El Gray Eagle	6	1		0	
17. El Hueso (Wesley area)	2	1		2 yrs.	
18. La India	20	4		8 yrs.	
19. Lake	200	12	2 Ghost Town	15 yrs.	
20. Los de la Loma	3	0		3 yrs.	
21. Mafia (Circle)	5	3		5 yrs.	
22. Menchaca	10	3		2 yrs.	
23. Mirasol	25	13		8 yrs.	
24. Mirasol (Las Palmas)	90	12		8 yrs.	
25. Los Mosquitos (Dot)	3	1		1 yr.	
26. Tigers	80	14		4 yrs.	
27. La Tripa	8	2		5 yrs.	

*Two other members of the Ghost Town Gang have been shot and killed -
one by the owner of a local Drive-Inn and one by the police.

Gang activity as recorded by the Good Samaritan Center, 1959–1967 as a "gang-war outbreak." This acknowledgment came reluctantly. When Adam Torres was shot and killed in the front of the Good Samaritan Center after a dance (on March 19), social worker Roy Valdez noted that Torres was "a loner" and not involved in any gang activity. A detective said that Torres was "an innocent victim of a shooting by a bunch of drunk youths." But Frank Runnels, principal of Rhodes Junior High School, said that police cannot ignore the fact that Torres died at the demarcation line between

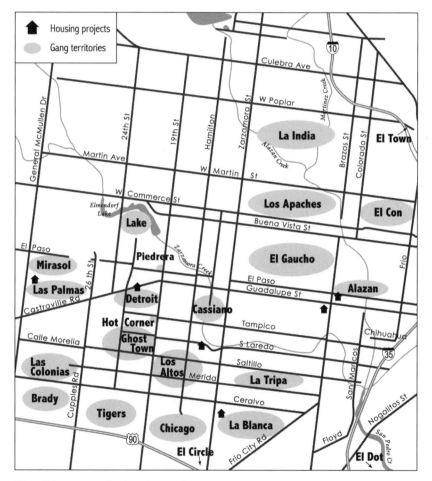

West Side gang territories, circa 1966.

the Ghost Towners and their rivals El Alto. "You cross 18th Street west, and that's Ghost town territory where it's open season on the Altos gang." A suspect later said the shooting was triggered by an incident in which a neighborhood girl was slapped by a boy from another neighborhood. The shooting had been a random act of vengeance.[9]

Over the next two months, drive-by shootings dispelled any doubt that a gang war was taking place. The shootings were frequently random; many of the targets were simply young people walking in particular neighborhoods. By the end of May, San Antonio newspapers were reporting on "shooting links" and "gang links."[10]

One West Side mother of four children, in apparent desperation, penned an open letter to gang members after a spate of such shootings:

> Here it is Friday night again and now for the third weekend in a row we are due for the usual terrifying experiences that have been plaguing our neighborhood. We have had people shot at for no apparent reason, cars brought here from other places and stripped, and needless to say, robberies from right to left.

The West Side mom then ventured to predict a nightmarish future for the boys:

> Now, let's suppose that one of your cars goes by shooting and since yours is random shooting, one or more bullets strike a house. Suppose, just suppose, that one of your bullets strikes an innocent baby sleeping in a crib near a window. Would you all then be satisfied? Think your friends will have respect and admiration for you? You know they won't. Think how you'd feel when the headlines would greet you: "West Side Baby Shot to Death from Passing Car."
>
> Ask the boys which one of you is going to fulfill this prophesy. Who will fire that shot and wake himself the next morning into a nightmare?[11]

With the assistance of concerned (and anonymous) residents, the police strengthened their patrols and carried out group arrests. On June 5, 1966, police arrested nine members of La India, and the following day they arrested fourteen "self-styled juvenile gang members" of El Alto.[12] These were the first of several roundups.

Later, in speaking of this and other outbreaks of gang violence, Roy Valdez asked his fellow workers at the Good Samaritan Center why they had not seen "the writing on the wall." A tone of exasperation was evident:

We cannot say that we did not expect it. The warnings came to us and the community last year, year before that and who knows how long before that. We heard of the fights in school. We saw the boys get kicked out of school. We witnessed some of the shootings in and around the Center. . . . We heard of visits by the gang in our area going into both [Public] Housing projects. Remember that exchange of bullets fired on Sandy Court and Colima Street? The windshields broken on both sides and the break in at the school. Does this pattern ring a bell in your ears and mine?"[13]

THE WAR COUNCIL

While police cracked down on the gangs, settlement house workers acted to defuse tension in the West Side. The settlement houses expanded their outreach program of group or gang workers, and they reactivated a "war council," composed of principal gang leaders, which met regularly in an attempt to de-escalate and prevent future gang warfare. The Good Samaritan Center reported that it was working with the Lake boys, La Blanca, the Alto group, the Ghost Town, the Cassiano, the Detroits, the Tigers, "the Chicago Boys," and the Barricas.[14]

Journalist M. Ruiz Ibáñez of the *San Antonio Sun* recorded one of the first meetings of the reactivated war council. Roy Valdez at the Good Samaritan Center had managed to bring representatives of eight gangs together in "a history-making meeting without precedent." The meeting got underway, Ibáñez noted, "in a tense and explosive atmosphere, which could have erupted into one of the bloodiest free-for-alls ever to have taken place in western San Antonio." But the forty-two boys in attendance had given their word to Valdez that there wouldn't be any violence, so "besides occasional verbal bursts, things went as smoothly as could be expected."[15]

When the boys were asked about the causes of gang violence, one of them answered impatiently: "Can you understand that there's too much pressure . . . that we are in foreign territory?" As Ibáñez explained to his readership, because the groups claimed jurisdiction over certain territories, some youths were afraid to attend school because they would have to pass through "foreign territory." Another boy remarked that "It's a plain case of revenge. If they beat one of our boys, we'll catch one of theirs and even things up." Asked if they might want to try a different approach to solving issues, a boy who had "kept silent" asserted that "We've got it in for each other. There are too many deep scars to just forget about it." Another remarked that most of the incidents flare up when members of the other groups get drunk and "remember old grievances"; then they go out and look for whomever "they have it in for." Soon several of the gang leaders were talking about their negative school experiences with teachers who showed them no respect or understanding. "We've been pushed around in school too often" was one comment. Another noted that a teacher had him "kicked out of school" because he asked a question: "The thing for us to do is not to shut up . . . we have rights and we want those rights respected." This echoed several complaints.[16]

After arguing back and forth about what to do next about gang violence, most of the boys indicated that they would be willing to meet again at a neutral site to continue talking about setting up a grievance committee to negotiate their differences. There was hope that the needless violence might eventually be eliminated. Ruiz Ibáñez noted:

> Contrary to the common belief that those groups are composed of "punks" and hoodlums, we found most of them (members of eight different and warring groups) to be alert, bright, and with a high sense of loyalty and pride. What a reproachful squandering of natural abilities and talent, which could pay high dividends if properly directed![17]

The journalist laid the blame for the lack of direction belonged on many— parents, teachers, religious and civic leaders—who believe that "problem boys" are beyond help. He then asked, "Where are the legions of anthropologists and writers who of late have become so eager to write about the Mexican Americans?"[18]

The Social Scientists Explain

In the 1960s several anthropologists, social psychologists, and sociologists were busy writing about—and often misunderstanding—Mexican American youths in the Southwest. Although all of the researchers were concerned about the problem of juvenile delinquency, most of them considered segregation and inequality as insignificant or "given" conditions. With such external factors removed from consideration, explanations for the problems of Latin youths tended to focus on the internal failures of Mexican American culture. Sociologist Celia Heller, for example, argued that the "excess of juvenile delinquents" in Southern California was not due to deviants from Mexican American culture, "but rather [to] boys who over-conform to this pattern."[19]

Social psychologist Ira Iscoe from the University of Texas at Austin used a Laredo study to arrive at conclusions similar to those of Celia Heller; namely, that delinquency stemmed from the youths' unwillingness to accept the status quo.[20] Iscoe's findings were based on an ethnic preference test he conducted among "Anglo, Latin-American, and Latin-American Juvenile Delinquents" in Laredo in the mid-sixties. This research was one of a series of studies based on the ability of children to recognize the ethnic origins of names and make name choices for certain situations—of the "who would you invite to dinner" variety.

Iscoe's most revealing question was "Which person has the best chance for a good job?" The choices given the seventeen-year-olds were "Perkins, Torres, Raginsky or Levine." In response to his question, nearly three-quarters (or 72 percent of twenty-five) of the *non-delinquent* Latin Americans believed that Perkins would get the job, and only 16 percent thought that Torres might get it. In contrast, nearly three-quarters of the *delinquent* Latin Americans (68 percent of twenty-five) thought that Torres would get the job, and only 24 percent thought that Perkins might get it. Iscoe reasoned that the delinquents had neither recognized reality nor accepted it:

> The [non-delinquent] Latin-American children, in contrast to the delinquents, recognized early the social and economic situation, and this increased with age. They perhaps had come to realize that Anglos most likely would get better jobs. No such recognition took place for the Delinquents.[21]

Iscoe believed that this lack of realism might account for some of the delinquents' difficulties:

> The Latin-American boy who is well adjusted and achieving in school is more likely to recognize the social realities and strive upwardly to reach the Anglo majority. He does this in terms of associations and reaching out. The Juvenile Delinquent group is not readily cognizant, or perhaps they are too cognizant, of the state of affairs. They reach out for their own group, or to be more explicit, they do not depart from it.[22]

Inadvertently, it seems, Iscoe had hit on a key point. Were the delinquents not aware of reality? Or were they perhaps "too cognizant"?

In San Antonio, another social psychologist, Idel Bruckman of St. Mary's University, believed that poverty was "a vicious cycle" and that, of all racial and ethnic groups, this was especially true for Mexican Americans.[23] By and large, sons and daughters did not take jobs that differed much from those of their parents. The problem was how to break this particularly vicious cycle for Mexican Americans. Unlike Iscoe, who believed that well-adjusted Latins were those who accepted the social reality of Anglo preference, Bruckman argued that children needed "to stretch their imaginations, their dreams, their aspirations." She described how she directed a counseling and guidance program for San Antonio high school students:

> I took as my theme song for the program "To Dream the Impossible Dream" from the theater production *Man of La Mancha*. And I told the children about old mad don Quixote—of how wild he was to believe many things—for example, he thought that a woman of ill repute was really his Dulcinea, a lovely damsel in distress.

Quixote was "really crazy" to do the things he did to protect Dulcinea's virtue, Professor Bruckman noted,

> but at least he had a dream! And I tried to encourage these children to dream the impossible dream—for only when it is dreamed (incorporated into the self) does it become capable of attainment.[24]

Only with such an "impossible dream" could Mexican American youths break the cycle of poverty.

Dreaming was not a problem for the barrio youth, it turns out. But the dreams could take nightmarish turns, as the social psychologists and sociologists studying barrio youths in the late 1950s and early 1960s quickly discovered. Both the Sherifs and the Wesley Center sociologists had to confront the problem of gang violence. Interestingly, both research teams eschewed any notion of cultural deficiencies.

THE ECOLOGY OF NEIGHBORHOOD CONFLICT

Social psychologists Muzaf and Carolyn Sherif were interested in understanding group interaction and individual self-esteem among high-rank and middle-rank Anglos, and middle-rank and low-rank "Latins" in San Antonio. The Sherifs found no differences between Anglo and Latin youths of different ranks with respect to desires for material goods. In addition to comfortable housing, the symbols of success for these adolescents included a car, telephone, television set, transistor radios, fashionable clothing, time to enjoy them, and money to provide them. But when stated by low-rank boys with no occupational or educational plans, these material desires acquired "a fantasy character." This may have "something to do," the Sherifs added, "with the fact that these boys, who had so little in the way of possessions, had no qualms about stealing from those who had some."[25]

In the process of describing the environment of "low rank Latins," the Sherifs elaborated a compelling ecological explanation for gang conflict. Basically, the lack of transportation and vigilant police practices heightened the importance of local neighborhoods. On one hand, only a small fraction (29 percent) of low-rank boys could drive, and hardly any (2 percent) had cars. In comparison, two-thirds (66 percent) of the high- and middle-rank Anglo boys could drive, and one-fourth had cars. On the other hand, the police were a significant part of the everyday lives of the low-rank boys: "Leaving the area involved not only considerable physical effort or planning to get a ride, but subjected the boys to suspicious eyes of the police in other areas and occasionally to questioning about their presence."[26] The Sherifs also noted that their two Anglo youth samples rejected "Latins" more frequently than any other ethnic/racial group, including Blacks. Thus the "ecology of the immediate neighborhood" was a "much weightier matter" for low-rank Latin boys than for higher-rank boys. This also made for greater solidarity among the youth groups in low-rank neighborhoods.[27]

Gang conflict, then, was the result not of "disturbed personalities," but of competition for resources (entertainment, drugs, and so on) between groups in restricted spaces. Over time this competition had created hostilities, and this hostile relationship had become formulated as one between enemies, which in turn justified the preemptive use of violence. Competition for facilities and resources was reduced only by a group claiming and defending a territory:

> Thus, groups in low rank areas were aware of other neighborhoods and their boundary streets where they could not go without danger of incident or even violence. They were also aware of friendly groups who could be counted upon to leave them alone, provided they did not interfere with their activities, try to crash their parties, or compete for girls.

These were the conditions, the Sherifs concluded, that provided the foundation for alliances and conflicts between neighborhood groups.[28]

The alignments and hostilities between groups did not follow strict racial or ethnic lines.

Thus the Vargas Cats had friendly relations with Negro boys in their neighborhood and avoided other Latin groups outside it. Los Apaches kept a distance from Negro groups, but did not fight them. They counted on support from the Negro boys in possible clashes with "Anglos," but not with other "Latin" groups.[29]

There seemed to be no pattern. Los Apaches, for example, had frequent encounters with the Lakeside gang, but had friendly relationships with another large group called "the Spooks" (aka the Ghost Towners) and another called "Los Colonias." The Spooks and Los Colonias, on the other hand, were "violent rivals with each other."[30]

Nonetheless, emphasized the Sherifs, a major concern of every group that engaged in violence was "avoidance of conflict." Whenever Los Apaches went into a public place, they sent someone in first to be sure no Lakesiders were there. Another group always chose seats at a ball game as far as possible from any members of a rival group who might be present.[31]

MEDIATING CLASS-BASED CULTURAL CONFLICT

While the Sherifs had focused on the ecology of neighborhood-based conflict, the Wesley group had talked about class-based cultural conflict. Due to its extended work with conflict gangs in San Antonio, the Wesley team felt that they had come up with some "relatively new methods" and ideas about delinquency and gang-work.[32]

The "new theory" of the Wesley Youth Project sociologists held that delinquency should be seen "as a product of a series of life-cycle confrontations between normal lower class patterns of behavior and middle class institutions." Rather than reflecting a frustration at not being able to achieve middle-class values (as many argued), delinquency was the result of conflict with those values and expectations. Behaviors that were seen as normal from a lower-class perspective were defined by middle-class institutions as "abnormal." To complicate matters further, the general inability of the lower class to understand "bureaucratic behavior" fostered "attitudes of distrust and suspicion" and "a conspiracy theory about the larger community." In this context, delinquency was a manifestation of class-based cultural conflict.[33]

One step in resolving this conflict called for teaching lower-class youths how to deal with bureaucracies. This highlighted the need for settlement house workers or "gang workers" who could act as mediators between lower-class male adolescents and middle-class authorities. The principal middle-class institution of concern was the school, where most gang boys experienced a great deal of trouble, consisting of truancy and failure at a relatively early age, usually "prior to a move into the conflict gang." While the gang worker tried to help the gang boy "accept the fact that there are certain behaviors he must perform (or quit performing) if he is to get along in the larger community," the worker attempted to persuade institutional representatives "to be a little more flexible toward the gang boy."[34] A more vigorous formulation called for the gang worker to learn how to manipulate middle-class bureaucracies.

The "gang worker" experiment was so successful that the Wesley project sociologists began to envision them not simply as mediators but as "responsible ward-heelers." Unlike the "social reformer or social action model" of clergy and lawyers, the responsible ward-heeler employed strategies that were "not foreign to the style and perspective of the lower-class."[35] In this regard, Farris and Hale noted:

> Among the Mexican-American, his style here is more of the "Don" or "Padrone." With the lower-class person or group, the worker's goal is to help them to properly present themselves in the various situations. Thus he may take a person to get a job or to go back to school.[36]

The gang workers were aware, naturally, of their influence over barrio youths and of the critical intermediary role they played in barrio society.

The Gang Workers Explain

What was actually innovative about the Wesley approach was its decision to utilize "indigenous workers" in its gang outreach activities. This strategy was influenced by practical cultural considerations. Gang workers were needed to work "with males from lower-class Mexican-American families," because males from both the "stable working class" and the "bottom problem" families ran in clicas. As Farris and Brymer noted, ". . . indigenous personnel were thought to be the best agents of change, since they knew the people, and their words would carry more weight."[37]

Roy Valdez, who would later become director of the Good Samaritan Center, represented the group worker strategy of the settlement houses and the practice of crisis intervention. Jesse Sauceda, Mariano Aguilar, Ben Guajardo, Domingo Bueno, and Joe Rendon, among others, were "indigenous" group workers who had grown up around Good Samaritan as teenagers and were now involved in social work in their neighborhoods. Mariano Aguilar, whose family helped build the Good Samaritan Center, noted that the Center's missionary work was to develop leadership.[38]

The view or theory that the gang workers elaborated was that it was normal for guys to hang out in peer groups. Eduardo Villarreal, who worked with Muzafa Sherif in the early sixties, preferred a neutral term like "clicas" over that of "gangs":

> Clicas form primarily for socializing; it's a very normal social activity of a peer group. People tend to ignore the "controlling" aspects of clicas, that they many times would keep the batos in line.

Villarreal further noted that in contrast to the image of authoritarian gang leadership, authority shifted when the group's major task shifted:

> The leadership depended on what type of activity was going on for the group at a particular time. In time of peace, which was 90 percent of the time, certain gregarious characteristics would predominate, and the bato who displayed them was the leader or one of the leaders. In time of war, the batos who showed more courage or fighting abilities would provide the leadership.[39]

In other words, the group dynamics surrounding decision making were flexible and "generally an unconscious process." The leader would use more intelligent batos for advice and planning, but everyone would attribute credit to the leader. "La perica era de aquellas [the conversation was great] and would last for hours, and planning—some call it dreaming—would always be going on." The conflict, or "pedo," mainly came from some aggressive guys who were sometimes not even in la clica: "But you have aggressive groups just like you do in politics. It's natural and the problem is how to channel aggression, not to focus on the 'inherent pathology' of gang conflict."[40]

Former gang worker Mike Bustamante likewise stressed that the great majority of gangs were not aggressive: "Ninety percent of the gangs are just hanging around. Only 10 percent get into conflict." And conflict, added Bustamante, often mobilized otherwise latent gang identities: "A gang in the South Side only became a gang in time of conflict. Otherwise, there were just several cliques living in the same general area."[41]

Such complex terrain was evident in the West Side as well. Roy Valdez summarized the situation by noting that some groups went under two or three names, and that many known conflict gangs were actually composed of subgroups. "Sometimes, one large area will be known under one gang name to outsiders, but as the gang worker begins to know the area, he may find many gangs in one small area." Thus the famous Ghost Town gang comprised five smaller gangs (e.g., the Hot Corner gang) "grouped together under one banner." Valdez further explained that most boys joined self-identified gangs because of neighborhood conditions: "They base it [gang membership] in reality, the things they can't control because of the environment, or would like to, but don't know how to control." Given such unpredictability, these boys usually carried knives even during times of relative tranquility, in order to protect themselves if need be.[42]

In this context, the approach adopted by the group workers made good sense. For the self-identified gangs, they had devised a "war council" of gang representatives to diffuse tensions and to handle specific grievances. But for the great majority of barrio youths, the group workers tried to help the boys "develop and maintain the public identity of a social palomilla—rather than a gang group." This also meant preventing the "tagging" or "labeling" of a clica as a gang by another group or by authorities. Thus the group worker was not just interacting with adolescents, but often mediating on their behalf with institutional representatives, especially the police and teachers, to see the group as a "social clique."[43]

The overall mission of the group or gang worker, then, was to maintain the status quo of latent group identities. Thus, Eduardo Villarreal believed in a "naturalistic approach to social work." This type of approach called for de-emphasizing poverty as an explanation and accepting it as an "uncontrollable" element that had to be dealt with in the best possible way. Likewise, Mike Bustamante explained the goals of the gang worker plainly: to eliminate hate toward society, to provide positive ego support, and to "buy time." By that, Bustamante was referring to both the "cooling off" mediation that gang workers engaged in, and to the notion that most of the boys would settle down once they reached adulthood.[44]

These views would change later as the social workers became involved in the Chicano movement. Poverty would come to be seen not as natural, but as an imposed condition, and "hate" toward society would become a sentiment that could be harnessed in a social movement determined to end that poverty. In fact, the group workers would play a key role in passing on movement ideas and lessons to barrio youths.[45]

Los Batos Explain

As explained by the gang workers and sociologists, the clicas were natural groupings of teenage boys, many of them with familial ties, and almost all of them with neighborhood ties. The "fighting gangs" were organic formations in this sense. Gene Vasques, who joined Los Tigers in 1956, when he was twelve, recalled that the members were "camaradas [friends] from the barrio, and I started hanging around with them." Gene stayed until he was nineteen. Ernie García, who belonged to La India between the ages of fourteen and nineteen, said: "Pos la clica had been around for many years because my older brothers had been part of it . . . and the gang fights came from wanting to show other barrios that they were the big guns for the pedo." Juan Guajardo became part of the Ghost Town gang because "It was already formed. I grew up with the guys and that's how I knew them." Victor, from the Circle, said the members of his Los Osos gang were "los batos de mi bloque" (the guys from my block).[46]

Only a few clicas were self-identified gangs; most of them had no name or stable identity. In fact, group identity and group formation itself owed much to negative interaction with other clicas or with authorities. Groups became "tight" in bad times, and "loose" in good times. Arturo Delgado, for example, from the barrio of La India, described himself as a loner as a teen.

> *Q:* How did you defend yourself then, when there was so much gang fighting?
>
> *Arturo:* No andaba ni tan solo, andaba con los camaradas todo el tiempo. [I wasn't so alone, I was with friends all the time.]
>
> *Q:* Wasn't this a gang or a clique?
>
> *Arturo:* No, we were just camaradas, you know, we just hung around here and there. The only time que se comenzó el pedo de atiro era cuando 'tabamos en el tenth grade, es cuando comenzaron hacernos pedo a nosotros, you know, they started forming together y todo, pero nosotros we were just minding our own business too, you know, pa' defendernos nosotros mismos. Venían otros batos acá y hacían pedo.[47] [The only time that shit really started was when we were in the tenth grade, that's when they started provoking us, you know, they started forming together and all that, but we were just minding our own business too, you know, to defend ourselves. Other guys would come over and would start trouble.]

Arturo was describing the tensions of 1966, when he was in the tenth grade and joined with friends for self-defense. Clearly conflict or the threat of conflict was often responsible for group formation. When conflict spilled over to affect all youths within certain neighborhood zones, they would form groups for self-defense.

Even when the memory of a group identity was passed down from older cohort to younger, identity seems to have become salient only during times of conflict. The trigger, again, was usually a run-in with another group or with authorities.

EL DETROIT

The case of El Detroit, the gang of Villa Veramendi Courts, provides a good example of how gang identities could be formed and loosely maintained. Frank García recalled the founding of El Detroit back in 1958, when he was thirteen.

> En la noche tú sabes, no teníamos nada que hacer. Y una vez estábamos platicando—y tú sabes, uno se quiere levantar más que el otro, y la chingada. De todos los chavalos, y nomás éramos de los courts, no nos llamábamos nada. Y sale Homer con la idea de que "Vamos a hacer una ganga." Entonces era cuando andaban los chavos del Chicago en chinga, poniendo su nombre en el papel cada rato, dándole en la madre a chavalos, balaceando y la chingada, y dice este bato, "¿Si acaso hay una ganga que se llama Chicago, por que no va a haber una que se llama Detroit?" Entonces dijeron los batos, "Órale!"[48]
>
> [You know, at night we had nothing to do. And one time we were talking—and, you know, one wants to rise up higher than the other, what the fuck. Of all the guys, and we were all from the courts, we didn't call ourselves anything. And Homer comes up with the idea that "we should form a gang." At that time the guys from the Chicago (gang) were all over the place, getting their name in the paper a lot, beating the shit out of guys, shooting up everything around, and this guy says, "If there's a gang called Chicago, why shouldn't there be one called Detroit?" Then the guys said, "Alright!"]

Later they ran into some guys from Ghost Town at a dance, and a fight broke out. Some Ghost Towners were beat up. The next night the Ghost

Town came and shot up the Veramendi Courts. The police announced to the press that a "new gang," El Detroit, was mixing it up with the Ghost Town. "Ahí entonces agarraron los batos la onda" (Then the guys understood the idea).[49]

Lalo, Sancudo, and Chale were members of the cohort that followed García's. In 1961 they belonged to the Little Detroit gang of the Villa Veramendi Courts. Their recollections illustrate the fluidity, or ambiguity, of clique or gang identity. How did the gang form? Lalo recalled, "Well, it was already El Detroit gang when the older batos used to hang around there so we just took over. We were the young batos who lived there." Lalo was thirteen at the time. Chale, then twelve, likewise said, "Ya 'taba, nomás crecías y te metías, y te quedabas hasta que te cansabas" (It already existed, you just grew up and joined, and you stayed until you got tired).[50] On the other hand, Sancudo, thirteen back then, after acknowledging that he once belonged to a gang, resisted giving it a name.

> Well, we were from los courts and to tell you the truth we didn't have a name but the name that was left before was El Detroit. And those guys [Hot Corner] thought we were the Detroits. But we didn't consider ourselves a gang or part of that.

Most of the time the guys "just hung around the courts, and we played it cool, drank a couple of beers and did our own thing, or we would play football with los batos de los courts." But the guys from the Hot Corner, Sancudo added, "would come over to our barrio every weekend all drunk, stoned or whatever, spray can y la fregada . . . and we would have to get ready." One time there was conflict with the batos from El Corner gang who "came over to our barrio looking for trouble, so there were batos filiorados [guys knifed] from both sides."[51]

THE CIRCLE

The case of El Detroit, confined to a housing project, illustrates the fluidity of gang identity over time. The Circle gang, which was spread over twelve square miles on the deep South Side, illustrates the fluidity of gang identity over space. In contrast to the much older and denser West Side, the Circle area—roughly bounded by Division Avenue on the north, SW Military Drive on the south, Roosevelt (Highway 281) on the east, and the Expressway (I-35) on the west—was a sprawling, unzoned development of the 1950s. The Circle gang reflected this topography: it had a huge territory and, in the words of social worker Mike Bustamante, "was a big, ambiguous cluster of small groups."[52]

In a similar vein, Victor and Java, two ex–gang members from the Circle, made clear that there was no "Circle gang" as such, only a defined area with small clicas that often fought with each other but that might, under special circumstances, become mobilized as a larger grouping. Victor and Java recalled the time in 1960 when the Dot gang killed Juliano from the Circle.

> *Java:* [El Circle] era un barrio bien chingón . . . había batos de la Calle Division, de la Calle South San, de la Calle Zarzamora, asina me entiendes . . . y cuando ibas al escuelín pues se miraba uno al otro . . . allí nunca hubo ringleader . . . habían muchos batos, como 400 o 500 guys . . . y está cabrón controlar un chingo de batos.
>
> *Victor:* Controlabas un cierto area . . . dos, tres calles.
>
> *Java:* Y nos dabamos en la madre y todo, pero cuando caía pedo como cuando mataron al camarada Juliano, se juntaron todos, compa' . . . yo estaba chavalón . . . se juntaron todos en la escuelín . . . chingos de batos.[53]
>
> [*Java:* (The Circle) was a fucking big barrio . . . there were guys from Division Street, South San Street, Zarzamora Street, and the like, you understand . . . and when you went to school, well one would see the other . . . there was never a ringleader . . . there were many guys, about 400 to 500 guys . . . and it's damn hard to control so many guys.
>
> *Victor:* You would control a certain area . . . two, three streets.
>
> *Java:* And we would fight each other like the mother and everything, but whenever there was conflict like when they killed comrade Juliano, everyone joined together . . . I was a kid then . . . everyone at school got together . . . so many fucking guys.]

In the absence of such polarizing conflict, the various barrio gangs that made up the Circle would end up fighting one another. Colorado, so-named because of his red hair, used to run with Victor in Los Osos gang and had his share of scars and knifings. Colorado was a "bien hecho" (hard-core) gang fighter from the seventh through the ninth grades. He said the gang-fighting happened because there were many barrios then. One couldn't walk in another barrio without fearing that one would be beaten up. You needed a gang to defend you. If not, everyone, including those from your barrio, would beat you up.

We couldn't go the Circle Drive-In without the guys because there was always fighting with the other barrios. The guys from the other side of Southcross were called Changos, those from this side were called the Memorials. At the Circle Drive-In, they would throw blows, and when the police would arrive, everyone would jump the fence.[54]

Other gangs from the Circle area that Los Osos had to contend with were El Charco and La Mafia.

In short, the history of El Detroit and the Circle suggest that gang identities were fluid and could expand or contract depending on relations with other groups. Likewise, from an individual perspective, whether one became a "loner" or sought friendships often depended on whether gangs were at peace or at war.

THE PLAY OF MALE PRIDE

The batos were clear that male competition and pride were often factors in the gang rumbles. Given no constructive channels for their expression, the result at some point had to be bad. Guajardo of the Ghost Town explained that gang fighting came from the fact that "there was nothing to do. The guys just hung around until there was something to do." Frank García, an old veteran of the Detroits, waxed eloquently on this point:

Porque entonces no había una chingada que hacer. !No había nada que hacer! 'taba en los courts chingao, 'taba una bola de animales ahí. Era yo y diez, quince chavos más, de mi edad, sin nada que hacer en la noche. Nomás se sentaban ahí y nowhere to go, nada que hacer nomás que sentarte y maderiarte and try to build up your own male ego a la madre! Que yo me aviente, que yo me cogí a esa vieja, que yo esto, que yo el otro. Y todo el tiempo viene alguien que le hicieron pedo en un baile y ahí vamos todos pa' probarles quien es más hombre. Y en el otro lado, en los otros courts o en el Ghost Town o en el Lake allá están los batos igual que tú, same fucking thing! Nothing to do y las churches were closed, schools were closed, no había nada de social action program."[55]

[Because then there wasn't a fucking thing to do. There was nothing
to do! Fuck, that was in the courts, there was a pack of animals there.
There was me, and ten, fifteen guys more, of my age, with nothing to do
at night. They would just sit there with nowhere to go, nothing to do but
sit and bullshit and try to build up your male ego to the max! That I was
great, that I screwed this chick, that I did this, that I did that. And all the
time there would be someone who had trouble at a dance, and there we
all go to prove who is more manly. And on the other side, in the other
courts or in the Ghost Town or the Lake, the guys are [in] the same [situ-
ation] as you, same fucking thing! Nothing to do and the churches were
closed, schools were closed, there was no social action program.]

Victor, a veteran from the Circle, acknowledged the element of power
that at times fueled the male competition for resources (including honor):

cuando eres miembro de una gang, you have a sense of power . . . tú
dices si me catean a mí, tengo todos estos batos atrás de mí . . . a veces
no había classification . . . no te decían "Joe, Ramiro, Juan es member"
. . . no había ese jale, bato . . . si necesitas esquina, ellos están allí auto-
máticamente . . . pero si había batos aprovechados, batos que si miraba be-
neficio para ellos, they would take advantage of it.[56]
[when you're a member of a gang, you have a sense of power . . . you
say, if they beat me up, I have all these guys behind me . . . at times
there was no classification . . . one didn't say, "Joe, Ramiro, Juan are
members" . . . there was no such thing, bato . . . if you needed backup,
they were there automatically . . . but there were opportunistic guys,
guys who if they saw some benefit for themselves, would take advantage
of it (the backup).]

What contained such display, in part, were the compromises that the
gangs were willing to make. The gangs represented a certain politics. As
Lalo put it:

they [El Detroit] let the guys from La India come to a party and La India
would let them go the Texas Theater, and so on; only the Ghost Town
thought they were superior [cabrones]. They didn't go with anyone, until
the other gangs got together and fucked them up.[57]

The "onda" (idea) was that "my barrio counted." Outsiders had to respect the neighborhood, a posture that at times garnered some support from barrio adults.

Ernie of La India, for example, remembered that "many batos from outside the barrio would come and shake down the older people for money. So the guys started getting together to stop ese jale."[58] In a similar vein, Gene Vasques recalled that one main rule of Los Tigers was

> no chingar con gente grande, tú sabes. A muchos chavalos les gusta catear viejitos y la chingada. Nosotros los respetabamos, tú sabes. Si necesitaban ayuda, nosotros les ayudabamos y la chingada, tú sabes. Y la gente del barrio, las señoras y todo la gente grande, nos hacían chingo de esquina, tú sabes. Si nos traiban en corrida los perros, nos metían pa' los cantones de ellos, tú sabes, pa' esquiniarnos, tú sabes. Si nos traiban los perros a puro pedo ahí en la calle, salían las señoras y nos hacían esquina, tú sabes. Les tiraban al pedo [a la policia] que nos dejaron, que no estábamos haciendo nada, tú sabes.[59]
> [don't fuck with older people, you know. Many young guys liked to beat up old people and what the fuck. We respected them, you know. And the people from the barrio, the women and all the older people, would give us a lot of fucking support, you know. If the dog police had us on the run, they would take us into their homes, you know, to back us up, you know. If the dog police were harassing us in the streets, the women would come out and back us up, you know. They would give the dog police shit about leaving us alone, that we weren't doing anything, you know.]

Gene recalled how once when two or three of them were surrounded by fifteen or twenty batos from other gangs, that a "señora" named Pancha and her daughter Sulema came to their aid: "aquella Sulema traiba un filerón chingonote, y la señora traiba una pipa chingada y un cuchillo. Y le echaron a andar la pompa a los batos" (that Sulema had a fucking big knife, and the woman had a fucking big pipe and a knife. And they made the guys walk on their butts).[60]

Such support was an understandable response in the context of protective neighborhood and family ties between adult residents and barrio youths. But when gang warfare escalated into drive-by shootings of homes, support from barrio adults tended to evaporate. In terms of how gang members were seen or treated within barrio society, the situation was as ambiguous and complex as the question of gang identity.

Many Barrio Worlds

To return to the original question: How does one reconcile the "latency" observation of the Wesley Center researchers—namely, that gang identities were "latent identities" of loosely organized groups—with evidence of cyclical gang violence?

The preceding review of various explanations suggests complex and diverse patterns of youth relations. At the level of the individual, whether or not one belonged to a "clica" could be ambiguous and changeable. At the level of the group, most clicas were casual groupings and had no name, and even those with names were not necessarily gangs. Self-identified gangs were a very small subset of the barrio youth culture, and in contrast to their image, they generally sought to avoid conflict. However, when conflict between self-identified gangs did break out, it had the potential of spilling beyond its localized origins and mobilizing formal and informal clicas as well as unattached individuals to strengthen group ties for self-protection and possible retaliation. Every other year in San Antonio, it seemed, group identities would be activated by some conflict that had rippled beyond its local origins, reverberating along familiar neighborhood boundaries. Authorities, usually the police, would compound the problem by seeing most clicas or groups as gangs.

Framing the dynamics of youth relationships in such layers, then, suggests that there was no contradiction in believing that most clica identities were latent, despite the periodic outbreaks of gang violence. The complexity and diversity of youth relations allowed ground for both. Clearly the pattern of cyclic violence pointed to neighborhood rivalries maintained by successive cohorts of adolescents. The Wesley Center team understood this. Delinquency was tied to an age-specific stage, meaning that boys moved into delinquency, or at least into gangs, with the transition to junior high school, at around thirteen to fourteen years of age, and stopped being involved in gang and delinquent activities between the ages of eighteen and twenty. Only about 5 to 10 percent went into adult crime, specifically narcotics addiction. For social work practice, this meant getting adolescents through this stage "with as little damage as possible." Specifically, this meant making sure that youth cliques did not adopt a gang identity and that they were not tagged with such an identity by other cliques or by authorities.[61]

The barrio youths were certainly aware of the complexity of their social environment. In a provocative comment, Lalo, a West Side Beret and former member of El Detroit, described the fragmented reality in terms of "bubbles of familiarity," or places where people spent most of their lives. In these "bubbles," people knew and understood one another. Before the Chicano movement, his world was the West Side, and he didn't go to the South or North sides, preferring to stay in his own barrio:

> But what has happened now [1975] is that everyone sees only one big barrio. Now we can go to the South Side without having to be on alert, and they can come over here. Just because you're in a bubble doesn't mean that you can't get to know guys from another bubble.[62]

Lalo's notion of "bubbles of familiarity" suggests the sociological concept of "social worlds," or the local, everyday environments that individuals grow up in and experience. Such local worlds have immediacy and regularity, and provide the framework for identity, behavior, and action.[63]

The poor barrios were a complex aggregation of such local worlds. In San Antonio, and other cities throughout the Southwest, some of the better-defined youth cliques, organized around kinship and intimate peer relationships, cooperated and competed for the barrio's scarce economic and status resources. Sometimes this competition could take a nightmarish turn. A minor misunderstanding, or some affront to male pride, could escalate into a scuffle, and that, in turn, could escalate into still more serious conflict. "An eye for an eye, and a tooth for a tooth" was the law of the land in west San Antonio, according to gang members. This primitive concept of justice made for "endless feuds, bloodshed and continuous strife."[64] And it meant that barrio youths were always ready to mobilize their clicas, those with names as well as those without names. The atomized nature of barrio youth society facilitated both escalation and mobilization.

This helps us understand why, despite the seeming homogeneity of the barrios, a unity of class or even of ethnicity could not be assumed. Indeed, one singular achievement of the Chicano movement was the creation of such unity for a few short years. Under the unifying mantle of cultural nationalism, the neighborhood loyalties and class distinctions of many barrio youths would become largely irrelevant.

ORGANIZING UNITY

3 **FROM THE MID-FIFTIES** through the mid-sixties, gang warfare had broken out in San Antonio every two years. Then, in 1969, such incidents ceased for nearly a decade. The common causes of troubles (pedos) were still around, and gang activity was still taking place, as group worker Jesse Sauceda noted, but it was "not as explosive as before, porque [because] it doesn't involve ten to fifteen guys on each side but maybe just one or two guys." The gang identity was still there, but it had been "weakened as far as numbers are concerned." There were more things for young people to do; they could get involved with their cars, with clothes, "with more material kind of things." Ernie García of La India said the same thing about the weakening of gang identity:

> The guys have calmed down and they have learned, many of them, that the jale [activity] we were in wasn't worth three cents of a bottle deposit. Even though there are guys who say they're from La India, it has practically died. Only the name remains. It was a name that was respected.[1]

Both police officers and social workers claimed credit for restoring calm among the Mexican barrios, but whether their claims were valid cannot be ascertained. Both had made concerted efforts at intervention and containment previously, but with little effect. The Chicano movement, on the other hand, was arguably a major factor in the calming of the barrios at this time. College activists and politicized social workers successfully introduced the notions of brotherhood and unity to barrio youths. In this chapter, I begin to outline the campaigns and projects that provide substance to this argument.

Explaining Barrio Peace

Several explanations for this period of barrio peace are possible. The war in Vietnam, for example, may have had a dampening effect. In the mid-sixties, as the Southeast Asian conflict expanded into a war, barrio youths volunteered to serve at high rates, and those who did not volunteer were subject to the draft unless they had a college deferment. The influence of the Vietnam War would have been indirect, however, since most gang members were young teens ineligible for the military. Yet perhaps the absence of older brothers and other eighteen- and nineteen-year-old acquaintances may have weakened the passing on of kin- and neighborhood-based feuds. The only suggestion of the impact of the war on the barrios comes from the casualty rates. According to data compiled by Congressman Gonzalez's staff, in 1966 almost two-thirds (62.5 percent) of the casualties from San Antonio were Spanish-surnamed, at a time when Spanish-surnamed people made up just 41 percent of the city's population.[2]

The veteran social workers also mentioned a change in drug use as a factor in tranquilizing the gang youths of the barrios. Mike Bustamante believed that "pill-popping in the late fifties and early sixties stimulated violence; since then, mota [marijuana] and carga [heroin] have calmed everyone down." Eduardo Villarreal said that he saw no pills around in the mid-sixties: "the only drugs being used were beer, mota, wine, pisto, glue and gasoline." But he agreed that television and heroin had tranquilized all conflict. Villarreal related an example from La India, of "one bato, a gregarious leader, se prendió en carga [he got hooked on heroin] and he dropped out." Villarreal said that this happened to several batos. "Mientras estás en carga, no piensas en nada más. The batos themselves would exclude tecatos from la clica. No valían para las actividades de ellos." (While you're on heroin, you don't think of anything else. The guys themselves would exclude addicts from the group. They weren't of any use to their activities.)[3]

Ex–gang members disagreed about the impact of heroin. One said that he had always seen "chiva" in the bar scene; another said heroin was hardly mentioned or noticed in the early sixties (compared to the seventies). A third opinion emphasized the heavy influence of marijuana:

ahora casi todos los chavalones se prenden. . . . ahora vas a un baile en
donde hay chingos de chicanos y los batos se pasan toques . . . "Hey, carnal, gracias" . . . la mota ha ayudado traer carnalismo . . . porque la mota
te ayuda olvidar tus problemas . . . por que los batos se ven y "Hey, tienes
rolling papers?" y "Porqué no rolas tú," y riaaata, todos están juntos.[4]
[today almost all the kids get high . . . today you go to a dance where
there are a lot of Chicanos and the guys are passing around joints . . .
"Hey, brother, thanks" . . . marijuana has helped bring brotherhood
around . . . because marijuana helps one forget one's problems . . . because the guys see each other and "Hey, do you have rolling papers?" and
"Why don't you roll?" and riaaata, everyone is united.]

The role of marijuana and heroin, in particular, in sedating barrio conflict merits further investigation. Local law enforcement estimated that
there were "more than five thousand addicts on the streets of San Antonio,
acting as both pushers and users in most cases." The Alamo City was a
major distribution point for narcotics across the country.[5]

The collapse of strict segregation, including the police monitoring of
these boundaries, must figure in as a general circumstance. Such segregation, the backdrop for the everyday life of the working and lower classes,
had often functioned like a "pressure cooker," accentuating and provoking tensions within the poor districts. This had been the ecological-social-
psychological argument of the Sherifs. This is what ex–gang member Lalo
meant when he said, "There was a lot of pressure in los barrios that you had
no choice but to get frustrated with one another and get into trouble. Now
it's better because today youths can go anywhere."[6]

We still do not have a compelling explanation for the demise of gang-
associated violence in the late sixties and early seventies. All of the above
factors—Vietnam, the breakdown of segregation, drug use, and police
crackdowns—likely combined in some fashion to make for an uncustomary
calm. To this mix of explanatory factors, however, one must add the Chicano movement as the key element.

What was new in the late sixties were the political organizing efforts
directed towards barrio youths. The farmworker strike led by César Chávez
and Dolores Huerta had set off a chain reaction in organizing activity that
from the beginning reached out to urban youths for support. In San Antonio and South Texas, the strike attracted the first-generation college youths
from the working-class barrios. In turn, these activists, along with the group
workers from the settlement houses, began to work with high schoolers

and street youths, preaching the gospel of "carnalismo" (brotherhood) and "raza unida" (united people). The lower-class slang word "Chicano" became invested with a new sense of pride and self-assertion. Before this overarching identity of Chicano and Chicana, local identities were weakened and broke down. To summarize the argument: basically the restlessness of barrio youths was channeled toward social protest under an identity greater than that of the neighborhood.

The broader civil rights movement and, to a lesser extent, the War on Poverty influenced the development of a critical consciousness and activism among Chicano and Chicana youths, particularly college students. What I want to emphasize here is not the "temper of the times," but actual practice and networking. What must be taken into account were the deliberate efforts of movement activists, particularly the politicized social workers, to convert barrio youths to "la causa," the cause for social justice and equality. Dedication to such a cause meant, for batos locos in particular, that the practice of carnalismo would become paramount.

Former Ghost Town leader Juan Guajardo agreed that gang conflict has decreased, but he didn't believe that it was largely due to the Chicano movement or to drugs. As he noted in 1974: "It's died down quite a bit. The last conflict was when some guys from Ghost Town shot some guys from El Detroit and the Lake. That was back in 1968. The movement has had some impact, but not much."[7]

Yet, as we shall see, Guajardo's own life trajectory from the Ghost Town to the Brown Berets suggests the influence that the Chicano movement had among some gang members. Guajardo would become the founder of the Brown Berets, whose prime directive called for the philosophy and practice of carnalismo. Their work with the most active and self-conscious gangs—those with names and legacies—did much to calm the tensions that would occasionally flare up and reverberate through the barrios.

Such organizing began to challenge the established gang boundaries. Alicia Martínez, a leader of welfare mothers, recalled that many of their protest marches, which included gang members, had to cross several barrios. In one instance:

> We marched from the House of Neighborly [Services] to the Good Sam, and some of the boys de la Espiga couldn't march because that was Ghost Town . . . so the women, you know, las señoras, marched with them and it was okay then. Los del Ghost Town los dejaron pasar [let them pass].[8]

MAYO: An Organization of Organizers

The Mexican American Youth Organization (MAYO) was unquestionably the prime mover of the Chicano movement in San Antonio and Texas during this time. Indeed, it is possible to trace the development of one thick branch of the Chicano movement through the history and evolution of MAYO. The group, which saw itself as an "organization of organizers," was for a time able to create an infrastructure supportive of its social change agenda. For a while it was the umbrella that brought together college students and street youths. Organized by Chicano college students, MAYO appealed to the barrio youths with its tough talk about "the gringo." Between 1967 and 1970, MAYO engaged in several protest marches, encouraged and supported high school walkouts, worked with youth gangs, and organized several statewide conferences. Through these activities, MAYO brought barrio residents, gang members, politicians, and college students together, "rubbing shoulders and learning from each other." By 1969 MAYO was one of the most active and most militant Chicano organizations in the Southwest, with more than forty chapters in Texas alone.[9]

MAYO had its origins in 1967 on the St. Mary's University campus in San Antonio, where the founding members—José Ángel Gutiérrez, Willie Velásquez, Mario Compean, Ignacio Pérez, Juan Patlán—were students. Gutiérrez and Patlán, who had rural, middle-class backgrounds, were from the Winter Garden region, some ninety miles southwest of San Antonio. Velásquez, Compean, and Pérez were working-class products of San Antonio's West Side. A key politicizing event for all of them had been the farmworkers' strike in California and Texas. The core group of MAYO had initially been farmworker support people. Mario Compean recalled that he and Angel sounded each other out: "How would you like to start an organization like SNCC? Yeah." It took several months of constant meetings, two to three each week, until finally on July 4, 1967, they announced the formation of MAYO with a picket in front of the Alamo. The goals of the new organization was to promote the idea of "la raza unida" (the united people).[10]

MAYO members took the task of developing a "liberation strategy" seriously. They engaged in a survey of power structure research, social movements, community organizing, and the Black liberation movement. They read the works of Fanon, Che, Lenin, Saul Alinksy, and later, Pablo Freire and Antonio Cabral. They visited Chicano and Black leaders—including César Chávez, Reies López Tijerina, Corky González, Stokely Carmichael, and H. Rap Brown—to learn from their political organizing experience.[11]

They recruited members through their existing networks. Willie Velásquez, as the local coordinator of the farmworker support efforts, brought in several who had been involved in the Valley strike. José Ángel Gutiérrez met Richard Jasso, who would recruit many street youths from Ghost Town through his work with the San Antonio Neighborhood Youth Organization (SANYO). Another bato, Norman Guerrero of La India, at the time a Trinity University student, just walked into the MAYO office at the Mirasol Courts. Luz Gutiérrez, José Ángel's wife, described the approach used by MAYO organizers as follows:

> They would get the leaders of gangs like Richard [Jasso] . . . and they
> would tell him, "Trayte tus camaradas" [bring your friends], we're going
> to meet at such and such a place and such and such a time. So Richard
> would get his five leaders. They were the one ones who controlled the
> whole thing. All they did was get this one guy and he would control the
> rest. So se sentaban y hablaban [So they would sit down and talk]. They
> would get tired of just bullshitting and they would start talking about the
> real meat of the whole thing. . . . What was MAYO?[12]

In October 1967, MAYO introduced itself to the established Mexican American organizational field. In reaction to being left out of a White House–sponsored Interagency Conference on Mexican American Affairs in El Paso, some six hundred Mexican American leaders from throughout the Southwest convened their own rump conference only a few miles away. Here, as journalist Leo Cardenas of the *San Antonio Express & News* described it, the "business suit-types" of the established organizations such as LULAC, the GI Forum, and PASO met with an "impatient new breed" of leadership. The two groups, according to Cardenas, were "as different as tortillas and sandwich bread." Those attending the meeting heard for the first time about MAYO and its work with barrio gangs. The MAYO leaders told the old leadership: "We have studied and seen your ways of improving the lot of the Chicano. We are not impressed. If nothing happens from this [conference], you'll have to step aside or we'll walk over you."[13]

The MAYO leaders rejected the conventional protest strategy of the "old guard"—that of writing letters, holding press conferences, and using diplomacy. Their strategy instead called for an eclectic blend of Black Power tactics and Saul Alinsky's "confrontation politics." One favorite MAYO tactic followed Alinsky's fourth rule: "Ridicule is a man's most potent weapon." Closely related was Alinsky's ninth rule: "Pick the target, freeze it, personalize it, and polarize it."[14]

Whether the result of study or simply a natural skill, the MAYO leaders quickly demonstrated their mastery of ridicule and polarization as tactical tools. José Ángel Gutiérrez believed that such language and posturing was necessary to break the veil of fear and inferiority that silenced many Mexican Americans. MAYO was able to accomplish this, especially among barrio and college youths. But these confrontational tactics alienated many potential supporters among the Mexican American community, while at the same time alarming the Anglo establishment.

In the year following the rump session, MAYO demonstrated its seriousness in organizing the barrios and youths. On January 6, 1968, the first La Raza Unida conference was held at Kennedy High School in San Antonio with some 1,200 delegates from the Southwest in attendance. Two more conferences, in Laredo and Houston, followed that year. With MAYO assistance, high school students began staging walkouts and boycotts to protest the lack of a better education. This tactic had already been primed, so to speak, by the walkout of 10,000 students from East Los Angeles high schools in March. The following month, 700 students from San Antonio's Lanier High School were threatening to walk out; they demanded a tougher curriculum, including such courses as chemistry, physics, algebra, trigonometry, calculus, and computer programming. The next month, 600 students at Edgewood High School walked out; they wanted more discipline, qualified teachers, and cleaner restrooms. Rumbles of protest were also heard at Fox Tech High School. Later there would be walkouts in Edcouch-Elsa, Kingsville, Uvalde, Falfurrias, and Crystal City. Between 1968 and 1970, MAYO would organize or be involved in thirty-nine high school walkouts.[15]

The high school walkouts were dramatic events that kept the name of MAYO in the newspapers and galvanized support from barrio youths. More critical to the success of MAYO, however, was the creation of an organizational infrastructure to carry out its programmatic vision. To confront the many problems of the barrios, the MAYO leadership had developed an ambitious vision of community empowerment, economic development, and alternative schooling. Pragmatically, MAYO sought to create jobs for its organizers, but they knew that they could never secure funding directly from foundations or government sources. Thus the college-educated activists began working on several grants that would create front organizations to implement the various aspects of MAYO's wide-ranging program.

By August of 1968, its inaugural year, MAYO had put in place the Mexican American Unity Council (MAUC), chartered as a tax-exempt, nonprofit economic development corporation. MAUC would be the vehicle through which Ford Foundation monies would be funneled to MAYO and its various projects. MAUC's explicit mission was to promote economic development and to provide services to the Chicano barrios of San Antonio. Its implicit mission was to provide jobs for the MAYO organizers working in San Antonio.[16]

The Social Workers Become Political

One of MAUC's first mini-grants went to MAYO, which used the funds to open an office close to Mirasol Courts. Another mini-grant went to the settlement house workers who were on strike. These social workers formed Barrios Unidos and shared MAYO's office. Thus the striking settlement house workers can rightfully claim that they were part of the initial nucleus of movement activity in San Antonio. As Jesse Sauceda of Barrios Unidos put it,

> They [MAYO] started in the educational aspect. They wanted to reform the school system. Well, we started in the social system, in the social welfare institution. That's where we started our movement, making changes. So we all started together y luego for the first Raza Unida Conference in Kennedy High School in early '68, we [group workers] went as a delegation of about ten guys.[17]

Sauceda added that the founding members of Barrios Unidos and MAYO were mostly first-generation college students from the West Side enrolled at St. Mary's University.

The settlement house workers proved to be a natural link between MAYO college activists and barrio youths. As college students themselves, the group workers basically introduced and translated the movement ideas in circulation to the street youths. They knew how to speak to the batos, and they had a long experience of working with them.

To diffuse gang tensions in the barrios, the group workers had set up a "war council." Jesse Sauceda recalled that the purpose was "to get the leadership of the gangs together to discuss things." The group workers then steered the council to create an all-season sport league. "That was a vehicle," explained Sauceda, to get them "to discuss rules of the tournament or of the league":

From there, we kicked off, we started introducing things like settling affairs, fights y todo eso [and all that]. Getting them to work it out instead
of out here in the streets. Sometimes it didn't work. Sometimes it back-
fired on us, but we had to pick up things and start again.[18]

Ghost Town member Juan Guajardo, who was active in the war council in
1963–1964, when he was fifteen and sixteen years old, credits the idea to
Roy Valdez, director of the Good Samaritan Center. "But it wouldn't have
happened," he added, "without the batos":

> Every club had two representatives, and because the Ghost Town was
> chingón [really big] we had lots of representatives. The group workers
> would get us together regularly, but would leave us alone in the meeting.
> The idea was to calm the tension between the gangs, but it didn't work.
> Right there in the same council meetings, we would start fighting. But
> sometimes it worked. We made all the rules. If someone got way out of
> line, his own camaradas would come down on him.[19]

Likewise, Sancudo and Lalo, from El Detroit, recounted how Valdez got
them involved in a sports league. "We became more active in sports," Lalo
recalled, "so we didn't have any fights. After a while we were not considered a gang any more. Then I joined the navy." Sancudo added that he
"didn't leave [the clica]. It just disappeared. Some guys got married, some
left Texas, one guy was killed."[20]

The settlement workers became politicized, and they in turn began politicizing los batos. Sauceda recalled, "At first we're just keeping them busy
with athletics. . . but then the movement hits." As the gang workers of the
Good Sam Center "started getting en la onda del movimiento [into the spirit
of the movement]," they kept introducing "new ideas, new philosophies."
According to Sauceda,

> we would be having a discussion and the guys would, se arrimaban y
> comenzaban a oír [they would get close and start to hear]. Se metían a la
> plática [they would get into the conversation] and would ask questions:
> "What do you mean here, 'raza unida'? What do you mean, 'carnalismo'?
> What do you mean, 'Chicano'? What do you mean, 'gringo'? What do
> you mean, 'vendido,' 'malinche'?" Eso lo explicábamos [we would ex-
> plain] and they started también, "Brown Power y que." Pero, it was more
> through personal influence than method.[21]

One of the first politicizing moments was raised by the Volunteers in Service to America (VISTA), a domestic "peace corps" program and an integral part of President Johnson's War on Poverty. There was tension between the college-educated white kids coming to help people in the barrio and the "indigenous" settlement house workers. Mariano Aguilar recalled that the first VISTA volunteers were mainly Anglo kids from the North who were antiwar and couldn't understand the patriotism of Chicanos. Because of criticism about the Anglo VISTA volunteers "bringing in their own values," social worker Gil Murillo wrote a proposal to recruit Chicanos to become VISTA volunteers to work in the barrios of South Texas. As a result, a VISTA Minority Mobilization Project was created, and these "community VISTAS" began working through the settlement houses. When Roy Valdez secured a major job with VISTA, he took along a number of gang workers.[22]

This change in job title for the gang workers did not lessen the tension at the settlement houses. The VISTA Minority Mobilization Project, with its emphasis on community organizing and Chicano assertion, quickly ran afoul of the settlement houses and other agencies working in the West Side. Jesse Sauceda recounted the growing conflict between the Chicano gang workers and the Good Samaritan Center:

> The agency had a different philosophy. They didn't particularly care about working with the hard to reach. They liked the publicity and the money, but they didn't like the individuals hanging around the area. They made it hard for us to continue working with the gangs, because they themselves didn't support that kind of work. While they were making a study and getting money, they wholeheartedly supported it, but once the money was cut off, well, they had other interests like a preschool and things like that.[23]

In mid-1968 the gang workers presented a list of demands to the Good Samaritan Center based on the premise of "self-determination." As one supporter explained it,

> Tenemos que ver la realidad. Por muchos años, ha habido gringos en la area de trabajo sociales. El único que puede ayudar al pachuco y a la gente pobre del barrio es otro Chicano.[24]
> [We have to see reality. For many years, there have been gringos in the area of social work. The only one who can help the pachuco and the poor people of the barrio is another Chicano.]

The premise, of course, was unacceptable to the Good Samaritan Center and to the network of antipoverty agencies. One concerned agency director described the "disgruntled Good Sam employees" as representing a "brown power" reaction to the "Negro" community's Black Power rallying cry for change.[25]

Because of this disagreement, the Chicano social workers walked out of the agency. After that, Sauceda noted, the Good Samaritan Center never did gang outreach again, and the war council was dissolved. But the "disgruntled" gang workers took all the street clubs and organized them into Barrios Unidos. They moved into the West Side office of the recently formed Mexican American Youth Organization (MAYO). There all sorts of barrio elements were brought together—college students, social workers, high school dropouts, ex-cons, and just street-corner guys—all undergoing the experience of a Chicano renaissance in the same office, if not in the same organization.

Although the gang workers had left the settlement centers, the demands on the centers being made by their West Side "client base" seemed to increase. At the Southwest Conference of the National Federation of Settlements and Neighborhood Centers, held at the Inman Christian Center on September 18–20, 1969, barrio youths in attendance criticized the 300 delegates from five states for "sitting behind a desk" and handling each problem by "taking a case study." The newspaper account quoted a MAYO youth to the effect that "Chicano people are going to have to define their problems and likewise are going to have to be the ones to solve their own problems." Another MAYO member, "who wore a brown beret and carried a large cane which he thrust to make points," said, "We've got plans," and, moreover, "we know who's keeping us down and we're out to get them." The climax to the two-day conference came, fittingly, at the final session, when Barrios Unidos spokesmen Ernest Gómez, Gil Murillo, and Mariano Aguilar, former Good Sam and Wesley Center social workers, demanded that the church-supported settlement houses turn control of their programs over to barrio residents.[26]

Adding Method to the Movement

The energy generated by this mix of activists from different walks of life resulted in an ambitious and aggressive program of action. The students of Alinsky and Black Power, the college guys, had joined forces with gang workers of the settlement houses, "the most organizationally sophisticated guys at the time," in the words of one MAYO leader. The street youths recruited by MAYO and Barrio Unidos were thrown into a cauldron of activity. Protesting or picketing were regular actions, meetings were daily events, and proselytizing about unity was ongoing. With the West Side of San Antonio as its base, MAYO would export its brand of community organizing throughout Texas. There was no lack of targets in the segregated environment of the late sixties, with schools, police departments, and city councils among the most obvious ones.

These community-organizing efforts received a tremendous boost when MAYO maneuvered to influence VISTA'S Minority Mobilization Program. The program had been launched with a budget of $1.5 million in June 1968. MAYO gained control of much of the allocation, including some supervisory and administrative positions. Mario Compean, then vice president of MAYO, was hired as a recruiter and trainer for the effort within Texas. Many young MAYO members became VISTA volunteers.[27] Compean explained to political scientist Armando Navarro how MAYO benefited:

> MAYO had two hundred people employed. We had a budget. We had salaries for people. We had transportation. We had telephones. We had travel monies. Consequently that really allowed MAYO to expand. We knew that it was only a one-shot deal. So we used it to the maximum.[28]

Compean went to Del Rio, Cotulla, Laredo, the Valley, San Antonio, and El Paso, and set up thirty volunteers at each site to be community organizers. Basically MAYO was using the Minority Mobilization Project to organize community groups for la raza unida throughout the state.

Back in San Antonio, MAYO–Barrios Unidos, along with other service workers and teachers, had organized an independent "war on poverty" entity, the Mexican American Neighborhood Community Organization (MANCO), which represented "a radical departure from the way the traditional agencies operated in the West Side."[29] For one thing, MANCO members understood that they could not fight poverty simply with grant proposals. So within a few months of its formation, it in turn organized the Committee for Barrio Betterment (CBB). Its purpose was to select a slate of candidates for city council—an entry into the political arena that would alarm the city's establishment.[30]

Equally alarming were the various grassroots projects launched by MAYO and Barrios Unidos to deal with the problems of gang conflict and juvenile delinquency. The MAYO leadership was explicit about converting gang members to la causa through another MAUC-funded project, a "freedom school" for street youths. Through political education classes at their La Universidad de los Barrios (LUB), MAYO activists intended to add "method" to the politicization process.[31] This experiment would be closely monitored by the local authorities.

The MAYO leadership divided up responsibilities according to their interests. Mario Compean and Nacho Pérez focused on VISTA, Willie Velásquez and Juan Patlán concentrated on MAUC, and José Ángel Gutiérrez concentrated his organizing in his home town of Crystal City, in the heart of the Winter Garden region, about ninety miles southwest of San Antonio. A second tier of activists, led by Norman Guerrero and George Velásquez (Willie's brother), headed up the LUB project. This division of labor was also meant to decrease the developing tension among the MAYO leadership. The Velásquez brothers and Patlán questioned the tactics and rhetoric of confrontation, whereas Gutiérrez, Compean, Pérez, and Guerrero asserted that militancy was the only way to awaken the country. This mirrored the general tension within the Chicano movement between moderates and radicals. Both righteously pressed for Chicano power but differed over strategy and language.[32]

La Universidad de los Barrios: A Freedom School

The MAYO leadership understood the need to provide political education classes for its members, particularly for street youths. Toward this end, MAYO established La Universidad de los Barrios as an outreach center and made a concerted effort to work with gang members. The school's full name was "La Universidad de los Barrios, Colegio de los Batos: Escuela de Libertad" (The University of the Barrios, College of the Guys: School of Freedom). "The origin of La Universidad," according to one of its grant proposals, began in 1967,

> when several Mexican American college students, themselves products of San Antonio's predominantly Mexican American West Side, befriended members of several conflict gangs. These youths, though a long process of talking and associating with the college boys, became convinced that a dedication and commitment to "La Causa"—the Mexican American social movement toward justice, was the only purpose that could prevent them from a life of prison and violence.[33]

Four ex–gang members, supported by funds and guidance from MAUC, began organizing among five West Side gangs: La India, Ghost Town, the Lake, Los Tigers, and Los Mirasoles. The organizers were constantly harassed by rival gang members and by the police. This initial organizing phase lasted through most of 1968 and was "filled with perils." The barrio youths passed through "a period of trial and error"

> as they began changing their dependence on former destructive ghetto lessons. As they went through this personal purgatory they began talking with other youths about their discovery, i.e., commitment to "La Causa" is a far better way to prove yourself; getting high and gang conflicts were KID STUFF.[34]

Commitment to la causa was framed in terms of acquiring manhood and self-respect: "The real challenge is making the Anglo respect you as a man, and a man sees that his people in the barrio, his parents, his brothers and sisters get what they have coming."[35]

The "perils" of working with street youths surfaced publicly within a few weeks of the founding of the "freedom school." In October 1968, a group of batos began meeting formally as La Universidad de los Barrios. Norman Guerrero of La India, a philosophy major at Trinity University, served as the first "dean" of LUB and kept minutes of these meetings. The first set explained the purpose of La Universidad:

> The main function of LUB is to try to bring together the various gangs so that they can identify their problems. Once identifying their problems the barrio youth are encouraged to then seek solutions to the particular problems that they identify.[36]

The group "liked the idea and wanted some way to participate and keep off the streets." A suggestion was made that LUB have "a central place in 'La India' where the batos could get together and then try to establish other places in other barrios."[37]

By November, with some seed funding from MAUC, the group had acquired a house for its university at 133 Rounds, deep in the West Side. It was a two bedroom, one bath, wood frame house, common to the neighborhood. The group put up posters and drew political graffiti on the walls. About fifteen batos, with nicknames such as Gafas, Sapo, Chi-Chi, and Lampo, were now meeting regularly and talking about politics. Many of

La Universidad de los Barrios, January 1969. Gonzalez Collection,
Center for American History, University of Texas at Austin.

the batos "hanging out" at LUB wore berets and were aware of the Brown
Berets of Los Angeles and the Black Berets of Albuquerque, but at this time
they were MAYO members.

According to the second and third sets of minutes, the group had decided to "participate in Voter Registration and concentrate in precinct of 'La
India'" and to "explain their work and try to talk with batos from El Ghost
Town, Tiger and The Lake."[38] A serious crisis then nearly brought the entire project to an early demise. Mirroring the experience of the settlement
houses, MAYO organizers discovered that providing space for barrio youths
often meant providing space for conflict.

On the night of January 10, 1969, less than two months after LUB had
opened, an altercation outside the school resulted in the stabbing death of
a student nicknamed Gafas by a nonstudent, a neighborhood bato, over a
question of money. This provided the occasion for a police investigation of
LUB.[39] The homicide investigators, Detectives Roy Aguilar Jr. and S. Salas,
reported that one of the LUB students, Joe Castillo, age eighteen, had said

that the house was "for the young boys in the neighborhood to have meetings, to air out their differences and try to contact other Barrio Clubs to
have a little harmony among the Latins." But the detectives had seen the
interior of the house and were struck by its "political tint":

> It had literature in regards to the Brotherhood of Packing Houses, voter
> registration cards. Had our president LB Johnson dress[ed] as a Hippie
> ridding [sic] a motorcycle, Humphrey dressed like Tarzan ridding [sic] a
> Rhino, had several cards saying not to buy grapes, had a big sign show-
> ing our president elect Nixon stomping his feet on some grapes and indi-
> cating they were Latins and saying that if La Raza (Latins) do not unite,
> Nixon would stomp La Raza.[40]

Several quart bottles of beer back in the kitchen indicated that a lot of
drinking was going on. In the summary opinion of the detectives, the place
was "deplorable" and in need of "a good cleaning,"

> and for all this [sic] young kids in the neighborhood to hang out around
> this club under the disguise of Latinos Unidos, Barrios Unidos and the
> such, showing big pinup pictures of naked girls, a nun showing her
> thigh, is just a trouble spot and lacks supervision.[41]

Along with their written report, the detectives submitted photos of the
graffiti-covered walls. The graffiti reflected a mix of political statements,
high school exhortations, and individual "tags," and the drawings ranged
from a life-sized Brown Beret to a beautiful "Mary Jane." Written at the top
of one wall was a call to "Raise your weapon, Chicano!" (Alzate! Chicano!
La Arma!) by the "Project of the Society in Defense of My Culture" (Proyec-
to de la Sociedad en Defensa de Mi Cultura). At the bottom of the same
wall was a poetic slogan dedicated to Che Guevara: "We must grow tough,
but without losing our tenderness." On the side of the window frame was
a tag by "El José de los Brown Berets." (Many batos were already dressing
as Berets even though the group had not been formally organized.) Clearly
this was no settlement house.

A few days after Gafas's death, the group gathered at the LUB house for
a special meeting to discuss what had transpired. The bare, laconic tone of
the minutes is especially pronounced at this point:

> The death was discussed. The question was asked why the death had to
> occur. It was discussed if and where any blame is to be laid. It was de-

Crime scene, La Universidad de los Barrios, January 10, 1969. Gonzalez Collection, Center for American History, University of Texas at Austin.

Police photo of the interior of La Universidad de los Barrios, 1969. "Alzate!" (*upper left*) means "Rise up!" Gonzalez Collection, Center for American History, University of Texas at Austin.

cided that if La Universidad is to work with and among the barrio youth
this type of incident while to be avoided is nevertheless to be expected.
In order to avoid any further pressure from law enforcement it was decided to temporarily close the place and continue to work on voter registration in the best manner possible.[42]

But the damage was done. The fact that this was a political center and
not a "social work" oriented place made this death special for some observers. Indeed, LUB had already been under police surveillance before the
stabbing. Days after the murder, in the first of several negative portrayals,
the *San Antonio Express & News* juxtaposed an article on the slaying at "Barrios U" next to one on groups funded by MAUC's $100,000 budget. The
point was made: La Universidad de los Barrios, Colegio de los Batos, which
the article translated as "College of the Punks," was one of MAUC's irresponsible projects.[43] LUB members were naturally irate at the newspaper
article and decided "to avoid further notoriety" by keeping their organizational efforts "as indiscreet [sic] as possible."[44] The LUB house closed for a
few months.

A Blown Cover: The VISTA Minority Mobilization Program

With access to VISTA's Minority Mobilization funds, MAYO had expanded
beyond its San Antonio base to more than a dozen sites in South and West
Texas. MAYO organizers within VISTA had a dual role, and in this way pro-
tected their grants. As Compean put it, "When you raise hell, you're MAYO,
not VISTA. The cover was blown in Del Rio."[45]

MAYO's use of the VISTA MM program came to light in February 1969,
when three VISTA volunteers in Del Rio were charged with taking part
in MAYO-sponsored activities. Dr. Fermín Calderón, head of the Del Rio
VISTA, fired the individuals involved and defended the program before
some agitated Val Verde County commissioners. The commissioners nonetheless asked the governor, Preston Smith, to request the national Office of
Economic Opportunity to withdraw the twenty VISTA workers in Del Rio
because staffers had been involved in political activity in violation of federal guidelines. The governor concurred.[46]

In response, MAYO leaders decided to raise the stakes and make the Del
Rio situation a symbol of the system's treatment of Chicanos. The Del Rio
City Council, anticipating trouble, quickly passed an ordinance prohibiting
marches and demonstrations without a proper permit, excepting funerals.

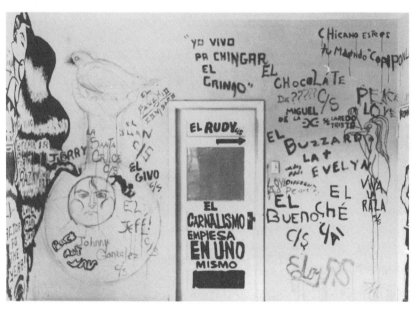

LEFT: Police photo of Brown Beret figures on the wall of La Universidad de los Barrios, 1969. Gonzalez Collection, Center for American History, University of Texas at Austin.

BELOW: Police photo of the interior of La Universidad de los Barrios, 1969. The sentence above the door, "yo vivo pa' chingar el gringo," means "I live to fight the gringo." Gonzalez Collection, Center for American History, University of Texas at Austin.

In mock defiance, on March 15, MAYO staged a funeral procession for a rabbit named "Justice" to protest the requested termination of the Del Rio VISTA program. Thirty-two people, mostly teenagers, were arrested. The MAYO leaders then raised the stakes even higher and began planning for a massive protest to take place on March 30, Palm Sunday.[47]

A broad organizing committee that included elected officials, clergy, and prominent civil rights leaders was formed. Bexar County commissioner Albert Peña arrived on March 16, the day after the arrests, to take the lead in planning the march. A few days before Palm Sunday, the coalition held a high-profile press conference in Washington, D.C. Peña revealed that "El Plan de Del Rio" would be up for adoption at the Sunday meeting. The plan involved a Mexican American bill of rights, a Mexican American declaration of independence, and "full restoration of our dignity and identity," Peña said. He added that this was no longer a Del Rio problem, but "an insult to all Mexicanos."[48] José Ángel Gutiérrez added more vinegar to the public statements, noting that MAYO had asked Governor Smith "to send the symbol of gringo injustice, Ranger Capt. A. Y. Allee, to stop us."[49]

MAYO's belligerent rhetoric had previously stirred anger and fear among some middle-class Mexican Americans in San Antonio and elsewhere in South Texas. Now the "hate literature" and rhetoric had spread 150 miles westward to Del Rio, a border town of some 25,000. Del Rio, which prided itself as "a fine example" of good community relations, had gradually been dismantling its segregated order. In 1969 the city was still experiencing the convulsions of court-ordered school integration, but it was no longer a border town run solely by an Anglo elite. It was a town in transition. The city's first Mexican American mayor, Dr. Alfredo Gutiérrez (no relation to José Ángel Gutiérrez), had been elected, and five of the seven city council members were Mexican American. Although many vestiges of segregation still remained—the local country club still had a "Whites only" policy—Mexican American businessmen were taking a more active role in city politics. This conservative, elite group was determined to protect a fragile progress from outside interference. Del Rio mayor Gutiérrez defended the removal of the VISTA volunteers because they had joined with MAYO in printing and distributing literature that blamed the "smiling, blue-eyed gringo" for the "miserable plight" of the Chicanos. Mayor Gutiérrez asserted that all people in Del Rio had equal opportunity, noting that some groups, such as the Volunteer Women's Organization, did outreach work in the barrios "to help with recreation, beautification and human relations problems." In response, the Mexican American Legal Defense and Education Fund (MALDEF) filed a lawsuit against the Del Rio Country Club for its "Whites only" membership.[50]

To the surprise of many, Congressman Henry B. Gonzalez of San Antonio jumped into the fray two days before the march. Gonzalez, who had been defending the status quo in San Antonio for over a year, understood the division within the Mexicano community of Del Rio. Although he had earlier refused to become involved in the farmworkers' strike in the Valley because it was "out of his district," the congressman now joined in the Del Rio controversy and began a vigorous counterattack against MAYO.

In a televised interview, Gonzalez blasted the young Chicano activists as racists and Communist-inspired extremists. Referring to confidential information he had received, he charged that "Cuban trained revolutionaries" had infiltrated the ranks of Mexican Americans planning a massive demonstration in Del Rio. In the words of the congressman: "Castro and the Cuban government has [sic] heavily subsidized trips by 50 to 100 young men of Mexican descent from California. They have come back heavily indoctrinated and are the ones who have been preaching this racial hatred of 'gringo imperialists.'"[51]

The march had been infiltrated by "some returning flaming radicals," Gonzalez said, adding that he was investigating "the extent of this involvement, but it has been considerable." In actuality, the congressman had only impressionistic information at this time, but he believed that "a premeditated, directed drive was being made in the Southwest to polarize the situation."[52] The major reaction of the activist community to Gonzalez's sweeping and alarmist statements was one of disbelief.[53]

An Untelevised Challenge

Against the backdrop of dramatic charges and countercharges about the upcoming Palm Sunday march, a vigorous local challenge to the old order was virtually ignored in the San Antonio news media. The long-dominant Good Government League (GGL) was being challenged in the city council elections by the Committee for Barrio Betterment (CBB), a West Side slate organized by the combined efforts of MAYO and Barrios Unidos. MAYO leader Mario Compean, schoolteacher Darío Chapa, and businessman Candelario "Candy" Alejos were on the ballot for the April 1 election, to be held two days after Palm Sunday. Social worker Mariano Aguilar was the campaign chair.

The MAYO–Barrios Unidos partnership had entered the political arena in January 1969 after a heated meeting at Karam's Restaurant, where the West Side liberals—Albert Peña, Johnny Alaniz, Pete Torres, Joe Bernal, and others who had long opposed the GGL—regularly gathered for Friday lunch.

Alaniz insulted the activists by asking them to act as "the kamikazes," after which "the politicians" would move in. Upset at such paternalism, Mario Compean, Nacho Pérez, Jesse Sauceda, Cruz Chapa, and Mariano Aguilar left the meeting and met at a tavern, Salon Social Tea, down the street, where they began talking about their own agenda. Thus was born the Committee for Barrio Betterment, formed to run a slate for city council in the spring of 1969 against the Good Government League.[54]

According to political scientist Rodolfo Rosales, the CBB was a coalition of barrio organizations, including MAYO, that rejected "the middle class politics of the Anglo community as well as the coalition politics of Albert Peña and others." Peña, Bernal, and their associates, who were considered "radical" by the GGL and Congressman Gonzalez, were now dismissed as too timid. From the cultural nationalist perspective of MAYO–Barrios Unidos, "a middle class Chicano from the north side" was "just as incapable" of representing the West Side as a middle-class Anglo. Compean, who was challenging Mayor McAllister, summarized the CBB platform as one of eliminating the "gringo rule" of the Good Government League.[55]

CBB strategy, according to campaign manager Aguilar, was to focus on the barrios and use "mimeograph and ditto machines" and groups such as the Teatro de los Barrios and "neighborhood networks, bautismos and quinceañeras" to reach out to people.[56] The staff consisted of women volunteers from various barrio clubs, and the fieldworkers included several ex–gang batos. This was clearly a low-budget affair.

The Good Government League and the mainstream news media basically ignored the CBB. It was not considered a serious challenge because of its ethnic rhetoric, its paltry budget, and its barrio-oriented campaign. In an oblique reference to the CBB, the GGL featured footage of the 1968 Chicago riots in its televised political ads. But the CBB campaign was not televised or reported on in any significant way, remaining largely invisible to San Antonians outside the West and South sides. In the spring of 1969 considerable organizing was taking place in these barrios as activists simultaneously mounted a city council campaign and planned a mass protest event in Del Rio, 150 miles away. These were frenzied times.

Although the LUB house had been closed, the batos had continued meeting regularly, taking minutes, and working on the school's articles of incorporation so that it could secure future funding from the Mexican American Unity Council. They had participated in a voter registration drive and in the CBB campaign itself. The March and April minutes mention the Del Rio situation and "its effect on La Raza and La Causa"; however, no mention is made of the press conference held in early April—in part to clear the name

The march in Del Rio, Texas, on March 30, 1969, was attended by more than 3,000 people from throughout the state. Photo by Shel Hershorn, *Texas Observer*, April 11, 1969.

of LUB—where LUB dean Norman Guerrero had menacingly pounded the table and declared that the gringo system had not produced "angels."[57] Instead, the minutes are laconic, showing no indication of the maelstrom gathering around LUB, MAYO, and the Chicano movement in general.

¡Que Viva Max!

The Del Rio controversy competed for front-page attention in the San Antonio newspapers with another simmering conflict that appeared to test the tradition and symbols of the old order. Montmorency Productions of Hollywood wished to film the satirical comedy *Viva Max!* on the grounds of the Alamo. The film featured Peter Ustinov as Maximilian, a modern-day Mexican general who decides to recapture the Alamo. Over the objections of the Daughters of the Republic of Texas (DRT), the "traditional" guardians of the old mission, the city council had given the Hollywood company permission to film on city land that fronts the Alamo. Attempting to block the filming, the DRT barricaded the gates of Long Barracks with a concrete bench and some flower pots. Several genealogical societies throughout the state rallied in support of the DRT. The *San Antonio Express* commented wryly that "the DRT battle to stave off a second taking of the fortress-shrine was as determined if not as bloody as the original battle in 1836."[58]

"Some heroes are born . . . some are made . . . some are mistakes."
Poster for the movie *Viva Max!*

"General Max" leads the charge against the Alamo, 1969. *San Antonio Express & News* Collection, University of Texas at Austin Institute of Texan Cultures, L-6412-B-34.

Thus, on Palm Sunday in 1969, while 3,000 young Chicanos were marching in Del Rio to protest inequality and injustice, a platoon of Hollywood extras dressed in Mexican army uniforms, led by Peter Ustinov on horseback, marched down Houston Street in downtown San Antonio on their way to recapture the Alamo. The photographic coverage of the *San Antonio Express* captured the drama of the march as well as "the final assault" led by General Max, mounted on a white steed at full gallop. "Teddy Roosevelt at San Juan Hill had nothing on General Max at the Alamo when it comes to enthusiasm." Such was the surreal juxtaposition one saw in front-page news during this time. Whether from angry protests or satiric comedy, the traditions and symbols of the old order seemed to be under assault.[59]

MAYO activists, naturally, had long before targeted the Alamo for symbolic attention. The group's founding had been announced via a picket in front of the Alamo. When MAYO activists began to publish a newspaper, they named it *El Deguello*, after the trumpet call by Santa Anna that had given the signal to take no prisoners. The reasoning given was blunt and provocative: "El Deguello must again sound out its war cry to all Chicanos that we must rise up against the gringo again. He has had his last chance."[60]

A CONGRESSMAN REACTS

SPEAKING BEFORE CONGRESS, Henry B. Gonzalez described, with a tone of bewilderment, the panorama that he saw unfolding in his district:

> We see a strange thing in San Antonio today; we have those who play at revolution and those who imitate the militance of others. . . . We have those who cry "brown power" only because they have heard "black power" and we have those who yell "oink" or "pig" at police, only because they have heard others use the term. We have those who wear beards and berets, not because they attach any meaning to it, but because they have seen it done elsewhere. But neither fervor nor fashion alone will bring justice."[1]

It was Congressman Gonzalez's fourth House speech on the subject in the month of April 1969. He was determined to douse the fervor.

"The troubles," as the congressman explained later to his biographer, Ronnie Dugger, started in 1966 or 1967 when the farmworkers went on strike in the lower Rio Grande Valley. Texas state senator Joe Bernal had asked him to join a group traveling to Rio Grande City to protest the use of the Texas Rangers as strikebreakers. Gonzalez said that he could not venture into the politics of another congressional district and break "an unwritten rule." Several months later, Gonzalez recalled, he heard that several political figures, including county commissioner Albert Peña and ex-protégé Willie Velásquez, had denounced him for having turned his back on Mexican

Americans. Then he learned that Velásquez had helped organize a Chicano conference (in January 1968) where some speakers had advocated sabotage at Kelly Field and the planting of a bomb at the city's Public Service Board. The worrisome activity continued apace. In April and May, more than a thousand students walked out at two West Side high schools, Lanier and Edgewood, demanding college prep classes, a culturally relevant curriculum, and clean restrooms. Then, in August, the social workers of the settlement houses walked out and moved into the office of the upstart militant organization MAYO. Gonzalez felt profoundly disillusioned.[2]

The activists, for their part, felt equally disillusioned with the congressman. "Yeah," acknowledged George Velásquez, "criticism of Henry B. had been mounting. After every confrontation—the Texas Ranger incident in the Valley, the walkouts at Lanier and Edgewood high schools—we would ask, 'Where is Henry B.?'" Gonzalez was being taken to task for his silence and inaction. And he was being confronted publicly. In December 1968, at a West Side community meeting attended by 300 people, fifty walked out after Gonzalez refused to answer their challenging questions.[3]

About that time the congressman began receiving "intel" reports from the San Antonio Police Department (SAPD). La Universidad de los Barrios (LUB) was the focus of one of the first police intel reports that Congressman Gonzalez would receive. In a January 3, 1969, report, Sgt. Rafael López of SAPD observed that among those at a meeting called to protest the police killing of Eloy Vidal was MAYO member Norman Guerrero, who was also the dean of LUB. Norman was accompanied by one of the school's students, Ramiro "Lampo" Ledesma, who had "a record of three murders and one assault to murder."[4] "Henry B.," who was known for his remarkable memory, would catalog this fact for later use.

In an effort to understand what was happening in his district, Congressman Gonzalez began to draw sketches of the networks and links between various movement organizations, or what is known in sociology as an "organizational field." The pace of political activity in San Antonio's West Side and in other barrios throughout the Southwest seemed like a veritable explosion. The new acronyms alone—MAYO, MAUC, MALDEF, LUB, MANCO, CBB—were difficult to keep track of. Later, when he assailed the Ford Foundation for having subsidized the creation of new militant organizations with "questionable leadership," Gonzalez observed that "the proliferation of new organizations over the past year has made it all but impossible to determine which is and is not funded with foundation money, let alone to know even if the foundation is aware of how its money is being used."[5]

Protest against Captain Allee of the Texas Rangers during the U.S. Commission on Civil Rights hearings at Our Lady of the Lake University, San Antonio, Texas, January 8, 1968. *San Antonio Express & News* Collection, University of Texas at Austin Institute of Texan Cultures, E-0017-64-f34, courtesy of the Hearst Corporation.

Gonzalez's quandary was understandable. Like most large-scale social movements, the Chicano movement was characterized by a thick, ever-changing organizational web. Overlapping memberships and overlapping organizational goals were commonplace, and it was sometimes difficult to distinguish "head or tail," much less a genealogy, of the movement. Often, especially in a movement's early years, different organizations with distinct styles and strategies are confounded, mixed, or joined in one or two offices. Such was the case with the Mexican American Youth Organization (MAYO).

Because this was an emergent movement, Gonzalez's diagrams of the organizational field would go through several drafts.

The Thin Skin of Henry B.

The tension and conflict between Gonzalez, the liberal congressman from San Antonio, and Chicano movement activists had been evident long before the Del Rio incidents. In 1968 Gonzalez had begun to speak out against Chicano militancy and in defense of San Antonio's public image. That year he criticized a CBS special program on hunger in San Antonio and the civil rights hearings held there, when only a few years earlier his speeches could have served as compelling testimony in both the exposé and hearings.[6] "Henry B.," as he was popularly known, seemed to have changed.

It was difficult for many in the Mexican American community to understand Congressman Gonzalez's negative attitude toward the emerging Chicano movement. Gonzalez had earned a heroic status in the Mexican American and African American communities for his aggressive challenges of Jim Crow segregation in the 1950s, first as a San Antonio city councilman and later as a member of the Texas Senate. His record-setting filibuster of thirty-six hours, which defeated most of the senate's segregationist bills

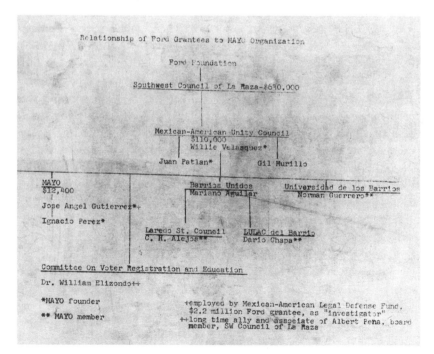

Congressman Henry B. Gonzalez's diagram of Chicano movement relationships, 1969 (Gonzalez Collection, Center for American History, University of Texas at Austin).

in 1956–1957, was legendary. The *Texas Observer* had hailed Gonzalez as "the new State orator, champion of his people and others oppressed, and a man of magic mind and voice." First elected to Congress in 1961, Gonzalez proved to be a resolute liberal in his voting. He continued to speak for the "common person" and was an unabashed friend of organized labor. In 1962 he introduced a bill to repeal the poll tax and another to abolish the Bracero program for Mexican immigrant workers. The following year he opposed additional appropriations for the House of Un-American Activities Committee, thereby incurring the wrath of many conservative groups. In 1964 he was one of a handful of southern congressmen to vote for the Civil Rights Act. Henry B. was not afraid to take unpopular stances. As a friend of labor, he had been present at the 1966 Labor Day rally that celebrated the conclusion of the farmworkers' march from the Valley.[7]

After such a courageous record of progressive work, the mounting criticisms of his inaction must have been a bitter and insulting sting. Could it be, as historian Richard García asked of the Mexican American middle class, that "the hunger and militancy" of their 1950s civil rights movement had become "somewhat diluted," or, as many critics of Gonzalez put it, compromised?[8]

By the late 1960s, Gonzalez appeared to be a defender of the Anglo-dominated status quo. As newspaper commentator Paul Thompson put it, Gonzalez was liberal in the area of civil rights, but conservative when it came to taxes and spending. Moreover, Gonzalez had worked "unstintingly for state and local business projects," thus earning the support of San Antonio's business community and "a whole heap of Anglo-Americans on the north side."[9] The most ambitious project championed by Gonzalez was the planning and financing of HemisFair, an event timed to commemorate the 250th anniversary of the founding of San Antonio. HemisFair's executive committee, according to one observer, read like a roster "of old rich San Antonians." Set to open in the summer of 1968, this world's fair was a public-private venture that was intended to put San Antonio on the national map.[10] This may explain Gonzalez's sharp criticism of anything that threatened to highlight the city's poverty and segregation.

At the local level, Gonzalez's compromises with the establishment and years of personal infighting had made him many friends and enemies. The bitterest animosities surfaced among former political allies, including county commissioner Albert Peña, state senator Joe Bernal, and ex-protégé Willie Velásquez. Peña had played a key role in Gonzalez's 1961 election to Congress. Joe Bernal, who served in the Texas House from 1964 to 1966

Congressman Henry B. Gonzalez at the 1966 Labor Day rally in Austin, Texas. Father Henry Casso is standing behind Gonzalez, on the right. Gonzalez Collection, Center for American History, University of Texas at Austin.

and the Texas Senate until 1972, had considered the congressman one of his mentors. Velásquez, who had worked three summers at the State Department, courtesy of Gonzalez, was once part of Henry B.'s political family.

The falling out with Willie Velásquez was perhaps the bitterest disillusion of them all. George Velásquez, Willie's brother, recalled that "Henry B. saw himself as Willie's mentor. He was preparing Willie to run for political office. But they disagreed over too many things—the farmworkers, the student walkouts. When Willie broke away, Henry B. felt betrayed."[11]

In the fall of 1967, Willie Velásquez told Gonzalez that he was returning to Texas to help "los mexicanos." Later Velásquez recounted that the meeting was taken up by a Gonzalez monologue about his critics and enemies, naming Peña, Bernal, and city councilman Pete Torres. Velásquez said that they were "good people doing something," but Gonzalez responded by saying, "You can't expect cooperation from me if in fact you're consorting with my enemies." Juan Sepúlveda, Velásquez's biographer, notes that the breakup between Velásquez and Gonzalez was more than just a misunderstanding between a "naïve idealistic kid" and a "seasoned politician." It had the overtones of a familial dispute—"like a father reprimanding a slightly rebellious son."[12]

Although county commissioner Albert Peña had helped get Gonzalez elected to Congress in 1961, he had soured on his support by the mid-1960s. Noting the fund-raising efforts of the Good Government League on Gonzalez's behalf, Peña commented: "For a long time many of us have known that Gonzalez has forgotten the people who elected him." Peña, who had accompanied state senator Bernal to the Lower Rio Grande Valley to support the striking farmworkers, asked why Gonzalez had kept quiet "when Texas Rangers were kicking people around in South Texas?"[13]

To the thin-skinned Gonzalez, such criticism was a declaration of war. Once provoked, he did not hesitate to trade verbal insults. Commenting that Peña had always wanted to be the "Super Mex" on the West Side, Gonzalez said that he would contribute to build a "monument to Super-Mex in the middle of the West Side, provided Peña learns how to keep the restrooms clean at Mission County Park in his precinct."[14]

The Gonzalez-Peña feud picked up steam in 1968 and became the subplot behind many of their public statements and positions. In 1968, a CBS special, "Hunger in America," focused an embarrassing spotlight on San Antonio, noting that it was one of the poorest cities in the country, where 100,000 people went hungry. The timing of the exposé was not good. Hemis-Fair, a business showcase project that had been several years in the making, was set to open in the summer of 1968, and this nationally televised documentary was a public relations disaster. Congressman Gonzalez, defending San Antonio's image, blasted CBS for "fraudulent" inaccuracies. Taking a swing at Peña, Gonzalez added, "If CBS had known that the commissioner it relied on was at the time engaged in a political contest and desperate for an audience, it might have suspected that his statements would have been dramatized for their benefit."[15] Subsequently, with Gonzalez's apparent approval, the FBI stepped in to interrogate the poor families highlighted by the CBS documentary.[16]

Timing, however, would not be kind to the HemisFair. Two days before its opening on April 6, 1968, Martin Luther King Jr. was assassinated, setting off a wave of urban riots. While rioters and soldiers faced off in several cities across the country, San Antonio was hosting a party. But these were not happy times in the city's restive barrios.

Congressman Henry B.
Gonzalez opening San An-
tonio's HemisFair, April 6,
1968. Mrs. Louise Straus,
wife of Chamber of Com-
merce president David
Straus, is to his left. Zintgraff Collection, University
of Texas at San Antonio
Institute of Texan Cultures,
z-1088-001-1, courtesy of
John and Dela White.

Gonzalez clearly did not like what was happening back in San Antonio,
and he went after the prominent figures, such as Albert Peña and Joe Bernal, the "so-called older radicals," who were supporting the Chicano militants. He warned them against polarizing the climate and asked them to disassociate themselves from the "orators of race and hate." As for the young
activists, who considered him "a hopeless, passé reformist," Gonzalez's first
public comments, expressed just before the Del Rio march, labeled them as
"Castroites" and Communists. Later he would call them "hate mongers" and
"punks."[17]

The Chicano activists counterattacked. "Of course," recalled George
Velásquez, "we threw stuff right back. They would respond, and then we
would answer back. We went back and forth like that for a year." Velásquez

added, "To our parents and their generation, Henry B. was a hero, a pioneer. They couldn't understand our criticism. Tony the neighborhood grocer asked us if we knew what we were doing."[18]

Del Rio, 1969: "Are You With Me, Henry B.?"

Gonzalez's widely publicized remarks about Castro-trained activists being involved in the protest did not dampen enthusiasm for the Del Rio march. An estimated 3,000 Mexican Americans gathered on Palm Sunday (March 30, 1969) at the Del Rio Civic Center for a rally of speeches and then marched three miles through the city, heralding "a new decade for the Chicano." Following their Alinsky training, MAYO leaders seemed to have turned defeat into victory. The Palm Sunday march drew thousands, and also put the Raza Unida movement in the national spotlight as all three major television networks and newspaper reporters from the *New York Times*, the *Los Angeles Times*, and the *National Observer* were on hand. The rally became a general indictment of the system's treatment of Chicanos.[19]

One skeptical reporter, Leo Cardenas of the *San Antonio Express & News*, couched his coverage in sarcastic terms. According to Cardenas, José Ángel Gutiérrez of San Antonio, leader of "the young, serape-clad organization" MAYO, shocked the marchers with his belligerent talk about oppression and tangling "with the 'gringo' anywhere he wants to." The other aspect that struck Cardenas was the prospect that the Black civil rights movement was spilling over into the Mexican American community. He noted the words of state representative Curtis Graves of Houston, who told the crowd that "La Raza is not alone" and that Black men "will march with you to victory and will not stop until all are free."[20] When Gutiérrez tacked "The Del Rio Manifesto" onto a wall of the courthouse, Cardenas observed that he had been joined by R. L. Hayes, an African American activist from Houston. Cardenas's words suggested the taint of Black radicalism:

> A brown hand and a black hand joined efforts here on this sunny Palm Sunday afternoon to pin a "warrant for justice" on the doors of the Val Verde County courthouse. . . .
> "Viva la Raza!" the crowd yelled.
> The red flag of the militant Mexican-American Youth Organization (MAYO) was raised then on the courthouse courtyard.[21]

Cardenas sardonically concluded his report by noting that "The poverty stricken, about whom the orators spent thousands of words to describe their plight during the morning hours of the mass meeting, apparently stayed home."[22]

Despite anxiety and apprehension about possible trouble—Commissioner Peña recalled that the Department of Public Safety had been present with machine guns—the atmosphere at the rally and march was one of peaceful determination and a resolve to seek justice. The Del Rio Manifesto, authored by Peña, MAYO leader Juan Patlán, and Reverend Henry Casso from the San Antonio Archdiocese, was essentially a "Mexican-American Declaration of Independence and Bill of Rights." The manifesto touted La Raza as "the affirmation of the most basic ingredient of our personality, the brownhood of our Aztec and Mayan heritage." The unifying coloration of "brownhood" was explained in the language of Catholicism:

> As children of La Raza, we are heirs of a spiritual and biological miracle wherein family blood ties unite the darkest and the fairest. It is no accident that the objects of our veneration include the black Peruvian St. Martin de Porres, the brown Indian Virgin of Guadalupe, the blue-blood European Madonnas, and the Jewish Christ of Indian and Spanish features."[23]

The speakers in general offered moderate visions of change. Reverend Casso, one of the march organizers, declared that if "we can't help self-determination in Del Rio," then it is time for the United States to call the Peace Corps volunteers throughout the world to come home. Dr. Hector García of Corpus Christi in his remarks mentioned the sacrifice of Mexican Americans in Vietnam and in previous wars. "Ya Basta!" (This is enough!) was the prominent theme of the mass meeting.[24]

Another theme was sounded by the chant "Are you with me, Henry B.?" as various speakers responded to Gonzalez's charges that the meeting had been infiltrated by Cuban Communists. Retired army major Raúl Gutiérrez held up his glass case of eleven medals and said, "I was trained here to go to Cuba and not in Cuba to come here." Senator Bernal, the keynote speaker, started his speech by noting, "I am not here from Cuba. I just got in from San Antonio." He described the struggle as "not an Anglo versus Mexican battle, but it's a bad-Anglo against the Mexican. Likewise the fight is not Mexican versus Mexican, but instead elite Mexican versus the peon."[25] In his speech,

Bexar County commission Albert Peña, in outlining details under which La
Raza Unida banner would fly, pointedly noted that "there are two kinds of
people the group will not tolerate: the Anglo American who plots his strat-
egy so that one Mexican-American will battle another Mexican-American.
Even worse, the Mexican-American who 'sells out.'" Peña then shouted,
"Are you with me, Henry B.?"[26]

The following day, Gonzalez responded by saying, "Not only no, but hell
no, Albert P." He then expounded on his earlier remarks, noting that MAYO
for a year or so had been infiltrated by students and others from California,
and that they had been subsidized by Castro for trips to Cuba. Gonzalez
also excoriated MAYO literature that condemned the "blue-eyed gringo" and
used the slogan "the ballot or the bullet," saying, "These sheets reflect the
language of Castro and incorporate language that is alien to our area of the
country."[27]

Gonzalez said that he didn't know why the speakers were out to blud-
geon him, but that both Peña and Bernal were probably interested in his
congressional seat. Of Bernal, Gonzalez said, "I don't know why he chose to
ridicule me, but he who laughs last laughs the best."[28] The feud was getting
personal, and it was being played out openly through the newspapers.

Peña responded by saying: "I want to state categorically that I'm not
after his seat, or any other part of his anatomy." He added that Gonzalez
had maligned the 4,000 people who had gathered to protest on behalf of
Mexicans, as well as leaders such as state representatives Bob Vale, Carlos
Truan, Raul Muñiz, and Lauro Cruz, and state senator Bernal, and such organizations as LULAC, the American GI Forum, and PASO. Peña surmised
that "It has become more and more obvious that anyone or any group organizing on behalf of the civil rights of Mexican Americans, if not cleared
with Henry B., are suspect." Peña denied he had called Gonzalez "a sellout."
"What in the world ever made Henry B. think I was talking about him?"
Peña said, obviously tongue-in-cheek.[29]

Bernal replied that he had no intention of running against Gonzalez
and that he didn't even live in Gonzalez's congressional district. "This does
not limit me to be critical when I think he has been wrong. . . . I think he
was wrong in making blanket accusations. . . . I resent the implication that
people attending the Del Rio conference had anything to do with Castro."
Bernal said he had spoken up for Gonzalez when he was maligned during
the McCarthy witch-hunts, yet now Gonzalez was using similar guilt-by-
association tactics. Bernal added, "I got very critical of people who were
calling him a 'pink' when he first ran for Congress." Gonzalez responded
the following day, calling Bernal a "liar."[30]

"El Voto o La Bala!" (The Ballot or the Bullet!) From the February 1969 issue of the MAYO newspaper, *El Deguello*. Gonzalez Collection, Center for American History, University of Texas at Austin.

"¡¡Ya Basta!!" (Enough!) In this cartoon, Congressman Henry B. Gonzalez is portrayed as the "malinche," or traitor, of Landa Park, who has turned against poor Mexicans. The mention of Landa Park is a historical reference to Gonzalez's much-publicized encounter with segregation in New Braunfels in the mid-1950s. The last frame asks rhetorically, "Were we born to shine the shoes of 'others,' Henry???" The answer: "This is enough!! Where is the pride? Where is the anger? Where is the shame, people?" From *La Nueva Raza* (San Antonio), September 1969. Author's collection.

The tactics employed by Gonzalez were severe—involving arrests, surveillance by FBI and undercover informants, public innuendos and denunciations, and suggestions of criminality and violence, most based on information that was never produced. Gonzalez sought and received intelligence from the San Antonio Police Department, the Texas Department of Public Safety, and the FBI, none of which supported the charge of Communism. Many citizens, upset about the activities of Mexican American organizations, volunteered information to Gonzalez on what they considered to be suspicious or un-American activities. Several Catholic and Protestant clergy who were intimidated or angry about the Chicano movement also kept the congressman abreast of suspect activities. Father John Yanta, director of the San Antonio Youth Organization (SANYO), forwarded a "confidential file" of typed summaries of various meetings he had attended with "disgruntled" settlement workers and other movement activists. Father Fritz, chaplain of the Newman Student Center at San Antonio College, reported that a student newsletter criticizing the congressman, called "El Pinche Buey" (The Mean Ox), was "a hate sheet, nothing more or less."[31] The predominantly "Anglo" and "Irish" clergy, who played a critical supporting role in the farm worker cause, were in no position to provide logistical assistance or moral leadership once "la causa" had taken a nationalist turn. Ironically, many key leaders of this movement were graduates of the Catholic school system.[32]

Losing Control of the West Side?

In the month following the Del Río march, the exchange of charges and countercharges between Gonzalez and Peña and Bernal became more intense. Adding fuel to Gonzalez's fire was the fact that the "militants" seemed to have surprising popular support in the barrios. Two days after the Del Rio protest march, its organizers and supporters had received an unexpected endorsement of sorts. In a maverick campaign against the incumbent and dominant Good Government League—in power then for fifteen years—the three Committee for Barrio Betterment (CBB) candidates received between 20 and 30 percent of the vote in the at-large San Antonio City Council elections. Although they never campaigned outside the barrios and had little money, they had nearly forced two GGL incumbents, including Mayor McAllister, into run-off elections.[33]

CBB candidate Mario Compean, one of five challengers for McAllister's mayoral seat, received only 12,000 votes to McAllister's 31,000, while the four other candidates pulled in slightly less than 19,000. But noting that

A caricature of Congressman Henry B. Gonzalez as "Don Quijote . . . of Money,"
sent by his aide Albert Bustamante, May 2, 1969. The "Fritzee" statement is a reference to Father Louis Fritz, director of the Newman Student Center at San Antonio
Community College, who was at odds with some of the Chicano students on campus. Congressman Gonzalez is riding to rescue Fritz from the pesky MAYO bird.
Gonzalez Collection, Center for American History, University of Texas at Austin.

he had beaten the incumbent mayor in all the West Side boxes, Compean proclaimed his victory as mayor of the West Side.[34]

The GGL had run scary TV ads featuring scenes of urban riots in Cleveland, Washington, and Chicago while a voice-over warned of "radical racism" and "brown power." Councilman Calderón, running for a third term, declared that the most important problem facing San Antonio was "the presence of a small, but militant violence-oriented group seeking to divide the community by pitting race against race for the purpose of gaining total control of the city." While the GGL never had any doubts about the election outcome, the strength of the "anti-gringo" CBB slate in the West and South sides took it by surprise.[35] CBB's "success" created doubts about the GGL's dominance, and it moved Gonzalez to redouble his efforts to discredit the Chicano movement.

On April 3, in a speech before the House of Representatives, Gonzalez attacked MAYO for "spreading a message of hate" among Mexican Americans. Its members were "Brown Power" advocates who liked "to costume themselves in brown berets, combat boots, serapes, rolled blankets slung over shoulder and chest in campaign style, moustaches and-or beards."

Table 4.1.
Mayoral Race by Select West Side Precincts, 1969

Precinct	Location	Compean (CBB candidate)	McAllister (GGL incumbent)
103	Brackenridge Elementary	144	36
106	Immaculate Conception Church	162	41
107	Inman Christian Center	214	41
108	Crockett School	198	108
109	DeZavala Elementary	170	83
110	Ivanhoe Elementary	211	42
111	Rhodes Jr. High School	314	38
112	Barkley Elementary	187	21
202	Bowie Elementary	131	51

Source: *San Antonio Light,* April 2, 1969.

Gonzalez also blasted "so-called older radicals who lend their assent and even support to the orators of race and hate." These people, he added, need not "wonder why their integrity is questioned." The congressman noted that he had been attacked repeatedly during his tenure in office by right-wing extremists as a Communist, a "Nigger-lover," and as a "dirty Meskin" because he believed in equality for all, but "Ironically, I now find myself attacked from the left as well as from the right."[36]

Gonzalez stated that he would not hesitate to say that it is just as wrong for an ethnic minority to succumb to hate and fear as it is for anyone else to do so. Now he had watched "with alarm" as new Mexican American militant groups formed, because some of them have "fallen into the spell and trap of reverse-racism." Gonzalez specifically charged that "members of the W. E. B. DuBois Club and rabble rousers" had been attending La Raza meetings, and that a participant had called for a "Castro-type uprising."[37] Black and Cuban revolutionaries were the two "outside" influences feared by the congressman and others opposed to the Chicano movement. This view was an undercurrent in the news reporting.

In an apparently coordinated effort, the San Antonio Express published an editorial that warned about the "destructive seeds" being sown by MAYO:

> The Mexican American Youth Organization, whose goals may be entirely
> worthy and supportable by all of us, has let its organization become
> a sponsor of papers attacking "blue-eyed whitey" and challenging the
> members to use "brown power," give "no quarter," and reclaim what "the
> gringo" took away: "The gringo took your grandfather's land, he took
> your father's job, and now he's sucking out your soul."
> Aside from being patent nonsense, that last line is designed to stir
> mindless hatred.[38]

The editorial dismissed MAYO as representing "a handful of malcontents" who "know very well that San Antonio is a veritable melting pot of the races and cultures" and that the city "offers opportunity and less racial prejudices than found in nearly any big city in America, if not the world."[39]

Paul Thompson, the controversial muckraking columnist for the San Antonio Express & News, joined the fray, backing Gonzalez. Thompson noted that MAYO was circulating "the worst kind of vicious, inflammatory word-slinging" leaflets on the West Side. This material, "which savagely goes to work on 'blue-eyed whitie' and the 'Gringo establishment,' calls on the 'chicano' to fight, fight, fight—even if it means death." Thompson rapped Peña and Bernal because they had hesitated "to do or say anything that might offend these MAYO youths with their serapes and slogans and steady hate spewing."[40]

The following day Senator Bernal publicly disassociated himself from "hate literature." While affirming his support for MAYO, he called on all organizations to quit using hate as an approach. At the same time, he called on Gonzalez to "come up with names of all those people that he claims were trained in Cuba and who participated in the Del Rio conference. Or else he ought to disassociate himself from this type of McCarthy guilt by association harangue."[41]

In response to reporters' questions, Bernal described the hate literature as a "misguided attempt" to "tell it like it is." It is hard to desist, Bernal noted, "when you are refused a haircut in West Texas, because you happen to be Mexican. Or when you cannot enter a swimming pool in Marlin. . . . Or when the San Felipe Country Club in Del Rio bars Mexican-Americans, even if one does happen to be the mayor." Bernal insisted that MAYO could continue to write about injustices without using "inflammatory words."[42] However, that belief would soon prove to be mistaken. Bernal had underestimated the degree of impatience and anger of the MAYO leadership.

Gonzalez broadened his attack to include the Ford Foundation and La Universidad de los Barrios. Now irresponsibility and criminality were added to the charges of Communism and race hatred. On April 7, Gonzalez announced that he would submit information concerning the hate literature to the congressional committee investigating the Ford Foundation, whose monies had "underwritten and paid for the circularization and printing and general dissemination of the hate literature and the clearly calculated activities intended to arouse public passion and civil disorder." He charged that the Ford Foundation, in trying "to help set up a national organization of Mexican-Americans similar to the NAACP of the negro minority," has turned over "in excess of $135,000 as a starter . . . to a 24-year-old." This "24 year-old," continued the congressman in reference to his former protégé, Willie Velásquez, "has astounded people by turning over fistfuls of money" to the University of the Barrios, "where drunken revels occurred and at whose entrance a 19-year old youth was stabbed to death."[43] Moreover, Velásquez had "facilitated over $10,000 in Ford Foundation money for Gutierrez and MAYO." Then Gonzalez noted that it was ironic that Gutiérrez, "the loud-mouthed, self-styled revolutionary head of MAYO who says he hates gringos," had no qualms about accepting "gringo Ford Foundation dollars." Calling Gutiérrez and Velásquez "self-imposed leaders," Gonzalez predicted that when the Ford money ran out, they would go home—and not to the barrios.[44]

April 10, 1969
1.30 PM to 2:45 PM
Tello T.V. appliance
1009 S. ZARAMORA st.

EMD 222   (sac sticker 3876)
2Y 9353   Truck
GJF 50
GKG 590   press
GMR 925
GJM 911   (Nielsen supporter)
HVB 120
GFC 343
GYR 760
GDV 926   priest
GVB 311
~~GJR 340~~
GRG 185   appeared again
GHG 76   * state car
GTR 369   50154
GVT 411
GHK 586   Lake Realtor
HPF 802
GTR 369   out of state
GDM 909   CONN. FR.-7475
GRG 185

Record of surveillance of MAYO headquarters, April 10, 1969. The note at the left margin reads "4/9/69 Two A-Saxon Bearded type," and above that, "appeared again." (Gonzalez Collection, Center for American History, University of Texas at Austin).

Willie Velásquez's take on all this? On one hand, he could understand Gonzalez's concerns. The congressman was concerned about losing political power and control in his district. In this sense, Gonzalez was like many other politicians around the country who were feeling the same pressure from community action programs created by the War on Poverty. So Gonzalez was targeting the Ford Foundation, the funding sponsor of MAUC, MAYO, and MALDEF. On the other hand, Velásquez could not understand the vehemence of Gonzalez's reaction, which seemed grossly out of proportion to what was actually happening. Neither MAUC nor MAYO, despite the strident rhetoric of the latter, had instigated riots or violence.[45]

But Gonzalez and the intelligence unit of the SAPD were taking no chances. The MAYO headquarters at Tello's T.V. Appliance Store at 1009 South Zarzamora Street was regularly watched. After MAYO scheduled a press conference, ostensibly to respond to Gonzalez's accusations, a congressional staffer monitored and recorded the license plates of those visiting the group's headquarters.[46] According to the surveillance, on April 10, from 1:30 to 2:45 p.m., a few hours before the press conference, twenty cars had parked at the headquarters. One had been driven by a priest, another by someone supporting Nielson (an independent candidate for city council), and another by "two A-Saxon Bearded type[s]" who had visited there the day before. Little did Gonzalez know that such covert surveillance would be unnecessary. The incriminating evidence that he sought would be provided by the MAYO leadership at a press conference they had organized.

KILL THE GRINGOS!

5   **EMBOLDENED BY** their performances in the Del Rio protest and the San Antonio city election, the MAYO leadership decided to respond to Congressman Gonzalez's charges by turning up the rhetorical heat. The strategy seemed to follow Alinksy's ninth rule for radicals: pick a target, freeze it, personalize it, and polarize it. This, in any case, was what MAYO leaders successfully pulled off through a press conference in which they called for the elimination of the "gringo" and questioned the manliness of a certain congressman. Of the two charges, the second was arguably the more consequential.

The MAYO Press Conference

Held on April 10, 1969, at the MAYO office in the heart of the West Side, the press conference was attended by at least a dozen reporters, believing that MAYO wished to respond to the charges leveled against it by Gonzalez. Sitting behind a table were attorney Juan Rocha of MALDEF, bespectacled and dressed in a suit; José Ángel Gutiérrez, the president of MAYO, looking and dressed like a graduate student; Mario Compean, MAYO's vice president, looking indifferent, his hand under his chin; and Norman Guerrero, dean of La Universidad de los Barrios, wearing the signature sunglasses of the bato loco. Rocha was present only to advise the MAYO members. Gutiérrez and Compean, along with Guerrero, wanted to use the press conference to explain MAYO's aims and to express their dissatisfaction with the "gringo system."[1]

"A gringo," Gutiérrez explained to the gathered reporters, "is a person or institution that has a certain policy or program or attitudes that reflect bigotry, racism, discrimination, and prejudice and bias." These "gringos and their institutions" had inflicted "vicious cultural genocide" on la raza and were obstructing Mexican Americans' "right of self-determination." If nothing else worked, warned Gutiérrez, the gringo might have to be "eliminated." Gutiérrez added that most Anglos in Texas are gringos.

Asked to explain what "eliminating the gringo" meant, Gutiérrez expounded:

You can eliminate an individual in various ways. You can certainly kill him. That is not our intent at this moment. You can remove the base of support that he operates from, be it economic, political, or social. That is what we intend to do.[2]

Pressed on whether he intended to kill all gringos, Gutiérrez countered that "if worst comes to worst" and the Mexicano had to resort to "killing gringos," it would be in self-defense. Gutiérrez then warned of the possibility of violence, rioting, or "serious social unrest" as the result of gringo policies.

Asked to respond to Congressman Gonzalez's remarks, Gutiérrez tried to skirt the issue by saying that MAYO would not engage in controversy with fellow Mexicanos regardless of how unfounded and vindictive their accusations might be: "We realize that the effects of cultural genocide takes many forms. Some Mexicanos will become psychologically castrated, others will become demagogues and gringos as well." Upon further questioning, Gutiérrez said that a Mexican American can be a gringo, and that Congressman Gonzalez had demonstrated tendencies that would fit in the gringo category.

Mario Compean tried to steer the press conference back to a discussion of MAYO's objectives. He noted that in the process of developing youth and barrio leadership, "political and other types of patrones will be eliminated and the barrios will be able to choose their own leaders and run their own communities." Among its many community activities, Compean noted that MAYO had been working with gangs to channel the energies of their members to meaningful and constructive projects.[3]

Guerrero, dean of La Universidad de los Barrios, defended the school from Congressman Gonzalez's attacks by blaming the criticism on ignorance. He said that Gonzalez did not understand the school's function, which was to make students understand the manner in which la raza had been injured by the gringo system. "We do not deal with angels," he noted.

"Kill the gringo" press conference: *left to right,* Juan Rocha of MALDEF, José Ángel Gutiérrez and Mario Compean of MAYO, and Norman Guerrero of La Universidad de los Barrios, April 10, 1969. Courtesy of the *San Antonio Express & News.*

Guerrero said that he and his staff of two were out in the creeks at 2 and 3 a.m., talking to dropouts and dope addicts. The students at La Universidad were dropouts and drop-ins—the "hard-core youth out on the streets." The police called the school's students "pachucos," and they in turn called the police "perros" (dogs).

When questioned about the curriculum, Guerrero pounded the table and said that bigoted, prejudiced gringos had put Mexican Americans in the deprived position they are in today. "After years of the psychological degradation we have encountered, the system has not produced angels," Guerrero said in further support of his students.[4]

The press conference predictably ignited a firestorm of reaction, with local newspapers featuring sensationalist and unsympathetic accounts. "MAYO Head Warning of Rioting, Violence," "Elimination of Gringos May Become Necessary," "We'll Crush Any Gringo Who Gets in Our Way," and "Gringos Gotta Go" blared the headlines. Lost in the militant talk had been the stated objectives of MAYO: "to secure our human and civil rights, to eliminate bigotry and racism, to lessen the tensions in our barrios and combat the deterioration of our communities."[5]

The talk about eliminating the gringo was not actually new. Compean and Gutiérrez had been using this rhetoric publicly for months. When Compean had announced the Committee for Barrio Betterment (CBB) campaign a few months earlier, he had pledged to "pursue a course plotted to overthrow the gringos." At the Del Rio rally, Gutiérrez had shocked some protestors by declaring that "we have been oppressed for too long and we will tangle with the gringo anywhere he wants to." But two weeks later, in the press conference called to respond to the charges of hate and racism leveled by Congressman Gonzalez, such language instead appeared to confirm the accusations.[6]

Gutiérrez's statements were quickly seized to embarrass the other leaders of the Del Rio march, Albert Peña and Joe Bernal, and to back up Congressman Gonzalez. Paul Thompson, political commentator for the *San Antonio Express & News*, had a field day with the MAYO press conference.[7] He started his front-page column with the following:

> When Jose "Angel Face" Gutierrez opened his mouth, a large one, and told the community how he was REALLY looking at things, it must have jolted some of our more conventional Mexican-American leaders.
>
> Like County Com. Albert A. Peña and State Sen. Joe J. Bernal, who had been praising this articulate little speechifier.

"With public utterances of the kind that out-rap Rap Brown," Thompson continued,

> this kid could be regarded as funny were it not for the fact that other young fellows who are also educated beyond their intelligence have been saying the same things.
>
> And saying them in areas where there's already a certain amount of unrest.

Then Thompson egged on the authorities to act:

> But how long can law enforcement authorities allow the war-like mouthings to emanate from the Angel Face without at least trying to quiet him down?[8]

Thompson concluded emphatically, saying that *"Somehow, some way, young Gutierrez has got it into his head that by preaching hate against 'blue-eyed whitie' and calling for 'gringo elimination' he can do his people some good."* Gonzalez was right, Thompson said. *"If anything, Gonzalez didn't go far enough."*[9]

But the congressman was not through. On April 11, the day after the MAYO press conference, he called a press briefing to disclose that a "concentrated effort" to disrupt the annual King's River Parade was being planned. Under the bold heading of "Gonzalez Says Fiesta Disruptions Planned," the *San Antonio Express* reported that Gonzalez had information "that militant Mexican American elements are making plans to disrupt Fiesta Week activities and that 'young toughs' plan to stand along the river bank and hurl objects—as well as epithets—at the participants." The congressman had again associated the movement with hooliganism. Gonzalez did not reveal any specifics; he said he would add this information to what he had amassed "if he and district judges decide it should be brought before the grand jury."[10]

At the same briefing, Gonzalez noted that his wife had received three phone calls threatening his life during the past week. Gonzalez said "the only reason" he mentioned the calls at all was that they had "the same tenor" as statements made by a MAYO leader about how it might ultimately be necessary to eliminate "gringos" by killing them. Gonzalez called Gutiérrez's remarks "false, noxious and poisonous drivel," and he called on county commissioner Albert Peña to "disavow" them. He also called on Bernal to either reaffirm his support of Gutiérrez, which he had announced publicly only a few days before, or to also disavow Gutiérrez's utterances.[11]

Both Peña and Bernal responded, as they had previously, that Gonzalez was using McCarthy-ite tactics in associating them and the protests with Fidel Castro.[12] Willie Velásquez hastily organized a community meeting to respond to Gonzalez's charges and to contain the damage caused by the "kill the gringo" press conference. At the meeting, attended by 200 people, Velásquez asked Gonzalez to name the Communists and Communist sympathizers in the Mexican American Unity Council (MAUC). Velásquez said the tactic of claiming Communist subversion was "a gross form of McCarthyism" and had been used "many times to destroy the lives of many people by his unfounded charges." Mrs. Guadalupe Ibarra, youth chair of the Cassiano Park Neighborhood Council, stated that "It is a shame that our congressman is fighting Mexican-Americans who come to help us help each other." She explained that her group worked with "boys who have no place to go and who would otherwise be in the streets."[13]

In a related action, LULAC Council No. 2 condemned "all vicious, malicious and despicable hate charges and counter-charges being leveled between local and so-called community leaders." While not naming individuals, the statement clearly sided with Congressman Gonzalez and called on all responsible and respectable citizens to unite with the council's position. Otherwise San Antonio would be seen as a city "seething and breathing with racism, radicalism and hate." LULAC leaders feared that the result of inaction could be "utter chaos" and "an untimely violence never experienced before in a major city."[14] And from Del Rio came word, via the *San Antonio Express*, that Dr. Fermín Calderón, who had launched the original protest against the removal of VISTA volunteers, had accused Gutiérrez of making "irresponsible statements." Calderón said he was disassociating himself from any connection with the militant group.[15]

When no disturbances marred the King's River parade April 14, Gonzalez took credit for preventing them. "I think we scared them off," he said. Nonetheless, Gonzalez said he was investigating links between Mexican American extremist groups and Black militants who had created a downtown mob disturbance. Gonzalez theorized that those incidents were aimed at provoking police to arrest the demonstrators, who wanted to echo the "usual worn-out police brutality charges." A police group, in the meantime, offered to provide security for the congressman.[16]

In the ensuing month, Gutiérrez tried to back off from the implications of his press conference statements, emphasizing that he meant killing the "gringo system" and not individuals, but the damage had been done. As Ronnie Dugger has noted, although Gutiérrez came close to saying "kill the gringo," he did not say it, "but he never succeeded in erasing from the public's mind the idea that he had."[17] Nor were the militant MAYO members in a mood to accept Gutiérrez's semantics. At a rally held in support of 116 persons arrested at a school walkout in Kingsville, when Gutiérrez told "a crowd of 400 cheering sympathizers that the militant group will 'kill gringos' economically and at the polls—not physically," shouts of "Kill!! Kill!!" came from the crowd.[18]

A View From the Cockpit

The political section of the *San Antonio Express* was titled "The Cockpit" and was appropriately framed by images of two fighting cocks. In a town governed by an Anglo business elite, this was simply a picturesque nod to Mexican culture. The editors of "The Cockpit" generally saw themselves as commentators standing above the political fray of the moment. On occasion, however, "The Cockpit" could take on the role of cheerleader, as in the contest between Congressman Gonzalez and MAYO.

"The Cockpit" elaborated Gonzalez's criticism of the Ford Foundation, directly naming its president. Its featured opinion piece noted, somewhat chagrined, that president McGeorge Bundy didn't know what his left and right hands were doing. The Ford Foundation had earmarked millions of dollars for a new goal, "Reducing Racial Tensions," while at the same time MAUC, with $110,000 in Ford funds, had "fostered a host of militant groups [and] . . . passed along $8,500 to get the gringo-hating Mexican-American Youth Organization off the ground." In contrast to the expressed aim of Ford's grants to reduce racial tension, the recent press conference remarks of the leaders of "the Ford-funded MAYO would convince almost any rational observer that the group is doing the opposite."[19]

"The Cockpit" writers were also upset at the Ford Foundation for having abetted or encouraged militant challenge through its "leadership" programs. Pointing to that year's city election, the opinion piece noted that Mario Compean, the vice president of MAYO, "bagged nearly 12,000 votes in a race against Mayor McAllister—almost enough to force a run-off." Although Compean received no MAYO funds, his campaign illustrated "the close relationship" between what the Ford Foundation labels a "minority leadership" program and political action. "The Cockpit" writers were worried that the MAYO message—and the curriculum of La Universidad de los Barrios—had "succeeded in arousing dangerous passions in all too many San Antonians."[20]

This salvo marked the beginning of a two-week offensive in mid-April by Gonzalez. In a series of speeches from the floor of the House, the congressman assailed the entire civil rights advocacy network in San Antonio—MAYO, MAUC, LUB, MALDEF, the Southwest Council of La Raza—and the Ford Foundation, which he claimed had financed them all. He also set his eyes on VISTA.[21] The San Antonio newspapers carried daily reports about Gonzalez's speeches and actions.

Gonzalez again attacked MAYO and their "reverse racism" tactics. What appeared most disturbing about the new racism, Gonzalez said, was that it demanded "an allegiance to race above all else" so that "Anyone deviating, anyone criticizing, anyone questioning is tainted with having gringo tendencies or having sold out the cause."[22]

Without naming Willie Velásquez, Gonzalez noted that MAUC was "headed by a very young and peculiar man whose attitudes appear to be more or less racist."[23] He also noted that La Universidad de los Barrios had "as its dean a young college junior and its purpose—lacking a curriculum or classes—is said to be working with delinquents and others to create constructive action." Questioning the project, Gonzalez said:

> The problem with the "university" is that its headquarters have served as a sort of hangout for tough characters, and it has been the scene of drinking bouts and wild activity. Neighbors have been terrorized; one person who called in the police reported to me that her home had been stoned and her son's life threatened.[24]

Gonzalez allowed that the Ford Foundation wanted to see progress in the Southwest, but "rather than fostering brotherhood, the foundation has supported the spewing of hate." He called on Ford to fund "genuine, bona fide Mexican Americans rather than the so-called extremist leaders they have foisted on the community."[25]

Back on the home front, the congressman asked Bernal to repudiate MAYO and Gutiérrez, pointing out that "Sen. Bernal realizes that over half his constituency are 'gringos' and these are the people Jose Angel Gutierrez means to kill." Gonzalez continued:

> Sen. Bernal says I get excited about this; and because I get excited about advocates of killing gringos, he accuses me of McCarthyism.
>
> Of course, I get concerned when some irresponsible juvenile with a tamale on his shoulder starts inviting a whole segment of the population to knock it off. That's the game we stopped playing around here 30 years ago.[26]

Bernal countercharged that he was being made a "scapegoat-whipping-boy" in Gonzalez's "latest campaign of self-laudation." Bernal said he saw only two possible reasons for Gonzalez's "diatribes." On one hand, Gonzalez seemed to be suffering from "a case of paranoia. He does not seem to feel he has job security and anyone disagreeing with him . . . he sees with distrust and suspicion." On the other hand, speculated Bernal, Gonzalez could be "trying to build his own image [by] calling attention to his past efforts in behalf of the downtrodden."[27]

Congressman Gonzalez's actions were confusing to some Anglos, especially conservatives. One ultraconservative, Bard Logan, chairman of the American Party of Texas, smelled a conspiracy—otherwise why would Gonzalez be talking "like a member of the John Birch society" while his voting

record reflected 100 percent support for measures "which have foisted so-
cialism and furthered the cause of international and domestic communism"?
Logan reasoned that Gonzalez was assuming a new conservative image because pending congressional redistricting would place more-conservative
voters from San Antonio's North Side in his district. Indeed, Gonzalez's
high-profile attacks on the Chicano militants endeared him to conservative
Anglos who might otherwise have opposed him.[28] The congressman garnered support from Anglo officeholders, many of them staunch conservatives, in his "anti-hate campaign." The County Commissioners' Court, led
by A. J. Ploch, commended Gonzalez "for taking the lead in exerting every
effort toward the elimination of hate among the citizens of the U.S." Several
Texas representatives joined Gonzalez in denouncing the "hate campaign"
sponsored by Ford Foundation money. Representatives O. C. Fisher of San
Angelo, Abraham Kazen of Laredo, Kika de la Garza of Mission, and Jake
Pickle of Austin all praised Gonzalez for "exposing" the activities of MAYO
and allied groups.[29]

Gonzalez said his fight with militants was not a partisan political issue,
and he suggested that all parties and all citizens should take a position with
him against the force threatening the welfare of the community. "We have
to forget about being Democrats and Republicans, and renew our faith in
the system of democracy." Gonzalez noted that he personally had seen what
can happen from a lack of communication and the breakdown of "man to
man" relations in other cities. "We are threatened with it happening here,
a lack of communications and letting a handful of misguided, almost per-
verted, individuals preaching violence and hatred taking over literally."[30]

Toward the end of his campaign, Gonzalez was at times moved to pained
hyperbole. In his fifth speech to the House of Representatives on the subject, he again criticized the Ford Foundation for enabling "a zealot, misguided and as wrong as sin, to have this tremendous amount of money in an
attempt to disturb the public peace and order." Gonzalez then referred once
more to the stabbing death that had taken place outside of La Universidad
de los Barrios in January:

> This has led to murder. It has led to homicide. . . . Because it would be
> one of these half-baked projects in San Antonio funded through this or-
> ganization [MAUC] and from the Ford Foundation that established what
> they called the Universidad de los Barrios, that is the university of the
> neighborhoods and the colegio de los batos, that is the college of the
> punks.[31]

Gonzalez repeated his charge of Communism, adding that he knew that members of the DuBois Club in California, an organization sponsored by the Communist Party of the USA, had participated in Raza Unida meetings. One revolutionary, according to Gonzalez, had advocated sabotage of the computers of Kelly Air Force Base. Gonzalez then called on Velásquez, the organizer of the Raza Unida meeting, to divulge the names of the outsiders who "came for the purpose of inciting disturbances and riots." In response, Velásquez defended the meeting, asking whether all 1,200 people in attendance should have been checked for their Americanism. "We want to spread the word on such things as patriotism," said Velásquez. "We have never had a turncoat."[32]

Congressman Gonzalez was not just making speeches. He met with Wilbur Mills, chair of the powerful House Ways and Means Committee, and Wright Patman, chair of the House Banking Committee, both of whom were investigating the activities of tax-free foundations, and repeated his charges about the Ford Foundation, MAUC, and La Universidad de los Barrios. Gonzalez said that tape recordings of the "kill the gringo" press conference and of the Del Rio Palm Sunday protest would be turned over if requested. He then "fired off" a request for a complete review of the OEO-VISTA Minority Mobilization project in Texas by the U.S. comptroller general. Gonzalez also requested that the commissioner of the Internal Revenue Service fully review the Ford Foundation's tax-exempt status. Before the congressional session ended, he helped pass, as a member of the Banking and Currency Committee, the 1969 Tax Reform Act, which was created in part to prevent foundations from ever funding groups like MAYO again.[33] Gonzalez did his best to contain the movement, and these efforts at first glance appeared successful.

Los Pendejos

In late February 1970, *San Antonio Express & News* gadfly Thompson introduced his readership to the Spanish word "pendejo." Literally, it means "groin hair," but figuratively it refers to a very stupid person, an idiot. In Mexican culture, the word is generally considered a fighting word. The occasion for this Spanish lesson was "a fist-swinging, name-calling scene" during a speech by Gonzalez at St. Mary's University on February 27.[34]

As the congressman was being introduced to the St. Mary's audience, he recognized the faces of his young MAYO adversaries seated at the front, and sensed that he had walked into a trap. Rather than present his prepared remarks, he began to lecture the students on the false and limited promises of the Chicano movement. He noted that he was "an American without prefix, suffix or apology," a comment that struck many in the largely Mexican American audience as condescending.[35]

After listening to the congressman's impromptu remarks for several minutes, a dozen or so audience members began to walk out in a prearranged protest. Gonzalez taunted the protestors, and they responded by calling him a "cabrón vendido" (bastard sellout). In response, Gonzalez unleashed "a barrage of guttural expressions": "Pendejos! Babosos! Bola de animales!" (Idiots! Dummies! Pack of animals!) The livid congressman then challenged George Velásquez, who was among the last to walk out, "Si eres hombre, ven para acá." (If you're a man, come over here). Velásquez took the challenge and went onstage. Willie Velásquez and Albert Gamez turned to follow George. According to Gonzalez, Willie stopped about three feet away, and Gonzalez warned him, "Willie, if you take one step further, you take your glasses off and I'll knock the shit out of you." Velásquez started to take them off, but just then Albert Bustamante, Gonzalez's aide, appeared from behind the stage curtain and threw a punch at George Velásquez, whom Gonzalez then pushed. Before George could respond, Willie Velásquez and Albert Gamez grabbed him.

George Velásquez remembers the incident well:

> There were about thirteen of us walking out. I was the last one. Henry B. was just cussing, egging us on. I turned around and walked onto the stage. I kept asking him why he wasn't supporting the high school students who were walking out. All of a sudden, I get hit from behind. It was Bustamante, Henry B.'s aide. I'm 6'2", 250 pounds, a linebacker. I was about to respond when Willie grabbed me and held me back."[36]

The Velásquez brothers and Gamez then left the stage, and the walkout resumed.

Predictably, the reporting in the San Antonio newspapers simply recounted the congressman's version of the incident. According to the *San Antonio Express & News*, a young man jumped on the stage and made a threatening move "as if to pull a weapon," at which point Gonzalez's aide slugged him in the head. Gonzalez wasted no time in characterizing the protestors as "paid organizers for Albert Peña," "racial fanatics," "MAYO hotheads," and "coiled rattlesnakes poised to strike." He associated them with criminality by dramatically singling out a Ramiro Ledesma, "a known

felon," for particular attention. Ledesma, Gonzalez said, had been responsible for several homicides and had criminal charges pending against him—
and "that he is now a free man I do not doubt since he was among those
that disrupted my recent appearance at St. Mary's University." Knowing
that the modus operandi of this individual was "not knife, but gun," Gonzalez said he moved the microphone closer to the side of the stage so he
could duck behind the curtain in case he was fired on. Gonzalez put a nice
finish to the story by noting that he had wired San Antonio district attorney
Ted Butler to ask what assurances a San Antonio citizen might have for his
safety "when there is apparently no accountability for criminal behavior."
The very next day, Ledesma had his probation on a two-year-old charge of
aggravated assault revoked. He would be sentenced to the maximum two
years.[37]

The problem with Gonzalez's explanation was that Ledesma had not
been present at the protest. The congressman had pulled information from
his "intel" reports and the arrest records given him by the San Antonio Police Department to fabricate a presumed threat. Ledesma, Ledesma's mother, the Velásquez brothers, and others involved in the walkout emphatically
denied Gonzalez's accusation, but to no effect. "Henry B. was vindictive,"
said an understated George Velásquez:

> He was getting intelligence reports from the beginning, and using that to
> go after people. And they made stuff up. They said that Lampo was one
> of the protestors. They played this up to make us all look like criminals.
> Lampo wasn't at the St. Mary's event, but they revoked his probation
> and he served two years. We didn't have any influence over the media.
> Chinga'o, we were only nineteen, twenty years old.[38]

Willie Velásquez, age twenty-six, countered as best as he could. In an open
letter, he noted that of the thirty-three individuals who eventually walked
out on the congressman, five were seminarians, seven were teachers, three
were social workers, four were law students, two were professors, eight were
undergraduates, one had been in the convent, and three were workers:

> Those in the walkout weren't thugs. They weren't riffraff. They were
> clean kids or they wouldn't have been there. The riffraff don't go to
> speeches. These are the kinds of kids who are presidents of their classes
> and officers of the Young Democrats.[39]

These were the people, Velásquez said, that Gonzalez had called idiots, dummies, and animals.

Had the protestors stayed to listen to Gonzalez's speech, they would have heard little that was new, and little to be happy about. Gonzalez noted that "a Raza Unida Party can have local success, but that success will be limited" and that "gaining political power requires more than winning symbols." He concluded his speech by saying: "Violence by a few against the many is foolhardy, and can result only in tragedy for the innocent."[40]

In the aftermath of this incident, Gonzalez criticized the report released by the Texas Advisory Committee to the U.S. Commission on Civil Rights as faulty, mediocre, and highly biased. Referring to those members appealing for reform as "crybabies," Gonzalez elaborated as follows: "If I were belly-aching like those crybabies I would complain my civil rights were violated by a member of their committee, Willie Velásquez, who not only wanted to interrupt but to interpose physical objection to my right to speak."[41]

Crosscurrents of Class and Generation

An assessment of the political climate of the Mexican American community in the late sixties and early seventies would have found contradictory crosscurrents. On one hand, there was anger and resentment, especially among the barrio youths and college students. On the other hand, an older, middle-class generation, confident about their politics of gradualism, saw no need for such militancy. Class and generational differences divided the Mexican American community. Much depended on whom one spoke to.

In June 1970, the *Wall Street Journal* added to the speculation about "likely trouble" in San Antonio in an article titled "The Angry Chicanos: Deepening Frustration of Mexican-Americans Stirs Fears of Violence."[42] Noting that most Mexican American groups deplore public demonstrations, even nonviolent ones, the *Journal* reported that nonetheless some militant groups were organizing. A federal observer warned that

> There are "brown power" militants who are as full of hate and violence as anything the black power movement ever saw. It wouldn't surprise me to see things really come to a head in San Antonio. Maybe here before anywhere else.

In support of this assessment, the article focused on Beto Martínez, "an unemployed high school dropout who wears a goatee and shabby clothes, and rarely takes off his sunglasses even in the darkest bars." Martínez was "minister of war" for the Mexican American Nationalist Organization (MANO), a clandestine group that held that all Anglos should be driven out of the Southwest, by force if necessary. Things were calm right now, Martínez noted, because they had seen the political reaction to José Ángel Gutiérrez and MAYO. And they had seen the police repression of Black activists in Cleveland and Chicago. "Right now, we're strictly for self-defense. We're just waiting," Martínez said. He claimed that MANO had 300 members, but no more than four or five met at any time. "We're not so stupid. We went underground right after the cops murdered all those Black Panthers," said Martínez. He told his recruits that MANO was following the successful strategy of the Minutemen, a secret right-wing paramilitary group:

> Get guns wherever you can, preferably from addicts who steal them. Don't buy them if you can help it. And don't carry them. Stay off dope. Don't use the telephone. Don't make public speeches. Get a job, if you can, and try to look harmless. This is how the Minutemen have survived. We will, too.

Others discounted such talk. The San Antonio Police Department described MANO as "nothing to be afraid of—just Beto and a few crazy kids." Mayor McAllister, chastened after barely avoiding a runoff with a MAYO challenger, likewise dismissed such fears: "I don't expect trouble. Americans of Mexican descent here have made real progress in recent years."

But the *Wall Street Journal* took note of the "seemingly hopeless poverty" of San Antonio's barrios—"a sprawling collection of dilapidated wooden houses . . . jammed with big families." The yards were "tiny, often surrounded by fences and decorated with birdbaths and plaster religious statues." Unemployment was nearly 30 percent. Complaints about police abuse were commonplace. These might become the root causes of any possible violence. Or so believed MAYO president Gutiérrez, who was quoted as saying that "the chances for violence are better than ever." Gutiérrez was still pushing the rhetorical envelope: "It's too late for the gringo to make amends. Violence has to come."[43]

This kind of rhetoric, along with the protests and marches, had brought an uneasy feeling not only to the Anglo community, but also to moderate and conservative Mexican Americans who saw no need for such strident

militancy. One survey conducted in 1972 for CREEP, the reelection campaign committee of President Richard Nixon, found that the Spanish-speaking community of San Antonio reflected stability and "a high order of self-
confidence." There was "a great deal of typical middle class neighborhood
concern and a relatively high amount of sheer content."[44] A special *San
Antonio Express* report on the Chicano movement put it more prosaically.
The middle-income group has

> given up a lot of sweat and burned a lot of midnight oil to move to
> Highland Hills and North San Antonio. This type of Mexican American
> is willing to help the Chicano lot in his conservative way, but he's not
> going to march or call his neighbor a "gringo."[45]

Conservative Mexican American leaders were concerned that Mexican
Americans might start acting like the "rioting" Blacks. As journalist Cardenas noted, many of them warned in "barbershop conversations" that organizations such as MAYO "could stir some people's mind to trouble." One
barbershop patron asked Cardenas rhetorically: "How long can you keep
telling the troops there's going to be action without stirring an atmosphere
of uneasiness?"[46]

Congressman Gonzalez had issued several such warnings. He did not
want San Antonio to experience the riots of Detroit or Washington, D.C.
Thus he raised the alarm about race hatred. He "red-baited" Chicano movement activists by accusing them of Communism, and he "class-baited" them
by associating them with the toughs, delinquents, and punks who were
seen as prone to violence. Gonzalez's warnings scared the Mexican American middle class.

Even the label "Chicano" offended or at minimum mystified many middle-class Mexican Americans. Columnist Paul Thompson delighted in explaining to his English-reading audience that "Chicano" was a slang term
among lower-income people of the barrios and that many Mexican Americans hated the word. Thompson quoted their sentiments:

> "Chicanos are Mexican-Americans who do not think about the future,
> are lazy and not ambitious." . . . "It is a word just as 'Pachuco', although
> now they do not use 'Pachuco' but 'Chicano.'
> . . . "People who call themselves Chicanos are those who do not
> think of getting a job like other people."[47]

Finally, Thompson touched on the dilemma of many older Mexican Americans, citing their own words: "Those of us who have fought the use of ugly tags (pachuco, hippies, yippie) wonder why our own champions persist in calling us Chicanos. Why do they identify us this way?"[48]

Some older, middle-class Mexican Americans, on the other hand, were quietly supportive of the Chicano movement. One self-identified "oldtimer from Henry B.'s generation," writing anonymously in one of the many community newspapers that sprung up during this period, tried to explain the turn of events to his age peers. The author acknowledged that LULAC, GI Forum, and PASO had accomplished much in the way of bettering race relations after World War II, but noted that they had become somewhat complacent since then.

> We started something right after the war—it was a good thing. It helped make changes; but for the last 15 years after things got a little better for us—after we got good jobs, a law degree, a doctor's license, a nice home, a new car—we let up.[49]

Thus the young people "have grown up in a period where change has been very slow. They didn't know segregated schools as we did. They didn't know blatant discrimination everywhere you turned if you left the barrio. But we did." Instead, the youths—"our youngsters"—looked at the remaining segregation, the poor schools, and the lack of job opportunities and then told their elders, "You've talked about change. You've had your chance and you've failed. Move over because we're going to get it—now." The reaction of the elders? "We are horror-struck. Because our young men—and especially our young women—aren't supposed to talk that way—and act that way. But are we right?" The youth were "ruffling feathers—including some of ours"—but they were saying in public "the things we used to say in private"; they were challenging authority—and "some of that authority is ours"—but they were challenging it. And they were getting results.

> They have opened segregated swimming pools, helped change the school system in San Antonio, organized barrio people to get what's coming to them, registered voters in record numbers all over South Texas, and most important, I suppose, they have given our youngsters a new dignity.

In short, the anonymous author didn't think that "any of us can stand aside and point our fingers at the young men and women of MAYO. They are

doing what they are doing because we failed them. We must take responsibility for that.[50]

Thus even middle-income Mexican Americans felt some pressure to be
more aggressive. "More militancy, instead of less, appears probable," journalist Cardenas concluded, as "even the older, more conservative Mexican-
American organizations" were becoming more vocal in order to "siphon off"
Chicano youth from the controversial group MAYO. LULAC, for example,
had investigated and challenged San Antonio's Public Service Board for
equal employment opportunity for Mexican Americans. "A LULAC organization of the 1950s or the early 1960s would never have gotten this militant," noted Cardenas. The established organizations such as LULAC, the
GI Forum, and the Mexican Chamber of Commerce "more or less openly
concede that they feel this [firmer approach] is necessary to retain the following they have and keep any dissidents from drifting over to the potentially dangerous Mexican-American Youth Organization."[51]

The Chicano activists were certainly aware of the class differences within the Mexican American community. Speaking of San Antonio, Raza Unida
organizer Armando Cavada observed "an antagonism on the part of the
middle class toward the lower class."[52] In Cavada's assessment, the middle
class still felt insecure and inferior:

> They can't quite bring themselves to accept the poor people as human.
> They are afraid that if they commit themselves to the downtrodden, the
> wretched, they may contaminate themselves. The middle class Chicano
> is always struggling to get away from inferiority. They see the gringo as
> superior because he has power and money. So they are constantly trying
> to imitate him."[53]

Thus, in Cavada's view, any support that the movement might receive from
the middle class should not be considered reliable. He did allow, however,
that the movement had been so focused on the poor that they had not given
much thought to this middle-class issue.[54]

Willie Velásquez, on the other hand, had given this topic a great deal of
thought. He was against all the "kill the gringo" talk because the rhetoric
was alienating the Mexican American middle class. He believed—correctly, it turned out—that there were provocateurs on the government payroll
who were pushing MAYO in a more militant direction. And he was against
the idea of forming a separate political party because it was bound to fail;
moreover, it took away any possible compromise with middle-class Mexi-

can American Democrats. Velásquez was already separating himself from MAYO by early 1969 and was not present at the "kill the gringo" press conference in April. In 1970, after MAYO decided to form La Raza Unida Party, he withdrew from the organization.[55]

At first sight, it appeared that Congressman Gonzalez had succeeded in blunting the Chicano movement. By the end of summer 1969, most MAYO members had been purged from the VISTA program. The Ford Foundation had cut off funding to MAYO, "persuaded" MALDEF to move its headquarters from San Antonio, and put MAUC and its La Universidad de los Barrios project under strictures to focus on "hard" programs such as housing and job training rather than on "soft" activities such as voter registration and community organizing.[56]

On the personal-political front, Gonzalez's public foes were in a short time removed from their positions of influence. MAUC director Willie Velásquez, under pressure from his former MAYO allies on the MAUC board, resigned in November 1969, and county commissioner Albert Peña and state senator Joe Bernal went down in defeat in their respective elections. In 1971, a year after the St. Mary's altercation, Gonzalez's slugging aide, Albert Bustamante, ran against and defeated Peña in a nasty campaign. The following year, Bernal lost his Senate seat to a conservative challenger— endorsed by Congressman Gonzalez, naturally—by 99 votes out of 40,000 cast.[57] The old guard seemed to have won.

Ever defiant, Albert Peña commented, even while MALDEF headquarters were being relocated to San Francisco, that "the Washington mad man" and the (Mayor) McAllister forces would not quash the Chicano movement in San Antonio. On this point, Peña proved to be right.[58]

THE BERETS RISE UP

6 IN THE FRENZIED TIMES of the late sixties and early seventies, even an apparent failure could generate more social movement activity. Put another way, there were no failures, only experiments. So long as a core group remained committed and energized, the formal closure of one project or the disbanding of an organization ironically forced its activists to contemplate the next step, the next reincarnation, of their activism. The Chicano movement seemed to be like a resilient snake, growing bigger while shedding surface skins.

MAYO was a prime example of such growth. Even as it was losing its foundation and government resources, MAYO was evolving into a political party called La Raza Unida (The United People). The relative success of its electoral challenge to the Good Government League slate in the April 1969 city council elections, with a bare-bones campaign focused entirely on the Mexican American barrios, had persuaded activist leaders that an ethnic-based strategy might work in South Texas where Mexicanos constituted solid majorities. In December 1969, the delegates at the national MAYO conference (held in Mission, Texas) enthusiastically endorsed the resolution of make the formation of a Chicano political party, El Partido de la Raza Unida, a priority.[1]

The resiliency of movement activists also can be seen in the response of La Universidad de los Barrios (LUB) to its 1969 crisis. The impact of Congressman Gonzalez's intervention was plainly evident. As a result of Ford Foundation directives, the MAUC-funded school could no longer engage in "soft" programs such as voter registration or other political activities. The major project of its new "hard" direction was to turn gang members and school dropouts into entrepreneurs and have them run a fast-food Mexican restaurant called "El Chaleco." The restaurant was to be run by twenty former gang members with the help of several college students. Like many small start-up businesses, El Chaleco did not survive its inaugural year and closed at the end of 1970. LUB, the West Side center that MAYO had set up to educate and politicize barrio youths, and the lightning rod for much of Congressman Gonzalez's ire, closed its doors shortly after. It was a curious passing, for La Universidad metamorphosed into several projects and organizations that would endure for many more years. One such organization was the Brown Berets.

The Hard Agenda of La Universidad de los Barrios

In late May 1969, La Universidad reopened at a new site with a new leadership team consisting of seventeen youths and thirty other peripheral members. The core faculty consisted of Tito Moreno (economics), Norman Guerrero (philosophy), Chista Cantú (art), Ruben Sandoval (law), José Morales (karate), and George Velásquez (theater).[2]

The new leaders, all MAYO activists, were filled with ideas about projects and a renewed vision for La Universidad. One summed up the school's ultimate goal as that of discovering "el oro del barrio," or the spirit and pride of the West Side, and others proposed that liberation classes be held "from the street corner to the classroom." The school's political philosophy remained one of instilling pride, awareness, and brotherhood in its Chicano students. The new leaders, obviously well read in the work of Pablo Freire, Franz Fanon, and Che Guevara, called for expanding the idea of brotherhood, or carnalismo,

> so that Chicanos can see through man-made borders that separate us from our oppressed brothers in Mexico, in the jungles of Bolivia and Vietnam, and visualize our barrios as the same entity. Our Barrio then becomes the world of the oppressed, an experience which allies and unites us with the wretched of the earth.[3]

Some MAYO members, inspired by the theatrical skits they had seen at a youth conference in Denver, began to work on "developing a street theatre, guerrilla theatre" that they named Teatro de los Barrios. The group used a

MAYO faculty and activists at La Universidad de los Barrios, circa 1970: *left to right, front row*: Edgar Lozano, Lupe de León, Chista Cantú, Andrea Gámez, George Velásquez; *second row*: Albert Gámez, Ernie Olivarez, unidentified; *third row*, Rogelio "Smiley" Riojas, Roman Ramírez, Robert Cabrera. Courtesy of George and Andrea Velásquez.

technique called "banda loca" in which teatro members dressed up in costume and marched down the streets of the barrio playing drums and other instruments. In this manner they announced themselves to the neighborhood and simultaneously excited the kids to come and see the performance. The calaveras (skeletons) who "dressed up in the American flag while dancing to spectral movements" were an especially "awesome and gruesome spectacle." Tito Moreno, who had a background in drama and music, "put it all together." Moreno also started a movimiento band at La Universidad called the Distant Dream.[4]

All this talk about liberation pedagogy and philosophy, of guerilla theater and movimiento music and art, soon took a back seat to discussions of employment and business development. The first point on the new "hard"

El Teatro de los Barrios parading through the streets, circa 1970.
Courtesy of photographer César A. Martínez.

agenda of La Universidad was an economic development plan that included
the Mexican fast-food restaurant El Chaleco, a project that soon became the
school's primary focus.[5] The restaurant enterprise was touted as a venture
that would not only train batos in small business management and practices, but also had the potential to turn a nice profit. Such was the vision.

In the summer of 1969, representatives of LUB began pitching their
funding plea, and within a year they had talked to "nearly fifty predominantly Anglo groups," primarily church groups. The churches had proved
responsive. In a feature article published in the *Texas Presbyterian*, Reverend Tom Cutting praised La Universidad de los Barrios, noting that its
membership of seventy-five young men included college students, teenage
gang members, high school students, and dropouts. What held this diverse
group together, Cutting noted, was a commitment to "La Causa," or "the
social movement for justice and dignity among Mexican Americans," a
commitment "which transcends individual West Side neighborhoods and
gangs." While acknowledging that some considered the men of La Universidad to be "a threat to the community," Cutting argued that it was precisely

their "Chicano self-consciousness" and commitment that gave them "the potential for overcoming deep-seated alienation among West Side youth" and for providing "an impoverished community a means for solving its own problems."[6] The San Antonio Archdiocese of the Catholic Church, the United Methodist Church, the Lutheran Church, and the Presbyterian Church granted or lent "Industrias de la Universidad" a total of $28,000 to open the restaurant.[7]

Despite the loans and grants, El Chaleco closed after just a year of operation, and La Universidad closed shortly thereafter. Organizational meetings after July 1969 were dominated by discussions of how to keep El Chaleco up and running ("Who will cook the 80–90 heads of barbacoa needed?"). The last meeting of "the Core guys," on December 30, 1970, underscored La Universidad's organizational problems, mainly its loss of membership. According to the minutes, Tito Moreno believed that "the loss of membership was not due to things we got into, but to a shift of power. Before guys were involved in decision-making, now they are just used." George Velásquez pinned the problems on El Chaleco: "the guys received no pay for months, and they still had dedication after all that." Artist Chista Cantú "went into a rap of what he thought the Universidad's philosophy was—la Universidad de la Gente." The meeting ended inconclusively, with a restatement of the roles of the school's deans and chairs.[8]

With the closing of La Universidad, another experiment with "self-determination" fell short of its goal. The school's association in the public mind with "batos locos," as one of its founders put it, had made it vulnerable to facile, negative portrayals. Its survival in the face of "the hysteria, indifference of the general public, and harassment from many quarters," had been "a miracle."[9]

Had La Universidad been successful, as the *Texas Presbyterian* had put it, in overcoming the "deep-seated alienation among West Side youth"? Had it redirected the energy of batos locos in a positive way?

Ironically, if any bato associated with the school represented a dramatic success story—a rescue from "deep-seated alienation"—it would have been Ramiro "Lampo" Ledesma, the young man Congressman Gonzalez had publicly identified as "a menace." Ledesma had the profile of the bato loco that La Universidad intended to rehabilitate through a commitment to "la causa."[10]

Lampo Ledesma lived in Cassiano Homes, had a long juvenile record, and had hung out with a violent crowd. In January 1968, prior to becoming a student at La Universidad, Ledesma had been involved in a couple of shootings. He had just started hanging out at the school when another charge of aggravated assault was no-billed because someone else confessed to the crime. Ledesma was clearly on the SAPD radar and, to cite the dean of LUB, he was "no angel." According to his police record, Ledesma was arrested eight times on charges of drunk disturbances or malicious mischief between 1968 and 1969, which overlapped with his time at La Universidad. But he committed no violent acts while he was involved with the school.[11]

Ledesma was a student at La Universidad for two years. He was present at its first meeting in October 1968 and faithfully attended its monthly meetings through 1969. Apparently his participation led to his election, in July 1969, to the school's board. Further suggestion of his development comes from a note in the LUB scrapbook. Written in the margins of a thank-you letter from Grace Presbyterian Church, the note says, "It was the first time I ever heard Ramiro speak in a presentation."[12]

Where these inklings of development might have led is open to conjecture. In Ledesma's case, it was cut short, not so much because of his police record, but because of his association with MAYO and the Chicano movement. Once Congressman Gonzalez identified him as a participant in the walkout at St. Mary's, Ledesma's probation was immediately revoked. In March 1970 he began serving a two-year jail term.[13] He subsequently vanished from movement circles.

Also cut short was the collaboration between college students and batos locos. La Universidad de los Barrios had been an experimental space where college students, activists, and street youths could engage in discussions about history, philosophy, politics, art, and theater. The school had offered a sense of community and political purpose. The unequivocal evidence that this space had a politicizing influence is the founding of the Brown Berets.

The Birthplace of the Berets

La Universidad de los Barrios provided a space where street youths could hang out to discuss and learn about the Chicano movement. The Brown Berets of Los Angeles and the Black Berets of Albuquerque were of particular interest, as evidenced by a life-sized Brown Beret on the graffiti-covered wall of the LUB house. Many of the batos, in fact, were wearing berets long before the San Antonio Brown Beret chapter was founded, but at that time they were MAYO members. Once the MAYO leaders decided, in December 1969, to transform the organization into a political party, the street batos begin to have several discussions about charting their own course. It would be at a meeting at La Universidad during the summer of 1970 that the MAYO batos decided to form the Brown Berets.

The life trajectory of the San Antonio group's founder, Juan Guajardo, suggests the links between the settlement houses, MAYO, VISTA, and La Universidad.[14] His political development was like that of many movimiento batos. As a high school senior, Guajardo, a Ghost Town leader and member of "the war council," had followed the settlement house workers when they left the agencies and moved in with the upstart organization MAYO. Upon graduating in 1968, he was hired by the Good Samaritan Center to be a group worker as a VISTA volunteer. "I didn't know anything about VISTA," Guajardo recalled. "I was a high school graduate who was looking for work." He was with them for only three months before being drafted into the army, but during that short time he met MAYO organizers and other batos involved in the Chicano movement:

Jijo, que esos tres meses me voltearon mi cabeza. [Jijo, those three months turned my thinking around.] My time with VISTA opened my eyes. It made me think. And that's when I started to wear the beret. There were no Brown Berets; I was just wearing it. I had read of the Berets in California in various Chicano newspapers, and I liked their onda [idea]. But I didn't know much about them.[15]

Guajardo was drafted three months after graduating from high school. "Como chicano del barrio, entonces creía que debería ir, como todos pensaban entonces. Comoquiera seguí chavetiando." (As a Chicano from the barrio, I then believed that I should go, like everyone then thought. In any case, I continued philosophizing.) In Vietnam, Guajardo got together with the Chicanos of each company, "from every state—Califas, Nuevo Mexico, Texas—and it didn't matter what barrio you were from. You looked for the ten, fifteen guys who were in your company. Talking to them, I learned a lot." One lesson impressed upon Guajardo in Vietnam came from

little kids who were ready to die killing us, while back in the barrio we were killing each other for stupid things. You know, when you were always close to death in Vietnam, you start to think a lot about your life, about what you want to do with it.

After five months in 'Nam, Guajardo was badly hurt when a soldier in front of him stepped on a land mine. He returned home and joined other

Vietnam vets in discussions about carnalismo and the pressing problems of the barrio.

The MAYO batos had been looking to do something on their own for a while. Guajardo recalled:

> When several of us returned from Vietnam, we started to talk more about the movement. There were about fifteen batos from different barrios, guys we knew from work, from the bars, from the war, but we didn't know what to do.[16]

After months of discussion at La Universidad during the summer of 1970, the batos talked to Tito Moreno, the school's director, who arranged to bring Tomás Atencio and Luis Jaramillo from New Mexico for a brainstorming session.

Atencio was a social worker, barrio philosopher, and cofounder of La Academia de la Nueva Raza, a community learning center and research institute in Dixon, New Mexico. Atencio was into discovering "el oro del barrio"—the gold or wisdom of the community—through dialogue ("resolanas"), and then "using the sayings and memories of the people to politicize them." Jaramillo, a priest on leave from the Catholic Church because of his radical leanings, was a Black Beret at the time. From his readings of the evolutionary philosophies of theologian Pierre Teilhard de Chardin and José Vasconcelos, Jaramillo had distilled the notion of "la nueva raza" (the new people).[17]

After the guys heard Jaramillo and Atencio talk about "the nueva raza" and building the "knowledge base of la gente," the batos decided to form the Brown Berets. According to Guajardo, it wasn't until that meeting in August 1970 that they decided what to do:

> The task was to organize the barrio so that it could defend itself. We also wanted to stop the conflict among ourselves. If we were going to die, it was going to be for the movement and our people and not for some stupid thing.[18]

Thus they formed the Brown Berets, a paramilitary organization committed to protecting the barrio—specifically, from the police.

The Berets later issued a formal statement that explained the reasons for their existence:

As batos in the barrios, we were a tightly knit family hanging around at
el parque, el rec, or just costiando en la esquina con un frajo [just hanging out on the corner with a cigarette]. At night, we would buy some
jumbos and get a little drunk. Some of the batos más locos would smoke
a leno [joint] and drink some wayakan [wine] and really get high. This
was typical of all batos locos in the barrios of San Anto.[19]

But there was an obvious negative side to this life. They couldn't find decent jobs and were "constantly harassed" by the police. "A lot of the batos
were sent to la pinta [prison], some were killed in fights, and a lot of us
thought that the best way out was to go into the service." After their time in
the army and Vietnam, they came back to find that things had not changed
at all.

The barrios were still the same. Gang wars were still going on, the poverty was and still is here, we still could not get a decent job, we found
out that although we went to defend our so-called country, the people
still did not give a damn about the Chicano.[20]

Facing such problems, a group of batos decided to get together to discuss
what was going on in the barrios.

After "months of rapping," they decided the best approach would be
"to promote Carnalismo, meaning brotherhood, in all the barrios." The first
order of business was "to stop all the senseless killings of all the batos in the
gangas." The Berets acknowledged that they might not succeed in putting
an end to gangs, but they felt that "if we could get the gangas to look at each
other as carnales, instead of 'un bato de los courts' or 'un bato del Ghost
Town,' it would be a step in getting our 'Raza Unida.'"[21]

The Berets adopted military khakis as their uniform and structured the
organization in military fashion, with ranks from private to major and, at
the top, prime minister and field marshal. As to the symbolism of the beret
and its patch,

All members of this organization wear a brown beret with a round patch
on the left side and crossed rifles on the front. The patch is colored red,
black, and brown. The red color stands for the Chicano blood that has
been shed in this nation's streets and wars. The color black is the eagle
of "La Huelga." In the center of the patch is the Chicano handshake
and it is colored brown to show the color of our skin and our unity. The
crossed rifles speak for themselves.[22]

The crossed rifles symbolized how far the Berets were willing to go in order to protect the rights of Chicanos.

Using the War Council Networks

The first cohort of 1970–1972 were older batos, Vietnam veterans in their early to mid-twenties who had already been attracted by or involved in the Chicano movement. Calling on their old war council relationships to spread the word about the movement, the Brown Berets expanded rapidly, from a handful of members to seventy by 1972. As individual guys from different clicas got "turned on," they would "rap" to their clica about the Beret "onda" (idea), and the clica would join as a unit. In this manner, the first Brown Beret organization evolved as a confederation of chapters made up of ex–gang clicas.

Former "Detroit" gang leader Lalo Martínez learned about the Los Angeles Berets and rapped "with batos who were in the movement" while serving in the navy in the late sixties. Upon his honorable discharge in 1970, he joined the United Farm Workers' support group and enrolled in college. He also worked for a brief time at the Guadalupe Community Center. He knew the group workers at the other settlement houses, many of whom would become Berets: "Everyone already knew one another because they had gone to the school together at one time or another, also because they had joined the rumbles." He knew Juan Guajardo from school, so when Guajardo organized the Berets, he was one of the first to join. When they began accepting select nonveterans and women into the organization, Lalo Martínez brought in David "Sancudo" Martínez.[23]

Like Lalo, Sancudo had already been "turned on" to the movement. As an artist, he was a member of Los Pintores de la Raza (Artists of the People), whose work dealt with the themes of la raza, carnalismo, and so forth. "In '68, '69, I was reading newspapers from Califas and hearing that the barrios over there were organizing. I was really interested in that jale [activity]. Then I went to a meeting of Barrios Unidos right around the corner." He knew Lalo from having grown up with him in the San Juan housing project. Sancudo joined the Berets, but only when he saw that they were disciplined batos and not "pistoleros" (gunmen), and that they were "calmados" (calm) and not "batos de puro pedo" (guys full of bull). He noted that a lot of kids were going around smelling glue and spray paint, and that the Berets could reach them better than a social worker.[24] Because of Sancudo, other batos joined the Berets. Recruitment generally followed a network of neighbor-

Brown Beret recruitment poster from Chicago, circa 1973. Beret chapters sprang up throughout the county. Author's collection.

hood friendships from the settlement house days of the war council. That was the way, Lalo recalled, that the Detroit, La India, and the Lake gangs became Beret chapters.[25]

Ernie García, of La India, joined when he ran into an old running partner who "turned him on" to the Berets. García had already left the "clica": "I understood that the jale [activity] I was involved in was not right—no more beating one another up, or killing our brothers. I learned this when I started to work with the people of my barrio." He had learned about the Chicano movement from working with *Chicano Times*, an underground newspaper published in 1968–1969, but he had no opinion about the San Antonio Berets. He had seen them on television and didn't know if they were like the "militantes" from Los Angeles. Such militancy did not appeal to him because in his opinion one must first speak well before engaging in "haciendo desmadres" (mayhem). Then he ran into the Berets at the school where he worked as a janitor:

Me puse a platicar con ellos. A uno de ellos ya lo conocía de hace
mucho, anduvo en la clica conmigo desde las gangas, y él comenzó a
decirme de la clica de los Brown Berets.[26]
[I started talking to them. One of them I had known for a long time, he
had been in the clica with me during the gangs, and he started to tell me
about the clica of the Brown Berets.]

García joined in November 1971 "porque los Brown Berets estaban traba-
jando con la juventud, los chavalones, tirándoles historias de nosotros, y
haciéndolo por quebrar la clica de las gangas" (because the Brown Berets
were working with youths, the kids, telling them our history, and trying to
break up the gang cliques). He also wanted to show the people what kind
of government the state of Texas and San Antonio had: "to show them that
the clica de perros [dog police clique] is a nasty clica that doesn't care for
Chicanos, that doesn't want us to rise. They don't want to see one of us rise
to any high position." Like Sancudo, García felt for the first time that he was
really going to do something for the people.[27]

Basically individual batos from different clicas would get turned on to
the Berets, and they in turn would "rap" to the clica about the Beret onda,
and then the entire clica would join as a chapter. The clica, now a Beret
chapter, would then recruit among former clica associates. Thus during the
first two years of Beret organizing in San Antonio, 1970–1972, the Berets
were organized by clica boundaries. The batos from Little Detroit had their
own chapter with their own prime minister. The batos from La India had
their own chapter, although there were two clicas, one from Big India and
the other from Little India, just like Upper and Lower Ghost Town; these
all had their own prime ministers. In the past, during times of general barrio warfare, the various clicas had sometimes rumbled against each other,
but now they were united as Brown Berets. Essentially, the first Beret organization was a confederation of chapters superimposed over the old gang
boundaries of West Side San Antonio.

Not all recruits had been part of a clica or gang. One of the first to join
was a "loner" from the East Side, José Morales, an energetic, articulate man
who, at thirty, was among the older members. His biography reflected the
trajectory of many Beret leaders. He had stabbed a guy when he was fifteen
and spent a year in youth corrections. When he got out, he wasn't allowed
to enroll in school; they didn't want him. His parents and a judge then
made arrangements so that he could join the army; thus, at the age of sixteen, he was inducted into the army by court order and served for six years.

One of them, however, was in military prison because he had knifed four "gringo" soldiers in Germany. He volunteered for Vietnam in order to erase his record, but he wasn't there long before he was injured. When he came out of San Antonio's Wilford Hospital, he began hanging out at La Universidad de los Barrios; his image and placa (insignia) were clearly visible in the LUB police photos of January 1969. In 1970 he met Juan Guajardo at a meeting at La Universidad. After hearing of Morales's military experience and martial arts expertise, the Berets voted him in and made him their spokesman. Morales's main problem had been tecata (heroin), but he gave up the habit for the Berets.[28]

Not all batos were receptive to the Berets. Morales tried recruiting on the East End, but the guys there did not want the formal discipline of the Berets. Even lifelong friends of individual Berets might shun an invitation. This was apparently the case with Hippy and Bird, two good buddies of Berets Lalo and "Chale." Lalo and Chale explained why their friends from Little Detroit hadn't joined the Berets.

> *Lalo:* You can't tell a pachuco "look at the onda [thing] we're in, come join us" because the bato will say "You know what, don't tell me about your thing or I'll shoot you," and that's the way the guys are. They're bien locos [very crazy]. With Bird you can't bother him because he'll take out his gun and he'll use it. He told me a long time ago, "Don't tell me about your onda and I won't tell you about mine." I told him, "Está bien, bro, así la jugamos." [That's okay, bro, we'll play it that way.] Hippy is also in the onda about living well, about making it.
>
> *Chale:* Bird needs the fifty to one hundred bucks he wins playing pool every week; he wouldn't make it without that cash. Also, for Bird, playing pool is second only to his job. Hippy also anda pa' arriba y pa' abajo [hustles] for work. He has a small house painting company. He and Bird have another onda and we leave them alone.
>
> *Lalo:* In other words, they don't have the security to sit down and talk about the movimiento like we do; they don't receive a VA check every month so that you can just think.
>
> *Chale:* Those guys are with us [in the movement] but now they have to work. If something heavy comes down, they'll be with us.[29]

Beret prime minister Juan Guajardo said that the Berets were not for everyone. Guys of conflict ("batos de pedo") didn't join the Berets because they had personal things to take care of, and some guys just wanted to run with a clica. Other batos, such as Hippy and Bird, recognized the Chicano movement, but they had other goals and interests.[30]

Bringing Peace to the Barrio

The Beret leaders readily identified the reasons for insecurity among barrio youths: the constant threat of run-ins with hostile youths, and the constant threat of run-ins with hostile police. Accordingly, they established two priorities: one, to reduce gang conflict, and, two, to monitor police conduct in the barrios.

The first priority they tackled in the fall and winter of 1970–1971 by recruiting members and preaching the word of carnalismo in the West Side barrios. While La Universidad was struggling to stay open, the Berets were gaining public attention and praise for their "progress in breaking up gang warfare." So reported Frank Trejo for the *San Antonio Light*. Working with gangs in the Barkely-Castroville Road barrios, the Berets had minimized the activities of "the famous Detroit gang." Former gang members were helping the Berets tackle other barrio problems: helping families get food stamps and jobs, getting teenagers off glue-sniffing and back into school, getting "tecatos" (addicts) into the methadone program. Beret leader Guajardo explained to newspaper reporter Trejo that "We are not a gang, a social club or a car club, we are just a group of young men from the barrios trying to help our people."[31]

Beret field marshal José Morales explained that they were preaching carnalismo, brotherhood, telling each Chicano that "it doesn't matter what barrio you're from," that we want to unite every barrio. "We would tell the guys from the gangs, 'Calm the conflict and we'll get the dog police off your back.' 'Órale,' they would say." "The big event," Morales recalled, "was when we got 200 batos from five gangs—Lake, Ghost, India, Detroit, Dot—to hand in their weapons at the Good Sam. This was evidence of carnalismo."[32] Two hundred batos giving up weapons! The Berets had scored a major victory. The spirit of carnalismo had brought peace, if not unity, to the barrios.

With a gang truce in place, the Berets turned their attention to their second priority, the problem of police harassment and brutality. Barrio youths had long complained of mistreatment by police, but the Berets said that such mistreatment was a community-wide problem that impacted all West Side residents. They argued that people had become accustomed to police harassment. Fear and perhaps plain discretion kept folks in line.

One of many short-lived community newspapers of the time, *El Portavoz*, conveyed this line of reasoning:

> After a while, people stop noticing what policemen do. The fact that they
> wear a uniform and carry a weapon lends authority to their actions.
>
> Through the years, the people of San Antonio became used to scenes
> like those where several policemen would drag, shove, beat some
> wobbly-legged old man into a patrol car, right downtown, in front of the
> tourists.

The worst cases of suspect police behavior were hidden in the "back sections" of the two city newspapers:

> In the back sections of the newspapers, one would occasionally find
> a story about a 14-year-old boy "assaulting" a 6-foot-two, 210-pound
> policeman and getting shot in the back of the head for his folly. In self-
> defense.[33]

Stories that might indicate a form of low-intensity warfare between gangs and the police rarely found their way into newsprint:

> Like the time a group of boys ambushed a police officer in one of the
> housing projects who had been harassing them and sent him to the hos-
> pital. Or the other half of the story—how each boy paid for his crime,
> alone, and at the hands of policemen in dark, unreported incidents.[34]

This was the backdrop for a protracted Beret campaign against police brutality. The year-long effort, launched a few months after the disarming of some West Side gangs, involved major protests and the organization of community patrols to monitor arrests in the barrio.

In midsummer of 1971, lawyers from the Mexican American Legal Defense and Education Fund (MALDEF) presented six documented cases of police misconduct to the San Antonio City Council. Much to the disappointment of MALDEF and concerned community leaders, the city council issued a clean bill for the police. Immediately after the decision, about two dozen Brown Berets, carrying placards that said "Stop Police Brutality" and chanting "Viva la Raza," led a demonstration in front of city hall and the police department.[35]

The following month, in August, the Berets, several community leaders, and other West Side residents formed the Committee on Police Practices

(COPP) to monitor police conduct in the West Side and gather evidence. COPP members were "disturbed" with official investigations that always reported a lack of evidence. As a result, COPP announced that members had been assigned "to trail police patrol cars on Saturday nights through 'poverty pocket' areas." The practice would continue each Saturday night in order to get "first-hand information" for use by official organizations.[36]

Police practices kept the issues of brutality and the need for a police review board on the front burner. A few weeks after the September 16th celebrations, when the Berets had formally introduced themselves to the public, police killed a teenager fleeing a break-in at an ice house. The Berets sought a policy statement from police chief Emil Peters on rules and procedures regarding the apprehension of fleeing suspects. Morales, spokesman for the local Berets, commented pointedly, "We feel there is more caution in handling the Viet Cong than there is in handling our Chicano boys." He added that "an officer who practices firing his gun periodically should be able to hit the suspect in the leg."[37] The Berets promptly organized a march and rally, and began making plans for an even bigger protest.

In mid-November, the Berets, along with Reverend Edmundo Rodriguez of Our Lady of Guadalupe Church and Mario Cantú of Mario's Restaurant, organized a lively protest against police misconduct. More than 500 persons marched peacefully through the West Side and rallied in front of the Alamo. More than thirty-five organizations were represented. Berets from Houston, Dallas, Austin, and Los Angeles had also come to lend support. The Berets and the police escort "cooperated well in keeping the marchers orderly," according to the *San Antonio News*. Chants shouted in a litany-like manner by the demonstrators included "Chicano power," "Viva Zapata," "Viva Tijerina," and "Raza sí, gringo no." The reporters observed that the "largely Mexican American crowd" displayed a minimum of antipolice signs and even included one "thank you" sign for the police escort.[38]

The police brutality issue garnered the Berets considerable media attention, including a half-hour television "rap session." By the end of 1971, the group had become recognized publicly as part of the emerging Chicano movement for "racial parity." The Berets heard that "the SAPD would tell their patrols every morning that there are Berets out there—don't mess with them."[39] In the barrio, the citizen patrols also earned the Berets considerable respect and even authority. According to Juan Guajardo,

> The people started seeing us as cops. They would come to us to tell us
> of troubles and conflicts—with drug pushers, with the police, with their
> sons, and so on—to see what we could do. It was inspiring.[40]

For some barrio residents, the Berets represented a neighborhood police force. This was indeed high praise. It would be the high point of the Brown Berets' history.

The Berets had no chapter historian, but they left behind a scrapbook for the year 1971 that suggests an intense level of activity. Among the miscellaneous items contained in the scrapbook are the following:

—newspaper clippings about the gang work of the Berets in February, with a photo of the guys from El Detroit raising clenched fists in the air;

—a letter by José Morales, April 30, 1971, concerning a family whose house had burned;

—newspaper clippings about the July picketing of the police station;

—more articles in August about the police monitoring set up by the Berets;

—another August article about the planning of a Houston school boycott, with a marginal handwritten note indicating that thirty San Antonio Berets had attended;

—September ticket receipts indicating their sponsorship of a dance headlined by Jimmy Edwards to help the Villa Coronado Clinic, with a handwritten comment "money made after expenses: $60.00";

—the September 16th program for La Semana de la Raza celebrations;

—an October news clipping (October 19, 1971) about the half-hour KENS TV show on the Berets;

—and, finally, various news clippings about the major police brutality protest in mid-November.

Around the wide margins of one undated clipping (about a "Good Samaritan" Beret) are extensive notes, handwritten in careful penmanship, about the Brown Beret Pledge and purpose:

As a member of the Brown Beret organization, I have committed myself to be a dedicated sincere servant to my community and to my people. By all means necessary, therefore, it is an absolute must that I conduct myself in a mature manner, at all things. I must remember that I am a Brown Beret twenty-four hours a day.

On the bottom half of the copy, the Beret motto "to serve, observe, protect" is defined, again in a clear, block-style handwriting:

To Serve . . .

To give vocal as well as physical support to those causes which will help the people of the Chicano community.

Observe . . .

To keep a watchful eye on all federal, state, city and private agencies, which deal with the Chicano, especially the law enforcement agencies.

Protect . . .

To protect, guarantee and secure the rights of the Chicano by all means necessary. How far we must go in order to protect these rights is dependent upon those in power. If those in power are willing to do this in a peaceful and orderly process, then we will be only too happy to accept this way. Otherwise, we will be forced to other alternatives.

This eloquent, gracefully handwritten statement concludes the Beret scrapbook.[41]

Measuring the Impact on Barrio Youths

For a few years, the ideas of "brotherhood" and "the united people" calmed the internecine conflict between San Antonio's barrios. The Chicano movement, it seemed, had interrupted the cycle of gang warfare. Beret founder Juan Guajardo, sounding like a sociologist, agreed that "yes, the movement had some impact, but how do you measure it?" An excellent question— there was no survey of Chicano youths at the time; no direct quantitative measures exist.

Fortunately, the annual statistics compiled by the San Antonio Police Department about "Anglo," "Latin," and "Negro" juvenile offenses over a fourteen-year period (1959–1972) shed some light on the matter.[42] Examining these police records reveals some suggestive patterns about the intensity of conflict within the barrios. Moreover, these records of juvenile arrests also shed light on the policing of the Chicano movement. A longitudinal look at juvenile arrests, in other words, might tell us something about both youth conflict and police control.

There are problems with using police statistics to measure youth conflict because it is possible that they simply reflect police deployment, tactics, or policy decisions. Delinquency offenses might also be redefined or recategorized, as happened in 1974 when the Bexar County Juvenile Department assumed responsibility for record keeping. Even when we limit our consideration to those offenses most likely to indicate youth conflict—aggravated assault, simple assault, and affray—these at best offer an indirect look at changing levels of conflict within the barrios. Nonetheless, they permit a rough test of the argument.

One would expect that appeals for "carnalismo" and "raza unida" might be reflected in a reduction of the number of assaults and affrays among Latino youths. A cultural-nationalist movement would have influenced Latino youths throughout the city. Most impacted would have been those in the deep West Side districts, where half of the "Latin" delinquents lived and where most of the movement organizing took place. Thus, if the juvenile arrest rates for these offenses remained constant or increased during the movement period, then my argument about movement influence might be seen as problematic, and much more difficult to advance. If, on the other hand, the number of assaults and affrays declined during the movement period, then my argument is not proven; it is simply *not refuted*. There are a couple of other plausible explanations—or claimants—to any such decrease in delinquency.

During the 1959–1972 period, "Latin" delinquency accounted for about 60 percent of all delinquency, "Anglo" for 25 percent, and "Negro" about 15 percent (Table 6.1). Offenses involving physical violence constituted a small but prominent number of juvenile arrests, and were most likely to have been committed by Latin youths. The greatest number of Latin juvenile arrests stemmed from shoplifting, burglary, and vapor sniffing.[43]

When one studies the arrests for assaults and affrays over time, one can spy indications of increased or decreased conflict for the various groups. The arrests of Latin juveniles for assault and affray suggest increased conflict in 1959–1960, 1962, 1965, and 1969, a periodization that corresponds roughly with the memories of the batos and social workers about gang conflict. The arrest patterns of Anglo and Negro juveniles over this period do not demonstrate the same "peaks" and "valleys" of conflict. Moreover, the number of Latin juvenile arrests for assaults and affrays was frequently quadruple that of Anglo or Negro juvenile arrests, an indirect indication of the intensity of youth conflict within the barrios.

That some type of change was taking place in the barrios in the late sixties and early seventies can be seen if one charts the number of arrests for assaults and affrays for the period 1959–1972 (Table 6.1). The number of such offenses committed by Latins had remained roughly constant between 1966 and 1968 at 114–125 offenses, but rose steeply in 1969 to 162 offenses—an indication of one "last" gang outbreak. It then declined sharply in 1970 (93 offenses) and 1971 (65), and remained low in 1972 (71). In three

Table 6.1.
Select Juvenile Arrest Statistics for San Antonio, 1959–1972

	1959	1960	1961	1962	1963	1964	1965	1966	1967	1968	1969	1970	1971	1972
ARRESTS FOR ASSAULTS & AFFRAYS														
"Latin"	209	173	146	201	140	101	146	123	125	114	162	93	65	71
"Anglo"	56	33	46	42	35	31	39	44	40	44	16	37	30	32
"Negro"	42	33	45	21	25	18	39	33	29	38	58	32	17	23
ARRESTS FOR DISTURBING THE PEACE														
"Latin"	126	99	178	129	134	154	187	112	84	73	96	139	285	84
"Anglo"	37	37	47	82	55	53	52	49	42	29	25	37	58	55
"Negro"	42	36	43	42	41	33	33	31	41	78	31	70	48	27
ALL JUVENILE ARRESTS														
"Latin"	2,831	2,347	2,194	2,650	2,677	2,379	2,301	2,386	2,205	3,001	3,466	3,111	3,491	2,713
"Anglo"	1,096	916	875	1,064	1,182	867	903	1,007	1,106	1,218	1,192	1,180	1,415	1,443
"Negro"	507	574	495	436	423	439	615	455	501	754	767	702	631	884
TOTALS	4,434	3,837	3,564	4,150	4,282	3,685	3,819	3,848	3,812	4,973	5,425	4,993	5,537	5,040

Source: San Antonio Police Department Annual Reports, 1959–1972.

Assaults & Affrays, 1965–1972

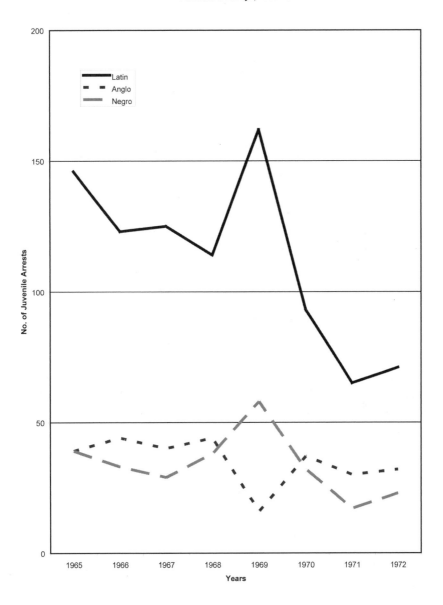

Juvenile arrests for assaults and affrays, 1965–1972.

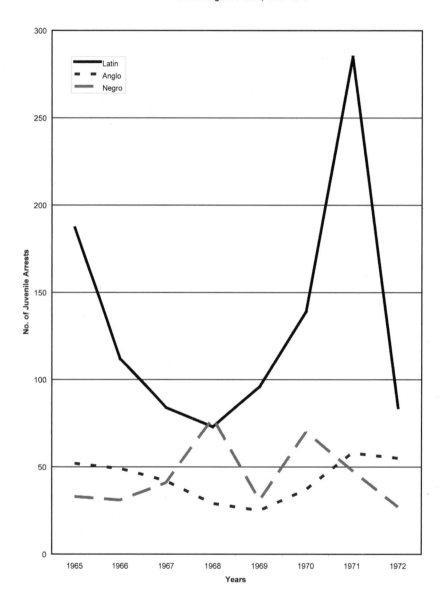

Disturbing the Peace, 1965–1972

Juvenile arrests for disturbing the peace, 1965–1972.

years, the number of arrests for assaults and affrays had been halved. In
1971 and 1972, arrests for these offenses reached their lowest points in over
a decade. The trend line for Negro juvenile arrests slightly mirrors that of
the Latin, suggesting some interaction effect, but the predominance of the
latter is clear.

The role of the police in monitoring and containing the Chicano movement is vividly suggested by arrests for "disturbing the peace," a common
charge used against activists and supporters (as shown in the figure on page
138). This was a favorite crowd-control method of the police and had been
used during the high school walkouts and various protest marches. When
the number of arrests for disturbing the peace are charted by ethnicity
for 1965–1972, what immediately stands out is the striking increase in the
number of "Latin" juvenile arrests, from 96 in 1969 to 139 in 1970, and then
to a high of 285 in 1971. This 200 percent increase in two years parallels
the growth and intensification of the Chicano movement. The precipitous
drop from 285 arrests of Latin juveniles in 1971 to 84 in 1972 likewise suggests a policy change—perhaps a result of the citizen patrols and the police
review campaign waged by MALDEF, the Brown Berets, and others. The
striking "roller-coaster" pattern of Latin juvenile arrests for "disturbing the
peace" from 1969 through 1972 can readily be read as a police reaction to
the Chicano movement. There is no correspondence with either the Anglo
or Negro arrest patterns.

To return to Juan Guajardo's question about measuring the movement's
impact, an overlay of the "Latin" arrest patterns (shown in the figures on
pages 138 and 140) during 1965–1972 illustrates in sharp relief the impact
that the movement may have had on barrio youth. One sees a distinct pattern after 1969: a decreasing number of arrests of Latino youths for fighting,
and an increasing number of arrests for "disturbing the peace." Were both
the result of movement activism? The most parsimonious explanation for
this striking pattern points to movement activism. Organizing among West
Side youths began in earnest in 1968, peaked in 1971, and had dissipated
by 1974. The batos from La Universidad formed the Brown Berets in 1970
and began to work extensively with barrio youths. By early 1971 they had
achieved a truce among various gangs, and they monitored police conduct
from mid-1971 through 1972. In short, the Berets and the movement had
their most discernible impact among barrio youths in the early seventies.
One thing seems certain: the two- to three-year cycle of gang warfare had
clearly been interrupted.

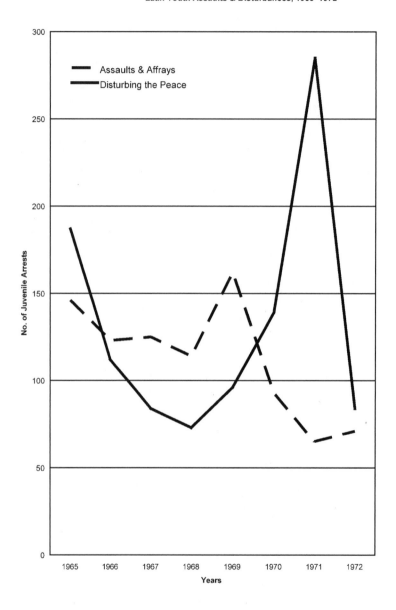

Latin Youth Assaults & Disturbances, 1965–1972

300

━━━ Assaults & Affrays
━━━ Disturbing the Peace

250

200

No. of Juvenile Arrests

150

100

50

0

1965   1966   1967   1968   1969   1970   1971   1972

Years

Arrests of Latin youths for assaults and disturbing the Peace, 1965–1972.

Juan Guajardo *(foreground)* and other Brown Berets leading a march against police
brutality, San Antonio, November 20, 1971. *San Antonio Light* Collection, University of Texas at San Antonio Institute of Texan Cultures, L-6568-A-12, courtesy of
the Hearst Corporation.

Naturally, alternative explanations for a reduction in juvenile delinquency exist. The police and social work agencies stood ready to claim responsibility for any lessening of crime and delinquency. The Bexar County
Juvenile Probation Department, for example, attributed the drop in overall
juvenile delinquency in 1972 and again in 1973 to the opening of a branch
office in the Alazan-Apache Courts in August 1970 to focus on the West
Side, "where as much as one-third of the referrals originated."[44] Another
contributing factor was the establishment in the same area of a Youth Service Project in October 1971, a preventive program designed for children
referred for "minor, non-adjudicable offenses."[45] Detective Ralph Lopez of
the SAPD told Beret spokesman José Morales that the Berets shouldn't take
all the credit for the delinquency drop.[46]

Unfortunately, there is no way of knowing if delinquency or, more specifically, assaults and affrays increased after the Berets fell out in 1973 and
disbanded in 1974. After 1973, the SAPD recorded only aggravated assaults
and ceased recording simple assaults and affrays, perhaps because, with

the creation of the Youth Service Project, the latter were seen as "minor, non-adjudicable offenses." The Bexar County Juvenile Department, for its part, did not maintain consistent annual statistical reports. The 1974 report, however, noted a puzzling 10 percent increase in overall delinquency referrals from 1973. The Bexar County juvenile officials were befuddled: "For the first time in four years Bexar County experienced an increase in delinquency referrals." The department found solace in the fact that most of this increase was due to "new referrals," while recidivism rates continued a downward trend "due to increased supervision and better counseling services being rendered."[47] In other words, a new cohort of youths—one not exposed to movement influences—was responsible for the unexpected increase. Despite the overall increase in delinquency, gang activity remained negligible. References to "gangs" do not reappear in any public document until 1978, when social workers noted that some youths might be returning to the "old gang culture."[48]

There is no need, of course, to deny the positive influence of expanded juvenile probation services or of changes in police policy toward juveniles. Some of these improvements, as suggested earlier, may have been the result of movement pressure. Some Berets were ready to acknowledge the change in police behavior. Frank García, the old veterano of El Detroit, said in 1974 that the reason things had died down was because of the social programs:

> Take El Detroit. Now it's a club and the guys have formed a band. They hold street dances and the cops close the streets so they can dance in the streets! The cops are community relations, and together with the social workers, they are doing a beautiful job. It really works! By the mere fact that they are there, they have deterred un chingo de gang fights.[49]

The social workers, police, and juvenile probation officers clearly had a role in shaping the lives of lower-class Latino youths. But for a few years, the batos themselves, organized as Brown Berets, took the lead in providing a sense of security for San Antonio's Mexican West Side. A robust explanation for the decline of gang fighting must give due credit to Beret activity and movement politics.

Even though the Brown Berets were an offspring that the settlement houses would likely not claim, their particular imprint was evident. The old war council network helps explain the rapid conversion of gangs into Beret chapters, with membership based on the old gang boundaries. With a new identity and a new purpose as "soldados de la raza" (soldiers of the people), the former gang leaders and batos locos had assumed the settlement house mission of calming gang warfare. Even the early Beret "rap" about learning how to manipulate the bureaucracy was a bit of sociology they picked up from listening to the gang workers and sociologists at the Wesley Center. But the message about "la raza unida" and "carnalismo"—this was new.

These ideas had been introduced and elaborated in the countless "rap" sessions and classes held at La Universidad de los Barrios, the "freedom school" set up by MAYO college activists in 1968. The school closed in 1971 after unrelenting pressure led by Congressman Gonzalez. Who knows how this experimental meeting space for college students and street youths might have developed? Ironically, because of his prominent role in closing La Universidad, Gonzalez ended up playing an important part in the rise of the Berets.[50]

Before it shut its doors, La Universidad spun off pieces of itself or provided the foundation for important new organizations. El Teatro de los Barrios, which had gained a following through its theater work in the housing projects, would survive as an entity for another ten years. The GED program would be reincarnated as the Colegio Jacinto Treviño, an Antioch-sponsored alternative college. And the batos locos, after listening to a radical social worker and priest from New Mexico, would fashion their own organization, the Brown Berets.

PART TWO

Marching through the West Side, circa 1972.
Courtesy of George and Andrea Velásquez.

MARCHING TOGETHER
SEPARATELY

IN SEPTEMBER of 1971, an extraordinary but little noticed political event took place in San Antonio. A few key Chicano businesses and organizations representing a broad political spectrum—Mario's Restaurant, LULAC, the GI Forum, MAYO, and Mungia's Printers—organized La Semana de la Raza, a week-long celebration of movement politics and culture. Two aspects made this celebration important. It broke the monopoly of the Mexican Consulate and the San Antonio Chamber of Commerce on the celebrations of Mexican Independence Day (September 16), thus underscoring the emergence of a distinct Chicano voice. In addition, by cutting across the ideological spectrum of the Mexican American community, the event captured the sense of unity symbolized by the phrase "la raza unida." With financial backing from an amalgam of local beer distributors and small businesses, a wide-ranging array of political and cultural organizations, labor organizations, musical and theatrical groups, radio and television stations, a bishop, and several professors pieced together an impressive celebration of culture and movement. This rendition of the 16th of September was not just a commemoration of the Mexican cry for independence from Spain in 1810; the day was also a reminder that the movement for equality and justice for the Mexican community had a long history and was continuing. A reading of the souvenir program provides a good overview of the complexity and diversity of the Chicano movement during one of its best years.[1]

Held at Mission County Park on the South Side, La Semana de la Raza proved to be a huge success. There was a full calendar of events for eight days. Thousands jammed the park each night to hear music and speeches. The first day, September 11, featured music from three rock groups, speeches by Mario Cantú of Mario's Restaurant, Antonio Orendain of the United Farm Workers Organizing Committee, MAYO leaders Mario Compean and Carlos Guerra, Rodolfo "Corky" González of the Denver Crusade for Justice, José Ángel Gutiérrez of La Raza Unida, performances by three theater groups—El Teatro de la Universidad from San Antonio, El Teatro Chicano de Aztlán from Austin, and

Los Mascarones from Mexico City—and a closing performance by the band El Chicano from East Los Angeles. Each of the following six days of La Semana were as filled as this first day.

The chair of Semana de la Raza, Mario Cantú, noted in his editorial for the souvenir program that the purpose of the fiestas was to create a stronger community and to underscore that the Rio Grande was a geographic line that could not erase or destroy the fact that Mexicans and Chicanos were one people with one historical heritage and one future. In his statement, Américo Paredes, a professor at the University of Texas at Austin and one of the nine honorary chairmen of the event, explained that the "grito de independencia" of Padre Miguel Hidalgo y Costilla was "a cry for social justice—justice not limited to 'whites only' but embracing the mestizo, the village Indian, and the Negro slave." Also mentioned in the program are other professors: Rudy Acuña of San Fernando Valley State College, Rudy Alvarez of Yale, Julian Samora of Notre Dame, and Jacinto Quirarte of the University of Texas at Austin—all of whom had presented a series of informal lectures in a new field called "Chicano studies."[2]

Chicanas were not yet in the forefront of the movement. The women were conspicuously absent from the honorary chair positions of La Semana, and not a single women's group was featured in the souvenir program.[3] The program did include a one-page article on Chicanas and their role in the movement, but the article, written by Enriqueta Chávez, had apparently been copied from a Chicano newsletter from San Diego, California, and inserted into the program. Given this context, the article's statement that Chicanas were "no longer inclined to merely fill secondary positions" was somewhat ironic.[4] The local women of the movimiento, although much involved behind the scenes, had not yet visibly exercised their influence or asserted a distinct group identity. This would change shortly.

MAYO had a page in the program explaining that "killing the gringo"—the daring declaration made two years before—was a task that was going to require more preparation and work:

> No hemos abandonado nuestra intención de matar al gringo pero hemos llegado a entender que será una tarea que requerirá nuestra dedicación total. . . . A la preparación nos dedicamos.[5]
> [We have not abandoned our intention to kill the gringo but we have come to understand that it is a task that will require our complete dedication. . . . To that preparation we dedicate ourselves.]

José Ángel Gutiérrez penned two pages on the "Chicano Revolt in the Winter Garden," describing how a "raza unida" was seizing control of city and county government from an old Anglo "oligarchy." Gutiérrez also announced that he was seeking "voluntarios de Aztlán" to work in Zavala County.[6]

The Brown Berets also had a page, where they emphasized that they would protect the rights of Chicanos "by all means" necessary:

How far we must go to protect these rights is dependent on those in power. If those in power are willing to do this in a peaceful and orderly way, then we will be only too happy to accept this way. Otherwise we will be forced to other alternatives. VIVA LA REVOLUCION![7]

Next to such talk about "revolución" and "killing the gringo" was a full page describing the League of United Latin American Citizens (LULAC) and the "LULAC Code" about loyalty to the country and respect for citizenship, and another page about LULAC's sponsorship of classic pianist Adrian Ruiz. Another page was devoted to San Antonio's auxiliary bishop Patricio F. Flores, and still another announced a mass for the memory of Ruben Salazar, a journalist killed by deputies during the August 1970 Chicano Moratorium in Los Angeles. These were followed by articles featuring activist Corky González of Denver and radical UCLA professor Angela Davis.

The representation of such a broad spectrum of the Mexican American political field suggested a striking unity. It was all the more remarkable given the stock views of a highly fragmented Mexican American leadership.[8] La Semana of 1971 brought people of various political persuasions and backgrounds— rural and urban working classes, small businesses, professionals, college students, and batos locos—together for a brief but intense period of celebration.[9]

While the sense of unity was impressive, more striking was the fact that of the political and cultural organizations represented, only two—LULAC and the GI Forum—had been in existence for more than five years. A veritable explosion in mass activity and thought had taken place since the California and Texas farmworker strikes of 1965–1966. The souvenir program suggested an unprecedented scale of interaction. Bands and professors from Los Angeles, theater from Mexico City, speakers from Denver and New Haven, an intersection with the Black civil rights movement—these indicated a wide-ranging national and international network. Commemorations of the massacre of students at Tlatelolco in Mexico City in 1968 as well as the death of journalist Salazar in Los Angeles in 1970 illustrated this expansive network.

What was taking place in San Antonio was taking place throughout the Southwest and Midwest—in Los Angeles, Albuquerque, Denver, Chicago— wherever substantial numbers of Mexican Americans lived. A nationalist sentiment that preached unity and celebrated Mexican American culture was being voiced in barrios throughout the country. Community newspapers, conferences, workshops, countless meetings, and fiestas—all served to refine and elaborate consciousness and political perspective. An expanding organizational field circulated ideas and tactics. Protest actions in one locale could set off similar actions elsewhere in an apparent domino-like chain reaction. Thus the East Los Angeles "blowouts" of March 1968 were followed within weeks by San Antonio high school walkouts. The frustration with barrio schools was such that the Mexican American Youth Organization (MAYO) would organize or "inspire" thirty or so high school actions within the year. The hyperactivity of the emerging networks indicated a growing awareness among Mexican Americans of their status as a distinct national group.[10]

In the following section, I examine this surge in activity and political consciousness by focusing on the organizational "structuring" that took place as MAYO evolved from a community advocacy group into an official political party. MAYO, from its beginning in 1967, had a diverse group of members: college students, batos locos, high school students, men and women. Within three years of its founding, this self-conscious "organization of organizers" had in fact created or inspired several organizations. At the Semana de la Raza celebration of 1971, MAYO could claim to have given birth to the Mexican American Unity Council (MAUC), the Raza Unida Party (RUP), the Brown Berets, and El Teatro de los Barrios. Some of the organizations created by the MAYO leadership were tactical and existed for a specific purpose. Others, however, were formed independently of MAYO and reflected a deeper and distinctive social base.

Herein lies the dynamic that I wish to explore: that the movement, through the medium of ethnic consciousness, gave rise to consciousness of other differences—differences that found expression in organizational form. Organizational growth of the movement was shaped, of course, by functional need, aesthetic taste, ideological debate, and simple personal ego. But much organizational structuring mirrored the emerging signs of gender and class consciousness within the race-ethnic nationalist movement. In other words, the initial sense of unity provided by cultural nationalism, by a common "causa," gave way in a short time to organizations or groups built on particular shared life experiences and interests. The formation of various women's groups and of lower-class men's groups from the one initial organizational foundation of MAYO illustrates this dynamic. Essentially, the "intersections" of race, class, and gender unraveled into distinct parts.

Taking Different Paths

How does one identify the factors or events behind a "structuring" of a social movement along class and gender lines? In the case of MAYO, one could arguably point to its electoral challenge to the Good Government League in the 1969 city council elections as a key moment. The relative success of its Committee for Barrio Betterment (CBB) campaign, based primarily on ethnic appeal, had persuaded MAYO leaders to apply this electoral strategy in the rural Winter Garden region around Crystal City.[11] By the time of the September

16th celebrations of 1971, local "raza unida" slates in the Winter Garden area had already won quick and resounding local victories. MAYO activists, excited by these victories, were determined to expand their strategy beyond a regional basis. A few weeks after the Semana de la Raza celebrations, Raza Unida–MAYO activists held a state convention in San Antonio where they voted to organize an official statewide political party, El Partido de la Raza Unida, as an alternative to the Anglo-dominated Democratic Party. In preparation for this move, and partly in response to the furor of "kill the gringo" rhetoric, MAYO leaders began to talk about facing reality and leaving the "romanticism" behind—meaning the "long hair, beards, and berets."[12]

Most of MAYO's leaders and cadre made a transition to the Raza Unida Party—but not all of them. "Los batos del barrio no," Mario Compean explained. By then, many "college boys" had entered MAYO and the Raza Unida Party.[13] "Los batos," faced with the closing of La Universidad and casting around for a more appealing direction, decided to form the Brown Berets. Thus one division within the movement pointed to class difference, with most college student activists embarking on an electoral strategy for change, while the bato locos organized a paramilitary force to protect the community.

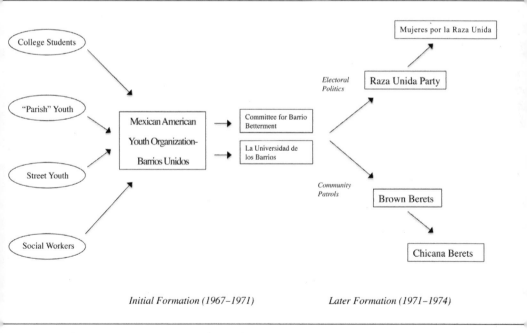

Initial Formation (1967–1971)   *Later Formation (1971–1974)*

Sketch of Chicano movement structuring.

Semana de la Raza Souvenir Program, cover, September 16, 1971. Author's collection.

Regardless of the path taken, tensions around gender—yet another difference—would soon surface as women activists began to assert themselves. Within MAYO and, later, the Raza Unida Party, women activists pressed for equality based on the key movement motif of "la familia." Within the Berets, a small Chicana contingent worked to expand the notion of "carnalismo" to include "sisterhood" and to claim some autonomous space; they appealed as well to the unity of la familia.

While the women acted to create organizational space for self-development and to promote women's issues, the batos acted to gain legitimacy for the space they already had as neighborhood clicas. The success of both groups rested on whether or not a significant change in behavior accompanied their emerging group consciousness. For the women of the movement, this meant departing from a "traditional" backstage supportive role and insisting on visible front stage leadership. For the batos of the movement, this meant departing from gang-related and other antisocial behavior by practicing carnalismo while insisting, also, on a front stage role.

In this section, I look at the play of gender and class consciousnesses within the Chicano movement, the organizational forms in which they found expression, and the identity and behavioral changes resulting from such expression. This process will also allow me to sketch out, in the barest terms, some history of the young barrio women and men involved in the movement.

In the concluding chapter of this section, I discuss whether "identity politics" contributed to a weakening of the Chicano movement. I take into account other factors—such as tactical decisions, philosophical differences, and police actions—that contributed to the fragmentation of the Chicano movement.

WOMEN CREATING SPACE

THE PATRIARCHAL aspects of Mexican culture have been much examined and need not be detailed here. Open to question is the variability of gender relations behind closed doors—that is, in the private world of the family.[1] Publicly, women were expected to act in subordinate backstage support roles, and this was generally true in the early years of the Chicano movement. This expectation, however, was repeatedly exposed by women as a contradiction in a political movement dedicated to equality and social change. Moreover, a growing "women's liberation" movement kept raising the question of male dominance, or machismo. Awareness of the contradictions led many Chicanas to examine and question their position in the movement. That this was an evolution or development over time is clear. That the questioning created bitter tensions between some Chicanas and Chicanos, and between "traditional, male-identified Chicanas" and "feminist Chicanas" is also clear.[2]

The assertion of an independent Chicana identity came gradually. As noted by sociologists Beatriz Pesquera and Denise Segura, Mexican American women active in the movement faced conflicting pressures. Chicano movement groups often organized around the ideal of la familia. The feminist movement, on the other hand, indicted the traditional patriarchal family as a primary source of women's subordination. Although Chicanas recognized the need to struggle against male privilege, "they were reluctant to embrace a feminist position that appeared anti-family."[3] Some, in deference to the goal of a raza unida, did not want to alienate the men. Thus, in spring

1969, at the first Chicano Youth Conference held in Denver, the Chicana caucus reported that "the Chicana woman does not want to be liberated." This was intended as a rejection of Anglo women's liberation struggle.[4]

Nonetheless, the gender question within the movement kept surfacing everywhere. In Crystal City, Texas, where the Raza Unida Party would take over in 1970, the activist women organized to press for equal representation.[5] In May 1971, women attending a Texas farmworkers' boycott conference formed a caucus that warned the main body that sexist attitudes and opposition to women's rights could divide the farmworkers' struggle. That same month, 600 women met in Houston at the first major Chicana conference and, despite dissension over strategy, asserted their distinct female consciousness and their desire for a voice. Gender divisions also surfaced within the university student organizations, leading some women to label "El Plan de Santa Barbara," the document that laid the basis for Chicano studies, as just another movement "man-ifesto." Gender tensions would arise as well within the teatro cultural groups.[6] In a short time, the deferential sentiment expressed at the 1969 youth conference had evaporated.

In San Antonio, the specific reason for tension between men and women within MAYO and its CBB campaign was plainly evident: women constituted the workforce of both, yet had limited or symbolic representation among the leadership. After the first CBB campaign, in 1969, the women began to press for representation on the slate. Leading and organizing a "wildcat" boycott of Mayor McAllister's bank, the San Antonio Savings Association (SASA), earned the Chicana activists two of the four seats on the CBB slate in 1971. Later, with the Raza Unida Party, they elaborated claims for equality based on the key movement motif of "la familia." The following is an account of the emergence of Chicana leaders within MAYO and the Raza Unida Party.

Women as the Foundation

In San Antonio of the mid-sixties, as in the rest of the nation, it was rare for women—white, black, or brown—to leave their private social worlds and seek elected office. One could read the newspapers of the time and not find a single reference to a woman politician, either as a candidate or spokesperson, much less as an incumbent. The public "official" side of government was essentially male business. Those reporting on politics—journalists as well as television and radio newscasters—were likewise all men.

Women of the Raza
Unida Party lead-
ing a march, circa
1971. Courtesy of
George and Andrea
Velásquez.

Nonetheless, women had occasionally challenged or ignored expected gender behavior. In fact, the most dramatic strike and boycott events in San Antonio history to that point—the pecan shellers' strike of 1938 and the Tex-Son garment strike of 1959–1963—had been organized and led by Mexican American women. These events had not ruptured the traditional expectation of female domesticity. Interestingly, the Tex-Son garment strikers, aware of this gendered expectation, had used civic arguments and the theme of motherhood to appeal for broad public support.[7] Unlike men, women labor activists had to explain why they had left the domestic arena of the home and were engaging publicly in strike and protest activity. The need to offer justification for such activism would disappear with the Chicano movement.

Mexican American women had long been involved in politics, movement activist Rosie Castro recalled, but before the seventies "the role that everyone maintained was a support role. . . . it was understood that men would be up front." Castro, a graduate of Our Lady of the Lake College where she had headed the Young Democrats, had been among the first to join MAYO. "The women at that point were not running for office," Castro noted, but they were deeply involved nonetheless:

The political machine built by Albert Peña was really nurtured by Olga, his wife at the time, everybody talked about that, everybody knew it, everybody had respect for her abilities, and yet there was never any recognition of that, a formal recognition saying "this woman is equal to this man." I can remember coming up with the wives of Pete Torres, Joe Bernal; now here were some women that were always busy in their campaigns, were always doing the work; not just sitting idly by but being very much a part of the political work, and yet there was no recognition of that.[8]

Castro speculated that one reason for this neglect of women's contributions stemmed from the kind of leadership practiced by women—"a leadership that empowers others, not a hierarchical leadership."[9]

Perhaps this non-hierarchical tendency explains the absence of women in the early leadership of MAYO, even though they were involved in the organization from the outset. Former MAYO leader Carlos Guerra bluntly described the situation then: "We would like to think that in the old days we were progressive about it [the role of women], but we were not. We were pretty sexist. They were essentially second-class participants by and large." Luz Gutiérrez, married at the time to MAYO leader José Ángel, concurred: "Women were not necessarily in a leadership capacity because at the time we really didn't demand to be recognized as leaders as we do now. We were just partners in the whole development of MAYO." The Chicanas, Gutiérrez explained, "didn't want the feminist issue to divide us. So we tended to want to be united for *la causa* as a family and not divided. We wanted to go forward together."[10]

The general situation was described candidly by Carlos Vásquez from Centro de Acción Social Autónoma (CASA), whose immigration rights network stretched from Los Angeles to Chicago and San Antonio. As editor of the CASA newspaper, *Sin Fronteras*, Vásquez was well positioned to assess the general circumstances confronting women activists in the movement:

> In the early stages of the Chicano Movement and throughout its later years, sexism was clearly present in many forms and on many occasions. There existed a double standard of work and social life among men and women involved in the same struggle. Women did the petty work, men did the leading. Women's opinions were belittled or ignored, and rarely was the woman allowed meaningful positions of leadership.[11]

At the same time, though, the women of the movement were exalted in romantic portrayals as revolutionary "Adelitas" and beautiful "Aztec princesses." Vásquez called such characterizations "artful attempts" to paper over the obvious tensions in the movement. "In another vein, we grabbed onto the concept of the traditional Mexican family and by this means sought to box the woman into a role of mother, housemaid, and little else."[12]

The women activists, however, proved to be skillful at rearticulating or reinterpreting the images and themes of the movimiento. The exaltation of la familia, for example, could point the discussion and negotiation about gender roles in an entirely different direction, as activist-intellectual Marta Cotera wryly noted. Cotera, originally from El Paso, had been one of the first "voluntarios de Aztlán" to relocate to Crystal City after the Raza Unida's stunning victories there.

Like other movement organizations, MAYO's ideology of cultural nationalism celebrated the ideal of la familia as the foundation of Mexican resiliency and strength in the face of oppression. From this position, the next, seemingly natural step, articulated in many early "man-ifestos," led to a reinforcement of traditional married roles and expectations (with reproduction being a major one). Cotera observed that although MAYO had identified the family and carnalismo as strategic elements, it was "still debatable as to whether MAYO organizers were aware that women and men who were family oriented would turn reality into an ideological statement and vice versa." The grassroots training of women and their families would establish "a consciousness of egalitarian values" in most movement participants.[13]

While the notion of "political familism," as Cotera called it, may have helped married women in renegotiating gender roles and expectations, single women faced a more delicate balancing act in dealing with their male relationships. Rosie Castro remembered the internal discussions that women had then about maintaining one's identity and one's name:

> Many times I remember going crazy because these women wanted to be Mrs. so-and-so, you know, Mrs. whatever, and we were the young ones coming up and saying "screw that shit, be who you are, you got a name."[14]

The women began "to buy into that," added Castro.

The men, on the other hand, seemed confused by such assertions of independence. Poet and writer Inés Hernández, who was active in the Houston MAYO–Raza Unida Party in the early seventies, recalled the words of a "true compañera" who told the women, "If you want the men to respect your word, don't go to bed with them." The compañera followed her own advice, and so when she spoke, the men were "reverent in their attention." In contrast, wrote Hernández in her "testimony of memory,"

> when we spoke
> they let the moment pass and continued
> as if nothing had been said,
> Remember?[15]

Basically, males and male privilege were confronted with the ideology of the movimiento as well with the grassroots participation of women. Working for egalitarian change created egalitarian expectations within the group, and this framed the context for numerous confrontations with male leaders. Cotera recalled one incident that set her off:

> In 1968 we had a conference in Houston, and not a single woman was on the stage, but it just made me very pissed off that of all of us who had done all the work, no one was there. I just knew that we were not going to take second-class treatment because we were not second-class people.[16]

Cotera added, chagrined, that "even she didn't realize" that her vocal reaction had been "a feminist act, but it was."[17]

In San Antonio, the women worked their way to the public forefront through their involvement and leadership in MAYO–Barrios Unidos. In 1969, when the group fielded a slate of city council candidates under the rubric of the Committee for Barrio Betterment, the women formed the core campaign staff. The Barrios Unidos staff consisted of social workers Mariano Aguilar, Cruz Chapa, and Jesse Sauceda, but, as Aguilar recalled, "the organization was all women, the leaders of each barrio club were women, señoras, the board was all señoras. They voted, phoned and got the people out, manned the polls, registration, they were the mothers, aunts, and so on."[18] Aguilar described las señoras as "the troops of the Committee for Barrio Betterment."

Leaving the Shawl Behind: The SASA Boycott

After the 1969 CBB campaign, the college women of MAYO–Barrios Unidos organized a group called El Rebozo (The Shawl) and published a newspaper with the same name.[19] The imagery of the shawl, suggesting modesty and tradition, gave the formation of a women's group a nonthreatening veneer. The initial issues had a reassuring dedication for the men: "Dedicamos nuestros esfuerzos a los hombres en este movimiento chicano que nos inspiraron a escribir este periódico" (We dedicate our efforts to the men of the Chicano movement who have inspired us to write this newspaper). A preamble further explained that the newspaper, "written by women, put out by women, distributed by women," had as its purpose the uniting of our people to work for "La Causa." The symbolism of the rebozo represented "la mujer completa" (the complete woman):

> El Rebozo—the traditional garment of the Mexican woman—with its many uses symbolizes the three roles of the Chicana portraying her as "la señorita," feminine, yet humble; as "la revolucionaria," ready to fight for "La Causa," and finally portraying the role of "la madre," radiant with life.[20]

"La mujer completa," in other words, combined femininity and motherliness with a readiness to fight alongside her compañero in the struggle.

Reassurances to the men aside, the women of MAYO–Barrios Unidos were pressing for recognition and representation. A declarative poem in the November issue of *El Rebozo* suggested their impatience:

> We have waited for a change,
> A change from being left out,
> A change from standing in the
>   background.
> We have waited too long to say
>   something.
> Yes, we have waited long enough.
> Something must and will be done
>   soon![21]

The opportunity for the women to assert their leadership and organizational skills came with a nationally televised insult by San Antonio mayor Walter McAllister on NBC's "Huntley-Brinkley Report" in late August 1970. In response to a question about the violence that had just taken place in Los Angeles during a Chicano protest march, Mayor McAllister commented that in San Antonio "our Mexicans" prefer to sing and dance. Moreover, the Mexican Americans in San Antonio were "not as ambitiously motivated as

DEDICAMOS NUESTROS ESFUERZOS A LOS HOMBRES EN ESTE MOVIMIENTO CHICANO QUE NOS INSPIRARON A ESCRIBIR ESTE PERIODICO.

EL REBOZO

NOVIEMBRE, 1969   SAN ANTONIO, TEJAS

THIS NEWSPAPER – WRITTEN BY WOMEN, PUT OUT BY WOMEN, DISTRIBUTED BY WOMEN WAS UNDERTAKEN FOR THE PURPOSE OF UNITING OUR PEOPLE TO WORK FOR "LA CAUSA".

INSPIRED BY THE MEN OF "EL MOVIMIENTO", WE, "THE WOMEN OF LA RAZA" WANT THE MEN TO KNOW THAT WE SUPPORT THEM AND THE COURAGE THEY HAVE ENDLESSLY DISPLAYED IN FIGHTING FOR "LA RAZA".

EL REBOZO – THE TRADITIONAL GARMENT OF THE MEXICAN WOMAN, WITH ITS MANY USES SYMBOLIZES THE THREE ROLES OF THE CHICANA PORTRAYING HER AS "LA SENORITA", FEMININE, YET HUMBLE; AS "LA REVOLUCIONARIA", READY TO FIGHT FOR "LA CAUSA", AND FINALLY PORTRAYING THE ROLE OF "LA MADRE", RADIANT WITH LIFE.

THIS NEWSPAPER HAS TRIED TO PORTRAY THE WOMEN OF "LA RAZA" IN THEIR DIFFERENT ROLES, FOR ALL THREE ROLES MAKE UP "LA MUJER COMPLETA".

Cover of the November 1969 issue of *El Rebozo*. The dedication above the title reads: "We dedicate our efforts to the men of the Chicano movement who inspired us to write this newspaper." Author's collection.

the Anglos to get ahead financially." McAllister also added that charges of police brutality at protests were "a common Communist cry."[22] The televised remarks sparked an angry and spontaneous protest outside his bank, the San Antonio Savings Association. The mayor's words had ironically served to bring the August 29 protest of Los Angeles to San Antonio.

Under the leadership of women, the spontaneous protest evolved into a long, messy boycott of SASA. The goal was to get Mexicanos to withdraw their savings. Alicia Martínez, a leader of welfare mothers, used the House of Neighborly Services as an organizing base for the boycott. Like many women, she felt that they had to respond to McAllister's insult:

> Everybody was upset and we decided to boycott SASA. People took off from work, they would go picket SASA, school children were there, the elderly, just everybody trying to get people to take their money out of SASA. I don't know if it worked or not, but it was the first instance that had called attention to the Chicanos and what was going on in San Antonio."[23]

For the first month, the number of picketers grew larger each day. On Wednesday, September 9, twenty-nine picketers, including county commissioner Albert Peña and Rev. G. J. Sutton, were arrested for disturbing the peace. Peña had designated the day as "'Business and Professional Men's Day' in the SASA picket line, showing that the middle-class Mexican American supports the protest against the mayor's racism."[24] Ten more picketers were arrested the following day after a "melee" that began when a security guard "bumped" into picket leader Andrea Gámez. Rosie Castro described the incidents:

> On one particular day a cowboy pushes Andrea Gámez out of the way. The pickets chased him into the Frost [National Bank] and cornered him in the elevator. The women formed a circle around the cowboy, between him and the guys. But a conflict occurred. Soon the melee began, the police began to bang people against the walls and sidewalks. A pregnant woman was beaten. The lawyers [for the picketers] arrived but then they all got thrown in jail. It was traumatic.[25]

They went back onto the streets, with even more picketers, and some got thrown into jail again.

Police photos in possession of Congressman Henry B. Gonzalez, of individuals arrested on September 9 and 10, 1970, during the SASA boycott. Gonzalez Collection, Center for American History, University of Texas at Austin. *This page, from top, left to right,* Albert Peña, county commissioner; G. J. Sutton, mortician; Mamie Lopez, housewife; Teresa Guerrero, housewife; Sylvia Rodriguez, social worker; and Angelita Burgos, student. *Opposite page, from top, left to right,* Hilda Cantú, secretary; Nacho Perez, no occupation; Gregoria McCumber, housewife; Frank Tejeda, no occupation; Gilbert Murillo, teacher; and Ruben Sandoval, attorney. *Items of note*: Perez was a MAYO founder and organizer; Tejeda would later become a congressman; Murillo was leader of the settlement house workers; and attorney Sandoval represented many Chicano organizations.

Over the long haul the SASA boycott was very difficult. A key organizer, Gloria Cabrera, recalled that at times only one person marched. But the boycott went on for months and finally forced Mayor McAllister to go on TV and apologize for the comments that he had made. In Castro's assessment, "The boycott raised the level of consciousness of the public." It was a significant event for the Mexicano community. But still, she added, "it was a very sad incident and almost no one has talked about it again."[26]

Taking the Electoral Path

After the SASA boycott, the women of MAYO–Barrios Unidos began to press for inclusion on the second CBB slate that would contest the 1971 city council elections. The question of representation became an issue. Gloria Cabrera, by virtue of her work on the boycott, became a CBB candidate. There was some opposition to placing Rosie Castro on the ticket because she was seen as too feminist and unconventional. But Castro, who represented the Chicana activists of El Rebozo, had already proven herself in previous campaigns.[27] Thus, of the four candidates on the CBB ticket—Mario Compean and Willie Benavides rounded out the slate—two were women. Cabrera and Castro would become the first Chicanas to run for city council in living memory.

CBB was now touted as more than a rejection of Mexican American middle-class politics of assimilation and gradualism: it was also a rejection of male patriarchy—or at least a symbolic gesture in that direction. Castro downplayed the gesture. The men had formed a selection committee but had trouble forming a slate:

Many men turned them down. So there was not a strategic plan, but it was the luck of the draw, who was available, and Gloria and I were crazy enough to say yes. They [the selection committee] had some respect for women, but it wasn't their intent to select us.[28]

The campaign had its highs and lows, Castro recalled, with support and criticism coming from unexpected places:

From the traditional Mexicano structure, there was some support, but there was a lot of "you're crazy; it's an impossible dream; but if you want to try it, go ahead, here is some postage, here's fifty dollars." There was incredible support from the women within the campaign.

But outside the campaign, many women did not take the candidates seriously; they were a stumbling block. "They would call us crazy kids that are impatient and don't know politics." Many women would not register to vote "without the men's permission." It was disheartening, recalled Castro.[29]

Regarding her 1971 CBB campaign, attorney Gloria Cabrera recollected that one of the questions the media asked her was if being a woman would hinder her in performing the job. "The way I handled it, because this was on live television, was to laugh it off and say, 'Fortunately it's a job that both men and women can perform.'" The question, Cabrera noted, revealed "the mentality in the 1970s." Cabrera felt that she was treated fairly by the Chicanos in circles that she was working with, "although definitely the men were in control of the entire movement."[30]

In the spring of 1971, the CBB again placed second in all their contests while winning the West and South Side precincts. The result was a foregone conclusion in at-large elections in a segregated city. But in the South Texas rural areas, where the Mexican American population comprised 70 percent or more of the total, an ethnic-nationalist strategy had yielded promising local results. In the Winter Garden area around Crystal City, an upstart "Raza Unida" had captured control in 1970 of the school board and city government, and the party was preparing for the 1972 county elections.

As in San Antonio, the women involved in these campaigns demanded representation. In Crystal City, the women were not satisfied with being shunted into the "women's auxiliary" of the main and male-only decision-making organization, Ciudadanos Unidos. They "stormed the dance hall" and demanded to be recognized as members on an equal basis. Luz Gutié-

Candidates of the Committee for Barrio Betterment, February 20, 1971: *left to right*, Willie Benavides, Gloria Cabrera, Rosie Castro, and Mario Compean. *San Antonio Light* Collection, University of Texas at Austin Institute of Texan Cultures, L-6502-A-11, courtesy of the Hearst Corporation.

rrez recalled that they had to say, "Hey, we don't want to be the tamale makers and . . . the busy bees. We want to be part of the decision-making process." Many men did not like the idea of their wives being in a dance hall with other men, but the women remained firm and won out. Within a short period of time, the women made up much of the group's elected leadership.[31] Although it took struggle, organizer Marta Cotera cited "the liberating experience of women in Crystal City" as something that set them apart from other women activists, who "despite movement rhetoric nationwide" were primarily relegated to logistics and "housekeeping" duties.[32]

Perhaps it was this background of *successful* struggle within male-dominated political formations that prompted the MAYO women of San Antonio and Crystal City to clash with those Chicanas who were determined to create autonomous organizations independent of men. The disagreement surfaced publicly at the first national Chicana conference in Houston in May 1971. Many attendees, such as Francisca Flores of the Comisión Femenil Mexicana in California, believed that women "are best served by their own effort through their own organizations within the total movement."[33] The disagreement boiled down to identifying the principal enemy: sexism or racism? The macho or the gabacho?

Whom to Target—the Macho or the Gabacho?

The first national conference of Chicanas demonstrated the rise of a distinct feminist consciousness along with a corresponding organizational network. Like most movement-inspired conferences, the meeting aimed to disseminate information, exchange views, reach consensus on basic principles, and ideally offer a plan of action or a vision for the future. The conference also offered the first opportunity since the 1969 national youth conference in Denver to revisit the question of Chicana liberation. The meeting broke up dramatically into two camps on this very question. This experience moved many participants to write about their observations and opinions, thus permitting a reconstruction of the event.[34]

More than 600 Chicanas from twenty-three states gathered in Houston over Memorial Day weekend in 1971 to participate in the first national conference of Mexican American women. In the workshops, Chicanas discussed and challenged every social institution implicated in their situation, from job inequality to their role in the home. They were questioning machismo, the double standard, the role of the Catholic Church, education discrimination, "and all the backward ideology designed to keep women subjugated."[35] Los Angeles participant Francisca Flores recalled that the workshops were so packed,

> only the most vocal and most aggressive could be heard discussing issues that interest women but which are shaking the men who feel threatened by women in action, women in leadership roles, women who are literally out of reach of the masculine dictum.[36]

After two days of meetings, the workshops returned several controversial resolutions, including one that stated that the traditional role of the

Chicana within the marriage context was no longer acceptable, another that called for the elimination of the double sex standard, another that called for free and legal abortions, and yet another that recognized the Catholic Church as an oppressive institution.

But then the storm, or "chubasco," as Flores described it, broke out. Disagreements that had surfaced in the Saturday workshops had continued through the night. By Sunday, the conference had divided into two groups. About half the women did not support the resolutions. Charging that the conference was being held at a "gringo" institution, the dissenters walked out and staged their own rump conference. These women felt that the emphasis should be placed on racism, not sexism—on "the gabacho, not the macho"—and that political involvement must "not detract from their family commitment." MAYO member Rosie Castro expressed the sentiment of those who walked out:

> Our people cannot come out of oppression unless we do it together. So it was not sexism but a race question. The White women's agenda had some relevance but not at the expense of our people. Job discrimination, for example, cut across the men and women in our community.[37]

The group that stayed and supported the "feminist" resolutions considered those who walked out as "male-identified" women. According to Flores, "the women who believed that women in the Chicano community must submit to the dominance of the men walked out. Much of their rationale was superficial."[38] The "feminist" group finished the conference, but the workshops on "strategies for the future" were cancelled. Two sets of final resolutions and evaluations were finally presented.

One of the conference organizers, Elma Barrera, from Houston, confessed her disappointment with the way things turned out. Although the women who walked out had claimed that the conference was being held in a gringo institution (the YWCA), and that the barrio people had been overlooked, Barrera noted that the "Y" was in the middle of six Houston barrios, and the organizers were all barrio women. They had developed the conference with "all the hopes and good intentions imaginable":

> How could we have deluded ourselves into thinking it would work out? It turned into a fiasco, with so many accusations directed to us. We really had no idea that women, Chicanas, could be so misinformed about one another."[39]

Nonetheless, she was sanguine about the conference's impact:

> [It] had a profound effect on some, it didn't faze others. But that weekend
> was only one weekend in our lives. A weekend no one will remember
> ten to fifteen years from now. Sounds a little bitter, but really, I'm not
> sorry we put it on. . . . We learned about us, about mujeres in the move-
> ment, about how some of us operate, right or wrong.[40]

Other conference attendees were more optimistic. Jennie Chavez, from
Albuquerque, said the conference had had an immediate impact. The meeting had emboldened a Las Chicanas group at the University of New Mexico
to have more confidence and to speak up for recognition. Prior to the conference, "Las Chicanas was being used as the work club by the other male-
run Chicano organizations in the city. . . . Every time they needed maids or
cooks, they'd dial-a-Chicana."[41] Francisca Flores concluded that the impact
of the Houston conference might not be fully realized for years, but that it
had given "greater impulse to discussion on the role of Mexican women."
She could not resist taking one more dig at the dissenters, expressing the
hope that "those women who wish to continue playing a secondary role"
would respect the rights of women who wished to organize independently
of men.[42] MAYO activist Marta Cotera, who had been among the dissenters,
tried to offer some grounds for reconciliation between the two groups:

> We feel, along with other Chicana women at the conference, that it
> makes no difference how many differences there are between what we
> think. The most important thing is to look at common problems, to get
> ourselves together, and even more important [to decide] what we're
> going to do.[43]

Regardless of the disagreement over whether to emphasize racism
or sexism, the conference made clear that Chicanas would be struggling
"around their own specific demands and through their own Chicana organizations."[44] The conference also showed that even the "male-identified"
Chicanas were pressing for significant change in gender relations. No longer content to simply play a supporting role, Chicanas would demand to be
part of the visible leadership.

The Raza Unida Party's Position on Women

Excited by the clear victories in 1970 in the Winter Garden district around Crystal City, the core members of MAYO were determined to go beyond local races and plunge into statewide electoral politics. On October 1, 1971, at Salon Social Tea on Colorado and Commerce streets, La Raza Unida formally became Texas's third political party. It was soon seen as encompassing and transcending MAYO and CBB, both of which were phased out.[45] Among the many tasks that the new party had to carry out was a drafting of a platform that explicated its position on key social issues, including that of women's rights. A close reading of the party's statement regarding women's rights suggests some of the friction that accompanied the rise of women leadership.

In 1972, its first year as an official party, the Raza Unida Party included a section devoted to "la mujer" in its platform. Party organizer Evey Chapa found inspiration in the platform's declaration that party development and "strength of unity" would be based on "*total* family participation," and that the party was committed to the political education and leadership development of women. The Raza Unida Party was the only political party in Texas to include a plank on women's issues in its platform.[46] Yet the caveats and tentative language that characterize the section on women point to an apparent tension within the drafting committee.

The platform committee prefaced its statement by noting that minority women found themselves in "an unusual position" since they could not speak of greater political participation, equal pay for equal work, or even control of their own bodies, because "all of these are denied in practice to all members of minority groups, male and female." This meant that minority women did not have "the luxury of dealing exclusively with feminism and fighting male chauvinism, as racism plays an even bigger role in suppressing peoples in the State of Texas."

The section further emphasized that the Raza Unida Party opposed second-class citizenship for all peoples, and thus the party did "not feel that a separate stand on the rights of women is necessary, as it is explicit that women are included in the fight for equal rights." Moreover, the party believed that "strength of unity" begins with the family. "Total family involvement" was touted as the basic foundation for the party, with "men, women and youth working together for a common cause."

Despite such declarations, in the end the platform committee essentially reversed direction and endorsed several resolutions on behalf of women:

"However, acting in good faith and realizing that women, as a group, are suppressed," the party resolved to support, among other things, the Equal Rights Amendment and the inclusion of women in the party's decision-making committees.[47]

In a sense, the men had little choice but to accede to the women, for as the new political party evolved, women continued to be "the backbone" of the organization. They handled everything, as organizer Chapa put it, from cooking, child care, and secretarial work to planning political events. From the beginning, women did the work that is essential to political organizing: door-to-door canvassing, office work, fund-raising, and so forth. Just as important, they provided volunteers for the party structure as well as candidates for political office. In 1972, over a third (36 percent) of the Raza Unida Party county chairs were women, and one-fifth of all precinct chairs were women. In a sign of commitment to women, Alma Canales, from the Rio Grande Valley, was chosen to be the party's candidate for lieutenant governor, making her the first Chicana to run for statewide office in Texas history. In the end, the women did "what had to be done," despite some resentment toward the men. But they negotiated concessions in return.[48]

Frequently, as Marta Cotera noted at the time, women felt they had to "retreat into more conservative stands" because of fear of being labeled a feminist or a "women's libber." They retreated even from activities that dealt "specifically with the special social needs of women."[49] Indeed, "outspoken women" often had to hold their tongues in order to preserve peace within the party. This was especially true whenever a critique of actions taken by the male leadership was involved.

One notable instance was triggered by a visit to San Antonio by Mexican president Luis Echeverría to dedicate the new branch of La Universidad Nacional Autónoma de Mexico (UNAM) in June 1972. Echeverría was widely regarded among movement circles as the architect of the Tlatelolco student massacre and Mexico's "dirty war" against political dissidents. Vocal protests were expected.

Picketers did greet Echeverría in San Antonio, but he unexpectedly agreed to meet with Raza Unida leaders José Ángel Gutiérrez and Ramsey Muñiz, as well as Mario Cantú, the picket organizer. After the meeting, during which Echeverría made a generous donation of medical and library supplies to Crystal City, Gutiérrez claimed that the president was "fantastic" and that he supported the ideals of La Raza Unida Party. Muñiz said that Echeverría was "very open" to the party and thought it a "wonderful idea" to be practicing democracy. And after Echeverría said that he would find those responsible for the student murders of the previous summer (June 10, 1971), Cantú called off the pickets in a "display of good faith."[50]

A clear, direct critique of the meeting appeared in the Chicano journal *Magazín* a few months later. The critic chose to speak her mind anonymously and simply went by the name "María." What had happened, she asked, to the solidarity with those struggling in Mexico? Echeverría, María wrote, "played a political game with our people and got what he wanted, support and approval of 'Chicano militants.'" She then cautioned movement organizers to "make sure that they are working with the people as well as for the people," and to "remember that we are not the only struggle for human and political freedom." María concluded her dissent with a concern: "The individualism and display of egoism among our people is only hindering the advancement of our movement internationally as well as nationally."[51]

A Concluding Note

In the early seventies, Chicana activists in the Southwest were busy dealing with the emerging women's liberation movement on one hand, and the continuing machismo of movimiento leaders on the other. Regarding the former, they withdrew from the national and local women's political caucuses because these were deemed insensitive to the concerns of women of color. With regard to the latter, they continued to organize women's groups to press for equality and influence within the movement. According to one count, thirty-two major Chicana conferences or workshops were held between 1970 and 1975, with a spike in 1972, when eight events took place.[52]

In Texas, the women of the Raza Unida Party continued to develop a cadre and network. They organized the first Mujeres por la Raza Unida statewide conference in San Antonio in August 1973. Almost 200 women from twenty Texas counties attended. As recalled by Evey Chapa, "The experience was phenomenal. The variety of lifestyles and ages represented were unique: high school students, college women, professional women, grassroots women, eighteen to eighty years of age, attended." The Chicanas who participated, with all their experiences and expertise, "demonstrated that the Chicano movement is stronger because mujeres are actively involved, and further, making decisions."[53]

Cotera, in her speech before the 1973 Mujeres por la Raza Unida Conference, noted with regard to women's liberation that an involved Chicana would "meet head on any alien feminist movement which attempts to recruit from her people" and that "any feelings or sympathy toward feminism" would have its force directed inward. It would "not be a contrary separatist course, or be directed by a non-Chicano terminology or leadership." On the other hand, with regard to machismo politics, Cotera warned that "disciplinarian," "purgist," or "protective" attitudes toward women attracted to feminism would be "tragic and detrimental to the cause."[54] The activist women argued that the goals of the Chicano movement and that of women's liberation were not mutually exclusive.

With her characteristic wry insights, Cotera noted that the women's liberation movement had actually made Chicanas take more conservative positions:

> Unfortunately, the only effect that Anglo feminism has on the Chicana
> has been negative. Suddenly, mujeres [women] involved in the struggle
> for social justice, who have always advocated for more and stronger
> women, and family participation in all political activities, are suspect.
> They are suspected of assimilating into the feminist ideology of an alien
> culture.[55]

Cotera concluded her assessment with a consoling thought about Chicanas: "we can face any feminist movement and still remain firmly within our Raza." The consolation was aimed as much at men as at women, for the women of the Raza Unida Party were attempting to carry on their work "without alarming the male leadership on the issue of feminism any more than the various Chicana conference resolutions were doing." To generate support from men as well as from women generally, the Raza Unida women emphasized the central unifying role of the woman in the Mexican American family.[56]

The 1973 conference resolved to work for the ideological and political development of women within the party. Over the following year (1973–1974), training conferences were held in San Antonio, Crystal City, Houston, Fort Worth, Austin, Kingsville, and Temple.[57] Chicanas soon stopped worrying about what the men thought. Indeed, they managed to keep the party afloat in the midst of the fierce infighting that erupted in 1974–1975. After winning control of Crystal City and Zavala County, the Raza Unida Party had begun to fray internally as pro-Gutiérrezista and anti-Gutiérrezista factions began fighting over ideology, tactics, and patronage. Cultural nationalism, which had provided the unity needed to depose the "old Anglo oligarchy," had provided no blueprint for governance.

Nor had it provided a sure blueprint for gender relations. Agreement on gender equity and inclusion in the political arena did not come easily or automatically; rather, it was the result of concrete struggle and political development among movement activists. Women came to the realization, as one activist put it, that it was "illogical to ask a woman to ignore and postpone her struggle as a woman."[58]

BATOS CLAIMING LEGITIMACY

8 MAYO WAS THE BASE for the formation of two very different organizations, each reflecting a distinct social class base. There was some overlap, but generally the militant college students went into the Raza Unida Party, and the batos locos into the Brown Berets. Many batos distrusted the college students. A typical sentiment was that of Lalo Martínez, a former gang member who described himself as "the first pachuco at the Lake [a local college]." Martínez described the middle-class Chicanos he ran into as aloof or in self-denial about their identity:

> That's a problem with many Chicanos; no se quieren dejar cayer la greña [they don't want to let it all hang out]; they're afraid to let go and be themselves. Me, I'm not afraid to be raza; I never had identity problems o nada, never had to go through that. There are some who are lost; they only want to escape and hide, that's all. They want to escape from the barrio and hide so they wouldn't have to think that they're raza and that the barrio has problems.[1]

In contrast, neighborhood loyalties were important for Martínez and the other batos, and now the immediate problems of their neighborhoods called their attention. Their concerns pertained to the police harassment and threat of gang violence that characterized everyday barrio life. In that context, electoral politics was a distant matter.

The batos thus had little patience with the mission or details of building a political party. "We can't waste our time with politics when the barrio needs organizing," some said.[2] What the batos wanted was an organization that would address the specific concerns of their social world. In this sense, the formation of the Brown Berets as a community defense group seemed like a natural development.

By 1972, the year of the last MAYO conference, the Raza Unida Party was well on its way to mounting a third-party challenge in statewide elections, and the San Antonio Berets counted some seventy soldados. Moreover, due to the influence of the San Antonio Berets, chapters had sprung up in Dallas, Houston, Austin, McAllen (the Valley), and several small towns surrounding San Antonio.[3] In all cases, they saw themselves as community guards concerned with the immediate issues of young males: clica rivalries, glue-sniffing addiction, and police behavior. The Brown Berets were a class-specific and, initially, a male-only formation.

Unlike the situation for the women who continued to struggle within the male-dominated MAYO–Raza Unida Party, whatever tensions the batos had sensed with college activists while in MAYO appeared resolved, at least in the day-to-day sense, once they formed their own organization. This, however, only threw into sharp relief the importance of forging a new identity and behavior. The problem faced by the Berets was how to gain acceptance as a legitimate organization or, more to the point, how to keep themselves from being seen as a new gang. Their commitment to la causa was not in doubt, but the devil lay in the details of everyday behavior. "Carnalismo," or brotherhood, was to supplant the conflict-oriented stance of the batos, and a set of rules was adopted to guide their everyday behavior. Such change was essential if the Berets were to become public actors. Thus their mobilization signified a change in identity and behavior—or at least a push in this direction—from the old gang milieu of West Side San Antonio. As was the case for the women of MAYO and the Raza Unida Party, this change in identity and behavior took place over time and somewhat unevenly. In the case of the Berets, some would argue that hardly any change took place.

One attempt to set themselves apart from a gang image was the decision to admit Chicanas into the Berets. This introduced, according to some males who had opposed the move, the gender problem into the group and ultimately led to the demise of the Berets.

The Chicana Berets

The Brown Berets first admitted women in 1972. Luisa, the first to be admitted, had come to know several guys who would later become Berets through her involvement with Barrios Unidos. She started dating one of the guys, and "he explained la onda de los Berets y de allí vine apañado la onda [the idea about the Berets and I learned from that]." After a year of hanging out with them, she became the first woman Brown Beret. Juan Guajardo was her padrino (sponsor) at her initiation. "For the first time," recalled Luisa, "I felt like I really belonged, that I had a place in the movimiento. No, nomás de andar bullshitting y ligando leaflets y todo como secretaria [Not just going around bullshitting and preparing leaflets and all that like a secretary]."[4]

Luisa was soon joined by Lety, Silvia, Queeny, Perla, Dolores, and Virginia—seven women joining some sixty male Berets. All of them were either sisters or girlfriends of Berets. Because their brothers or boyfriends had been gang members, they were familiar with gangs, but none of them had actually belonged to a gang. After three months of probation, Luisa was promoted to first lieutenant "para representar a las chavalas en las juntas con la gente" (to represent the girls in the meetings with the people).[5]

The soldaderas (female soldiers) created their own organization within the Berets, with their own screening procedures for new women members, and generally worked to expand the notion of carnalismo to include Chicanas. Many male activists interpreted the concept narrowly to refer only to men, as opposed to seeing it, as a Chicana Beret from Austin put it, as "a sign of solidarity in the struggle."[6] With support from their padrinos, the Chicana Berets were accorded respect and a good measure of equality within the West Side group. The harassment they experienced came from non-Beret males. As Luisa put it:

> Bueno, muchos se burlaban de mí porque guachaban una chavala en medio de muchos batos y creían que andaba como de puta, nomás vacilando, que nomás andaba de adorno. Yo les explicaba de los Berets, pero muchos batos nomás me oían hablar porque querían movidas conmigo. Y cuando no les capeaba, se aguitaban. Muchos decían que simón, sí somos iguales, pero era puro pedo. Más del tiempo los ignoraba.[7]
> [Well, many would laugh at me because they saw a girl in the middle of all these guys and they thought that I was a loose woman, just playing around, that I was just some adornment. I would explain the Berets

to them, but many guys would just listen to me because they wanted to make moves on me. And when I wouldn't respond, they would get bent out of shape. Many said that, yeah, we're equal, but it was a lot of bullshit. Most of the time I ignored them.]

More difficult to ignore were the "come-ons" and "put-downs" from new male Berets who had not learned (or been instructed) to treat the women Berets as equals. This created tension over gender relations, and several Berets would later cite this as the final breaking point for the organization. It was a reflection, however, of the general difficulty the Beret leaders had in maintaining a disciplined organization.

Leticia Gallegos, one of the original Chicana Brown Berets of San Antonio. Courtesy of Diana Montejano.

The Need for Discipline

Initially the Brown Berets were a community defense group comprised solely of Chicano veterans. Soon the ranks were opened to any bato or ruca committed to dying for la raza. A process was set up to evaluate such commitment. In Guajardo's words:

> We had a screening committee. The guys who joined the Berets were ready to give their lives for the people. Everything was placed in service of the people. Your personal life came last. Those we considered Brown Beret material. And those who joined because they liked the uniform, and those who didn't participate, we would throw them out.[8]

For the batos who had not served in the military, the discipline expected of them was new and sometimes resented. For many, this implied a change in personal behavior.

Like any formal organization, the Berets had rules and routines. Chapter meetings were held every week, and general meetings of all chapters every two weeks. They had classes to instruct the batos on how to manipulate bureaucrats and on how to present themselves in public. This was important because the Berets were assisting families in dealing with the welfare bureaucracy.[9] How they conducted themselves in public was also important because the Berets were making appearances before the city council and various community groups. Members were expected to attend all meetings, classes, and demonstrations. They were also expected to contact their officer once a day, and all officers were to contact the prime minister twice a day. They were expected to wear their berets at all times.[10] Thus the Berets were always exposed to scrutiny from the general public. Joining the Berets meant leaving one's private social world and entering the public arena.

Proper, respectable behavior, then, was expected of all members. This expectation was made explicit by the rules drawn up by the leadership (see the document reproduced on page 178). Of the thirteen rules, eight dealt with behavior; the other five dealt with organizational matters such as attending meetings. The prime behavioral rule had to do with the practice of "carnalismo," or brotherhood, "an absolute must" if a "raza unida" was to be achieved. Another important rule stated that Berets were not to lift a hand against another Chicano except in self-defense, and another said that Berets were not to speak against another unless he or she was present. Luisa explained why these behavioral rules were so important:

Por primera vez en mi vida, comencé a guachar como se portaban los
batos, como eran las rucas, como pensaba la mayoría de la raza acá en
los barrios. Aprendí porque se necesitaba la onda del carnalismo. Porque
sin carnalismo nos iba chingar el gringo. Nunca íbamos a hacer nada
porque todo el tiempo nomás nos andábamos peleando uno contra el
otro.[11]

[For the first time in my life, I began to see how the guys behaved, how
the women were, how the majority of the people in the barrios thought.
I learned why the idea of brotherhood was so necessary. Because without brotherhood the gringo was going to fuck us over. We were never
going to do anything because we were always fighting one another.]

Two important behavior rules prohibited public intoxication and the use of
heavy drugs. One Beret recalled that "La mota estaba de aquella, pero nada
más" (Weed was okay, but nothing more).

To those who thought the Brown Berets were just a gang dressed in uniforms, Luisa stressed the philosophy of carnalismo and the organizational
rules:

Bueno, porque no andábamos como ganga haciéndole pedo a otros barrios. Nosotros estábamos al contrario. Estábamos tratando de unir los
otros barrios. Nosotros teníamos batos de diferentes gangas que antes se
peleaban uno con otro pero que ahora aquí estábamos juntos tratando de
alivianar la raza . . . y alivianarnos nosotros también, al mismo tiempo.
No andábamos en las drogas. Esta era una de las reglas más estrictas que
teníamos. Y como batos de las gangas, you know, chingo de batos anda-
ban en ese jale. Se juntaban, se ponían locos, se daban un plomazo.[12]
[Well, we weren't going around like a gang making trouble with other
barrios. We were doing the contrary. We were trying to unite the barrios.
We had batos from different gangs that used to fight one another who
were now together trying to straighten out the people . . . and straighten
out ourselves also, at the same time. We weren't messing with drugs.
That was one of the strictest rules we had. And the guys of the gangs,
you know, many guys were into that thing. They would get together,
they would get crazy high, they would shoot each other.]

Discipline was important. The Berets would throw batos out if they used
the organization for personal pedo. "For personal conflict, you hang alone."
They would also throw batos out for heroin use, but sometimes there were

San Antonio Brown Beret Rules

In order for an organization such as ours to survive, we must have a love for our people, dedication, and discipline. If you really love your people, you yourself will straighten out. The following rules apply to each and everyone of us. These rules were not made to be broken.

Rules for the Brown Berets

The following rules are the San Antonio chapter of the Brown Beret Organization. Any member of the organization found guilty of breaking any of these rules, is subject to disciplinary action and will either be put on probation or permanently terminated from the organization.

1. Every member will attend all called meetings, rallys, pickets, or demonstration.
2. Any member absent from 3 consecutive meetings without a good excuse or failure to call in his excuse prior to the meeting will be ousted from the organization.
3. Every Brown Beret will be in uniform at all Brown Beret functions.
4. All soldados will contact their officer once a day and all officers will contact the Prime Minister twice a day .
5. Under no circumstances will a Brown beret indulge in the possession, sale, use or distribution of narcotics.
6. While in uniform, no Brown Beret will be seen in public while heavily intoxicated.
7. It is an absolute must that all Brown Berets preach "carnalismo."
8. No Brown Beret will speak against another carnal unless he is present.
9. Under no circumstances will a Brown Beret raise his fist against another Chicano, unless in self-defense.
10. All Brown Berets will show respect for each other and to the people at all times.
11. Any Brown Beret arrested for an offense not having to do with the causa, will swim alone.
12. Every brown Beret will always look and act his best.
13. All orders will be obeyed.

EL CARNALISMO UNE   –NO SEPARA

QUE VIVA LA CAUSE Y LA REVOLUCION

HASTA LA VICTORIA

Rules of the San Antonio Brown Berets, 1971.

A "bato loco" (crazy guy) before joining
the Brown Berets. *La Causa* (Los Angeles), April 1970.

A proud revolutionary after joining the
Brown Berets. *La Causa* (Los Angeles),
April 1970.

exceptions. Juan Guajardo recalled "one bato who got hooked on heroin
every time we kicked him out, but while he was with us he didn't have time
to think of la chiva."[13] On several occasions, the Berets were able to redirect
the desire for drugs to movement activities.

Vigilantes, Gangsters, or Communists?

Although the Berets had gained some visibility with their gang work in
early 1971, once they began attending city council hearings and monitoring
police activity in the barrio, as well as leading public protests, they attracted serious critical attention from the media. The "sudden" appearance of
the Berets—spokesman José Morales said they were 150 strong—provoked
some dismay. *San Antonio Express & News* columnist Paul Thompson called
them "vigilantes."[14] But the Berets, through their quick-witted spokesperson Morales, were able to disarm many with a sense of humor. The "rumor
mill" reporters of the local papers were willing to engage in sarcastic word-
play, sometimes lighthearted, sometimes not, with the Chicano activists.
Morales proved to be a master at this game.

The first publicized incident occurred shortly after the Beret protesters had left the city council chamber and patrolman Louis Pantuso noticed that his cap was gone from the table. A miffed Pantuso said that one of the Berets had taken it as "a mean-little-kid trick." The following day Morales responded that he had checked with all forty Berets who had accompanied him into the city council chamber, and "NOT ONE would admit to lifting the police cap of Patrolman Pantuso." He added that the Berets "are against stealing for any reason and we'll throw out the member who's a thief." He concluded by saying that "Until we get to the bottom of this thing . . . the Brown Berets are taking up a collection to buy Pantuso a new cap."[15] The last comment, a reader could surmise, had been said with tongue firmly in cheek.

In an exchange the following month, a news "short" commenting on the new political currents among Mexican Americans took as its example the "strange way" that the Berets greet each other. Several members of the Berets had walked into Mario's Restaurant and went up to former city councilman Pete Torres, Jr., who was having lunch. One of Mario's customers described what happened:

> I watched as the Brown Berets, one by one, lifted their right fists with the thumb extending straight up. Pete would grab the thumb—something like kids choosing up sides with a baseball bat—then extend his thumb for grabbing. After that, they would exchange normal handshakes.[16]

The reporter concluded this eyewitness account by commenting that it was "seemingly one more in the chain of intriguing little folkways that have started up here of late." The journalists were learning about the rituals of an emerging Chicano movement.

For the sake of the reading public, Beret spokesman Morales called in to correct the report:

> We first exchanged normal handshakes with Pete and said "Viva" which means "Live."
> Then came the mutual grabbing of upthrust thumbs to the salute "Carnalismo," which means "Brotherhood."
> And finally, we shook hands normally a second time and said "Para siempre" or "Forever." The whole exchange took about 10 seconds per man.[17]

This was the ritual handshake of the Chicano movement, Morales noted, and the way that participants identified and greeted one another. For San

Antonio, concluded the journalist who first reported the practice, this signified a whole "new ballgame."

The changed situation included civilian monitoring of the police by the
Brown Berets, which naturally created some tension. According to Morales,
police chief Peters had instructed his patrols to remember that "there are
Berets out there." The Berets self-consciously attempted to allay this tension
among the police and the larger barrio public through positive individual
and collective acts. One well-publicized incident involved an unidentified
"good Samaritan" Beret who rendered first aid to a hit-and-run victim before the police arrived. According to the newspaper accounts, when patrolman Joe Losoya arrived on the scene, "he found a crowd around the injured
man. Kneeling besides the victim was a Brown Beret giving first aid." Before Losoya could get his name, the Beret left, but "several people in the
crowd commended this Good Samaritan act." Patrolman Losoya concluded
that "this shows that police and the Brown Berets can work together."[18]

Nonetheless, despite some positive media coverage, the Berets constantly had to defend themselves against charges of being Communists or gang-
sters. Attorney Ruben Sandoval, member and legal adviser for the Berets,
defended the group from the charge of being "anti-cop" or Communist as
follows:

> We are not against police in general, but against the few who are repeat-
> ers of acts that amount to lawlessness. The Brown Berets are mostly vet-
> erans of Vietnam who work with deprived communities. We assist with
> social and welfare problems, break up gangs and get the kids on the right
> road to self-development. We are not Communists, or anything like it; we
> work for general improvements in the barrios.[19]

Apprehension about the Berets was not limited to law enforcement officers, politicians, or conservative Anglos and Mexican Americans. It surfaced
among other organizations within the broader Chicano movement as well.
Celebrating unity at a community fiesta was one thing, but directly participating in each other's activities was quite another, as the Berets would
discover. When dressed in full khaki uniform and boots, and marching in
military formation, the Berets could be an unnerving presence. Their offer
to provide security was often not welcomed. Beret leaders all had stories
about their support being rebuffed.

One much recounted story was about the time that the Berets went
down to the Valley to support the farmworkers who were on strike for

César Chávez.[20] They had traveled there with the intention of stopping the police brutality against the strikers. Lalo Martínez recalled, laughing, that they drove down in a van filled with old and dirty carbines and handguns. It turned out that the conservative farmworkers were shocked by the sight of the Berets and thought that they were Communists. So the Berets ended up doing nothing for the strikers. On the way back they were stopped by la migra [immigration officers] at a checkpoint. "Imagine," Martínez said,

> It [the van] smelled of mota and we had so many guns but they didn't say anything. They only wanted to know what organization we represented, and Juan told them "The Brown Berets." An official responded, "Just don't go raising hell down here; the people are peace-loving."[21]

Luisa recalled another example of how the people and the Berets did not always agree on certain actions. She remembered how beautiful everything was at a police brutality protest in 1973 at the state capitol in Austin when they raised the Mexican flag. There was a ring of uniformed Berets around the flagpole and a semicircle of Berets around the people, protecting them from possible retaliation from the police and FBI agents.

> It looked great. And then the people, the organizers, start talking publicly about apologizing to the governor for such acts. Chingado, we did it for la raza; that was the first time the Mexican flag has flown from the capitol since the war between Mexico and the United States.[22]

The Berets were rebuffed by the Raza Unida Party, the Mexican American Unity Council, and other movement organizations as well.[23]

Asked to explain such rejection, Raza Unida Party activist Pancho Velásquez said that many in the movement saw the Berets as a gang. Velásquez recalled the time when the Wesley Center was being burglarized about twice a week. The South Side Berets provided security for a whole week: "they slept there and everything." Velásquez and others would be playing basketball in the gym, and a Beret would come by to check things out. "Victor would walk slowly, very importantly, down the hallway, with an obvious cuete [handgun] in his pants, doing the bodyguard walk." There was a lot of role-playing, Velásquez noted, but it worked because word got around that the Berets were guarding the place. The South Side Berets had previously beat up a guy who was giving them a lot of "carrilla" (trouble), "so they were very persuasive in their role as security guards." Velásquez concluded on an important point: the movement organizations never provided the Berets a chance to break out or branch out beyond a security role, "and that's why the guys still see themselves only as bodyguards."[24] The "tough guy" look and behavior were the only "natural" resource that the batos brought with them as they entered the public arena of organizations.

There was negative reaction from barrio residents as well. The Berets decided not to go to "congales" (bars, lounges) with their berets on, according to Morales, "because batos viejos from the old gangs would try to raise trouble; they saw the Berets as a new gang." Lalo agreed that "había mucha carrilla de batos viejos, tecatos, et cetera, que veían a los Berets como una ganga que quería quebrar las gangas viejas" (there was a lot of friction with the old guys, the addicts, et cetera, who saw the Berets as a gang that wanted to break up the old gangs). At one bar, one old bato tried to knife Juan Guajardo. At another, some guys wanted to pick a fight, so one of the Berets got a shotgun from the car and had it ready; they thought of using it if necessary, but the other guys backed down.[25]

Sometimes conflict resulted from attempts to practice carnalismo. Big John recalled the time they were at a bar on Guadalupe Street, and a big group ganged up on a drunk guy who didn't want to pay for a beer. The guy was already down on the floor, and they were still kicking him and hitting him with a cue stick. That's when Big John and another Beret attempted to defend the drunk guy. The Berets tried to explain the concept of carnalismo, "pero no cayó bien" (but it didn't go over well). They had to fight a bit, but they took the drunk guy away from the cantina. John explained that this incident also showed that the Berets may believe in carnalismo but will fight if necessary.[26]

In short, the Berets never developed beyond a policing role, a role that reflected the power dynamics of the social world they knew as batos locos. The West Side Berets were in some sense an imitation of their adversary, the San Antonio police, whom they had monitored for more than a year (1971–1972). The Berets lost community support when they began to monitor and "pressure" the Chicano movement organizations. Intimidation was a natural but limiting resource for the Berets.

Demise of the West Side

Rejected by many movement organizations, and with no financial resources to sustain themselves, the West Side Berets finally fell apart. By 1973, the Berets, once a self-conscious vanguard of the movement, found that they had been left behind as movement projects became institutionalized as programs, and protest activity became channeled to electoral campaigns. Among the movement network, there was less need for their security services, and the Berets found themselves routinely excluded from a social service job market—a market they felt they had helped create. There was a bitter tendency to label these Chicano bureaucrats—sometimes referred to as "burro-crats" or "barrio-crats"—as having left or forgotten the barrio.

The Berets were particularly upset by the distancing of MAUC, which in its "hell-raising" days had funded La Universidad de los Barrios and hired several batos as field staff. Now MAUC was getting rid of all the guys without an education and bringing in "MAs," as José Morales referred to "college-educated Mexican Americans."[27] Guajardo, acknowledging the slowing down of the Chicano movement, cited MAUC as a prime example of what had happened:

> The government bought the movement and now controls it. There are
> no more protests or marches. I remember when the Mexican American
> Unity Council was starting. At that time, the job requirements called for
> barrio experience and knowledge; now they want college degrees and
> college hours y la fregada [and all that bothersome stuff].[28]

For the Berets, a prime example of a Chicano "burro-crat" was MAUC director Juan Patlán, with his coat and tie, and his insistence on protocol and "Robert's Rules of Order."

In turn, Patlán considered the Berets to be "a gang—that's all. The guys preach carnalismo but they're canibales"—meaning that they lived by eating other Chicanos. Patlán said that intimidation was "their style" and "their only resource." The Berets would come into his office and demand things, "as if without demanding they wouldn't have gotten what they wanted." Patlán said that he helped the Berets because he was committed, not because he was scared of them. In retrospect, Patlán concluded that most of the Berets were batos who never left the pedo (conflict); they simply had no discipline.[29]

Had the matter of class come back to haunt los batos? Long gone were the days when MAUC had supported MAYO and projects like La Universidad de los Barrios.[30] The loss of a space where college activists and street batos could hang out and interact—a center like La Universidad—now appeared especially significant, for the Berets were never able to develop beyond a monitoring or policing role. This and the ever-present problem of lack of discipline proved to be serious limiting factors.

Increasing isolation, particularly since the breakup of the broad coalition that had celebrated La Semana de la Raza in 1971, was an important
contextual factor in the decline of the West Side Berets. As important, and
certainly more immediate, were the internal tensions that surfaced within
the group. In this regard, the tactic of direct confrontation at times back-
fired and exposed differences between some Berets. Such was the case,
recalled Chale, when Guajardo mobilized the soldados to come down heavy
on MANCO, the Mexican American Neighborhood Civic Organization, at a
formal luncheon at Los Arcos Restaurant. Chale got upset at how the soldados were used in that action:

> The soldados didn't know what was happening; we were just told to
> meet at Los Arcos. Outside we were told that MANCO was getting off
> the track, that they weren't doing anything and were receiving big sala-
> ries, that they wouldn't let José Morales wear the beret, y así.[31]

The Berets then walked in, surrounded the MANCO luncheon, and got
involved in a bitter discussion led by Beret officers. Chale said they then
found out that the conflict was between one of the Beret officers and the
MANCO director, who was from El Detroit. Had they known, all the Berets
from El Detroit would have hesitated in coming down on MANCO.[32]

There were other complaints as well. Some were tired of "all this stuff
about stars, stripes, and rank"; they had been to Vietnam and "no longer
wanted to hear more about rank and all that." They were tired of the political education classes because the officers would just tell them the way
things were as if they didn't know or have any opinions or ideas themselves.
So El Detroit withdrew from the Berets and in the process took many others
with them.[33]

In José Morales's opinion, what broke things up was that each barrio
chapter began pulling for itself. La India would say that "they know what's
happening in La India. . . . Or the group wouldn't come to the meetings if
one of their guys couldn't make it."[34] Juan Guajardo would get upset:

> We had to stop this thing that you're from this barrio and I'm from that
> barrio, we had to start the thing that we're all Chicanos, it doesn't matter
> where I'm from, only that we're brothers. Carnalismo knows no bound-
> aries.[35]

To reinforce this message, Guajardo made a controversial decision to eliminate the chapter network in December 1972, about the time that the South

Side chapter joined the Berets. There was much disagreement over this move. The breaking up of the multichapter structure may have accelerated the demise of the West Side Berets.

Although the philosophy of carnalismo called for overcoming the parochialism of barrio boundaries, one can argue that the Berets were never able to do that—that barrio loyalties kept surfacing and creating tremendous tension. It would be misleading, however, to claim that such barrio loyalties were the principal cause of the organization's demise. The fissuring also reflected other fundamental problems.

According to several West Side Berets, Guajardo's failure to discipline the South Side chapter was a major factor. The two South Side leaders, brothers Victor and Frank San Miguel, had been kicked out of several organizations because they were seen as "pelioneros" (troublemakers) who were prone to violence: "They always wanted to shoot somebody," several West Siders commented. Because of this tendency, the batos from the South Side chapter were seen as weakening the practice of carnalismo.[36]

Nowhere was this more evident than in the area of gender relations. The women had built up a strong parallel organization with rules of sexual conduct and the right to determine their membership, thus fostering the development of Chicana politicization and an expanded notion of carnalismo. Luisa said that the South Side Berets broke two rules: they subverted the progress that the "rucas" (women) had made in developing their own parallel organization, and they broke the all-important rule about no dating between batos and rucas.[37]

South Sider Victor San Miguel, in pushing to admit Clara, argued that all Berets should interview and screen potential recruits, but the women countered that they should screen their own members first. In a skewed compromise, the women were allowed only five minutes to interview Clara, whereas previously it had sometimes taken a week, and sometimes they had rejected members. In short, the South Side undermined the veto power the women had over their own members.

Then it turned out that Clara and San Miguel were lovers, a violation of the second rule. This did not create immediate problems, but the wisdom of the rule became apparent later when the two broke up and San Miguel moved in with another woman. The fact that Clara was pregnant exacerbated the situation. At one point, Clara and the other Beret women went over and broke the windows of the house where Victor and his new girlfriend were living. "They wanted to get inside to make trouble," San Miguel recalled. The incident reinforced his opinion that women shouldn't be part of the Berets. For Luisa, this illustrated the collapse of carnalismo within the Berets.[38]

The problems with the new South Side chapter only hastened the departure of already disaffected West Siders. When La India dropped out, the Berets lost about ten batos. The Detroit chapter was next to withdraw, taking six more Berets. By late summer of 1973, Beret activity had slowed considerably, and everything was up in the air. The West Side batos were gradually leaving the Berets.

The final straw was a fight that broke out between a West Side Beret and a South Side Beret during the Semana de la Raza of September 1973, exactly two years after the organization's public introduction. After the near brawl, the two sides withdrew from each other. Seven months later, in April 1974, Juan Guajardo resigned, and the West Side Berets dissolved. "Cuando se salió Juan," noted Luisa, "me salí yo. Chingo de otros batos se salieron también, con Juan." (When Juan got out, I got out. Lots of guys got out also, with Juan.) Luisa offered the common explanation of the West Side group when people asked them what had happened. "Les digo que we went underground, que la estamos jugando fría porque se puso muy caliente el pedo, que al rato vamos a comenzar a emerge otra vez." (I tell them that we went underground, that we're playing it cool because the shit got too hot, that shortly we'll start to surface again.)[39]

Guajardo was philosophical about the withdrawal of the West Side Berets. There was too much envy, jealousy, and conflict within the membership, he explained:

> The Berets started falling apart because of pure personal conflict, that this guy did this to me, that this guy did that to my woman, just a lot of bullshit. The guys dropped out one by one. It wasn't just due to the entry of the South Side batos, because they believed in carnalismo; it's just that their discipline was different. And that's where I am at fault, because I believe that discipline has to come from within, that it's not useful to have someone disciplining you every moment. The rules don't work that way. But if I had to do it again, I would be more careful in the selection of the batos. Secondly, I would insist on discipline; you have to have discipline.[40]

There was unanimity among the West Side Berets on this point. Lalo was emphatic in saying that without discipline there is no brotherhood. Luisa recalled that at the beginning, the rules were followed strictly, but toward

A Chicana Brown Beret from Dallas marching in Austin, Texas, 1974.
Courtesy of photographer Alan Pogue.

Cover of the fall 1979 issue
of *La Onda Chicana* (Dallas,
Texas). Author's collection.

the end, the rules were broken more and more often. "Para una organización
como la de nosotros se necesitaba un chingo la disciplina, strict discipline,
algo estricto." (For an organization like ours, there needs to be a lot of fucking discipline . . . something strict.)[41] Political awareness was not enough.

The withdrawal of the West Side Berets mirrored the disbanding of
other Beret chapters throughout the Southwest. The Los Angeles Berets had
broken up in late 1972 because of internal conflicts due to police infiltration.[42] Beret chapters elsewhere had become inactive or had converted back
to clicas; in other cases, members had simply gone their separate ways. By
1973 the various FBI divisions throughout the Southwest were reporting no
Beret activities, although individuals wearing berets would regularly show
up at rallies. Thus although the Phoenix Division had within its boundaries
individuals who "profess to be Brown Berets," there was

no established meeting place nor are there any self-proclaimed leaders. Usually when a peace demonstration or rally takes place in Arizona a group of very young Mexican-Americans will take part and some will wear the standard garb of the Brown Beret, brown Khaki shirt and brown beret.[43]

Even when no Beret organization existed, wearing the beret remained a potent political statement.

The FBI reports turned out to be premature, however, at least in the case of San Antonio and Texas. Although the withdrawal of the West Side Berets signaled the end of participation by the group's founding generation, it did not mark the end of sustained Beret activity. In August 1974, the South Side chapter reestablished the San Antonio Berets. In fact, the general picture for the Berets in Texas was one of continuing organization and activity as chapters from throughout the state—from the Valley, Hondo, Austin, Dallas, Houston, San Antonio, and later Waco and Lubbock—began to participate in statewide meetings. The San Antonio Berets missed the first statewide Beret conference in McAllen in February 1974, but the South Side Berets represented San Antonio at the second conference in Houston in July 1974. A third statewide meeting took place in Dallas in October 1974, hosted by the new Dallas Ledbetter chapter. The Berets continued to hold statewide meetings two or three times a year well into the early 1980s. The deliberations at these meetings make clear that discipline, gender relations, and their search for a place within a weakening movement network would continue to be important issues.

FRAGMENTING ELEMENTS

9 IN THE PREVIOUS CHAPTERS, I have described the class and gender tensions that underlay much of the organizational structuring within the Chicano movement. Specifically, as MAYO evolved from a community organization to a political party, it gave rise to gendered and class-based organizations. Both the women and the batos locos involved with MAYO–Barrios Unidos used the language and symbolism of the movement to craft group-specific agendas and efforts. A lingering question—a residue, perhaps, of the days when Chicana feminists were accused of dividing the movement—is whether this kind of specialization, the result of what is often called "identity politics," contributed to a weakening of the movement. Certainly the women claimed that their independent and parallel organizing made the movement stronger, while the Berets saw themselves as "la punta de la flecha" (the tip of the arrow), the vanguard of the movement. Yet because these tensions have at times been associated with the fragmenting of the movement, some clarification and extended commentary is merited.[1]

It is best to return to the electoral path chosen by MAYO–Barrios Unidos and look at the obstacles standing in the way of success. This path was chosen at the height of movement enthusiasm, when the organizational network seemed to be expanding without end, and when a few small-town victories had sparked the idea of a national political party. The possibility of bringing the very different political activities of the Southwest—the land grant struggles in New Mexico, the organizing of urban youths and college students in Colorado and California, and the building of a third party in

Texas—under the single banner of "La Raza Unida" promised to elevate the Chicano movement onto the national stage. Thus the 1972 national Raza Unida conference in El Paso—where Reies López Tijerina from New Mexico, Corky González from Colorado, and José Ángel Gutiérrez from Texas had gathered their troops to draft a national plan of action—represented a critical juncture for the Chicano movement.

The national conference had promised to create an overarching communication and coordinating framework that could keep the expanding organizational network informed and ideally unified. The delegates, in fact, established a Congreso de Aztlán that could have played such a representational role. But the first and only meeting of the congreso collapsed in disagreements over its authority.[2] There never was a second national conference. A reexamination of the events in Texas, where the Raza Unida movement was the strongest, offers some insights into what happened.

My explanation about the fragmentation of the movement highlights influences that had little to do with identity politics and a lot to do with tactical decisions and philosophical and personality differences, as well as the role of police authorities. These matters have been discussed extensively elsewhere by journalists and scholars.[3] The following observations serve to add some notes to that discussion, while introducing these elements into my narrative explanation as open-ended questions.

A Question of Strategy

The MAYO leadership was well acquainted with the tactical limits of ethnic-based political campaigns. Such limits mattered little when Gutiérrez and the MAYO activists were focused on four Winter Garden counties with sizable Mexican American majorities. Within a two-year period, 1970–1971, local "raza unida" slates in the Winter Garden area had won a total of fifteen seats, including two city council majorities, two school board majorities, and two mayoralties.[4] Excited by such developments, MAYO activists from the urban areas became anxious to expand the electoral strategy. In October 1971, a few weeks after the September 16th celebrations, the core activists held the organizing convention of the Raza Unida Party in San Antonio and voted, over the objections of Gutiérrez, to organize at the state level. Gutiérrez believed that the party should consolidate and expand its rural base rather than expend its energy on a state party. As he recalled:

I felt we should build on solid ground, not engage in symbolic statewide exercises. This point offended many supporters in the urban areas because they felt I was leaving them out of the future of the political party.[5]

Mario Compean, on the other hand, argued that a statewide political campaign would invigorate the Chicano movement and introduce the success of Crystal City throughout Texas. Compean's appeal carried the day, and a statewide political party was born. The split vote of twenty-five "for" and fifteen "against" reflected an urban-rural division within the Raza Unida leadership. Gutiérrez recalled the moment with mixed emotions:

> the delegates voted against my proposal to form the political party county by county, a regional plan. They didn't listen, and voted with their hearts. They voted to go statewide with me knowing we would surely lose.[6]

As a harbinger of things to come, the first task for the Raza Unida activists called for gathering 23,000 notarized voter signatures in order to qualify as a political party. Learning the election code, selecting candidates, creating a statewide party apparatus, as well as organizing and mounting a statewide campaign for governor, would soon consume party activists' energies.[7] Rather than continue its community organizing and planning, the main movement organization in Texas turned its attention to achieving dramatic electoral results. Its significance would now be measured by the number of votes it could marshal.

This change in direction gave birth to what one sympathetic journalist described as "a quixotic war against the state Democratic establishment."[8] Since the activists knew they could not win any state offices, the best they could hope for was to act as a third-party "spoiler"—in effect, to deny the Democratic Party the governorship as well a few previously safe legislative seats.

In 1972, in its first statewide campaign, Raza Unida, with its charismatic gubernatorial candidate Ramsey Muñiz leading the way, demonstrated this "spoiler" potential. Muñiz received more than 200,000 votes, 6 percent of the state total, and made the contest between the Democrat and Republican candidates surprisingly competitive. Democrat Dolph Briscoe won with 48 percent of the vote, compared to 45 percent for the Republican candidate, Henry Grover. Muñiz had carried three South Texas counties and had come in second in another fifteen, thus demonstrating some rural strength.[9] However, more than half of Muñiz's vote had come from the urban areas outside of rural South Texas. For those looking for ways to increase the party's vote for the next election, that pattern of support held some unexpected implications.

In a 1974 article titled "Raza Unida Party and the Chicano Middle Class," party activist Armando Cavada, from Corpus Christi, offered a candid assessment for movement activists. When they started organizing in 1970, Cavada explained, "we had the idea que los de abajo eran los más importantes, a los que teníamos que llegarles, los que teníamos que organizer porque ellos iban a ser el Partido [that those from below were the most important, the ones we had to reach, the ones we had to organize because they were going to become the party]". The attention was directed to rural areas such as Cotulla, Robstown, Cristal, and other places where Chicanos were the majority. But when the party went statewide, Cavada noted, "we didn't necessarily develop another strategy."[10]

Thus Cavada was fascinated by the number of votes Muñiz had received from the Chicano middle class in urban areas. He believed that these middle-class supporters were "not the real professionals like doctors and lawyers, but bakery owners, construction workers, electricians, plumbers"—in other words, skilled workers and small businessmen. Cavada cautioned supporters that he did not see this middle-class support as solid. They might have voted for Muñiz, but their commitment to the Raza Unida was shallow: "they can't go along with the rest of the Party ideology."[11]

Nonetheless, the discussion within the leadership circles suggested a shift in the party's target population. As one party analyst wrote on a copy of the 1972 Texas voting results, "los pobres when they vote, vote for los Democratas."[12] Or perhaps, like the Brown Berets, they simply didn't bother with voting at all. It had become clear to the party's campaign staff that in order to get more votes, they would have to broaden Raza Unida's appeal beyond its Mexican American working-class base. With that decision, the transformation of MAYO–Barrios Unidos from a militant community organization to a political party had become complete.

In the second gubernatorial campaign, in 1974, Ramsey Muñiz and Raza Unida tried to attract support from middle-class Mexican Americans as well as African Americans and liberal Anglos in a "People Together" campaign. But this retooled presentation failed to generate much momentum or additional support. In fact, Muñiz received 25,000 fewer votes the second time around. Governor Briscoe was reelected by a comfortable margin, and

Raza Unida lost any symbolic influence it might have secured. Indeed, as we shall see, the loss made the party vulnerable to vindictive state police action.

A Question of Philosophy and Ego

Given the different circumstances under which the Chicano movement had germinated in the Southwest, it is not surprising that activists were divided over goals, tactics, rhetoric, and, of course, practice. The basic division was over the question of reformism versus revolutionary change. The tension between the "pragmatists" and the "revolutionaries" first surfaced in 1972 at the national Raza Unida conference in El Paso; it would grow increasingly shrill over the next two years. The "gringo" would no longer be the main target of activists, who now exchanged accusations of "selling out" and "opportunism" among each other.

The pragmatists, led by José Ángel Gutiérrez, believed in using third-party politics as a vehicle for gaining influence and patronage, particularly at the local level. Playing "gabacho Democrats" off against "gabacho Republicans" made sense, especially when the former constituted the long-time local elites. As far as the Republicans were concerned, the Raza Unida Party was a potential distraction for the Democrats. In a confidential memorandum, Alex Armendáriz of the Committee to Re-Elect the President (CREEP) noted that nearly two-thirds of the Spanish-speaking voters in San Antonio approved of the fledgling third party. Republicans were thus "in a good position" to help the Raza Unida Party:

> La Raza's strategy usually was denouncement of old-party politics. Any help given them would not be identifiable as Republican. McGovern could be exposed as an old-style politician especially since his recent visit to Wallace (who is vastly unpopular among Mexican Americans).[13]

The interest displayed by the Nixon administration in the Raza Unida Party was so transparent that the *Wall Street Journal* reported on it (April 11, 1972), titling its article "Señor Nixon Makes a Pitch for the Votes of Mexican-Americans." The GOP chairman of Texas, "Mr. Willeford," was quoted as saying he "wouldn't be surprised" if Republicans at the local level had "shipped" La Raza some money. In Washington, a Nixon aide acknowledged that "some people have been talking about financing La Raza." The party's Texas chairman, Mario Compean, acknowledged that Republicans "whom he won't name" had offered the party more than $25,000. But La Raza wasn't taking it, he emphasized. "We aren't going to prostitute ourselves."[14]

The revolutionaries, led by Corky González of Colorado, were vague about how to achieve radical change, but clear about their unrelenting opposition to capitalism and to any "deals" or compromises with the political establishment. They saw a party led by Gutiérrez as basically "catering to the system which the party was established to reform." Worse yet, Raza Unida was "becoming another tool used in controlling and pacifying the masses."[15]

This philosophical disagreement at the national level was mirrored at the local level. In Texas, the Raza Unida Party was severely criticized for its flirtations with the Republican Party and "the repressive administration" of Mexico's president Luis Echeverría. Mario Cantú, the former chair of the 1971 Semana de la Raza unity celebration, described these as "opportunistic collaborations." The Beret leaders likewise said that the party was simply creating a "three-headed monster," and that the Raza Unida in San Antonio did not work for the people; "they just believe in themselves."[16]

In response, according to a *San Antonio Light* account, state party chairman Mario Compean "lashed out at revolutionary critics of the party's all-out entry into electoral politics." Compean singled out San Antonio restaurant owner Mario Cantú in particular, noting his participation in such projects as "Free Angela Davis" and "Free Political Prisoners in Mexico." Compean added that

> Mario Cantú has never put a day in the party. The party principles have been upheld by leadership and by the rank and file. His revolutionary ideology is very prejudicial to the party.[17]

Indeed, many Chicano leaders and organizations had distanced themselves from Cantú because of his public revolutionary pronouncements.

The news media of San Antonio, on the other hand, seem to have made Cantú into a spokesman for the entire Chicano movement. Many activists wondered whether Cantú's public displays were simply driven by ego or by a plan to embarrass the movement. Regarding whether Cantú was a government agent or an egoist, George Velásquez said, "We decided that it didn't make any difference. His public statements on behalf of his one-man organization spread confusion. He undercut us [the other movimiento organizations]."[18]

José Ángel Gutié-
rrez (*left*)and Corky
González at the
National Raza
Unida Conference
in El Paso, Texas,
September 3, 1972.
Courtesy of pho-
tographer César
Martínez.

Velásquez was referring to Cantú's resignation from the Centro de Acción Social Autónoma (CASA) to work for the United Proletariat Party of
America, a new Mexican political party committed to the cause of Mexican
peasants and workers. In late 1975, Cantú, as the party's "presunto funda-
dor" (presumed founder), was the subject of sensational front-page news in
a Monterrey, Mexico, newspaper. The FBI was looking for Cantú, *El Norte*
declared, because he was supplying arms to the Alianza Internacional de
Terroristas, whose network included radical Communist groups in Mexico
as well as the farmworkers, La Raza Unida, CASA, the Brown Berets, and
other Chicano groups in the United States.[19] Cantú labeled the charges as
absurd lies and said that "something like that can get me killed." He also
claimed that the Alianza Internacional de Terroristas was an invention of
the newspaper. An FBI spokesman in San Antonio commented, "I haven't
the vaguest idea where the story could have come from."[20]

For several days, the news media of South Texas and northern Mexico were abuzz about the "Chicano leader" accused of being a "gunrunner." The confusion and "undercutting" that George Velásquez had warned about was in full display. The seeds had been planted: were the farmworkers terrorists? Was the "Partido Raza Unida" linked to the "Partido Proletariado Unido"? Within movement circles, doubts about Cantú multiplied: could this radical restaurant owner be doing the bidding of the FBI? Even the Berets, who often leaned on Cantú for financial support, wondered if he was "cutting deals" with the police.[21]

A Question of Police Control

The MAYO leaders suspected that they had been infiltrated by informants. Willie Velásquez believed that agent provocateurs were pushing MAYO toward radicalism. La Universidad de los Barrios, according to George Velásquez, Willie's brother, had an informer. For Mario Compean, the case of Los Angeles Brown Beret Frank Martínez was a prime example of government manipulation of the movement. In 1971 Martínez had revealed in California court proceedings that he was an agent for the Bureau of Alcohol, Tobacco and Firearms. Before he turned up in Los Angeles, recalled Compean, Martínez had been in Houston posturing as a MAYO militant, calling for arms, "only the guy was so stupid that he was discovered very easily." After he was run out of MAYO, Martínez tried to organize a Beret chapter in Houston. "In the end he was run out of state, but it wouldn't have gone so easy for the guy if they [MAYO] had known he would have turned up as an informer in East LA; they thought he had learned." In Los Angeles he joined the Berets. Known for his bravado in parading publicly with a shotgun—thus providing the pretext for a police raid on Beret headquarters—Martínez rose to be second in command. He eventually became cochair of the National Chicano Moratorium Against the War Committee, based in Los Angeles. Thus, for a time, an undercover agent led the national Chicano anti–Vietnam War campaign.[22]

All the major Beret chapters—Los Angeles, Albuquerque (Black Berets), Denver, Chicago, Dallas, and San Antonio—were under surveillance of some sort. When the Los Angeles Berets launched a year-long "reconquista" road trip through the Southwest in the summer of 1971, the FBI alerted various field offices and local authorities along the route to report on Beret activity. The FBI was able to document the entire journey of the "reconquista" from California through Arizona, New Mexico, and Texas. When the Los Angeles

Berets finally arrived in San Antonio, an "SAPD intel report" noted that they "did not demonstrate or parade" while visiting the city and otherwise "attracted little attention."[23] Their full-dress pose in front of the Alamo had apparently created no controversy. As for the San Antonio Berets, local FBI agents had earlier determined that they were a Mexican American civic action group "not affiliated with the West Coast militant group of the same name."[24] The San Antonio Berets were seen as posing no threat to security.

Nonetheless, various police agencies kept a close watch on the Chicano movement in San Antonio. The FBI had compiled a report on the 1971 Semana de la Raza celebrations, focusing on the Mexico City–based theatrical group Los Mascarones, "a group of students who are socialist oriented." The FBI source had even attended the after-hours party given Los Mascarones at the United Farm Workers Organizing Committee office, "starting at approximately 1:00 a.m. on September 19, 1971, until 6:00 a.m." This source, according to FBI memorandum, had "a comprehensive knowledge of the subversive element and organizations in the San Antonio, Texas, area and a comprehensive knowledge of the Chicano situation."[25]

Mexican authorities, naturally, were also concerned about any connections between Mexican student groups and Chicano groups. A prime suggestion of this concern surfaced in the "Nixon tapes," which recorded the following bit of intelligence offered to President Nixon by the visiting president of Mexico, Luis Echeverría, on June 15, 1972:

> When I was about to leave from Mexico for this trip, Mr. President, I
> was informed by my various people that groups of Mexicans had been
> in touch with friends of Angela Davis in this country. And that we were
> aware of the plans of the organization that Angela Davis heads to mount
> a key demonstration in San Antonio protesting the existence of politi-
> cal prisoners in Mexico. All of this is connected to people in Chile, with
> people in Cuba, with the so-called "Chicano" groups in the United States,
> with certain groups in Berkeley, California—they're all working closely
> together.[26]

Echeverría, who was scheduled to stop in San Antonio during a six-day tour of the United States, had been informed by his "various people" about the planned protests. He was worried about the attendant negative publicity. Among the groups Echeverría was concerned about was the "Free Angela Davis" committee led by Mario Cantú. Two days after his visit with President Nixon, however, five men were arrested for breaking into the headquarters of the Democratic National Committee at the Watergate complex in Washington, D.C. The news of the Watergate burglary crowded out that of Echeverría's tour.[27]

Years later, in 1977, the FBI released documents detailing the agency's counter-insurgency penetration of the antiwar and civil rights movements. Among the documents was a memo typed in large capital letters that suggested that the protest of Echeverría had been staged as a "baiting" tactic:

> [blank] has been encouraged to [blank] into organizing a march when [blank] arrives in order to bait other San Antonio area radicals in the Chicano community into identifying themselves by showing up. [blank] and carry out.

Although heavily redacted, the memo was linked to the arrival in San Antonio of President Echeverría, whose visit Cantú had protested. Cantú vigorously denied any FBI involvement with the protests. He decried the FBI's tactics as "fascist" and called for a congressional investigation.[28] Whatever the ultimate truth, the memo nonetheless indicated—as had the court testimony of "Brown Beret" Martínez—that undercover agents did not shy away from directing movement leaders or assuming leadership themselves if the situation merited it.

The use of such tactics was not limited to the "radical" element of the Chicano movement. The reformist elements were targeted as well. Insofar as political incumbents were concerned, reform could be as threatening as revolution. Despite the apparent internal difficulties of the Raza Unida Party, the conservative Democratic Party was concerned that the insurgent group held the potential to be a "spoiler" in statewide elections. Moreover, the 1970–1972 takeover by La Raza Unida of Zavala County and its county seat, Crystal City, directly threatened Democratic Party control in more than a dozen South Texas counties. Governor Dolph Briscoe hailed from Kinney County, one of those considered "threatened." Uvalde, Kinney's county seat and only forty miles from Crystal City, had become the center of an Anglo reaction to the "Mexican revolt." Governor Briscoe and attorney general John Hill were determined to use their powers to keep the Raza Unida Party contained.

In 1975 Hill launched a protracted, high-profile investigation in Zavala County, the stronghold of the Raza Unida Party, in a politically motivated campaign to undermine the party. He was not only trying to quash the upstart third party; he was also priming himself for a campaign for governor in 1978. These efforts would highlight his tough stance against corruption and ethnic militancy. Thus the Texas Rangers and the Department of Public Safety were constant observers of the Raza Unida Party and other movement organizations, and they harassed and occasionally arrested party organizers. Needless to say, the FBI also maintained an active watch on Raza Unida. The party had compiled "over forty cases of suspected illegal interference."[29]

In short, considerable documentation reveals that deliberate police action helped contain and disrupt the Chicano movement. How much of the movement's splintering and failure can be attributed to the counter-insurgency tactics of state police agencies cannot be answered; however, there is no question that overt and covert police activities contributed to internal tensions and divisions. Activists were arrested or threatened with arrest, and organizations were disrupted from within. As activists became paranoid and began suspecting one another, rumors about possible infiltrators abounded. Some rumors and suspicions turned out to have considerable truth. The movement had been thoroughly infiltrated.

Undercover agents were subversive provocateurs, especially when they acted not just as informants, but as leaders involved in decision making. Such infiltration contributed to the collapse of the Los Angeles Brown Berets and the National Chicano Moratorium Against the War Committee. It may also explain the ill-advised "occupation" of Catalina Island by a Beret troop, whose campground became a tourist photo-op for a few weeks. It was an embarrassing last hurrah for the Los Angeles Berets.[30]

Yet, as has been suggested, it was not necessary to infiltrate a movement organization to be an effective counter-insurgent. The creation of a vocal and visible revolutionary "dummy" organization, one with few if any members, was often sufficient to poison local movement activity.

Reconsidering Class and Gender

There is no question that tactical miscalculations, ideological differences, personal egos, and police action led to a weakening of the Chicano movement. The tensions generated by class and gender distinctions have to be placed in the context of these elements. My argument is the rather modest one that these "organic" tensions surfaced and influenced organizational formations. My discussion does not lend itself to an assessment of whether integrated, parallel, or independent organizational forms were best for maintaining unity and commitment within the movement. But some speculation is possible. The question can be framed prosaically: which works better for creating personal change—a rocky marriage or a separation?

For both the women and the batos involved with MAYO–Barrios Unidos, creating a distinct organization of their own signified a change in behavior. For the women of the movement, this meant departing from a "traditional" backstage supportive role and insisting on front-stage, visible leadership. For the batos locos of the movement, this meant departing from gang-related behavior by practicing carnalismo and insisting, also, on having a front-stage leadership role. The women who continued to work within La Raza Unida proved to be more successful than the Brown Berets in developing leadership and moving beyond a backstage support role. In contrast, the Berets, charting their own independent course, were unable to maintain discipline among the cadre and were never able to evolve beyond a security role.

One can only speculate on what would have happened had the batos remained within a movement organization with a notable college student presence. More concretely, what would have happened if La Universidad de los Barrios or MAYO had been able to maintain a space for frequent and continuous interaction? Divorced from the college activists, the Berets had limited opportunities for political and technical development. Basically, the independent path of the Brown Berets limited their movement role to a security force whose main resource was a façade of intimidation. Once their scarce resources began to dry up, they attempted to recoup by flexing their muscle within the Chicano movement. The result was a nearly complete loss of support.

Conversely, one can wonder whether MAYO would have become a statewide political party had the batos remained within its ranks. There would have been pressure, particularly on the urban activists, to maintain a focus on community matters—on police brutality and juvenile delinquency, for example—rather than undertake symbolic political campaigns. Perhaps the result would have been a deeply rooted organizational presence that could have withstood the state's predictable police actions.

One can also wonder whether the development of a Chicana contingent within the Berets might have led the organization in a different direction. In Austin, the Beret women organized a breakfast program for kids in spite of "the guys putting down their fund-raising ideas." In East Los Angeles, the Beret women created a free medical clinic, but only after a bitter split from the male Beret organization. Sociologist Dionne Espinoza, after analyzing this split, concluded that the gender consciousness of the Chicana Berets enabled them to develop a new movement identity based on "a feminist reconstruction of la familia."[31]

Such tensions, of course, were not unique to the Berets. Class and gender issues surfaced throughout the Chicano movement. They appeared within the militant organizations most critical of the "reformists." For example, CASA, a Marxist-Leninist organization that advocated for the Mexican working class (defined broadly to include Chicanos), was not immune to class and gender distinctions. The young activists who took over the immigrant social service centers in Los Angeles, Chicago, and San Antonio in the early 1970s, according to veteran organizer Bert Corona, "were not interested in the Hermandades [brotherhoods], which were dominated by recent immigrants, but in the CASAs, which were composed primarily of young Chicano professionals and students—people like themselves."[32] Corona described the young activists as follows:

> Many of them were children of immigrants, but they had lost the characteristics of immigrants. They were now English-speaking, young Chicano adults. Many were college students, college graduates, and professionals. They were looking for some political vehicle more commensurate with their own characteristics. They found that in the CASAs, which they believed would provide them with a working-class base that they—as more acculturated, educated, and radicalized individuals—would lead.[33]

The activists were more interested in ideological development than in maintaining the immigrant services of the CASAs, with the result that paid memberships declined sharply within two years. By 1978, the remaining CASAs ceased meeting.

Gender tensions also surfaced within the organization, as former CASA leaders Adelaida Del Castillo and Carlos Vásquez have made clear. Vásquez recalled "the double standard of work and social life" among men and women in the movement: "Women did the petty work, men did the leading." This double standard was the early norm for the "Third World left" of Los Angeles, as Laura Pulido has noted in a recent assessment. The more women and men worked together, observed Pulido, "the more apparent were the contradictions between the rhetoric of freedom and equality and the lived reality, and these in turn led to organizational conflict and change."[34]

In sum, to the extent that the Chicano movement can be said to have challenged many traditional cultural expectations about gender relations and roles, particularly in the political arena, the credit belongs to the conflict and negotiation initiated by Chicana groups. If men modified their "machismo," much undoubtedly had to do with a daily engagement with gender issues. As Vásquez put it, the "strong, persistent compañeras" who were prepared to struggle "made the difference among those [men] who came to change their attitudes of reactionary machismo and chauvinism."[35]

Many "strong, persistent compañeras," however, remain convinced that not much has changed. At one twenty-year reunion of Raza Unida Party activists, some forty women talked about past and present activism. Their comments confirmed, activist-writer Elizabeth Martinez noted, that

> indeed no national "Chicano movement" exists today, but hundreds of individuals and small groups are working at the community level on mostly local issues. Women in particular . . . gave sometimes incredible accounts of dogged efforts over long years.[36]

Yet the twenty-year activist reunion also confirmed, as Martinez put it, that "super-machismo lives." Real progress had been made, she allowed, but "when the subject of women was not on the official agenda, old-style practices and attitudes reasserted themselves." Martinez lamented that, twenty years after the movement, "chingón," or tough-guy, politics was still very much the norm among Chicano activists.[37]

A Concluding Note

By 1974 the organizational unity displayed three years earlier at the Semana de la Raza celebration in San Antonio had frayed into many different strands. The locations that year of community-based celebrations of September 16th suggested the fraying. LULAC, along with other old-line organizations, had reserved the downtown mercado site for its community celebration, whereas the movement activists—of MAYO/Raza Unida, Teatro de los Barrios, the Brown Berets, and a relatively new organization called TU-CASA, among others—had moved their celebration to the Ruben Salazar Cultural Center on the far West Side of town. The center, founded in 1972, had been named after the *Los Angeles Times* reporter killed by police at the Chicano Moratorium rally of August 29, 1970. Within a year of its founding, the activists themselves would split up over questions of process and practice.[38]

Throughout Texas and the Southwest, a similar fragmenting of the Chicano movement network seemed to be taking place. In California, a "mutual antipathy" would develop between the Raza Unida Party and the United Farm Workers led by César Chávez. As historian Juan Gómez-Quiñones put

José Ángel Gutié-
rrez crucified: a bit-
ing satirical cartoon
of Gutiérrez and
his supporters by
anti-Gutiérrezistas
in Crystal City, pub-
lished in *La Verdad*
("Cristal, Tejaztlan"),
November 20, 1975.
Author's collection.

it, the California Raza Unida Party felt that Chávez was "simply an arm of
the Anglo political establishment" and that he represented the "traditional
negotiating posture in politics." This, of course, conflicted with the Raza
Unida Party's rhetoric about self-determination.[39]

In Texas, both the Raza Unida Party and the farmworkers union experienced internal divisions. In 1974, in Crystal City, the stronghold of the Raza
Unida Party, political and personality differences had hardened into a bitter
division between Gutiérrezista and anti-Gutiérrezista factions. The party's
disappointing showing in that year's gubernatorial election sowed further
discontent.[40] In 1975, the Texas farmworker organizing campaign, the initial catalyst for the state's Chicano movement, split into two contentious
factions after years of internal conflicts over strategies and priorities. That
same year, Texas attorney general John Hill launched a high-profile investigation of Raza Unida officeholders and appointees, and maverick Mario

Cantú made an equally high-profile announcement of a new organization, the Partido Proletariado Unido. The Chicano movement was clearly under siege from various flanks.

The fragmenting and disbanding of Chicano movement organizations did not signify a change of heart among the activists, who maintained their critical political awareness and their commitment to "la causa." The inactive West Side Berets still claimed to be Berets, saying that they were "just laying low" and that they would reemerge if the situation called for it. In fact, in June 1975, more than a year after they had stopped meeting, the news that six striking melon workers had been shot by an irate grower moved the West Side to regroup for one action. At the invitation of the Valley Berets, they mustered a contingent and traveled to the Lower Valley to provide protection for the striking melon workers. They were prevented from doing so by a restraining court order but nonetheless gained national publicity.[41] In similar fashion, as the Raza Unida Party dissolved in the mid-seventies, many women activists simply took their philosophy and skills with them to the newly organized Mexican American Democrats. "A name is a name," said Ninfa Moncada. "We wouldn't have to change our philosophy or our politics or how we educate our kids just because we call ourselves Democrats."[42]

These women activists would lay the foundation for the emergence of a highly visible Chicana leadership in the city and state in the 1980s and 1990s. Among the most prominent was Irma Rangel from Kingsville, a key figure in Las Mujeres de la Raza Unida and the first Mexican American woman elected to the state legislature. Other Raza Unida notables included Alma Canales (McAllen), Linda Reyna (Edinburg), María Jiménez (Houston), Amalia Mendoza-Rodríguez (Austin), Marta Cotera (Austin), and Irma Mireles (San Antonio). These pioneering activists would set the stage for a "second generation" of women leaders who were "electable": San Antonio councilwoman María Antonietta Berriozábal; state representatives Lena Guerrero (Austin), Dora Olivo (Fort Bend), and Norma Chávez (El Paso); and state senator Leticia Van de Putte (San Antonio), to name a few. Some would imprint their commitment onto the next generation, as in the case of Rosie Castro, whose two sons, Julian and Javier, served San Antonio as mayor and state representative, respectively.[43]

The Beret experience also left an imprint on its members. In terms of individual achievement, Jimbo and Ben Guajardo had received their master's degrees, and Ben was working at the Good Samaritan Center. José Morales

Podium at the
National Raza
Unida Confer-
ence, El Paso,
Texas, September
3, 1972. Courtesy
of photographer
César Martínez.

was a "barrio professor." "Big John" finally had "a steady job," which was
"really something for this guy," and Luisa had gone back to school. "Yes,
there has been change," observed Beret founder Juan Guajardo, "but how
do you measure it? El Jimbo, Ben, and José had been talking about going to
school for a long time, and they would have done so without the Berets."
On the other hand, Chale and a few others had gotten "lost for a few years"
with la chiva (heroin) and had fallen by the wayside. For some, the discipline that comes from belonging to an organization—and from a commitment to a cause—was critical.[44]

PART THREE

Communities Organized for Public Service Conference, 1975. President Beatrice Gallego is speaking. *San Antonio Light* Collection, University of Texas at Austin Institute of Texan Cultures, L-6689-A, courtesy of the Hearst Corporation.

AFTER THE FURY

BY THE MID-SEVENTIES, the Chicano movement in Texas and the Southwest was largely exhausted. The reasons were many. Internal friction about leadership and tactics, and external pressure applied by police authorities, as discussed previously, were critical debilitating factors. On the other hand, some movement aims had become institutionalized and its activist elements accommodated. Some victories had been won. The "opening up" of universities to Chicano students and the creation of Chicano studies programs were important achievements. In the political arena, Mexican Americans had secured the kind of direct access and representation in decision making that movement activists had been pressing for. In particular, a vigorous organizational network, led by established movement organizations and their second-generation offspring, had developed a potent capacity to inform and mobilize voting blocs of barrio residents. In the "post-movement" era, the Mexican American community now had an organizational infrastructure with some political clout. Marching and protesting were no longer the only way to be heard.

The year 1975 saw two important legislative victories that symbolized the new order of things. The Voting Rights Act, originally passed in 1965 and itself a significant accomplishment of the Black civil rights movement, was expanded to include the Spanish-speaking communities of the Southwest. This provided Mexican American advocacy organizations new legal tools with which to break up electoral schemes (such as at-large elections) that had diminished proportional minority influence. The political framework of Jim Crow in the Southwest could now be challenged dispassionately and systematically in the courts rather than through the raucous mobilization that had often characterized ethnically polarized political campaigns. Threats of "the ballot or the bullet" could now be framed in the legal language of a voting rights lawsuit.

The second victory of 1975 was the passage of the California Agricultural Labor Relations Act, which extended labor rights and protections long accorded to industrial workers to previously excluded farmworkers. This had been the long-sought goal of the United Farm Workers. Since the act prohibited secondary boycotts, this victory ironically led to a sort of demobilization. The trade-off for securing labor rights entailed the dismantling of the national boycott committees that had been so critical to UFW strategy, and so influential to the Chicano movement. Thus an important training ground for urban activists had been shut down. As we shall see, however, ten years of training had inspired and produced many talented organizers who left an evident imprint on post-movement activity in the Southwest and elsewhere.

So what happened to the movement? A suggestion comes from the legislative victories, for while they provided a legal framework for addressing some of the core issues fueling the Chicano movement, they also effected a dismantling of the movement's organizational base. Any discussion of the demise or transformation of the movement must address this dual process of demobilization and institutionalization. In this final section, I wrestle with this question of transformation by highlighting the importance of agency, or what is often called leadership, in furthering demobilization or institutionalization. The following chapters maintain an eye on organizational matters but move the element of leadership to the center of the narrative.

Chapter 10, "Several Wrong Turns," highlights the biographies of key individuals in an effort to grapple with the charged issue of "unrealized leadership." By this I mean the inability, failure, or unwillingness of prominent individuals with a following or patron base to create or maintain an advocacy organization. To illustrate this point, and to suggest the wide range of potential leadership available for the barrios, I bring together for consideration the very unlikely grouping of Fred Gómez Carrasco, Ramsey Muñiz, and Henry B. Gonzalez. The first was a convicted drug lord, the second a fallen political star, and the third a respected congressman. What ties them together is that in the mid-seventies they were charismatic individuals, potential leaders, whose actions and decisions contributed to the decline of movement activity.

In contrast, Chapter 11, "A Transformation," looks at the rise of second-generation movement organizations as the result of "realized" leadership. I refer specifically to the Southwest Voter Registration Education Project (SVREP), founded by Willie Velásquez in 1974, and the Communities Organized for Public Service (COPS), organized by Ernie Cortés in 1973. Although the founders and charter members of these organizations de-emphasized or distanced themselves from militant Chicano rhetoric, their fundamental objective remained securing equality and justice for marginalized communities. Building on the legacy and lessons of movement activity, these second-generation organizations were able to fashion barrio residents into effective political pressure groups. This chapter, then, deals with the changed organizational field and the manner in which it empowered the barrio neighborhoods of San Antonio and, in particular, the women of these neighborhoods.

One significant measure of local success is clear. After all "the fury," the Chicano movement can be said to have brought down the paternalistic political order of post–World War II San Antonio. In its stead, it ushered in a more representative political system that included input from working-class communities. The exclamation point marking this change came with the 1981 election of Henry Cisneros as mayor, the first of Mexican descent since Juan Seguín in the 1840s. This election signaled an end not just of the political dominance of the Anglo business elite, but also of the conflictual ethnic politics that had so embroiled the city for nearly two decades.

Following the consolidation of their success in San Antonio, the second-generation movement organizations began to export their strategies and lessons throughout the Southwest and nation. Thus, rather than think of the demise or passing of the Chicano movement, it might be more accurate to think of its transformation.

SEVERAL WRONG TURNS

10 THUS FAR, MY narrative explanation has largely described the movement and the lives of those involved from an organizational perspective. Here I wish to shift focus and let the lives of a few key individuals—individuals who dominated the public arena in the mid-seventies—inform us about the pitfalls facing potential leaders. I am talking about a few charismatic individuals who, despite their obvious abilities, dissipated or undermined the political energy of the Mexican American working and lower classes. Although this chapter may read like a romantic tragedy, it is important to examine why such potential leadership went awry.

My selection of Fred Gómez Carrasco, Ramsey Muñiz, and Henry B. Gonzalez as examples of unrealized leadership may appear arbitrary and unreasonable. The first was a convicted killer and drug dealer, the second a fallen political star, and the last a respected liberal congressman. These individuals had different class origins and illustrate such different life trajectories that grouping them may at first appear contrived or forced.[1] What brings these disparate individuals together, however, is that in the mid-seventies they were front-page news, and in the racialized world of Texas they represented a "Mexican" voice or presence. Whatever the general public may have thought of these men, in the barrios they symbolized the aspirations, desires, regrets, and weaknesses of the working and lower classes. These men, different as they were from one another, were linked in the casual political conversations taking place in the barrios of San Antonio and

South Texas. For better or worse, they represented different paths leading up and away from barrio poverty and isolation.

The flawed journey of Fred Gómez Carrasco is rather apparent. His drug organization tranquilized hundreds in San Antonio and South Texas through heroin addiction, which had a direct impact on street youths and specifically on the Brown Berets. Just as tragic, perhaps, was the loss at an early age of Carrasco's potential leadership. Born in the West Side, Carrasco was seen by many in his barrio as a boy genius who went bad due to life circumstances. Relatively unknown outside the drug underworld, for a week in 1974 he became a household name in the state and nation when he attempted to break out from the Huntsville Penitentiary. By orchestrating his own death, prefaced with long interviews with the assembled press about what could have been, Carrasco ensured that he would not be dismissed simply as a ruthless drug lord.[2]

In contrast, Ramsey Muñiz, of Corpus Christi, Texas, was a high school and college football star, a graduate of Baylor University Law School, and had a brilliant future. From a poor family, his was a legitimate "rags to riches" story. As a two-time gubernatorial candidate for the Raza Unida Party, Muñiz inspired thousands in his campaigns for the working people of the state. Shortly after his second campaign, however, he fell victim to the temptation of drug money and self-destructed. Muñiz remains in prison.[3]

A thirst for wealth was not a weakness of Congressman Henry B. Gonzalez, perhaps because unlike Carrasco and Muñiz, he was born in comfortable circumstances. As a scion of an exiled elite Mexican family, Gonzalez was in fact expected to rule. In the fifties, as a young politician, he led a campaign against segregation and racism, earning him legendary status in Texas barrios and ghettos. His resolute "color-blind" view of the world later led him, in the sixties, to actively oppose the cultural nationalism and political activism of the Chicano generation. This vision, along with a stubborn pride, prevented him from recognizing or accommodating the progressive elements in the Chicano movement. These paralyzing sentiments also kept Gonzalez from providing any direct leadership for the Mexican American community.[4]

Although women would soon begin to enter the limelight as charismatic leaders and organizers, at this time they remained largely in the background, providing the base support for male-led organizations. This was the case, as discussed previously, for the women of the Raza Unida Party. This was also true of the Carrasco organization. Although much commentary on Carrasco focused, as one law officer put it, on "the machismo thing," the women in the organization, led by his wife, Rosa, were central to the operation. Sgt. Bill Weilbacher, who spent the better part of five years probing the Carrasco ring, commented pointedly that "The women are tougher, brainier, cooler and more vicious than any of the dudes in the outfit." Nonetheless, they stayed "off the streets."[5]

In this chapter I look at three men who stepped out into the streets but who somewhere, somehow took a wrong turn. Here I consider the lives of a bato loco, a college activist, and an established politician—in a sense, the major characters of this narrative history—to illustrate the different ways that potential leadership went unrealized in the mid-seventies.

For a Piece of Sugar Cane

Fred Gómez Carrasco could have been the South Texas model for historian Eric Hobsbawm's profile of a "social bandit." He was a flamboyant drug king who, upon imprisonment, vowed to escape or die trying. In 1974 he and two other inmates took control of Huntsville State Penitentiary library for a week, during which time he freely gave bilingual interviews to the news media, condemned the treatment of prisoners, asked for asylum in Cuba, and ordered Mexican food for the prison population. After being shot and killed trying to escape, he quickly became the tragic hero of many Texas Mexican corridos. Other than his nationalism—his son was named Emiliano after the Mexican revolutionary hero Zapata—little was known about Carrasco's political views until the Huntsville siege. Indeed, had it not been for the interviews he gave while holed up in the prison library, Carrasco would simply have been dismissed as a ruthless criminal.

In the early 1970s Carrasco was known to police authorities as the "narcotics kingpin" of South Texas and northern Mexico.[6] They had pieced together a biographical sketch which, when added to Carrasco's autobiographical notes, offers an excellent perspective on the individual.

As a teenager, Carrasco hung around Victoria Courts, next to downtown San Antonio. This was in the fifties, during "the days of gang wars and the 'red light' district," before the area was cleared to make room for Hemis-Fair. Between 1956 and 1958, he was a member of the Victoria Courts gang and was involved in several scrapes and shootings with the Ghost Town, La Loma, and the East End.[7] Writing his story in 1973, Carrasco proudly recalled the ambush of the Ghost Town seventeen years earlier, in 1956:

When things really got heavy was when our gang and the Ghost Town Gang let loose against each other. I've got to hand it to them because on one occasion they caught us unprepared and they blasted us with .12 gauge sawed-off shotguns. That time there were two wounded. And since they left as victors they returned the following week. We of course let them enter a previously selected street, and sprayed them so well with our guns that they forgot to return fire. The only thing on their minds was to get out of our trap. They finally got out and they didn't return again not even to pick up their change.[8]

"All of the battles," Carrasco said, "came from old grudges, and in the end we all lost. But at that time it was something to do."[9] Although he was arrested for several misdemeanors, none had to do with his gang fights.

In 1958, at age nineteen, Carrasco was charged with murder with malice for killing a teenager at a high school graduation dance. Over the next fifteen years, he would be in and out prison on both sides of the border as he built up an international narcotics organization called "Los Dons" by "using 'good-ole' American business enterprise." As the leader of Los Dons, Carrasco acquired a reputation as a "modern Pancho Villa and ruthless killer." He had no compunction about eliminating rivals or associates who became security risks. The authorities also knew that he hated "gringos" and dealt only "with his own race." A U.S. Customs official said, "He fancies himself as a bandido; the machismo thing is big. His people look up to him as an all-man type." The residents of his south San Antonio barrio described him as "polite and soft spoken" and caring of his parents.[10]

In 1972, while jailed in a Guadalajara prison, Carrasco made a daring escape using the warden's truck. An intense six-month manhunt on both sides of the border followed. The police looking for Carrasco nicknamed him the "ghost" and "phantom." The manhunt finally culminated in a dramatic shootout and capture at El Tejas Motel in San Antonio on July 22, 1973.[11] Although Carrasco was sent to Huntsville for a life term, the lawmen who knew him were not surprised when he attempted to escape.

Almost to the year after his capture, Carrasco and two accomplices seized the prison library and took more than a dozen hostages. For eleven days, from July 25 through August 4, 1974, Carrasco's breakout attempt captured national and international attention. It dominated the front pages of Texas newspapers, crowding out reporting about the congressional deliberations on the impeachment of President Nixon for the Watergate break-in. On day three (July 27) of the takeover, three major Carrasco stories surrounded the news that the House Judiciary Committee had voted for impeachment.[12]

Fred Gómez Carrasco
outside Guadalajara,
circa 1972. Courtesy of
Gregg Barrios.

For eleven days, Carrasco used the media, the hostages and their families, and prison and political figures to his advantage. He kept the authorities off balance, threatening the hostages one day, releasing one the following, and then springing a surprise on a third day. One detective described
Carrasco as a "master psychologist, an expert but brash con man."[13]

Carrasco was quite talkative on the phone with the prison officials, reporters, and attorneys who called him. He pledged to treat the hostages re-
spectfully and allowed them to have regular communication with relatives,
thus creating external pressure on Texas Department of Corrections officials
and governor Dolph Briscoe, to negotiate a peaceful settlement. Governor
Briscoe called him twice during the ordeal.[14]

In a phone conversation with one of his lawyers, Carrasco said he would rather die than live the rest of his life in prison: "What is the sense of living when you are caged up like an animal? . . . I'm not the type of man who can live life behind bars." To San Antonio reporter Gloria Delgado, he emphasized that "We're all men. And we're tired of being tied down. I will die if necessary for my liberty."[15]

Carrasco preferred to speak Spanish and, at one point, requested a list of reporters covering the situation so that he could call the Spanish-surnamed reporters directly. In one conversation with a Spanish-speaking newsman, Carrasco is reported to have said that he "could have become a doctor or a lawyer, but narcotics was his way to compete against the gringo on the same level." And he revealed that his favorite heroes were Emiliano Zapata, Pancho Villa, and Lucio Cabañas. In one of his longest conversations with a reporter, Sammy Rodríguez of radio station KTRH of Houston, Carrasco reassured the public that the female hostages had been respected because "el mexicano sabe respetar la hembra" (the Mexican knows how to respect the woman).[16]

Where would he go if he got out? "We are going where we will not see the face of the gringos again," said Carrasco to several news reporters. Specifically, he wanted to go to Cuba. Carrasco said that Fidel Castro would not turn him over to the United States or Mexico. "If I go to Cuba and Castro decides to shoot me, he would be doing me a favor," Carrasco said. "Maybe Castro would give me a piece of sugar cane," he told his lawyer.[17]

Everyone speculates that Carrasco knew that he was going to die; he knew that the authorities would never let him go free. On August 3, the eleventh day of the takeover, Carrasco, with his two accomplices and twelve hostages, attempted to board an armored truck for their escape. Carrasco had eight hostages form an outer ring, with another four as an inner ring. Upon leaving the library building, the hostage shield was blown apart by high-pressure water hoses, and in the ensuing gunfire, Carrasco, accomplice Rodolfo Domínguez, and two hostages, teacher Elizabeth Beseda and librarian Julie Standley, were killed "in a hail of bullets." Three other hostages, including prison chaplain Rev. Joseph O'Brien, were injured. Carrasco's third accomplice and seven other hostages were not injured. According to prison rumor, Texas Rangers executed Carrasco as he lay wounded.[18]

The Mexican American community expressed contradictory feelings about Carrasco. Many sympathized with Carrasco while at the same time condemning the violence and drugs of his lifestyle. Some took pride in the fact that a "noble criminal" had stood up against racist authorities, but felt depressed about the waste of a genius. The *Chicano Times* newspaper of San Antonio, in a feature article titled "Federico Gómez Carrasco—A Hero or a Criminal?" described Carrasco's takeover of the prison library as surrealistic. Carrasco had held "sway over a multitude of forces" that included a Texas governor, a prison warden, a prison director, and close to 200 news reporters, who were "baffled by the byzantine moves of Fred Gómez Carrasco."[19] For eleven days, Carrasco demonstrated his "unique ability to influence the situation instead of being a passive victim of events." And he demonstrated that criminals can be noble:

> Carrasco may be a criminal but he has exhibited other traits which men have admired in men for centuries. These include intelligence, daring, courage and chivalry. While some people may feel that it is inappropriate to comment on the attributes of convicted criminals, it does not necessarily negate their existence.

Was Carrasco a hero? The *Chicano Times* piece listed other fugitives from the law who had become heroes—Davy Crockett, James Bowie, Jesse James, Billy the Kid—and predicted that Carrasco would join Juan Cortina, Joaquín Murrieta, and Gregorio Cortez "in the pantheon of Mexican American folk heroes."[20]

Corridos, or ballads, extolling the exploits of Carrasco appeared shortly after his death. Literature professor Ben Olguín, who has studied these corridos, notes that one common story element was that Carrasco never had the opportunity to be honest and that the law in Texas didn't give a damn about Chicanos. More generally, Carrasco and his wife, Rosa, were the inspiration for a genre of "gato negro" (black cat) and "Camelia" corridos that revolved around the adventures (or misadventures) of drug running.[21]

Whatever the contradictory emotions, Carrasco acquired legendary status among some in the Chicano community. Poet Ricardo Sánchez, himself an ex-convict, lionized Carrasco for demanding, during the eleven-day standoff, "freeworld clothes / in the style of the pachuco warrior del barrio / como el bato de aquella que era [like the good guy that he was]." Most of the Brown Berets were equally enthusiastic. Lalo Martínez believed that the "narcos" and the FBI had found out that Carrasco had already established contact with Castro, and this was why they eliminated him. Ray Martínez, Lalo's brother, said that Carrasco was not a criminal; they only got him on charges of aggravated assault on a police officer, and that was in self-defense. Victor San Miguel said that the drug pushers were pushing carga (heroin) to the gringos, away from Chicanos. He added that Carrasco, in a different time, under different conditions, would have been a great leader, perhaps a lawyer, doctor, or politician, and the people knew that. But even among the Brown Berets there was some dissent. "Big John" told me later, in private, that Carrasco was a "matón" (killer) who exploited the people. "What of all the heroin he pushed on the barrios?" he asked rhetorically.[22]

The tragic tale of Carrasco's life elicited mixed reactions from the Mexican American community. Condemnation of Carrasco's lifestyle was tempered by an understanding of the circumstances that had framed his career. Even Anglo lawmen offered, begrudgingly, a nod of comprehension. The newspaper reporters on the scene, perhaps impressed by the articulate Carrasco, spun the operatic score. Thus the publics of Texas, the United States, and Mexico read about a boy genius who became a criminal because of circumstances—one of the costs of poverty and segregation.

For a Toke of Power

Marijuana has a long history in Mexican culture as a topical medicine, a tea, and smoking tobacco. During the Mexican Revolution, marijuana was celebrated in the song "La cucaracha" as the ingredient that made cockroaches (or soldiers) move. Associated with the lower classes, and particularly with the pachuco subculture that emerged in southwestern cities, marijuana possession was made a felony by legislation in 1937.[23] The act was intended to contain a Mexican vice, but to Mexicans of the popular classes, smoking marijuana was viewed with some ambivalence, if not tolerance. A clear distinction was drawn between smoking marijuana and doing other drugs, and between marijuana dealers and the "traficantes" of hard drugs. For the pachuco, or bato, marijuana was a recreational item much like beer or wine. Some batos, knowing how it was viewed in more respectable circles, seemed to enjoy flaunting its use. The official response to such public behavior has generally been to step up enforcement of existing laws or, as in the case of zoot suits and marijuana, to create laws making such things a crime.

It was natural, then, that when the first-generation Mexican American college students reached out to other barrio youths to become activists that the batos locos, now politicized, would reinforce the casual use of marijuana in the Chicano movement. In this case, it was relatively easy for barrio culture to morph into campus counterculture. Smoking marijuana was a common leisure activity among many MAYO activists and did not cease when MAYO became the Raza Unida Party. This casual practice ultimately made for the romantic-tragic story of Ramsey Muñiz.

At the time MAYO decided to form a third political party, the activists' main concern was to gather sufficient signatures in time to qualify for a spot on the 1972 ballot. The leaders had hardly considered whom they would endorse as the party's gubernatorial candidate. After great difficulty in finding a candidate, the party leaders "jumped at the chance to lure a young lawyer dedicated enough to the Raza Unida philosophy to put his future on the line for the good of the party and its platform."[24] The young lawyer was Ramsey Muñiz, twenty-nine years old, a MAYO activist and recent graduate of Baylor Law School.

Muñiz had all the makings of a Horatio Alger success story. In 1960, he had been the senior halfback on the Corpus Christi Miller state championship football team. In 1963, he had earned the Mr. Corpus Christi trophy, and in 1965, honorable mention in the Southwest Conference's all-star selection for his play as a lineman for the Baylor University football team. His athletic prowess and good looks had won him the title of "Mr. Baylor" for two consecutive years. Muñiz was indeed an unusual Mexican. At the time of his decision to run for governor, Muñiz was director of the Urban Community Development Corporation of Waco.[25]

As a dynamic and charismatic campaigner, Muñiz quickly transformed himself from a political novice into "a formidable gubernatorial candidate"— a Mexican American "John Kennedy," many thought. The Raza Unida party chair, María Elena Martínez, said of him: "Ramsey had a likable personality. People fell in love with him when they met him because he was so personable, so down to earth . . . straightforward, unpretentious. He was a perfect choice as a candidate." And party leaders were astounded at Muñiz's reservoir of energy and enthusiasm. Young Chicanos liked his direct style, his militancy, and some of his salty language. Notwithstanding his militancy, Muñiz also had the qualities that older, conservative Mexican Americans liked, according to historian Ignacio García: "middle-class respectability with his law degree, nice clothing, and [an] attractive spouse."[26]

Journalist Miguel Berry, who covered the Raza Unida Party's statewide campaign of 1972, described one of Muñiz's appearances at a fiesta in "the little rundown park in the Mexican end of town," in one of the countless little towns he visited that year.[27] The conjunto band had stopped playing, and the candidate had stepped up on the stage.

Ramsey begins to speak, softly, smiling a lot, almost shyly. . . . He's quiet, respectful, wanting to make a good impression. "Ahh," you sense the people thinking, "this man knows how to speak to us. Tiene educación [He is educated]."

Ramsey is into his speech now and he's talking about how he has to sleep in his car because there's no money in the state campaign fund to pay for a motel room. The people seem to collectively assent, "Yes, we know what it's like."

Ramsey's angry now. Really angry. He's gesturing and sweating profusely, pausing occasionally to wipe his brow. . . . The guys in the conjunto that form a backdrop for Ramsey are into the speech too. Tough-looking types all, they nod knowingly when Ramsey talks about how the educational system, the law, the military, the gringo politicians, the vendidos have all conspired to oppress the Chicano. . . . Ramsey says he intends to change this . . . all-out, up front, "con batos que no se aguitan" [with guys who will not back down].

Berry concluded his description by noting the feeling of solidarity, of unity:

It's all over now. The people are starting to leave but they're carrying the excitement with them. It's all been so natural; the afternoon, the beer, the music, the folks and for one startling moment, the knowledge that they were really together, as different as each one is. The knowledge that they are essentially together is something that cannot be taken away from them. Ever. Somehow, things are already different.[28]

To the surprise of most political pundits, Muñiz pulled in 214,072 votes—6.3 percent of the statewide vote and almost 20 percent of the South and West Texas vote. The Raza Unida activists were ecstatic. Journalist Berry gushed in the pages of *Magazín*, a San Antonio–based journal:

When someone asks, "What is the platform, what are the plans of the Raza Unida Party?" all one need say is that it is part of a dream La Raza has had of itself for centuries and that La Raza is making the dream a reality.

The meaning of that dream, the unfolding of that dream is happening before our eyes. We are the unfolders. And the dream is infinite.[29]

Muñiz quickly came to be seen by many as the party's standard-bearer. In the words of historian and Raza Unida activist Ignacio García, "In personal charisma he towered above most of the party cadre, and the less ideological delegates quickly became attracted to him."[30]

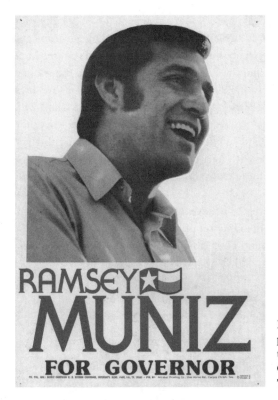

Ramsey Muñiz campaign
poster, 1974. Courtesy of
the Benson Latin American
Collection, University of
Texas at Austin.

In 1974, the Raza Unida Party adopted a "new look" and presented itself as the "United People Party" in an effort to broaden its appeal to middle-class Mexican Americans, African Americans, and liberal Anglos.[31] The strategy was to consolidate the party's strength in rural South Texas while expanding its influence to other regions of the state. But the shift in emphasis apparently did not work, and Muñiz in 1974 received 190,000 votes, 20,000 fewer than in 1972, a major disappointment to party leaders and supporters.[32]

Months before, Muñiz's campaign chair, Carlos Guerra, had confided in party organizer Evey Chapa that "If Ramsey doesn't get at least 750,000 votes, the political future of *all* of us is going to be dim, if not washed up." Guerra had no inkling of how dark the future would become for key party members. The state chair of the party, María Elena Martínez put it plainly: "People in La Raza were naive to think we could use the system and not have the system come down on us as hard as it did."[33]

Muñiz and other Raza Unida leaders were aware of the politically motivated police harassment and surveillance. During the 1974 campaign, Muñiz had asked Governor Briscoe to confirm or deny allegations that Muñiz, members of his staff, and the Raza Unida Party had been the subject of Department of Public Safety (DPS) investigations since 1968. A few days after that public request, Col. Wilson Spier, head of DPS, destroyed all DPS files of "non-criminal spying." In response, Muñiz charged the governor with participating in a scheme to "whitewash" DPS spying on individuals.[34] He also charged the governor with participating in a cover-up of evidence relating to the Carrasco shootout.

> We've heard too many stories to believe any of them. Now we understand that there are more than one set of videotapes and possibly some sound recordings of the event. First, how did these recordings disappear and then reappear? And second, why haven't they been released? The whole DPS matter stinks, and I feel the people have a right to know what is going on and why. We can't allow any more "in house" investigations and we can't allow any more evidence to be destroyed.[35]

Muñiz then called on Governor Briscoe to "quit covering up for the DPS."

The nightmarish problems with "the system" began to surface in 1975. Attorney General Hill, along with the Texas Rangers, organized and stationed a sizable investigative task force in Crystal City for some ten months. This investigation eventually resulted in the indictments, amid much fanfare, of three Crystal City officials on various charges of corruption. All of the charges would later be dropped or dismissed, but in the meantime considerable damage had been done to the Raza Unida Party.[36]

As damaging as such politically motivated indictments were, it was minor compared to that wrought by the drug-related arrests of prominent Raza Unida leaders. In 1975 Flores Amaya, the party's former senatorial candidate, was indicted and convicted of heroin possession. Although most Raza Unida leaders believed he had been framed, they nonetheless had expected some kind of drug-related action against party activists because of the casual use of drugs, especially in college-based chapters. Rural activists were bothered by this laxity, and it had become a matter of contention at the state conventions.[37] Yet few were prepared for the news that Ramsey Muñiz, the party's "golden boy" and former gubernatorial candidate, was engaged in drug dealing. For the Raza Unida Party, the other shoe had dropped.

On July 31, 1976, the *Corpus Christi Caller* carried a banner headline declaring, "Ramsey Muñiz sought for drug trafficking." The article described an eleven-count indictment, the result of an eighteen-month investigation into the activities of Muñiz and Fred Brulloths, Jr., a convicted drug trafficker already serving time in prison. Muñiz had apparently been under investigation by both the Drug Enforcement Agency and the Internal Revenue Service since the end of his second gubernatorial campaign in 1974. The illegal activities were alleged to have begun in June 1975 and were said to include conspiracy to smuggle slightly more than 1,000 pounds of marijuana from Mexico to Alabama.[38]

The response of party activists was one of shock and a feeling of betrayal that one who had been so popular had committed such a blunder. José Ángel Gutiérrez initially claimed that Muñiz's arrest on drug charges was a case of entrapment by government agents who had exploited the lawyer's contacts with his clients. But few among the party's top leaders believed that he had been framed. Historian Ignacio García noted that "Most had been privy to rumors that Muñiz had become involved in drug trafficking. . . . The party leaders had simply ignored the rumors in the hope that Muñiz would not get caught." One marijuana runner from Corpus Christi complained that Muñiz used to show up regularly at their hangout with "too much flash; he was always attracting attention." He was not surprised by Muñiz's arrest. For the Mexican American public at large, according to García's pointed summary, Muñiz's arrest confirmed the portrayal of Raza Unida members as "pot-smoking, long-haired sinvergüenzas (shameless ones) who were constantly in trouble with law enforcement agencies."[39]

In November 1976, things got worse when Muñiz failed to appear at the Corpus Christi federal courthouse, and the headlines read, "Muñiz jumps bond, may be in Mexico." Although Raza Unida leaders had argued that Muñiz had been framed, this defense now rang hollow. As Gutiérrez noted, once Muñiz jumped bail, it was "no longer politically feasible to defend him to the public." Muñiz apparently fled because state and federal narcotics officers had finally "smashed" the smuggling ring in which he was involved on November 2—ironically, election day. He was indicted on a second set of charges for attempting to smuggle 832 pounds of marijuana. Muñiz, it turned out, had been "in charge of the Mexican Side of the importing operation," which had apparently remained active even after his first arrest.[40]

Muñiz was captured the following month in Reynosa, Mexico, on Christmas Eve, 1976. Shipped back to Texas, Muñiz, then thirty-four, pleaded guilty and was sentenced to ten years in prison. He never offered any ex-

planation, and his side of the story remains a mystery. At the sentencing
on March 2, 1977, U.S. district court judge John Wood Jr. belatedly asked
Muñiz, who was already being led from the court, if he wanted to speak.
"Forget it," he said in a low voice.[41]

Muñiz's arrest and conviction on drug charges and bail jumping finished the Raza Unida Party. Alma Canales, Muñiz's running mate in 1972,
said that his arrest made them all look bad and guilty of drug trafficking.
People commented snidely about "la raza ruinida" (the gnawed people), and
the party never recovered its credibility or integrity. Shortly after Muñiz's
arrest, many activists left the party and joined the newly formed Mexican
American Democrats (MAD). In 1978, the Raza Unida candidate for governor, Mario Compean, received fewer than 15,000 votes. It was the last
time that the party would field a candidate for any state office. Gutiérrez,
speaking bitterly of Muñiz, said, "Many of us feel that he shamed us, nos
avergonzó, with his drug deals."[42]

Ramsey Muñiz was never able to pull out of his tailspin. He was released
from prison in 1984, but ten years later Muñiz was charged and convicted
on a third drug offense. This resulted in a sentence of life imprisonment
as a habitual offender. San Antonio attorney James Ingram, one of his old
teammates on the Baylor football team, commented:

> What's very unfortunate about this situation is that he came out of poor
> conditions, became a lawyer and had an opportunity to become a folk
> hero for his people. It's tragic when a guy like that bites the dust and
> violates the law.

Corpus Christi attorney Ruben Bonilla said that Muñiz's fall was devastat-
ing to the community: "It is far worse than a tragedy. It is the destruction of
a profoundly influential person."[43]

Muñiz never explained what led to the downfall. What could he say?
When asked about the past, he chose to focus on what the Raza Unida campaigns had meant to the common people.[44] Muñiz discounted talk about his
charismatic appeal:

> I don't know about the charismatic part of the campaign but I was a
> tireless campaigner and I travelled the entire state of Texas organizing
> people that had never been organized before in their lives. . . . Words
> cannot ever be found to express vividly the positive impact we left in the
> hearts of our people.[45]

Ramsey Muñiz outside Nueces
County Jail, December 1976.
Courtesy of the *Corpus Christi
Caller-Times.*

Muñiz noted that La Raza Unida had helped to liberate Mexican Americans by placing them in the political arena: "We won. We didn't win the
election, but we won like a people. That's the point everyone misses. We
didn't have to win the election; not in our position."[46] Muñiz was referring
to the creation of a sense of unity and solidarity, of peoplehood, that the
party and his campaigns had generated. "The biggest mistake that we made
during the times of organizing La Raza Unida," in Muñiz's estimation, was
the dissolution of MAYO, which represented "the voice for the youths, the
powerless."[47]

Writing from Leavenworth in 1996, Muñiz saw himself as a "mexicano
political prisoner" and "a soldier of Mexi." By this time he had become a
student of the indigenous history, culture, and ancient spirituality of the

Nahuatl peoples and was part of "a new Mexika movement." Mexi was the
Nahuatl prophet who "gave us our name and energies to live forever." Thus,
to the question about how he saw himself historically, Muñiz responded by
speaking of the prophet Mexi:

> I have never considered myself a hero knowing that my people are suf-
> fering and will continue to suffer under the oppression of this govern-
> ment. I have never considered myself a leader but only a soldier of Mexi
> for Mexi will eventually give us the direction that we must take in order
> to serve our people. Our declaration of independence is to serve LA
> RAZA. . . . We are all mexicano political prisoners and soldiers of Mexi.[48]

Muñiz saw "the creation of the party, the campaigns, the political movement of our people" as an answer to "the oppression of the American government." As a soldier of Mexi, he took this movement "so seriously that if
the sacrifice of my life meant a difference then so be it."[49]

For the Sake of Principle and Pride

"Trailblazing" and "quixotic" have both been used to describe Henry B.
Gonzalez's political career. As political commentator Michael King noted,
Gonzalez was "a man willing to lose for principle, as exemplified in his political epithets: the one crusader, the idealist, the eccentric, the 'maverick.'"
Columnist Molly Ivins likewise commented that "No one in Washington
seemed to understand Henry B.; he was always stigmatized as a 'maverick,'
a 'loner,' a 'lone wolf.'"[50] This solitary posture, as we shall see, stemmed
partly from Gonzalez's political philosophy and practice.

It might be said that Gonzalez, unlike Carrasco and Muñiz, was born
to rule. For eight generations Gonzalez's forefathers had been mayors of
Mapimi, a silver-mining center west of Monterrey, where they had operated several mines. Gonzalez described the family business as "the equivalent
of Wells Fargo." Gonzalez's father, Leonides Gonzalez Cigarroa, was the last
mayor and *jefe político* of Mapimi under the Porfirio Díaz regime. During the
Mexican Revolution, the family was forced to flee to San Antonio, arriving
in 1911. Henry Barbosa Gonzalez would be born five years later.[51]

Growing up in the Upson Street neighborhood, a diverse, generally middle-class area, Gonzalez experienced racism at school from the Anglo boys
and teachers. He remembered being called a "Mexican greaser" and being
thrown out of swimming pools and parks as late as the 1950s. Gonzalez

also got to know the West Side gangs. The Riverside gang was headquartered only a block away from his neighborhood, and they often caused him trouble. As he put it later, during a charged exchange in the Texas Senate, "I had to come up through the jungle of the West Side and I think I know how it is to have to fight alley-fashion."[52]

Gonzalez had a complex understanding of ethnicity; it was obviously a topic he had given much thought to. Like many of the World War II generation, Gonzalez fervently believed that the United States was the land of opportunity and fair play. His family roots were in Mexico, "but I am an American and my first and last loyalty is to America."[53] In a 1967 article titled "Hope and Promise: Americans of Spanish Surname," Gonzalez noted that Spanish-surnamed Americans have a unique problem in defining themselves, and that across the Southwest there was no "generally accepted name." Preferring the term "Americans of Spanish surname," Gonzalez believed that this problem of group identity led to a lack of goals:

> The Spanish-surnamed American group has problems in setting forth cogent goals, just as it does in finding an all-inclusive label. The group possesses no single program, no national goals and has not so far been able to coalesce into a single, meaningful whole, capable of speaking with a united voice. There is no national organization of Spanish-surnamed Americans that could be considered comparable to the NAACP.[54]

Thus, of the Ford Foundation's belief that the greatest need for Mexican Americans was to have an effective national organization, "This good desire may have rested on a false assumption: namely, that such a disparate group could, any more than our black brothers or our white 'Anglo' brothers, be brought under one large tent." Gonzalez noted that he and Congressman Kazen, from Laredo, "have many times disassociated ourselves from the descriptive phrase of being a Latin American spokesman or a Latin American leader, because this is a pluralistic group."[55] In fact, Gonzalez viewed claims to represent an ethnic constituency as "political brokering," which he equated with corruption. Gonzalez's beliefs left him in the strange position of eschewing any leadership role for the "Hispanic" community, even though he was one of the few Hispanics in Congress at the time.

Yet the congressman went beyond his beliefs to actively and consistently oppose any attempt to create a unified voice. His targets were not just the "hate mongering" MAYO and La Universidad de los Barrios, the "college of the punks." Gonzalez also organized a campaign to defund the Mexican

American Unity Council (MAUC), the Mexican American Legal Defense and Educational Fund (MALDEF), and the Southwest Council of La Raza, basically because he believed that it was wrong to practice the "politics of race." Gonzalez would not speak for the "Latin Americans," nor did he want anyone else to do so.[56]

Gonzalez made his views clear to fellow congressman William Clay in a letter of May 22, 1971, explaining why he would not lend support to a Black Caucus fund-raising dinner:

> I don't deny that any man elected from a minority ethnic group—as I am, and as you are—is often tempted to speak for a national constituency. That is a role that I have been asked to assume, and have refused, because I have never felt capable of speaking for the millions of people with whom I have a common ethnic heritage, but who in fact might not know me. It seemed to me that the only course was to represent my own district, and all the people in it.

Gonzalez then provided an insight into his political persona:

> Beginning with my decision not to attempt being a national spokesman or leader, *my feelings have been that I could not support others among my particular ethnic group who attempted to arrogate such a role to themselves.* [emphasis added][57]

Thus, continued Gonzalez, he could not contribute to the dinner "because I feel that the idea of a black or brown caucus is fundamentally defective." Gonzalez concluded that in his view, "the frail fabric of a pluralistic society demands that we develop trust for one another."[58]

Perhaps this "trust" requirement explains the maverick, loner image cultivated by Gonzalez as a political actor. Given the tenor of race and ethnic relations in the late 1960s and early 1970s, Gonzalez's philosophical position—of declining to assume leadership and of denying it for others—created many difficult moments.

Needless to say, Gonzalez had rocky ties with both the Hispanic Congressional Caucus and the Black Congressional Caucus. In 1969 Gonzalez opposed legislation by Sen. Joseph Montoya (D-NM) and Rep. Edward Roybal (D-CA) to maintain the Inter-Agency Committee on Mexican American Affairs; Gonzalez called it "a third-rate Bureau of Indian Affairs" and a political tool for the Nixon administration. In 1975 Gonzalez opposed the extension of the Voting Rights Act to language minorities, while Rep. Barbara Jordan (D-TX) championed its passage. He never wavered from his critique of the work of the U.S. Commission on Civil Rights.[59] These positions may have been philosophically principled, but it seems evident that they embodied considerable pique.

Henry B. Gonzalez's "Achilles' heel" was his sensitivity to criticism. Molly Ivins recalled that she once wrote that Gonzalez had "a barely perceptible accent," and he became "so infuriated by what seemed to me a harmless remark." He reacted viscerally to insults, and with the reflexes of a pugilist, which he had been. In 1963 he slugged a southern congressman who called him a "pinko" on the House floor. In the 1970 St. Mary's incident, he was set to punch a protesting student until his aide did it for him. At the time, Gonzalez noted that he had never tolerated insults and had "never turned the other cheek. . . . if someone calls me a 'vendido' (sellout) and I'm not, he's going to get a fight." And in 1986, at the age of seventy, he slugged a restaurant patron who called him a Communist. *Texas Observer* editor Ronnie Dugger summed up Gonzalez as "touchy, vengeful, quixotic."[60]

Add to this sensitivity an anxiety about radical movements among the lower classes, and one can begin to understand his reflexive and vehement rejection of the Chicano movement. State senator Joe Bernal believed that the apparent contradiction between Gonzalez of the 1950s and Gonzalez of the 1970s stemmed from his family's traumatic experience during the Mexican Revolution: "Seeing Mexican revolutionaries, he trips emotionally—I think he sees the same element in La Raza Unida and anybody who starts getting militant—he trips." And he goes "for the jugular."[61]

Gonzalez's paranoia about radicals had surfaced as early as the Del Rio protest in 1969, and it intensified over the next few years. Language on the floor of the House and in statements given to the press included exaggerations and some outright fabrications, much of it fueled by personal anger at Willie Velásquez, his former protégé. His intelligence gathering indicated that he was not against using whatever means necessary to undermine his detractors. His paranoia was apparent at the St. Mary's walkout in 1970 and again in 1973, when an unruly student audience at the University of Colorado prevented him from speaking at a scheduled engagement. Gonzalez had apparently feared for his life. He believed that the Boulder incident was an attempt to have him murdered, and that Willie Velásquez, social worker Gil Murillo, and councilman Bernardo Eureste were behind the plot. Velásquez discounted the charge as ludicrous.[62]

Although Gonzalez framed his opposition to the Chicano organizations as a matter of principle, critics questioned his motives. Perhaps his actions were not based on principle but were rather a calculated move to secure his congressional seat? His adversary Albert Peña believed that Gonzalez wanted to discourage any independent organizing among Mexican Americans. Peña noted that there was nothing new in the concept of ethnic organizations—remember the Irish, Italians, Poles, said Peña—"yet, when Chicanos organize and demand their rights, they are charged explicitly and implicitly with racism and un-Americanism."[63]

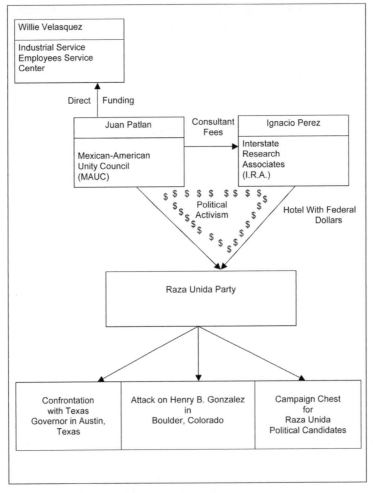

Congressman Henry B. Gonzalez's diagram of the Chicano movement organizational field, circa 1974 (Gonzalez Collection, Center for American History, University of Texas at Austin).

Bernal felt that Gonzalez had been "the biggest deterrent" to the Chicano movement because "white Establishment males" did not have to "put us down when they have him to do it." By opposing Chicanos, Gonzalez did not lose the Anglo liberals while gaining "great favor from Anglo conservatives, to whom he could say . . . 'if you don't like me, you may have to deal with them—the Chicano equivalent of the Black Panthers or the Stokely Carmichaels.'" Many "moderate-type Hispanics" followed Gonzalez's position, Bernal observed, "for they, too, want to cater to what they consider to be the ruling class." So by putting down Chicano militants, Gonzalez gained a lot of support. But his "greatest disservice," in Bernal's view, was the stultifying of potential leadership among the Mexican American community: "San Antonio could have very easily had its first Mexican-American mayor many years ago."[64]

Gonzalez's most substantive self-defense was his countercharge that the Chicano left tended toward anti-gringo rhetoric that was just as racist as any other racism. The left, Gonzalez said, wanted more than equality: "they want to get even. It's true also of the black. At that point I say 'Count me out.'"[65] José Ángel Gutiérrez defended MAYO tactics and rhetoric, noting that at that time "you didn't get anywhere by being mild and meek."

> People were afraid to speak out. There was no deference, no respect at all. People thought we were less than human. We were just here, as a labor commodity. We had to make the heap so they could be at the top. We certainly didn't have any history, either. We had no articulation, no speech.[66]

Likewise, Willie Velásquez, although he had disassociated himself from MAYO and the Raza Unida Party, did not hesitate in identifying Gonzalez as "the key person that has demoralized progressive leadership among Chicanos. . . . By the threat of using his power, he has made the Mexican-American community take much more moderate positions than it should [have]."[67]

In 1980 Ronnie Dugger interviewed Gonzalez and the Chicano leaders who had battled with him. At that time the latter had "not forgiven or forgotten, and neither had he." Gonzalez called the Raza Unida Party "the last refuge of Chicano scoundrels," and added, "They hate me, and the feeling is mutual."[68]

With the passing of time and a growing sense of mortality, however, there has been much reconciliation.

Congressman Henry B.
Gonzalez, circa 1986.
Gonzalez Collection,
Center for American
History, University of
Texas at Austin.

Que Descansen en Paz

This exploratory review of "unrealized" political leadership has focused on
three individuals who had a significant impact on the Chicano communities of South Texas in the mid-1970s. This impact might not have been what
they had in mind, or it might have been one that they later came to regret.
This exploration was not meant to impose a judgment. The intent was to
try to understand what the loss of these talented potential leaders meant for
the political situation of the barrios in the mid-seventies. More to the point,
how did they contribute to the demise of the movement?

Fred Gómez Carrasco, the chivalrous, polite drug "don," had been a
major heroin supplier for the barrios and ghettos of San Antonio and other
points in Texas. Despite the romanticization of his life as a narco-traficante,
Carrasco must be remembered as the genius organizer behind a drug operation that tranquilized and criminalized countless barrio and ghetto youths.
In short, Carrasco played a critical part in undermining the Chicano movement in the poor, working-class barrios. Yet his last-minute political testa-
ments, given before his staged death, suggests that there could have been a
different path.

Ramsey Muñiz, athletic star, charismatic leader, and two-time guberna-torial candidate for the Raza Unida Party, stumbled and then self-destruct-ed, taking along with him the fortunes of the party. What happened? Yes, it was a setup by the authorities, but how could Muñiz have walked into it? Was the temptation so great? Was it hubris? Ten years after serving time for his first two convictions, Muñiz was arrested and convicted on a third drug charge. As a result, Muñiz has been permanently incarcerated. The loss is irrevocable. What remains is a memory of those inspiring years in the early seventies when Muñiz moved 200,000 voters to believe in a "united people."

Henry B. Gonzalez, an American of Spanish-surnamed descent who held an idealistic "color-blind" view of the world, was so upset with Chicano eth-nic demands that he actively opposed the Chicano movement. He was suc-cessful in defunding MAYO, forcing MALDEF to move from San Antonio, and restricting MAUC activities. Was it principle that motivated his opposi-tion, personal pique at movement rhetoric, or simply interest in maintaining political control? Perhaps all three sentiments were intertwined. Gonzalez has been charged with undermining the Chicano movement, yet, as my nar-rative explanation has made evident, that responsibility must be partitioned among many.

Perhaps this does lead to a judgmental question after all. Can we judge which path was the most flawed? Is it the path of one who acquires politi-cal consciousness late in life, past a point of no return? The path of one who had consciousness but succumbed to temptation? Or the path of one whose consciousness refused to acknowledge ethnic identity as natural and legitimate? Which is worst: a flawed journey, a flawed decision, or a flawed vision?

Or should we pass judgment at all? In 2005 an e-mail sent to those "who have a benevolent attitude towards Ramsey" announced that Muñiz was seriously ill at the Leavenworth hospital: "At this point Ramsey does not need 'desprecios ni acusaciones' que realmente no sabemos como fué el caso de él. Y realmente no somos nadie para juzgar ['scorn nor accusations,' that really we don't know what his situation was like. And actually we are not someone who can judge]." The e-mail asked simply that we "pray for a fallen Warrior."[69]

Before Congressman Gonzalez died, he had made peace with most of the activists who had called him a "sellout." Both sides usually acknowl-edged that they had been carried away by the highly charged times. Even the bitterest of feuds could be set aside. Thus, on the eve of the posthumous awarding of the Presidential Medal of Freedom to Willie Velásquez, Gonzalez publicly recognized what Velásquez had contributed to American politics, noting that he had made an "enormous contribution" by creating "a movement that added enormously to the resources and political capability of Hispanics."[70]

Likewise, many of Gonzalez's old critics were quick to offer conciliatory eulogies upon the congressman's death in 2000. Activist and political theorist Andy Hernandez commented then, "In the long run, we've learned that we were both right, and both wrong. Ethnic-identity party politics had no future." Yet, added Hernandez, Gonzalez's ideologically liberal politics also seemed to be outmoded. "We have to find a common language in order to keep working for progressive goals."[71]

A TRANSFORMATION

11 *LOS ANGELES TIMES* columnist Frank del Olmo, reminiscing in 1997 on the twenty-fifth anniversary of the Raza Unida Party's national convention, commented that two events during the month of September 1972 marked both the zenith and nadir of the Chicano movement. He had traveled to El Paso to report on the convention, one of the few occasions that "Chicano icons" Raza Unida founder José Ángel Gutiérrez, Colorado activist Rodolfo "Corky" González, and New Mexican land grant leader Reies López Tijerina would gather to discuss a national strategy. The sense that this might be a "historic" moment had drawn the attention of the national news media. While at the convention, del Olmo received an urgent call about the Brown Beret "invasion" of Santa Catalina Island. According to the Berets, the Treaty of Guadalupe-Hidalgo of 1848 had not ceded the island to the United States.

> So they sailed to Catalina on tourist boats, put up a Mexican flag and claimed the island on behalf of all Chicanos. Their bravado got no support in Los Angeles, much less in Mexico City. I told my colleagues not to panic, and suggested they send another reporter to Catalina rather than bringing me back from Texas.

Del Olmo laughingly noted that his story on the Raza Unida Party ended up on page 3, while the story about the Beret encampment on Catalina Island was front-page news. Neither story of zenith and nadir, according to del Olmo, would leave behind a lasting memory.[1]

"In retrospect," concluded del Olmo, "I missed part of a bigger story in Texas." While the national news media was focused on the doings of the Raza Unida Party, "other Texas Chicanos were quietly doing the dull behind-the-scenes work needed to make political progress for Latinos." Del Olmo had in mind Willie Velásquez, whose Southwest Voter Registration Education Project (SVREP) was "signing up thousands of voters all over Texas"; Ernesto Cortés, whose public service organization had transformed "the barrios of San Antonio into a potent political force"; and Henry Cisneros, who would become the consensus-building mayor who would unite the Anglo business elite and the aroused Mexican American communities. Del Olmo would write about them later, "but only after all the sound and fury of La Raza Unida and the Brown Berets had faded."[2]

Unfortunately, del Olmo missed the point a second time. The "sound and fury" and the "dull behind-the-scenes work" were all part of the same messy, complex, and contradictory social and political activism known as the Chicano movement. Velásquez and Cortés were part of that movement. Both had been involved with the farmworker cause and had invested considerable energy in the MAYO-inspired Mexican American Unity Council. Both had extensive interactions with Gutiérrez, Compean, and other ranking Raza Unida Party activists. Both opposed the idea of forming a separate political party, yet both built independent nonpartisan organizations that at times played off the competition between Democrats and Republicans. Their detachment from militant Raza Unida rhetoric did not strip away their activist character and ideals, for their subsequent exploration of new and different ways to empower people reflected some fundamentals of the Chicano movement. Shorn of nationalist rhetoric, their goal remained, to cite the popular Black Panther phrase, to give "power to the people." Henry Cisneros would be the beneficiary of such organizing efforts, a fact that he has acknowledged many times. His political success and popularity were due in good part to the electoral clout that Velásquez and Cortés were able to develop through their respective grassroots organizations.[3]

Other political analysts who have studied the Texas scene have drawn similar false dichotomies as del Olmo. John Booth, for example, characterized the Communities Organized for Public Service (COPS), the organization founded by Cortés, as "not a Chicano organization per se" and "not a civil rights group," but instead as a coalition of pressure groups pursuing tangible improvements in everyday life.[4] Likewise, Peter Skerry reasoned that Cortés was successful because he focused on "non-ethnic issues": "After years of failure by Chicano activists to rouse the West Side with leftist slogans or racial appeals, Cortés succeeded in organizing around mud and floods."[5] Leaving aside the reasons for Cortés's success for the moment, the characterization of COPS as "not a civil rights group," and "mud and floods" as "non-ethnic," reflects a misunderstanding of Anglo-Mexican relations in Texas.

In a segregated context, all protest activity emanating from the barrios—whether around inferior schooling, police brutality, or "mud and floods"—were seen by the political establishment and "the better side of town" as ethnic or racial. This was a frame of reference that COPS deliberately and constantly subverted by emphasizing the class-based nature of their demands for public services. The framing of these community demands, in other words, was itself subject to public contestation. As Booth noted, local media commentaries were filled "with alarm" about the political organizing "of blacks and Chicanos under the leadership of groups like Communities Organized for Public Service." The demands by "formerly silent lower-class groups" had stirred "considerable unease among upper- and middle-class Anglos."[6] Indeed, some observers were concerned about whether the Mexican American community would "once again become dominated by patron-client politics" or if San Antonio would "become a Chicano-rule city only at the price—the same price paid by blacks in other cities—of having its more affluent population and its tax base move beyond city government's reach."[7]

In this concluding chapter, I describe the manner in which the Chicano movement and its second-generation offspring facilitated the collapse of the paternalistic rule of the old Anglo business elite and provided the basis for an open democratic system. This collapse has been described several times before. What is striking in these portrayals is their emphasis on the internal tensions within the business community and the political restructuring "imposed upon San Antonio from outside," while scant reference is made to the local Chicano movement.[8] This emphasis is reversed in my narrative explanation.

Bringing Down the Old Order

The hegemony of the Good Government League (GGL), the political arm of San Antonio's business elite, began to crack in 1969 and 1971, declined in 1973, and failed altogether in 1975, when it elected only three council members—a minority—for the first time since 1955. The GGL faced challenges from within its own elite business base and from the Mexican

American community. Political scientist Larry Hufford condensed the matter nicely: "The downfall was caused by a split between old money and new money, a debate on growth to the north outside the loop, and increased citizen organization on the west side of San Antonio."[9]

Tensions had been brewing between "the older, established business community and the younger, risk-taking developers who operated in the suburbs." The old guard was not willing to loosen its control over all commerce and development. Basically, the business community was split between "the Greater Chamber of Commerce, located in the heart of downtown," and the "suburban forces which held forth in the Northside Chamber."[10] Community organizer Ernie Cortés was less sanguine in his appraisal of the situation: the GGL was crumbling "in the face of a challenge from a bunch of builders and developers who simply wanted to make money." They wanted the city "to annex land, build new sewer and water lines, widen streets—let the city grow!"[11] In the meantime, no major infrastructural improvements had taken place in the West and South sides of town in thirty years.

Barrio residents were concerned about the annual floods, the lack of parks, poor municipal services, and other issues. The GGL was no longer able to contain their frustration and anger with GGL-anointed representatives. In 1969 attorney Pete Torres won a city council seat without GGL endorsement, and the Committee for Barrio Betterment (CBB), "an upstart Chicano slate of candidates with no money," won all the West Side precincts.[12] In 1971 the CBB again carried the West Side. In 1973 and 1975, with the CBB no longer a factor, independent Anglo candidates won these precincts over the GGL's "hand-picked" Mexican American candidates. Indeed, in 1975, when Henry Cisneros first ran for office as a GGL candidate, he failed to win a majority in the West Side.[13] This challenge from below, combined with a challenge internal to the business elite, finished the GGL.

The GGL did attempt to co-opt both the business challenge and the ethnic challenge. To bridge divisions within the former, in 1973 it placed a "new" developer, Clifford Morton, on its slate. To deal with the latter, it ran Roy Barrera for mayor. To appeal to women voters, an increasingly self-conscious group, it ran Lila Cockrell against an independent reform candidate. Cockrell and Morton won. Barrera lost to Charles Becker, an independent candidate backed by the North Side developers. It marked the first time that the GGL had lost control of the mayor's office in its twenty-year history.[14] Still the GGL had a majority (five of eight) of the council seats.

By 1975 the Good Government League's dominance had shattered. In a seemingly desperate move, the GGL placed four Mexican Americans on its electoral slate. All of them failed to win a majority in the West Side, and all except one, Henry Cisneros, lost the citywide vote. It was a sharp indication of the resentment Mexican Americans had toward the GGL, which too late sought to satisfy the impulse for ethnic representation. Recalled Cisneros, "The structure of the GGL was so decrepit, so atrophied, so arthritic that the GGL sort of stumbled to the finish line and collapsed."[15] Only three of the nine-member GGL slate won council seats. The GGL formally disbanded the following year (1976).

The final blow against the old order was delivered by the Mexican American Legal Defense and Educational Fund. MALDEF had been one of the Ford Foundation projects vigorously opposed by Congressman Gonzalez. Although MALDEF had been forced to relocate its headquarters from San Antonio to San Francisco, its lawyers still continued to influence matters back in Texas. In 1973 MALDEF had successfully challenged Bexar County's at-large, multimember state representative elections, which resulted in single-member districts and the election of several new Mexican American representatives. Then MALDEF challenged the at-large council districting of San Antonio and secured a favorable Justice Department review in 1976. The Justice Department, using the newly expanded Voting Rights Act, objected to the city's recent massive North Side annexation on the grounds that this had diluted the voting strength of Mexican Americans. San Antonio had two choices: fight the ruling in court or adopt a single-member districting scheme. The latter necessitated a referendum on changing the city charter. The city council, with Cisneros casting the decisive swing vote, decided to let the electorate vote on the matter.[16]

The campaign against council districting was waged, as expected, by former GGL stalwarts. These critics argued that single-member districts would intensify ethnic cleavages in city politics. In effect, they claimed that "increased Chicano participation would spawn ethnic conflict or racism in the political arena." With no sense of irony or contradiction, their campaign in the Anglo North Side distributed "propaganda appealing to racist fears of a possible Chicano takeover."[17] In the meantime, on the West and South sides of town, two relatively new organizations, SVREP and COPS, were hard at work registering and mobilizing the Mexican American electorate.

The referendum to adopt ten single-member districts, with the mayor to be elected at large, passed with a narrow margin of 52.7 percent of the citywide vote. The overwhelming Mexican American support—90 percent approval, according to one estimate—proved to be the critical factor.[18] The change to single-member districts had an immediate impact. In 1977 five

Mexican Americans and one African American were elected to San Antonio's ten-member city council. For the first time since the days of the Texas
Republic, Anglos constituted a minority on the council.[19]

Clearly the Voting Rights Act (VRA) had disturbed San Antonio's political landscape by laying the groundwork for single-member districts. This
has led some analysts to conclude that "these political and economic trans-
formations have been imposed upon San Antonio from outside—by civil
rights legislation, changes in voting laws, and restructuring of local government."[20] But the application of the act was the climactic moment of a
long legal campaign by MALDEF, and the passage of the single-member
plan happened only because of the huge turnout of long-frustrated Mexican American voters. Moreover, whatever potential was provided by the
single-member district structure had to be realized by Mexican American
organizing efforts. As political scientist Peter Skerry correctly observed,
the Voting Rights Act could not "*will* Mexican-American power into being."
Added Skerry, "All the VRA did was take the lid off a pot that was already
boiling, and allow Mexican Americans in Texas to achieve their political
potential."[21]

Once San Antonio moved to single-member districts, it was impossible
for any business elite faction to control the electoral slate. On the contrary,
single-member districts made the election of populist "muckrakers" such
as Bernardo Eureste possible. Eureste, representing a West Side district,
was variably described in the media as a "hothead" and "champion of the
underdog." His detractors saw him as "a bumbling, arrogant, uneducated
ethnic bent on destroying the gringo." At the height of his influence, the *San
Antonio Light*, in a feature article, asked, "Is Councilman Eureste a Racist,
a Hero, a Future Congressman—Or All Three of These?"[22] Eureste would
serve several terms on the city council.

Naturally, critics of the new council district system pointed to Eureste
as confirmation of their prediction of increased ethnic conflict in the political arena. Yet these structural changes, according to political scientist
John Booth, "had reduced a growing frustration felt among San Antonio
Chicanos."[23] Councilman Eureste himself believed that the 1977 districting
of the city council had headed off "serious disturbances" because Mexicans
would have felt "that they were not represented."[24] Had the at-large electoral system remained intact, the specter of highly charged political challenges by an increasingly aroused Mexican American community appeared
likely. The list of accumulated grievances had been voiced repeatedly in
council chambers for years before the adoption of single-member districts.

The "mud and floods" of each rainy season were a constant reminder of where things stood.

The single-member districts signaled newfound influence for the barrio districts and encouraged independent, neighborhood-based candidates. Kinship and friendship networks were now viable bases for aspiring working-class politicos.[25] Marshalling this influence were two movement-inspired organizations, SVREP and COPS.

Bringing in a New Order

The Chicano movement did not dissipate into nothingness. Some organizations—the Mexican American Unity Council (MAUC) and the Mexican American Neighborhood Council (MANCO), for example—have become fixtures among the economic development and social service agencies of Texas. MALDEF and the National Council of La Raza, formerly the Southwest Council of La Raza, survived their tumultuous birth in San Antonio and have become prominent advocates on the national stage.

While most movement organizations and projects were disbanded, such "demobilization" did not necessarily signify a loss of political commitment or energy among the core members. Many activists from the disbanded organizations simply took their consciousness and experience to other organizations. The best example of such migration was the crossing over of Raza Unida activists to the Democratic Party. As Raza Unida dissolved, ex-members joined with the Mexican American "yellow dog" Democrats and took control of local Democratic Party chapters. These combined groups formed the Mexican American Democrats (MAD), which quickly became a major player in the state Democratic Party and in Texas politics.[26] In retrospect, the Raza Unida Party may have facilitated the breakup of Anglo control in the greater border region as much through membership emigration as through direct electoral challenges.

The Chicano movement also inspired new political organizations that eschewed nationalist ideology but continued the basic quest for community empowerment. Among these "second-generation" organizations, the two most prominent in San Antonio were SVREP and COPS. The second generation, of course, did not have to resemble the first. What distinguished SVREP and COPS from movement organizations was the absence of Chicano power rhetoric and imagery. Their campaigns were basic, gritty ones—registering people to vote, getting streets paved, and so forth—in which ethnicity was a taken-for-granted reality. Although their public presentation differed from that of the militant movement organizations—SVREP was ethnic but not angry, COPS was angry but not ethnic—their target and objectives remained unchanged: to empower the working-class barrios of San Antonio and then export the lessons learned to other communities throughout the Southwest and, indeed, the country.

Another similarity with earlier movement formations was their stated independence from the two established political parties. The Raza Unida Party had attempted to do this by offering a third-party alternative, but this had merely sucked it into a predictably exhausting and losing battle at the statewide level. Both SVREP and COPS maintained a local focus and claimed strict nonpartisanship. Although nonpartisan, both were very engaged politically in the sense of promoting citizen activism and demanding accountability from elected officials. Their success at doing the former meant that they could accomplish the latter. In fact, in his training sessions, COPS founder Ernie Cortés sounded much like José Ángel Gutiérrez, sans reference to "gringos":

> It's unfortunate that fear is the only way to get some politicians to respect your power. They refuse to give you respect. They don't recognize your dignity. So we have to act in ways to get their attention. We don't always choose fear. In some areas, what we have going for us is the *amount* of fear we can generate. We got where we are because people fear and loathe us.[27]

This similarity in thought undoubtedly reflected not just a shared Alinsky philosophy, but also a shared experience of confronting an intransigent political system over many years.

THE SOUTHWEST VOTER REGISTRATION EDUCATION PROJECT

The idea behind SVREP was beguilingly simple: register Mexican Americans and get them out to vote. Founder Willie Velásquez believed previous registration and "get out the vote" efforts aimed at Mexican Americans had failed because most of the funds were tied to presidential campaigns and state races for the governor's mansion and the senate: "These campaigns would migrate to the Southwest and pick the crop of Mexican votes every four years or so, not to be heard of again until the next important national election."[28]

Survey research by SVREP had shown, however, that Mexican American voters were most concerned about basic municipal services and better schools. As Velásquez put it, "The tradition in the Southwest was that the Chicano side of town simply was not paved, had no drainage and suffered from second rate services. The second greatest complaint was about inferior education."[29] Such a finding had moved SVREP from the beginning to emphasize registration campaigns that were tied to local races—to city council, school board, county, and legislative races—rather than state or national ones. This reorientation of resources to local races, Velásquez believed, would become "the single most important factor in increasing Chicano registration and turnout."[30]

Under Velásquez's guidance, the organization initially modeled itself after the Voter Education Project (VEP), a nonprofit group in Atlanta dedicated to registering African Americans in the South. Velásquez praised John Lewis and VEP for the technical assistance VEP had provided in fund-raising and voter registration techniques. "Without them we never would have gotten off the ground."[31]

The strategy of SVREP was to work with the existing local leadership by providing legal and organizing expertise as well as basic funding. The laboratory setting was naturally San Antonio. For its first registration drive in 1975, representatives of forty different groups attended the initial gathering and signed on to help with the local drive. Olga Peña, the ex-wife of former county commissioner Albert Peña, was elected as chairperson. Nine more drives in small Texas towns would follow that first year. It was during one of those campaigns that Velásquez saw "his vision taking shape."[32]

What shaped that vision was Velásquez's experience in Fort Bend County, outside Houston. Dora Olivo, who would later become a state representative, had directed a very successful drive that ultimately resulted in the first-ever election of a Chicano judge in 1976. Velásquez became "captivated," in the words of his biographer,

> by the blatantly prideful expression of working-class "Mexicanness" that radiated from the small towns that made up Fort Bend County. He compared their leaders to "brash young gallos flexing their muscles."[33]

The campaign's leaders were "not polished operatives" like those who headed SVREP's campaigns in the large cities. Instead they were "ordinary people who had grown tired of their second-class status" and wanted to do something meaningful about it.[34] Andy Hernandez, SVREP's research director, elaborated: "We were training disadvantaged grassroots people to think about voter registration, politics, and campaigning in different ways. It wasn't civic duty stuff for Willie. It was all about creating the conditions out of which we could win." A majority of the grassroots organizers were women.[35]

The vision for SVREP was that of the campaña volante, a flying squadron of organizers and lawyers that would search for and target school districts, towns, and counties that appeared vulnerable to Mexican American community pressure. The strategy turned out to be highly successful. The annual number of voter registration drives increased from ten the first year (1975) to more than a hundred in 1982.[36] The field organizers were often on the road for months at a time. By late 1982, SVREP had conducted over 463 registration drives throughout the Southwest. As a result, Velásquez had become, as Los Angeles Times reporter del Olmo put it, "the man the Anglo establishment hates to see."[37]

To complement its voter registration drive and "get out the vote" strategy, SVREP created a litigation department that could file voting rights lawsuits against local government entities. Velásquez's memorandum to his board explained the need:

> The first sixty-six counties in a row that we investigated . . . were all, in fact, malapportioned and gerrymandered against Chicanos. Almost everything imaginable designed to steal Chicano votes has been thought of by the fertile brains of Texas politicians and actually tried.[38]

In addition to the sixty-six counties in Texas, SVREP research had found fifty-four counties in California that were racially gerrymandered against Mexican Americans. "That's why we didn't win in some cases," said Velásquez. "Redistricting is where they ate our lunch a long time ago." The appropriate federal and state agencies were doing nothing about the situation, and SVREP "was receiving so many complaints about voting abuses that we decided something should be done about it." In conjunction with MALDEF, SVREP filed eighty-five voting rights lawsuits between 1974 and 1984 in Texas alone.[39]

Skeptics of SVREP's "ostensibly unbiased, inclusive approach" were correct to suspect that Velásquez had a more ambitious agenda beyond increasing the Mexican American electorate. As his biographer noted, "Willie also wanted to develop a more progressive Chicano politics, one that unequivocally advanced the interests of working-class Mexican Americans."[40] Ve-

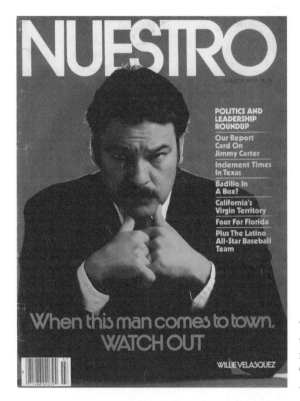

Willie Velásquez on
the cover of *Nuestro*
magazine, March 1979.
Courtesy of George and
Andrea Velasquez.

lásquez insisted that Mexican Americans were "a consistently progressive voting bloc." He was not surprised that West Side voters had not supported the GGL-sponsored Mexican American candidates. As Velásquez put it:

> Mexican Americans know how to vote even on complex bond issues. And we always vote for the betterment of our community even if it means supporting an "Anglo" over a Hispanic candidate. Despite our generally low socioeconomic status, we're remarkably sophisticated voters.[41]

Velásquez wanted to make sure that Mexican Americans had the best information available to them.

The deeper significance behind the simple idea of registering and informing Mexican Americans lay in the influence that Velásquez amassed by creating a regional network of local leaders. As a result of its registration campaigns and litigation efforts, SVREP had developed an extensive network of influential locals in 1,200 organizations in some 130 cities throughout the

Southwest and Midwest. In the early eighties, Velásquez was acting to have this network sponsor public policy forums on issues affecting Hispanics. Plans called for subregional meetings to discuss and formulate public policy positions. Velásquez predicted that key political actors from these 1,200 organizations would participate in these meetings.[42] Sitting at the center of the vast network he had created, Velásquez held the power of communication and persuasion. Clearly nonpartisan did not mean apolitical.

COMMUNITIES ORGANIZED FOR PUBLIC SERVICE

In 1973 Ernie Cortés organized COPS, a parish-based group that would transform the barrios into a potent political force for equitable public services and jobs. Disillusioned with government antipoverty programs, Cortés had left MAUC in 1971 to undergo training at Saul Alinsky's Industrial Areas Foundation (IAF) in Chicago. IAF's pragmatic approach of working on immediate issues and empowering people appealed to Cortés. After a two-year stint with IAF in the Midwest, Cortés returned to San Antonio and approached Father Albert Benavides of Our Lady of Guadalupe Church and other sympathetic Catholic clergy in the West Side. Cortés, Father Benavides, and other early leaders believed that the Catholic parish networks, with deep roots in the neighborhoods, could provide the ideal building blocks for an effective community organization. The parish networks included members of the parish advisory councils and others who ran the festivals and sports programs—the "natural leaders" that Cortés was looking for. Cortés would tap "the hub of community activity within the parish" for the leaders and members of the new organization.[43]

Following Alinsky's "iron rule"—"Never do anything for someone that they can do for themselves"—Cortés listened and learned, like Willie Velásquez, that what concerned the "altar society presidents and Kelly Field workers" were their living conditions and the quality of the schools. With the church's blessing and logistical support, Cortés was able to organize twenty-five local parish chapters on the West and South sides and focus "the accumulated anger and resentment" about the annual flooding of their neighborhoods into collective action. In a remarkably short period of time, COPS would grow to number more than 5,000 members.[44]

Cortés succeeded not only because of his exceptional organizing talent, but also because he had the institutional backing of the Catholic Church. Political scientist Peter Skerry, who studied the organization at length, called this "fully elaborated relationship with the Catholic Church" the most important innovation in IAF organizing. Catholic clergy and nuns oc-

Ernie Cortés (Industrial Areas Foundation) (*left*), Imelda Muñoz (Valley Interfaith) (*center*), and Rebecca Flores (United Farm Workers) at the state capitol, circa 1985. Courtesy of photographer Alan Pogue.

cupied important organizing positions, and nearly all chapters held their meetings in parish halls.[45] Unlike the nationalist stirrings of the Raza Unida Party, a class-based campaign that called for basic neighborhood improvements was a protest that the Catholic Church could support. Deteriorating neighborhoods signified deteriorating parishes. The creation of COPS gave the Catholic Church a means by which to address such deterioration. In general, working- and lower-middle-class Mexican American homeowners "with a clear stake in their parishes" formed the backbone of the organization.[46] And because many of the church activists were women, COPS training resulted in their leadership development, a point I return to later.

While the goals of COPS were the pragmatic, tangible ones of securing better public services, its style initially was that of "hard-nosed confrontation." COPS used the Alinsky "shock and awe" approach in dramatic and aggressive public actions designed to embarrass elected officials into action. Its members disrupted city council meetings with stinging satirical skits and pokes at unresponsive public officials. To get the attention of the business elite, COPS organized "tie-up" actions at banks and department stores—"overwhelming clerks and tellers with a flood of Mexican American customers." And as the COPS activists won tangible victories through their new organizational power, they began to see clearly the connection with "electoral power."[47]

From the beginning, COPS pursued an electoral strategy, registering voters and getting them out on election day. IAF organizer Arnold Graf said that COPS was

> as close to being a local political party as anybody is. We go around organizing people, getting them to agree on an agenda, registering them to vote, interviewing candidates on whether they support our agenda. We're not a political party, but that's what political parties used to do.[48]

By 1975, COPS was an established political force "whose leaders angrily challenged dominant institutions." When COPS demonstrated that it could turn out as many as 50,000 West Side votes on election day, it was able to instill fear among city officials who endured its infamous accountability sessions. In 1976 the *San Antonio Light* recognized COPS as one of the most powerful organizations in the city. "Working-class families looked at COPS with awe," in the words of Cortés's biographer, Mary Beth Rogers, "because for the first time in the history of the city, they had access to its decision-making structure."[49]

After the single-member district system was adopted in 1977, COPS was able to exert considerable influence over the five city council members in whose districts the organization had a presence. COPS, in effect, was able to influence the city's Community Development Block Grant process and direct millions of federal dollars to street improvements, recreational facilities, libraries, and even new private housing. In the ensuing decade, COPS would secure more than $500 million for West and South Side improvements, including storm sewer systems.[50]

The Election of Mayor Henry Cisneros

By the late 1970s, ethnic and class tensions in San Antonio politics had eased. After several years of locking horns over development priorities, COPS and segments of the business community had begun to work together to attract economic investment in inner-city neighborhoods. Henry Cisneros, then in his third term as councilman, had acted as the mediator between the two sides. The setting for a mayoral campaign looked favorable.[51] In the words of political observer John Booth, "the time was ripe" for Mexican American candidates who "could bridge the gap between the demands of COPS, Anglo environmental activists, and at least some factions of the politically active economic elite."[52]

Cisneros entered the 1981 mayoral race with a platform based on a "politics of consensus" and an economic plan that benefited all San Antonians.[53] This appealed to the "new" developers. They liked his thinking about economic development and inclusiveness. Developer Dan Parman, originally from Uvalde, decided to support Cisneros because, frankly, Cisneros represented peace:

> I saw what happened in Crystal City when the Mexican-Americans finally came to power. It was strictly confrontational. The confrontation had been building in San Antonio, and with Cisneros I saw a chance for peace. I liked what he was saying about economic development, and I guess I just believed that theory about a rising tide lifting all boats.[54]

Last-minute attempts by his opponent, millionaire businessman John Steen, to fuel Anglo opposition to Cisneros by linking him to "other, more militant Chicano council members" did not succeed.[55]

On election day, Cisneros won the mayor's race in a landslide with almost 63 percent of the 156,000 votes cast. He won 94 percent of the Mexican American vote, 75 percent of the Black vote, and nearly 40 percent of the Anglo vote. Mexican Americans had a turnout rate of 44 percent, compared to 38 percent for Anglos and 30 percent for African Americans.[56] For the first time in memory, the inner-city wards had outvoted the Anglo North Side.

Campaign manager George Cisneros attributed his brother's election as mayor to voter registration drives and a strong "get out the vote" effort on election day. Some 14,000 new Mexican American voters had been registered in the final months before the election. George Cisneros gave major credit for the success of the registration drives to two organizations: COPS and SVREP.[57] A slightly longer time frame would also trace this success to the gritty campaigns of the Chicano movement—to the challenges of the Committee for Barrio Betterment in 1969 and 1971, and the Raza Unida Party in 1972 and 1974. A thoroughly mobilized Mexican American electorate had provided the basis for the election of Cisneros as mayor in 1981.[58]

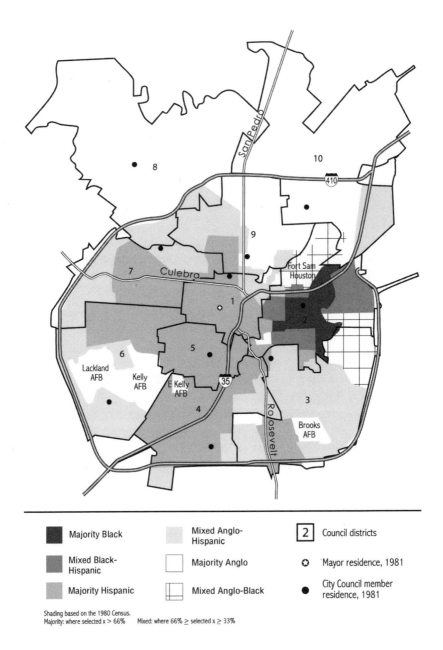

Residential patterns and residences of the mayor and city council members, 1981.

San Antonio City Council, 1981. *Left to right,* Bernardo Eureste, Frank Wing, Helen Dutmer, Joe Webb, Maria Berriozabal, Henry Cisneros, James Hasslocher, Van Henry Archer, G. E. "Ed" Harrington, Joe Alderete, and Bob Thompson. Zintgraff Collection, University of Texas at Austin Institute of Texan Cultures, Z-2156-29924, courtesy of John and Dela White.

Cisneros's philosophy of governance called for "giving everyone a stake by involving everyone—not just in the decision-making, but in the creation of the community ethic." Such an ethic would successfully guide San Antonio as it transitioned "from a city where . . . decisions were made at the Country Club by a handful, to a community where there are multiple power centers and in which successful policy is the outcome of negotiation between those multiple power centers." This meant that the mayor would play the critical role of "arbitrator"—"a mediating person between different centers of power—always with a personal agenda in mind, of course, but leaving that, in some sense, secondary to the process."[59]

Thus Cisneros, first as councilman and later as mayor, was able to bridge the interests of Anglo business and the Mexican American working class. By the 1980s a "coalition system" that featured Anglo business factions and Mexican American citizen groups was in place. "Developing a strong new sense of community unity," in the words of Cisneros's biographers Diehl and Jarboe, may have been his "greatest service" to San Antonio.[60]

The election of Cisneros and the subsequent rise of other Mexican American politicians were visible signs of a fundamental shift in ethnic and class relations in San Antonio. This new political order represented an "understanding," or convergence, between Anglo business interests and those of the Mexican American middle and working classes, with the former seeking support for their economic proposals, and the latter seeking support for their political ambitions. The new order also signaled a shift in gender relations, one highlighted by the entrance of Mexican American women into the political arena as community spokeswomen, candidates, and officeholders. The "grassroots" organizing by SVREP and COPS had created a new cohort of local women leaders, and they, along with several ex–Raza Unida women activists, would become very visible public actors in San Antonio affairs.

EXPORTING THE LESSONS

The success of the second-generation organizations that emerged from the Chicano movement had an impact far beyond the limits of San Antonio. Once the new city council district system was adopted, Cortés left the city to organize similar IAF groups throughout Texas and the Southwest. As with COPS, he relied on Catholic and Protestant church networks to lay the foundation for these community organizations. Within a few years, he had organized Valley Interfaith in the lower Rio Grande Valley, El Paso Interreligious Service Organizations, the Allied Communities of Tarrant (Fort Worth), the Houston Metropolitan Organization, and the United Neighborhood Organizations in Los Angeles. By the mid-eighties, COPS and its affiliates in Texas were exerting statewide influence through coordinated and highly visible civic actions and campaigns. That was the point behind the 1984 press announcement of COPS president Sonia Hernández that the IAF affiliates had registered more than 104,636 citizens "in a non-partisan drive through Texas neighborhoods that have historically had poor voter turnouts." The story about COPS in San Antonio had become, in the words of Mary Beth Rogers, "the story of more than 400,000 men and women who made up the network of Industrial Areas Foundation organizations in Texas." Political scientist Peter Skerry likewise considered COPS to be "the most important political development among Mexican Americans in Texas."[61]

In 1983, after the successful founding of the South-Central Organizing Committee in Los Angeles, Cortés believed the time was ripe for the IAF to expand into California. In his characteristically blunt fashion, he explained to Frank del Olmo that "Until Latinos in Southern California, and everywhere else, learn about political power in this country and how it really operates, the Decade of the Hispanic will be just so many beer commercials." Cortés envisioned establishing IAF organizations "from Stockton to San Diego."[62]

Willie Velásquez's strategic plan was no less ambitious. Although he passed away in 1988 at age forty-four, he lived to see the Southwest Voter Registration Education Project become a nationally recognized nonpartisan political organization. Its success in creating local coalitions of organizations to carry out registration campaigns had created a network that stretched from the Midwest to the Pacific. SVREP was undertaking and publishing its own polling and analyses of relevant policy questions, and it had begun to organize educational forums on the major issues facing the Latino community. Not only was SVREP beginning to intervene in domestic matters, but it had also begun to weigh in on international issues such as U.S.-Mexico trade and Latin American foreign policy. In the 1980s SVREP led several delegations of elected officials to Central America and Cuba on fact-finding tours. At the time of Velásquez's death, SVREP was already planning to move its major operations to Los Angeles. Like Cortés, Velásquez recognized that future organizing efforts had to be directed to California. In Texas, the Latino political machine had been sufficiently primed.

On the Question of Inclusion

In the 1980s the prominence of a Mexican American political presence became a widely accepted fact of life in San Antonio. COPS had become an established feature of the political landscape, relying much less on disruption and more on negotiating. In Skerry's assessment, "The business and political leaders of San Antonio, having initially fought this obstreperous newcomer, have learned not only to tolerate it, but to include it in their deliberations."[63] In short, the West and South Side barrios had been given a seat at the table of power. What did this mean?

Were the barrios better off as a result of the Chicano movement? Or was their inclusion merely an "illusion," as political scientist Rodolfo Rosales has argued?[64] Certainly, on the surface, there has been some progress. San Antonio has a vibrant intellectual and artistic Mexican American presence. Rosales himself, a product of both the West and South sides, is one of many tenured "Hispanic" faculty at the University of Texas at San Antonio, a "Hispanic-serving institution" that did not exist before 1973. Today the university is headed by President Ricardo Romo, another product of the West Side. Nonetheless, this begs the question, as activist intellectual Rudy Acuña put it in 1982:

Progress cannot be measured by how many professionals our community has, or how many judges and ambassadors have been appointed. The bottom line is whether there has been an improvement in the community as a whole. Are there less drugs than in 1968? Are there less gangs? Less Chicanos in prison? Less Chicanos who are functionally illiterate? Less police brutality? Is housing any better today than it was 14 years ago? Is there less unemployment?[65]

Such questions are not easily answered. There may be fewer gangs because there are more drugs; more literacy, but more Chicanos in prison; perhaps more police brutality, but more Chicano police officers, and so forth. The picture may be a complex one of uneven progress.

By the 1980s the barrios of San Antonio were no longer politically isolated. Or, to be more precise, the upper third of barrio society—the upwardly "mobile working class" of Buford Farris's typology—had been integrated into the political process.[66] COPS had organized the church-going, lower-middle-class homeowners with the result that basic city services and amenities, paved streets and sidewalks, flood control, parks, sanitation services, and so forth had been extended to previously neglected sides of town. Cortés's biographer Mary Rogers described the pride of COPS members at their accomplishments:

Today, riding around these districts in San Antonio with one of the women who became a leader in the movement, you are regularly invited to behold and admire the water drainage ditches that were built because people organized. You will also be shown other functioning monuments to people power—paved streets and sidewalks, new housing, an access to the freeway.[67]

Rogers's comment points to another important change brought about by COPS: the development of women's leadership. Although men had been involved in COPS from the beginning, most of the parish leaders who responded to Cortés's entreaties were women. As was the case for most barrio advocacy efforts, the women volunteers formed the backbone of the organization. "The women did most of the research," Rogers noted. "They set up the meetings, made the telephone calls, and got out the vote. They recruited their neighbors and organized their projects."[68] Women were attracted to COPS, Cortés explained, because

Many of the women leaders were real powerhouses in their private families. They had a lot to say about who does what. But that's not enough.
The public side of them didn't get developed because they are invisible
outside of the home. They may have gravitated to leadership in our organization because of the need to develop this aspect of their personality.
We offered them the opportunity.[69]

As a result of their work, women have dominated the powerful and very
visible position of president of COPS. Of the first six presidents, between
1974–1982, five were women. A common story was that of Beatriz Gallego,
from St. James Parish, who joined COPS when her South Side street became
a river during the flood of 1973. She would later serve a two-year term as
president in 1975–1976. Rogers noted that being president of COPS gave
these women

> the opportunity to make presentations before the city council, challenge
> officials at accountability sessions, or be interviewed on television. It was
> a new role for Hispanic women, who, with few exceptions, had never
> become active politically or in the women's movement.[70]

These women were now recognized in San Antonio as political leaders. As
a measure of inclusion, this clearly signified progress.

Less clear is the matter of progress for the bottom two-thirds of barrio society—the "stable working class" and the "maladapted," in Farris's
typology. These barrio residents certainly benefited from improvements to
infrastructure—more parks and sidewalks, better street drainage, and so
forth—and they directly benefited from the employment training programs
and new public housing brought about by COPS's pressure. The expansion
of social service programs during the movement years was another positive
development. Of the twenty-six community service agencies operating in
San Antonio in the mid-seventies, thirteen had been created between 1966
and 1974. Eight were social welfare and training agencies, funded mainly
by federal dollars, and five were advocacy organizations, funded primarily
by foundation monies. The settlement houses were no longer the main institutional provider of social services.[71]

Tangible signs of progress were evident in the Alazan-Apache housing
project in the deep West Side by the early 1980s. Two blocks from the old
Inman Christian Center on Colima Street, the Bexar County Juvenile Probation Department staffed a special Model Cities unit to better serve the neigh-

Table 11.1.
Community Service Agencies by Type, Time of
Establishment, and Funding, 1974

	1900–1950	1951–1965	1966–1974	Funding Sources
Advocacy Organizations	—	2	5	Foundations, Federal Gov't., Businesses
Social Welfare and Training Agencies	—	4	8	Federal Gov't., City Gov't., Foundations
Settlement Houses	5	2	—	Churches, United Way, Foundations

Source: Based on Directory of Community Service,
San Antonio and Bexar County, Texas, May 1974.

borhood. Around the corner from the probation office was the Guadalupe Cultural Arts Center, established with city arts funding as a result of pressure from the district's aggressive councilman, Bernardo Eureste. Now a new cultural center provided a place where Chicano literature, film, music, and dance could be celebrated. Adjacent to the cultural center was a new market place for small vendors and an open-air plaza in front of Our Lady of Guadalupe Church. Here was a public space for fiestas, meetings, and protests as well. Plans for revitalizing more of Guadalupe Avenue, the historic Camino Real, were on the drawing board. The Alazan-Apache neighborhood had become the hub of a cultural and commercial renaissance.

But did these improvements, the result of a new political order, have any impact on gang activity? Political representation and infrastructural improvements may have done little to change the tenuous situation of the "maladapted" families, the social base for delinquency of all types. In the following concluding note, I examine the question of gang activity in the immediate post-movement period. I return, then, to the subject with which I began this local history.

The Irrepressible Hand of Agency

What happened after the Chicano movement petered out in the mid-seventies? There was no immediate resurgence of gang activity, but as noted earlier, there are competing explanations for such absence. I have emphasized the influence of the Chicano movement, but alternative explanations range from the increased institutional presence described above to an increase in "sniffing." Cheap drugs and paint and glue sniffing, rather than movement ideology or social work, may have been the calming agents.

Neither drugs nor institutional presence, however, deterred the rise of gangs in the early 1980s. Interestingly, according to several observers, this renewed gang activity seemed to have no ties with that of the sixties. In other words, a break in the generational passing of gang identities and conflict had in fact occurred. Only the experience of the Chicano movement explains such a rupture.

Unfortunately, the Bexar County Juvenile Department, which took over the juvenile arrest record keeping in 1974, did not keep systematic or consistent records that might measure possible group or gang activity. Newspaper reporting through the late seventies does not mention gang activity. In 1978 an investigative report into the "local kid crime situation" listed shoplifting, vapor sniffing, and vandalism as items of concern. The only mention of gangs is a passing reference by social workers that some minority youth were resurrecting the old "gang culture" by burning symbols into their skin.[72] The local newspapers included no reports of any incidents until the spring of 1980, when troubles erupted at the San Juan Homes.

In response to the newspaper reports, Councilman Eureste said that gang activity in the West Side extended beyond San Juan Homes and that it seemed to have "blossomed" in the recent year, due in part to the fading economy. He warned that "roving youth gangs" were menacing many areas of the city. Fortunately, at this point, he said, "what you have are loosely knit gangs." They did not have "the well-defined structure and organization of the 1950s." But Eureste feared that it was only a matter of time before they acquired such organization.[73]

Although some dismissed Eureste's comments as exaggeration, it appears he knew what he was talking about. Journalist Richard West, writing in 1980 about San Antonio's West Side, had hinted at the loose-knit nature of current gangs compared to those of the fifties. In a *Texas Monthly* feature story, West spoke of a new gang called the "Whistling Warriors" that was vandalizing and burning vacant houses on the West Side: "These boys modeled themselves after the gang in the movie *The Warriors* and used an old barrio gang tactic of stationing members in trees to whistle when police or members of other gangs approached."[74] West named the new gangs whose graffiti had recently appeared on neighborhood walls: the Lords, the Night

The Brown Berets resurfacing, César   Brown Beret at the Alamo, César
Chávez Day March, San Antonio, Texas,   Chávez Day March, San Antonio, Texas,
March 9, 2008. Veteran Beret Victor   March 9, 2008. Photo by author.
San Miguel and immigration activist in
conversation. Photo by author.

Sinners, the Midnight Rats—names with no connections to the West Side's
past. Recently sociologist Avelardo Valdez, noting that San Antonio has
been a "budding gang city" since the mid-1980s, concluded that the gangs
are different from those before the seventies. The earlier gangs had been
linked multigenerationally, similar to the European-American ethnic gangs
described by William Foote Whyte and others.[75]

These observations—that the gangs of the 1980s had a loose structure
and few ties to the past—point to a generational break in the barrio youth
culture of San Antonio. Elders and their stories were not needed for gang
formation. The youths had the capacity to create new ways of being and
thinking, something they had demonstrated in the early seventies when they
had broken away from a legacy of inherited conflict and created the Brown

Berets. In the eighties, in the absence of such a legacy, the batos again demonstrated that they had the capacity to create new ways, or to re-create what appear to be new ways, by forming new gangs and new identities.

In this redrawn landscape, the imprint of the Chicano movement has at times surfaced in the actions of barrio youths. Such seems to have been the case in 1985, in what can only be regarded as a historical instance of déjà vu.

According to the *San Antonio Light*, "squads of Junior Brown Berets," ranging in age from eleven to fourteen, had recently started unarmed patrols at the Alazan-Apache Courts "to protect fearful elderly residents."

> Twenty Junior Brown Berets, some dressed in quasi-military khakis and topped with brown berets, marched to Our Lady of Guadalupe Catholic Church from the West Side housing project at noon yesterday to draw attention to their new organization and its goals.[76]

They carried placards echoing "the group's stance against drugs and in support of Christian beliefs." Father Edward Salazar, pastor of Our Lady of Guadalupe, explained that "One of the concerns we've had are the old folks who have been beat up, their checks stolen and their purses stolen." Cosponsor Jaime Martínez said that misconceptions had led some school officials to falsely label the Junior Brown Berets as troublemakers who were seeking confrontations with authorities. "This is no gang organization," said Martínez.[77]

The Junior Brown Berets planned to expand foot patrols at Plaza Guadalupe, the public park across the street from the church. Group members said they had detained several vandals and burglars for police arrest. They also wanted to paint pictures on dumpsters located around Alazan-Apache Courts. They figured that beautifying the dumpsters might decrease the incidence of fires set by vandals, and they planned to make a formal request before officials of the city's Parks and Recreation Department.[78]

Although these "Junior Brown Berets" explicitly supported Christian beliefs, the Beret veterans of the 1970s would have shaken their heads at the familiarity of the neighborhood setting, which seemed unchanged: the temptation of drugs, the need to protect the elderly, the likelihood of being labeled a gang and of having confrontations with authorities—all this would be familiar. But the idea of Brown Berets as an alternative to gangs, as a legitimate organization that could act as a community patrol to protect and serve the barrio had taken hold in the imagination of some youths. This was a hopeful sign, and a tribute to the memory of the original Berets and the Chicano movement.[79]

More than memories remain, however. For San Antonio, the Chicano movement brought about very real material and political progress for the Mexican American community. Just as important has been the dissemination of the civic culture of engagement that was seeded by movement activism and nurtured by the movement's second-generation progeny. In the early twenty-first century, the Southwest Voter Registration Education Project has an operational presence in all the western states as well as in North Carolina and Florida.[80] COPS has likewise replicated itself throughout the West; this progeny accounts for nearly half of the fifty-six affiliates of Alinsky's IAF network in the country.[81] All of these efforts to empower underrepresented communities can trace some part of their origins and tactics to the history of the Chicano movement in San Antonio, Texas.

THE PRESENT WORK represents an extension and deepening of the class and race-ethnic analysis outlined in my book *Anglos and Mexicans in the Making of Texas, 1836–1986*. Piecing together the local history of a social movement, however, called for some conceptual adjustments in my analytical framework. In *Anglos and Mexicans*, I outlined 150 years of history and ranged over vast parts of the state of Texas. The present narrative unfolded on a very different scale. Here I described a decade and a half and largely confined myself to the barrios of San Antonio. A few times my description ramped down to the block level. Personal relations and networks, rather than economic forces and structures, took the front stage. The language of class and race-ethnicity that had worked well when looking at long sweeps of time and over big swaths of land appeared thin and forced when the observations slowed to a few years and focused tightly on bounded neighborhoods. The adjustments merit some comments. The first is a methodological note on how to study social movements at the ground level. The second is a related comment about what this means for interpreting the Chicano movement as an identity shift. My final note calls for a broader, comparative perspective.

Navigating the Intersections

Unlike the panorama presented in *Anglos and Mexicans*, this local history called for a ground-level examination of politics in one place. Such an examination introduced complex actors, and thus had to recognize a number of attributes that people use to identify themselves and others: class, race-ethnicity, gender, sexual orientation, age or generation, religion, and even place of residence. The historian-sociologist on the ground must deal with the social construction of multiple identities. To complicate matters, a ground-level examination must also keep in mind that the salience of any particular identity will vary according to circumstance and context. In other words, individuals possess an array or hierarchy of identities, and they can invoke or emphasize one identity over another, and even "code switch," depending on circumstance and context.[1]

This notion of multiple identities surfaced from the research itself. Indeed, the ambiguity of the initial farmworker "causa"—whether this was a labor struggle or a race-ethnic civil rights cause—suggested such complex layering from the very beginning. Labor leader César Chávez and playwright Luís Valdez of the Teatro Campesino had different thoughts on the matter, and so the latter, as Carlos Muñoz put it, left the farmworkers' movement "precisely because Chavez did not agree with Valdez's efforts to locate the union in the framework of a Chicano nationalist ideology."[2] The framing of protest activity also helps explain much of the shifting, complex relationship of the Catholic Church with the Chicano movement. For the predominantly Anglo-Irish clergy could support striking farm workers or barrio residents upset about police misconduct, but support for racial-ethnic nationalism was quite another matter.

In a society marked by class and racial-ethnic segregation, appeals to either class or race had the potential to mobilize the Mexican American community, but other identities were also important. The periodic gang warfare in the barrios, for example, made it evident that neighborhood identity and loyalty were the most important markers for many youths. Because perceived neighborhood boundaries delineated a secure living space, place of residence had become a critical element of identity. Gang youths were conscious of their Mexican ethnicity, but this was submerged by neighborhood identities. For a time, the Chicano movement reversed the salience of these. The hierarchy or relative importance of various identities could change as a result of political discussion and work.

Likewise, rather evident class and gender differences within the Chicano movement challenged the view that cultural nationalism was the key that transcended all religious, political, class, and economic boundaries, as proclaimed at the Chicano Youth Liberation Conference of March 1969.[3] Race-ethnic nationalism could obviously coexist with other identities or perspectives.

Recognizing such identity politics did not displace a class framework. Rather, it meant that one had to think creatively about the interaction, or "intersections," of these identities when examining social action. A relaxed class analysis, one that acknowledges that society is organized on bases other than class, allows for multiple subjectivities. The more important question is that of significance.

Age or generation, for example, was certainly part of the mix of identities at play during the late 1960s. The public disagreement that surfaced within the Mexican American community over movement rhetoric and tactics was often portrayed as a generational dispute between stern elders and insolent youths. Noting the age differences added texture to the story but did not alter the central point that the dispute involved a conservative middle class and a restive working class.

In this sense, even the personal idiosyncrasies of individuals, or what we call "personalities," could be seen as adding deep texture to a story about a conflict between the haves and have-nots. To describe Congressman Henry B. Gonzalez as thin-skinned and vindictive, as a proud male, or as a boxer in his youth, for example, did not make his political philosophy any less representative of the Mexican American middle class. Acknowledging these attributes, on the other hand, helps in understanding his aggressive, pugilistic reaction to the Chicano movement.

The various facets of one's complex identity or identities have been described as "multiple locations" and "intersections." These concepts were elaborated by women activists of color who had to deal with their multiple subjectivities and associated contradictions on a daily basis. Chicana activists, attempting to deal with the contradictions, began to speak of multiple sources of oppression and validation and the intersections of class, race, and gender.[4]

Given, then, that a social movement may tap emergent, overlapping, or alternative identities, how can one navigate through the complex intersections? The organizational structure or network of a movement offers the blueprint for the researcher. Movement organizations represent critical signposts because they frequently reflect and emphasize a certain identity among their memberships. One must study the organizational life of a movement—that is, the changing informal and formal organizations and networks that make up a movement community over time. That is one of the key points underlying this narrative: that activists drawn to the race-ethnic appeal of "la causa" in a short time formed organizations based on other identities.

Conversely, which individuals and organizations might be mobilized depended on how an issue, action, or cause was framed or identified. An instructive case lies in the changing relationship of the Catholic Church with Chicano protest activity. The Church played a critical supporting role in the farmworker struggle, but once this struggle ignited the Chicano movement, the predominantly "Anglo" or "Irish" clergy were in no position to take part. Indeed, the nationalist turn of the movement frightened many clergy. Painting the statue of the Virgin Mary a bronze color—the climactic event at one Chicano youth conference—pointed to the tensions between clergy and the increasingly antagonistic youths, but this symbolic act paled before demands that unused Church property be turned over to "the cause." Simply put, the Catholic Church was not in a position to provide logistical support or much moral leadership for an emerging nationalist movement. Ironically, the best students of its school system often emerged as key leaders in the Chicano movement. It would not be until the mid-seventies, as the Chicano movement was fading, that the Church would use its parish network and resources to create an urban political pressure group for community public service.

Organizations, of course, are important because they are the critical linkages between individual agency and a given political environment. Organizations raise and define issues, and facilitate the elaboration of a common perspective or ideology. Organizations also empower and discipline individuals. Indeed, significant changes in identity and behavior generally come not from personal epiphanies or "awakenings," but from collective discussion, learning, and discipline—the stuff of organizational life.

In short, an emphasis on organization was the one clear way of tackling questions of identity formation and group interests. In the case of San Antonio, it was fortunately possible to trace the development of one thick branch of the Chicano movement through a history of the Mexican American Youth Organization (MAYO). MAYO evolved into the Raza Unida Party, spun off the Brown Berets, saw the emergence of women's groups, and laid the groundwork for second-generation organizations such as the Southwest Voter Registration Education Project. These second-generation organizations carried on the objectives of the Chicano movement long after the protests had ceased.

From Ethnicity to Race?

The foregoing methodological note about multiple identities informed my thinking about the Chicano movement as a transformational experience.

The most compelling theme in the literature on the Chicano movement has revolved around the striking fact of a resurgent consciousness and pride in indigenous Mexican identity. Generally this has been framed as a generational dispute—that, basically, the assertion of a Chicano and Chicana identity by the youths repudiated an older generation's claim of "whiteness."

The Chicano movement in this sense signified a dramatic break with the elders: the mestizo youths, insecure about their identity and with little sense of their history, rejected the assimilationist teachings of the older generation and began to reconstruct an indigenous heritage. Thus political scientist Carlos Muñoz places the movement in the context of "the politics of identity," seeing it as a "historic first attempt" to create a politics "on the basis of a nonwhite identity and culture." Historian Lorena Oropeza, in her study of the Chicano anti–Vietnam War movement, speaks of a "revamped racial identity." Legal scholar Haney López makes a similar argument while emphasizing the role of police repression in moving youths to increasing race consciousness.[5] The question of identity, of course, carried some political meaning. As Haney López explains,

> Older Mexican Americans, wedded to the ideals of white identity and assimilation, often shunned any association, actual or metaphorical, with blacks. Young people were more willing to learn from blacks, and this generation became the vanguard of the Chicano movement.[6]

The problem with this emphasis about the elaboration of a racial consciousness is that this experience may have been limited to college students and college-bound high schoolers. Identity was not a major issue for the other components generally thought to make up the Chicano movement: the striking farmworkers in California and Texas, and the rural land grant activists of New Mexico. Likewise, the lower classes of the urban barrios may have never given the question of identity much thought. The students on campuses, on the other hand, seemed to have been taken by Chicano identity issues. Even the formation of the Brown Berets in Los Angeles, which Haney López uses as a prime example of a shift from ethnic identity to racial identity, seems to confirm the college connection.[7]

In this instance, several college-bound youths, organized in 1966 as the Young Citizens for Community Action, within a short period of time metamorphosed to the Young Chicanos for Community Action (1967) and finally to the Brown Berets (1968). This was in large part the result of the police reaction to their peaceful protests. The Los Angeles Sheriff's Department and the Los Angeles Police Department systematically began harassing and intimidating group members and patrons of YCCA's coffee house, La Piran-ya. When YCCA members started wearing brown berets and field jackets to suggest an allegiance with the Black Panthers and the Puerto Rican Young Lords, the East L.A. sheriffs began calling them the Brown Berets. Accord-ing to Beret Gilbert Cruz Olmeda,

> We would hear it because every time they had us up against a wall we'd hear all the radio messages from the patrol cars, "Brown Berets here," "Brown Berets over here," and so then it stuck.[8]

This harassment, as Haney López summarizes it, "helped to shift the YC-CA's identity, driving away some members while further politicizing oth-ers." When the Berets issued their first program, they chose as their motto, "To protect and to serve," a mission statement as well as a satirical dig at the slogan of the Los Angeles Police Department.[9]

The explanation about a switch from ethnic to race consciousness may describe the political evolution of the Young Citizens for Civic Action into the initial Brown Beret organization. The street youths and gang members that the Beret leadership actively recruited as soldiers, however, may have had no need to experience such an identity transformation—or, better stat-ed, their experience might have been different. The Beret youths I inter-viewed generally had no qualms about their race-ethnic identity. Perhaps this certainty came from repeated police harassment, as Haney López has argued. Perhaps it came from the disdain that most segments of the Mexi-can American community directed at them.

What had been more important to the youths had been neighborhood boundaries and loyalties. Being Chicano or "raza" was a taken-for-granted identity, especially in a segregated setting. Chicano identity only became a potent influence once it was revamped with ideas of brotherhood and unity. San Antonio Beret spokesman José Morales put it this way:

> Carnalismo [brotherhood] differed from chicanismo. All the guys had the onda de chicanismo [idea of being Chicano] as kids. We would beat the gringos and raise hell with the perros [dog police], only we didn't think too much . . . and with the years our eyes opened and we began to see that it didn't matter what barrio you're from—that we're all carnales [brothers]."[10]

In this instance, the movement signified not a switch in race-ethnic identity, but rather an empowering redefinition or rearticulation of that identity.

Even when revised in this manner, the emphasis on race-ethnic identity has only modest value as an explanatory framework for the Chicano movement. Movement solidarity, as I have discussed in some detail, was subject to the centrifugal tensions of class and gender experience and interest. In other words, various identity shifts took place during the movement.

Moving Beyond Identity

The Chicano movement marked a fascinating turn in collective self-definition. The rediscovered indigenous consciousness of the Chicano student activists was an important moment in the political history of Mexicans in the United States. Yet the attention to identity should not detract from the fact that the Chicano movement was part of a greater struggle against segregation and discrimination. Ironically, many of the elders who were seen as assimilationist by Chicano youths had led a desegregation movement in the cities in the 1950s. At times identity did not seem to matter when it came to resisting inequality.

If we put identity aside for a moment and focus on the reality of racial segregation, then we can place the Chicano movement in a broader perspective. It can then be seen as part of a national history that stretches back to the early twentieth century when Jim Crow segregation became the "common-sense" solution to the problem of race. Focusing on the experience of segregation also provides the basis for a comparison of the African American and Mexican American civil rights campaigns and strategies.[11] Both communities organized parallel movements that expressed similar goals, experienced similar internal dynamics, and faced similar external forces.

Both the African American and Mexican American civil rights movements can trace their origins to the immediate post–World War II period when returning GIs began to press for first-class citizenship rights. Both movements began as nonviolent protests for civil and labor rights, and both evolved in the mid-sixties into militant, nationalist calls for autonomy. Both movements exposed differences between "gradualists" and "radicals" within their respective communities, but radical activists themselves developed differences over direction, philosophy, and identity. Both had to deal with emerging gender tensions, especially as race-ethnic nationalism became a prominent sentiment and ideology. Both also experienced an aggressive Anglo backlash as well as police harassment, infiltration, and subversion.[12]

Naturally there were differences between the two movements, reflecting the distinct histories and cultures of the African American and Mexican American communities. The New Mexican land grant struggle was a reminder of the nineteenth-century experience of annexation and dispos-session. As cultural nationalists, most Chicano activists drew on Mexican or Mexican American history and culture for inspiration. Nonetheless, the African American civil rights movement, especially in its "black power" phase, profoundly affected the emerging Chicano movement. The Chicano movement was not a "historical coincidence," as one black activist called it, but more an expression of the historical parallels of resistance to racial inequality in this country.[13]

NOTES

INTRODUCTION

1. See, for example, Manning Marable, *Race, Reform and Rebellion: The Second Reconstruction in Black America, 1945–1990* (Jackson: University Press of Mississippi, 1990); Clayborne Carson, *In Struggle: SNCC and the Black Awakening of the 1960s* (Cambridge: Harvard University Press, 1981).

2. See Rodolfo Acuña, *Occupied America: A History of Chicanos*, 5th ed. (New York: Pearson and Longman, 2002); Edward J. Escobar, "The Dialectics of Repression: The Los Angeles Police Department and the Chicano Movement, 1968–1971," *Journal of American History* (March 1993): 1483–1514; Ernesto B. Vigil, *The Crusade for Justice: Chicano Militancy and the Government's War on Dissent* (Madison: University of Wisconsin Press, 1999).

3. See Ignacio García, *United We Win: The Rise and Fall of La Raza Unida Party* (Tucson: MASRC, University of Arizona, 1989); Armando Navarro, *Mexican American Youth Organization: Avant-Garde of the Chicano Movement in Texas* (Austin: University of Texas Press, 1995) and *The Cristal Experiment: A Chicano Struggle for Community Control* (Madison: University of Wisconsin Press, 1998); Juan Gómez-Quiñones, *Chicano Politics: Reality and Promise, 1940–1990* (Albuquerque: University of New Mexico Press, 1990); Juan Gómez-Quiñones, *Mexican Students por la Raza* (Austin: Relampago Books, 1978); Carlos Muñoz, Jr., *Youth, Identity, Power: The Chicano Movement* (Verso, 1989); Ian Haney López, *Racism on Trial: The Chicano Fight for Justice* (Cambridge, MA: Belknap Press, 2003).

4. George Mariscal, *Brown-Eyed Children of the Sun: Lessons from the Chicano Movement, 1965–1975* (Albuquerque: University of New Mexico Press, 2005); Ernesto Chavez, *"¡Mi Raza Primero!" Nationalism, Identity and Insurgency in the Chicano Movement in Los Angeles, 1966–1978* (Berkeley: University of California

Press, 2002); Lorena Oropeza, *Raza Sí! Guerra No! Chicano Protest and Patriotism During the Vietnam War Era* (Berkeley: University of California Press, 2005); Armando Rendón, *The Chicano Manifesto: The History and Aspirations of the Second Largest Minority* (New York: Collier Books, 1971).

5. Acuña, *Occupied America*; Muñoz, *Youth, Identity and Power*; Gómez-Quiñones, *Mexican Students por la Raza*; Haney López, *Racism on Trial*; Navarro, *The Cristal Experiment*.

6. In my previous work, *Anglos and Mexicans in the Making of Texas, 1836–1986* (Austin: University of Texas Press, 1987), I emphasized the interests and actions of the Anglo business elite and the Mexican American middle class in supporting "desegregation." Here I focus on the mobilization of the working-class barrios and describe how it impacted the city's politics. See *Anglos and Mexicans*, 259–287.

7. Louis Mendoza, *Historia: The Literary Making of Chicana and Chicano History* (College Station: Texas A&M University Press, 2001), 245; interview with Juan Maldonado, November 20, 1999. Or as Peter Skerry has put it, San Antonio has been a net exporter of political talent. See Skerry, *Mexican Americans: The Ambivalent Minority* (New York: Free Press, 1993), 119.

8. Skerry, *Mexican Americans*, 176.

9. Author's interview with George Velásquez, February 24, 2002; also author's recollection of Tony, the grocer.

10. For Texas in particular, see José Ángel Gutiérrez, *The Making of a Chicano Militant* (Madison: University of Wisconsin Press, 1998); Juan A. Sepúlveda, Jr., *The Life and Times of Willie Velásquez: Su Voto Es Su Voz* (Houston: Arte Público Press, 2003); Ignacio García, *United We Win: The Rise and Fall of La Raza Unida Party*; Navarro, *Mexican American Youth Organization*; Rodolfo Rosales, *The Illusion of Inclusion: The Untold Story of San Antonio* (Austin: University of Texas Press, 2000); Kemper Diehl and Jan Jarboe, *Henry Cisneros: Portrait of a New American* (San Antonio: Corona Publishing Co., 1985); and the five-part "Henry B. Gonzalez—Conversations with a Congressman" by Ronnie Dugger in *The Texas Observer* (March 28, April 11, May 9, October 17, and December 12, 1980).

11. The papers of Congressman Henry B. Gonzalez, donated to the American History Center of the University of Texas at Austin in 2007, were particularly important for this project.

PART ONE: INTRODUCTION

1. "600 Negroes Flare Up," *San Antonio Light*, March 16, 1966, 1A; "New Violence Erupts in L.A. Negro Section," *San Antonio Light*, March 18, 1966, 6A; "Thousands March in War Protests," *San Antonio Light*, March 27, 1966, 1A, 12A; "Grape Strikers—300 Mile March Ends," *San Antonio Light*, April 11, 1966,

3A; "McKissick Warns of Racial Violence," *San Antonio Light*, May 16, 1966, 1A; "Tension High in Watts Area," *San Antonio Light*, May 20, 1966, 3A.

2. "Gang Link Sought in Shooting," *San Antonio News*, May 30, 1966, news clipping from Eduardo Villarreal's collection. Other news stories about gang violence in the Villarreal collection include: "Shot in Street: S.A. Student Slain," *San Antonio Light*, March 20, 1966; "Boy Held in Shooting," *San Antonio Light*, April 1, 1966; "Youth Is Arrested in Street Slaying," *San Antonio Express & News*, April 1, 1966; "Youths Fire Into House From Auto," *San Antonio Express & News*, April 2, 1966; "Gang Members Tell 'Their' Story," *San Antonio Sun*, May 19, 1966; "Mom Writes Letter to Members of Gangs," *San Antonio Sun*, June 2, 1966; "Police Crash 4 a.m. Teen Party," *San Antonio News*, June 6, 1966; "S.A. Gang of 13 Held in Breakin," *San Antonio Light*, June 6, 1966.

3. Dugger, "Henry B. Gonzalez: Conversations with a Congressman, Part V," 6.

CHAPTER 1

1. Richard A. García, *Rise of the Mexican American Middle Class: San Antonio, 1929–1941* (College Station: Texas A&M University Press, 1991), 314–315. According to the 1970 U.S. Census, the total population of San Antonio was 654,153. Of that, 39.2 percent was Anglo, 52.2 percent was Hispanic, and 7.6 percent was Black.

2. Buford Farris, "A Comparison of Anglo and Mexican-American Stratification Systems in San Antonio, Texas, and Their Effects on Mobility and Intergroup Relations," Ph.D. dissertation, University of Texas at Austin, 1972, 155, 157; see also "Mexican Americans in Texas," a special issue of *The Texas Observer*, December 9, 1966. For the "leaking caste" reference, see Leo Grebler, Joan W. Moore, and Ralph C. Guzman, *The Mexican American People: The Nation's Second Largest Minority* (New York: Free Press, 1970), 322–325.

3. U.S. Commission on Civil Rights, *Hearings Held in San Antonio, Texas, December 9–14, 1968*.

4. Skerry, *Mexican Americans*, 36, 47; Diehl and Jarboe, *Henry Cisneros*, 56.

5. Diehl and Jarboe, *Henry Cisneros*, 71.

6. The nine-member GGL slate included one Mexican American in 1955, and two from 1957 to 1971. Starting in 1964, the slate included one African American. Larry Hufford, "The Forces Shaping San Antonio," *Texas Observer*, April 20, 1984, 24–27; see also David R. Johnson, John A. Booth, and Richard J. Harris, eds., *The Politics of San Antonio: Community, Progress and Power* (Lincoln: University of Nebraska Press, 1983), 23.

7. U.S. Commission on Civil Rights, *Hearings Held in San Antonio*, 288, 294.

8. Albert Peña, "Needed: A Marshall Plan for Mexican-Americans," *Texas Observer*, April 15, 1966, 1, 4.

9. Ibid.

10. See Henry J. Graham, *History of Texas Cavaliers, 1926–1976* (n.d., pvt. printing), 11; Skerry, *Mexican Americans*, 43. In 1994 the Cavaliers, "a private, mostly Anglo club," tripled the number of Hispanics in the organization by admitting four, bringing the total to six. See "Cavaliers Enroll 4 More Hispanics," *San Antonio Express & News*, September 13, 1994, 9A.

11. "Middle class" is a "spongy" concept, since many among the working class feel middle class "in aspiration, hopes, and feelings." Richard García cites a number of variables—education, median salaries, citizenship, urban residence—to indicate that the Mexican American middle class grew between 1950 and 1960 in the Southwest. García, *Rise of the Mexican American Middle Class*, 313, 318.

12. García, *Rise of the Mexican American Middle Class*, 315. Voter turnout increased from 55.7 percent in 1948 to 68.7 percent in 1956 and 87.1 percent in 1964. For the funeral home incident, see Montejano, *Anglos and Mexicans*, 279.

13. See Montejano, *Anglos and Mexicans*, 278–282; García, *Rise of the Mexican American Middle Class*, 314–318.

14. García, *Rise of the Mexican American Middle Class*, 310, 312, 316–318.

15. Ibid., 317. Such conservative reaction had been evident during the late 1930s in opposition to the organizing efforts of Emma Tenayuca.

16. Peña argued that "The poor mexicanos can expect little help from this oligarchy. What is needed is a massive crash program, federally sponsored, that can break the vicious cycle of illiteracy, slum housing, disease, and unemployment." Peña, "Needed: A Marshall Plan," 1, 4.

17. Cited by Peña, "Needed: A Marshall Plan," 1.

18. Herbert Calderón, letter to the editor, "Not Needed: Mr. Peña," *Texas Observer*, May 13, 1966, 16.

19. Ibid.

20. García, *Rise of the Mexican American Middle Class*, 253–299.

21. Guillermo Hernández noted that the image of the pachuco was reduced to a few features: an argot, a stylized zoot suit, and unconventional behavior. Pachucos were also seen as juvenile delinquents, a feature emphasized by their detractors. Although Hernández spoke of Los Angeles, his comments could easily have been extended to San Antonio. See Hernández, *Chicano Satire: A Study in Literary Culture* (Austin: University of Texas Press, 1971), 21–22.

22. Octavio Paz, *The Labyrinth of Solitude* (New York: Grove Press, 1961), 14, 16.

23. "Spanish-Surnamed American Employment in the Southwest," Equal Employment Opportunity Commission, May 28, 1970; the next poorest city in the country was El Paso.

24. The barrios had been greatly underrepresented on the city council, with only two councilmen in the period 1955–1973 having lived on the West or South sides of town. Rodolfo Rosales, "A Case Study of the Mexican American Unity Council," master's thesis, Trinity University, San Antonio, Texas, 1972, 1–9, 12.

25. "Spanish-Surnamed American Employment in the Southwest," U.S. Equal Employment Opportunity Commission (Washington, D.C.: U.S. Government Printing Office, 1970); Sister Frances Jerome Woods, *The Model Cities Program in Perspective: The San Antonio, Texas, Experience* (Washington, D.C.: U.S. Government Printing Office), 51.

26. See Charles L. Cotrell, *Municipal Services Equalization in San Antonio, Texas: Explorations in "Chinatown,"* Southwest Urban Studies Series, Vol. 2, St. Mary's University, 1976, 16.

27. Ibid., 7–8, 23, 25. For photos of flooding, impassable streets, and lack of street and curb improvements, see U.S. Commission on Civil Rights, *Hearings Held in San Antonio*, 1145–1152.

28. These three neighborhoods essentially captured the diversity of the West and South sides of San Antonio. Buford Farris and Richard Brymer, "A Five Year Encounter with a Mexican-American Gang: Its Implications for Delinquency Theory," paper read at the April 16, 1965, meeting of the Southwestern Sociological Association. See also Buford E. Farris, Jr., and Richard Brymer, "Types of Families in Poverty Areas," Wesley Community Centers Youth Research Project, May 1967.

29. Buford E. Farris, Jr., William M. Hale, and Gilbert Murillo, "The Settlement House: Caretakers, Revolutionists, or Reluctant Social Reformers?" paper presented at the National Conference of Social Welfare, Dallas, May 1967, 8.

30. Ibid., 9.

31. Ibid.

32. The Sherifs, who were doing fieldwork in San Antonio in 1959, were struck as they drove from the high- and middle-rank neighborhoods to low-rank area by "the decreasing importance of the well-kept lawn and the appearance of flower gardens surrounded by bare dirt, in an 'Old Country' manner." Carolyn W. Sherif, "Self Radius and Goals of Youth in Different Urban Areas," *Southwestern Social Science Quarterly*, Vol. 42, No. 3 (December 1961): 261–262; also see Muzfer Sherif and Carolyn W. Sherif, *Reference Groups: Exploration into Conformity and Deviation of Adolescents* (New York: Harper and Row, 1964).

33. Sherif and Sherif, *Reference Groups*, 203–204, 227.

34. Buford E. Farris, Jr., and William M. Hale, "Responsible Wardheelers: Neighborhood Workers as Mediators," unpublished paper presented at the National Conference of Social Welfare, Chicago, May 1966, 7, 9.

35. Among these first-generation college students—Willie and George Velásquez, Ernesto Cortés, Rosie Castro, and Willie Benavidez, to mention a few key figures—the Chicano movement would find fertile ground. See also Rosales, *Illusion of Inclusion*, 122.

36. See Janie Salinas Farris, "A Study of Socio-Cultural Factors in 573 Case Records of Juvenile Delinquents in Bexar County, Texas," master's thesis, Worden School of Social Service, Our Lady of the Lake College, San Antonio, TX, 1962, p. 75.

37. Ben Guajardo interview, April 30, 2004; Richard West, "An American Family," *Texas Monthly* (March 1980): 169; Raúl Valdez, "The Writing on the Wall," Good Samaritan Center, unpublished paper, 1968.

CHAPTER 2

1. This observation is based on Eduardo Villarreal's collection of newspaper clippings as well as my own survey of San Antonio newspapers. "S.A. Opens War on Youth Gangs," *San Antonio News*, January 4, 1956; "Mysterious Shots Hit Second Boy," *San Antonio News*, January 4, 1956; "S.A. Gangs Ride High: Kid Thugs Have Murder and Mayhem in Their Hearts," *San Antonio News*, April 3, 1958; "Who's to Blame for Juvenile Delinquency? We Are, That's Who!" *San Antonio News* op-ed, May 13, 1959; "Behave or Be Jailed, Young Hoods: Ultimatum for Young Hoodlums," *San Antonio News*, March 18, 1960; "200 Hoods Prowl in Dozen Gangs," *San Antonio News*, April 26, 1960; "Youth Shot in Head Dies," *San Antonio Express*, May 28, 1962; "Youth Wounded in Café Shooting," *San Antonio Express*, September 24, 1962; "Shooting Victim Dies," *San Antonio Express*, December 17, 1962; "Frustration Labeled Key in Delinquency: New York Plan Told," *The Houston Post*, June 3, 1962; "Two S.A. Youths Shot," *San Antonio Light*, July 15, 1963; "S.A. Father Gets 99-Year Term in Gang Slaying," *San Antonio Express*, October 16, 1963.

2. West, "An American Family," 169.

3. Ibid. See also Woods, *The Model Cities Program in Perspective*, 51. The accounts of West and Woods owe much to the observations of Raúl Valdez. See Valdez, "The Writing on the Wall."

4. Carolyn W. Sherif, "Self-Radius and Goals of Youth in Different Urban Areas," 261–262. Also see Sherif and Sherif, *Reference Groups*.

5. Farris and Hale, "Responsible Wardheelers," 6; Farris and Brymer, "Five Year Encounter," 2. Gideon Sjoberg was an associate professor in the Sociology Department at the University of Texas at Austin, while Farris and Brymer, both UT doctoral candidates, carried out fieldwork at the Wesley Community Centers of San Antonio. Also see Ronnie Dugger, "To Work with the Poor," *The Texas Observer* (June 10, 1966), 1–6.

6. Good Samaritan Center, "Outline for In-Service Training Seminar," typescript, 1967. Valdez, "The Writing on the Wall," 50–59.

7. Ibid. After a conversation with two Ghost Town members suspected of making bombs, social worker Raúl Valdez noted the increasingly lethal weaponry of gang youth, developing over the years from rocks and knives to handguns and shotguns. Valdez, "The Writing on the Wall," 48–59.

8. Interview with Mike Bustamante, January 6, 1975. The map showing gang territories was created with help from Ben Guajardo and Darío Chapa, interviewed April 30, 2004.

9. "S.A. Student Slain," *San Antonio Light,* March 20, 1966; "Youth Is Arrested in Street Slaying," *San Antonio Express & News,* April 1, 1966.

10. "Youths Fire Into House From Auto," *San Antonio Express,* April 2, 1966; also "Gang Link Sought in Shooting," *San Antonio News,* May 30, 1966.

11. "Mom Writes Letter to Members of Gangs," *San Antonio Sun,* June 2, 1966.

12. "Police Crash 4 a.m. Teen Party," *San Antonio Express & News,* June 6, 1966; "SA Gang of 13 Held in Breakin," *San Antonio Light,* June 6, 1966.

13. Valdez, "The Writing on the Wall," 47.

14. Good Samaritan Center, "Outline for In-Service Training Seminar," 2.

15. Ruiz Ibáñez, "Gang Members Tell 'Their' Story," *San Antonio Sun,* May 19, 1966, clipping from Villarreal's collection.

16. Ibid.

17. Ibid.

18. Ibid.

19. Speaking of the lower Rio Grande Valley of Texas, anthropologist Arthur Rubel pointedly described the palomilla, or male friendship group, as machista and dysfunctional for family stability, because the family "interferes with the more manly activities" of the palomilla. Celia S. Heller, *Mexican American Youth: Forgotten Youth at the Crossroads* (New York: Random House, 1966), 76; Arthur Rubel, *Across the Tracks: Mexican-Americans in a Texas City* (Austin: Hogg Foundation for Mental Health, 1966), 107.

20. Iscoe studied three groups (fifty Anglo, fifty Latin American, and fifty Latin American delinquents from Laredo, Texas, divided equally between twelve-year-olds and seventeen-year-olds) in the mid-sixties. Ira Iscoe, "The Ethnic Preferences of Anglo, Latin-American, and Latin-American Juvenile Delinquents as Determined by Choice of Proper Names," unpublished paper, circa 1968.

21. Ibid., 4.

22. Ibid., 8.

23. Idel Bruckman, "Psychological Problems Involved for the Mexican-American in His Choice of Occupation," preliminary report, Southwest Educational Laboratories, Austin, TX, February 24, 1968.

24. Ibid., 3.

25. The Sherifs, with support from the Hogg Foundation for Mental Health, conducted an extensive comparative study of youth groups in San Antonio and Oklahoma City in the late 1950s and early 1960s. In San Antonio they obtained samples of 81 "High Rank Anglos," 113 "Middle Rank Anglos," 56 "Middle Latins," and 127 "Low Rank Latins." The median age was fifteen years, eleven months. Sherif and Sherif, *Reference Groups,* 199–200.

26. Ibid., 203–204, 227.

27. The highest degree of solidarity was found in groups that were the only locus of pleasurable activity, the only source of personal recognition, and the

only basis for stable relationships and a clear personal identity for its members. Ibid., 197, 240; see also C. Sherif, "Self-Radius and Goals of Youth," 269.

28. Sherif and Sherif, *Reference Groups*, 227–229.

29. Ibid., 227.

30. Ibid., 228–229.

31. With regard to avoiding conflict, a group worker recounted a somewhat humorous incident. Once when the group worker treated Los Apaches to a drive-in movie, the treat was almost ruined when they spotted members of a hostile group between them and the washroom. "For the entire intermission, they stayed in the car discussing strategies of how to use washroom facilities without making contact with the other group." Ibid., 231.

32. Farris and Brymer, "A Five Year Encounter," 1.

33. Farris and Brymer cite Herbert Gans's "urban villagers" as their model (3–4). See also Farris, Hale, and Murillo, "The Settlement House," 17; Gideon Sjoberg, Richard A. Brymer, and Buford Farris, "Bureaucracy and the Lower Class," draft ms., February 1, 1966, published in *Sociology and Social Research* (April 1966). One of the interesting aspects of Wesley-based research among lower-class Mexican Americans in San Antonio "points to the critical role of bureaucratic organizations in sustaining social stratification."

34. Farris and Brymer, "Five Year Encounter," 2–3, 6.

35. The ward-heeler notion was clearly not a new idea, but it stood in contrast with the dominant clinical approach that positioned the social worker as a "therapist" working to change the problematic behavior of the client. Farris and Hale, "Responsible Wardheelers," 3–5; see also Farris, Hale, and Murillo, "The Settlement House," 2, 10, 16.

36. Farris and Hale, "Responsible Wardheelers," 3.

37. Farris, Hale, and Murillo, "Settlement House," 14; Farris and Brymer, "Five Year Encounter," 4. Applying "street corner social work" to curb juvenile delinquency and gang activity, while not a new approach in other cities, was innovative for San Antonio. See Eduardo Villarreal, "A Study of Group Processes in Two Small Natural Groups of Latin-American Adolescents," master's thesis, Worden School, Our Lady of the Lake College, San Antonio, TX, 1962, 70.

38. Interview with Jesse Sauceda, May 25, 1974; Rosales interview with Mariano Aguilar, March 15, 1993.

39. Interview with Eduardo Villarreal, January 7, 1975.

40. Ibid.

41. Interview with Mike Bustamante, January 6, 1975. His observation was confirmed by ex-gang members.

42. Like the Ghost Town, the Alto and Las Palmas gangs were also made up of various subgroups that played different roles: "Some are the instigators, others are the backers, and some defend the area when things get hard on the smaller, younger subgroups." Roy Valdez, "Writing on the Wall," 11, 57–59; Ronnie Dugger, "To Work With the Poor," 4.

43. These institutional representatives included "teachers, principals, police officers, lawyers, judges, district attorneys, probation officers, pool-hall operators, labor union officials, welfare workers, bondsmen, public health nurses and doctors, and employers." Labeling theory was obviously relevant. Farris and Hale, "Responsible Wardheelers," 6–7, 9; Farris and Brymer, "Five Year Encounter," 5.

44. Interview with Villarreal, January 7, 1975; interview with Bustamante, January 6, 1975; Farris and Brymer, "Five Year Encounter," 4.

45. By 1974, Ernesto Gómez could write that a "central tenet" for barrio organizers was that Chicanos live as "an oppressed people within the context of a dominant Anglo society" and the "central principle" for barrio organization was to work toward "self-determination." Chicano social workers had obviously come a long way from the mediator and ward-heeler notions of social work. Gómez, "The Barrio Professor," 9.

46. Interviews with Gene Vasques, October 29, 1974; Ernie García, November 15, 1974; Juan Guajardo, April 7, 1975; Colegio Jacinto Treviño class discussion, October 31, 1974.

47. Interview with Arturo Delgado, November 16, 1974.

48. Interview with Frank García, December 7, 1974.

49. Ibid.

50. Interviews with Lalo Martínez, August 11, 1974, April 2, 1975; Carlos Garza, April 1, 1975; "Sancudo" (aka David Martínez), August 11, 1974.

51. Interview with Sancudo, August 11, 1974.

52. According to Mike Bustamante, "In the early sixties, there was no such thing as 'the Circle,' but congeries or small groups. . . . There were five general families in the South Side. El Circle was organized around these." Interview with Bustamante, January 6, 1975.

53. Java could identify South Side middle schools by the various barrio territories they served: "At Harris there were like four barrios, at Taft there were several barrios, and at Harlendale where many Anglos went . . . there were three barrios of Chicanos." Conversation during my Jacinto Treviño class, October 31, 1974.

54. Interview with Colorado, November 30, 1974.

55. Interview with Frank García, December 7, 1974.

56. Jacinto Treviño class discussion, October 31, 1974.

57. Interview with Lalo Martínez, April 2, 1975.

58. Interview with Ernie García, November 15, 1974.

59. Interview with Gene Vasques, October 29, 1974.

60. Ibid.

61. Farris and Brymer, "Five Year Encounter," 4. The classic work on barrio gangs argues that gangs were a substitute for family and identity formation. See Joan W. Moore, with Robert García, Carlos García, Luis Cerda, and Frank Valencia, *Homeboys: Gangs, Drugs, and Prisons in the Barrios of Los Angeles* (Phila-

delphia: Temple University Press, 1978); James Diego Vigil, *Barrio Gangs: Street Life and Identity in Southern California* (Austin: University of Texas Press, 1988); and Ruth Horowitz, *Honor and the American Dream: Culture and Identity in a Chicano Community* (New Brunswick, NJ: Rutgers University Press, 1983).

62. Interview with Lalo Martínez, April 2, 1975.

63. For use of "social world," see Horowitz, *Honor and the American Dream*. These reflections suggest the island metaphor chosen by sociologist Martín Sánchez-Jankowski to describe the isolated, self-sufficient gangs that formed like social archipelagos in an urban landscape. See *Islands in the Street: Gangs and American Urban Society* (Berkeley: University of California Press, 1991). For his argument that gangs are rational, Sánchez-Jankowski received the Robert E. Park prize from the American Sociological Association.

64. Ruiz Ibáñez, "Gang Members Tell 'Their' Story," *San Antonio Sun*, May 19, 1966.

CHAPTER 3

1. Interview with Ernie García, November 15, 1974; interview with Jesse Sauceda, Guadalupe Community Center, May 25, 1974.

2. As cited by Lorena Oropeza, *Raza Si! Guerra No! Chicana Protest and Patriotism During the Vietnam War Era* (Berkeley: University of California Press, 2005), 67.

3. Interview with Eduardo Villarreal, January 7, 1975; interview with Mike Bustamante, January 6, 1975.

4. Colegio Jacinto Treviño class discussion, October 31, 1974.

5. Cited in Wilson McKinney, *Fred Carrasco: The Heroin Merchant* (Austin, TX: Heidelberg Publishers, 1975), 19.

6. Interview with Lalo Martínez, April 1–2, 1975. Veteran social worker Villarreal believed that car ownership was a big key to calming the conflict between clicas. The lack of transportation before had been severe, and was made more pressing by segregation. In a similar vein, social worker Ernie Gómez suggested that if you made the West Side into an island, that the clicas would start again: "now the barrios are not so isolated like before." Interview with Ernesto Gómez, November 12, 1974; interview with Eduardo Villarreal, January 7, 1975.

7. Interview with Juan Guajardo, April 7, 1975.

8. Rodolfo Rosales interview with Alicia Martínez, September 21, 1992; cited by Rosales, *Illusion of Inclusion*, 110–111.

9. "Mexican-American Leaders Hold a Summit Conference," *Texas Observer*, January 20, 1967, 11–12; Armando Rendón, *The Chicano Manifesto: The History and Aspirations of the Second Largest Minority* (New York: Collier Books, 1971), 133; see also Navarro, *Mexican American Youth Organization*, 98, 106, 109.

10. Interviews with George Velásquez, April 5, 1975, and Mario Compean, April 20, 1974.·See also Sepúlveda, *The Life and Times of Willie Velásquez*, 44–49; Gutiérrez, *The Making of a Chicano Militant*, 99–102. During his senior year at Edgewood, 1965–1966, Compean read about the Delano strike in 1965 and got together with organizer Eugene Nelson when he came to Texas. He campaigned for Joe Bernal in 1966. He met José Ángel in the spring of 1967 at a university picnic.

11. Gutiérrez, *The Making of a Chicano Militant*, 103; Navarro, *Mexican American Youth Organization*, 86, 153.

12. Interview with Compean, April 20, 1974; Luz Gutiérrez cited by Navarro, *Mexican American Youth Organization*, 150–151. As political scientist Armando Navarro has detailed, MAYO sought to give the pachuco, or gang member, a cause that would displace gang rivalry and violence.

13. Leo Cardenas, "The Impatient New Breed Wants a Change—Now," *San Antonio Express*, April 14, 1969, 1A, 12A.

14. Saul Alinksy was a community organizer who advocated dramatic but nonviolent acts that would embarrass power holders. Dumping trash in front of city hall to protest unsanitary neighborhood conditions is a classic example of such action. See Saul David Alinsky, *Rules for Radicals* (New York: Vintage Books, 1971), 127–130; Navarro, *Mexican American Youth Organization*, 85, 97–103.

15. Kemper Diehl, "Lanier Student Walkout Hinted," *San Antonio News*, April 10, 1968, 2A. U.S. Commission on Civil Rights, *Hearings Held in San Antonio*, 190–193; "Walkout in Crystal City," *Texas Observer*, January 2, 1970, 5–7; Navarro, *Mexican American Youth Organization*, 99; Gutiérrez, *The Making of a Chicano Militant*, 142; Sepúlveda, *The Life and Times of Willie Velásquez*, 69–71; Rosales, *Illusion of Inclusion*, 108.

16. Initially, under the directorship of Willie Velásquez, MAUC's strategy was to encourage and coordinate the many fragmented efforts of various barrio organizations through minigrants and technical assistance. Although the minigrants consisted of only a few thousand dollars, the wide-ranging funding pattern meant that the Unity Council "came to be seen as a militant, hell-raising organization confronting city hall and other institutions as advocates on different issues." Rosales, "A Case Study of the Mexican American Unity Council," 28; Cardenas, "The Young Activists Lean Heavily on Grants," *San Antonio Express*, April 15, 1969, 1A, 18A; Navarro, *Mexican American Youth Organization*, 155.

17. Interview with Jesse Sauceda, May 25, 1974.

18. Ibid.

19. Interview with Juan Guajardo, April 7, 1975.

20. Interviews with Lalo Martínez, August 11, 1974; David Martínez, August 11, 1974; and Frank García, December 7, 1974.

21. Interview with Sauceda, Guadalupe Community Center, May 25, 1974.

22. "VISTA was a good funding source for Good Sam," recalled Mario Compean. Jesse Guzman and Janie Velásquez were also among the paid organizers for San Antonio. Interview with Compean, April 20, 1974; Rosales interviews with Aguilar, March 13, 1993, and Compean, January 23, 1993.

23. Interview with Sauceda, May 25, 1974.

24. Anonymous, *El Rebozo* (San Antonio, Texas), November 1969, 4.

25. "Confidential File of Father John Yanta," Henry B. Gonzalez Collection, Box SRH, Scrapbook, 1966–1969, Center for American History, University of Texas at Austin. There was tension between Yanta's poverty agency, SANYO, and movement-inspired community organizing. Father Yanta noted that "The Mexican American Neighborhood Civic Organization (MANCO) was started by three disgruntled Good Sam employees—Mariano Aguilar, Jesse Sauceda, and Roy Valdez, founder." Other principals behind such "radical" social work were Mike Bustamante and Gil Murillo, former Wesley employees.

26. "MAYO Pressure Social Workers' Meet" and "Workshop Chairman Chaired by Militants," *San Antonio Express*, September 19, 1969, 19D; "Barrios Demand Program Reins," *San Antonio Light*, September 20, 1969, in Gonzalez Collection, Box 127/64. MAYO objected to the newspaper coverage of their demands: "todo contrario a lo que se reportó en el periódico, este grupo presentó estas demandas de buena fe y *sin violencia*" (contrary to what the newspaper reported, this group presented the demands in good faith and *without violence*) (emphasis in original). "Qué es el Chicano Caucus?" *El Rebozo*, November 1969, 4.

27. Interview with Mario Compean, April 20, 1974; Rosales interview with Compean, January 23, 1993.

28. In Navarro, *Mexican American Youth Organization*, 154.

29. Letter from Father Yanta, February 19, 1969, in Gonzalez Collection, Box SRH, Scrapbook, 1966–1969. The initial grant proposals of Barrios Unidos, despite their references to "grass roots," were fairly traditional outreach programs fashioned after "the Chicago YMCA method," which held "that youths join gangs to seek recognition and status." The radical streak that would worry middle-class Mexican Americans and other San Antonians would come from MAYO. See Mexican American Neighborhood Civic Organization, "A MANCO Proposal to Model Cities Project," San Antonio, typescript, circa 1968.

30. Rosales interview with Mariano Aguilar, March 13, 1993; see also Rosales, *Illusion of Inclusion*, 118–121.

31. See Supplementary Report, San Antonio Police Department (SAPD) Intelligence, January 3, 1969, in Gonzalez Collection, Box SRH, Scrapbook, 1966–1969.

32. Ironically, the rift within the MAYO founding group would be exacerbated by the creation of MAUC. In the end, Velásquez pursued a "third way" with his Southwest Voter Registration Education campaign. See Sepúlveda, *The Life and Times of Willie Velásquez*, 57, 66, 73–74, 77, 101–102.

33. La Universidad de los Barrios (LUB) grant proposal, typescript, February 1970. The proposal was apparently the handiwork of Willie Velásquez. See Sepúlveda, *The Life and Times of Willie Velásquez*, 101.

34. Ibid.

35. Ibid.

36. There are monthly minutes from October 1968 through December 1970, but the minutes of each meeting consist of only of a page or two.

37. The La India gang territory was the area between Poplar Street on the north and Martin Street on the south. LUB minutes, October 21, 1968.

38. LUB minutes, November 25, December 30, 1968.

39. See Supplementary Report, SAPD, Homicide Investigation, 1-11-69, in Gonzalez Collection, Box SRH, Scrapbook, 1966–1969, Center for American History, University of Texas at Austin.

40. Ibid.

41. Ibid.

42. LUB minutes, January 14, 1969.

43. "Slaying at 'Barrio U,'" *San Antonio News*, January 15, 1969, 17A, in Yanta "confidential file," Gonzalez Collection, Box SRH, Scrapbook, 1966–1969.

44. LUB minutes, February 24, 1969.

45. Interview with Mario Compean, April 20, 1974.

46. The VISTA volunteers had participated in the protest of a no-bill decision by a grand jury regarding a highway patrolman who had beaten an Uvalde couple. See Navarro, *Mexican American Youth Organization*, 160–168; "Del Rio 'Manifesto,' March Slated Today," *San Antonio Express*, March 30, 1969, 2A.

47. Ibid., 1A, 2A. The ordinance was similar to the Birmingham, Alabama, ordinance struck down by the U.S. Supreme Court as unconstitutional. See Sepúlveda, *The Life and Times of Willie Velásquez*, 78–81; also Navarro, *Mexican American Youth Organization*, 161–162.

48. "Del Rio 'Manifesto,' March Slated Today," *San Antonio Express*, March 30, 1969, 1A, 2A.

49. "Castroites in March, HBG Says," *San Antonio Express*, March 29, 1969, 10A.

50. See "Controversy Over VISTA Continues," *San Antonio Express*, April 10, 1969, 19A; "Del Rio Mayor Hits Outside Organizers," *San Antonio Express*, March 29, 1969, 10A; also "Texas' Sleeping Giant—Really Awake This Time?" special issue of *The Texas Observer*, April 11, 1969.

51. "Castroites in March, HBG Says," *San Antonio Express*, March 29, 1969, 10A.

52. Congressman Gonzalez had no information about Cuban influence at the time of his allegations. A memo to Gonzalez from staffer Kelsay Meek dated "28 March 1969" regarding "Militant action" reads as follows:

I asked House Internal Security chief counsel Nittle to check into Cuban subsidies of student travel. No specific investigation has been made but available material is being assembled and hopefully will be delivered to you Monday.

Gonzalez Collection, Box SRH, Scrapbook, 1966–1969.

53. Twenty years after the Del Rio march, Albert Peña was still stunned: "I don't know what possessed him. I don't know why he did it. Joe Bernal, Matt García, Dr. [Hector] García, LULAC, were all there. Of course they were all put out about it. I made the speech with the theme, "'Are you with me, Henry B.?'" Dugger, "Henry B. Gonzalez: Conversations with a Congressman, Part V," 8.

54. Interview with Mario Compean, April 20, 1974.

55. Ibid.; Rosales, *Illusion of Inclusion*, 99–100, 118–121; Sepúlveda, *The Life and Times of Willie Velásquez*, 77.

56. Rosales interviews with Mario Compean, January 23, 1993, and Mariano Aguilar, March 13, 1993.

57. LUB minutes, 1968–1970.

58. "Max Troops Reach Alamo," *San Antonio Express*, April 2, 1969, 8A, 8E. The Maverick County Historical Society wrote in support of the Daughters of the Republic of Texas: "That precious bit of hallowed soil should never be subjected to the whims of sordid uses of the decadent and degenerate film industry." "Daughters Get Support," *San Antonio Express*, March 30, 1969, 2A.

59. "Max Troops Reach Alamo," *San Antonio Express*, April 2, 1969, 8A, 8E.

60. *El Deguello* (San Antonio), February 1969, 2.

CHAPTER 4

1. U.S. Congress, House, Congressman Gonzalez speaking on "The Hate Issue," 22 April 1969, *Congressional Record*, H 2928–2930.

2. Dugger, "Henry B. Gonzalez: Conversations with a Congressman, Part V," 6; also see Julian Samora, Joe Bernal, and Albert Peña, *Gunpowder Justice: A Reassessment of the Texas Rangers* (Notre Dame, Indiana: University of Notre Dame Press, 1979).

3. Interviews with George Velásquez, April 5, 1975, February 24, 2002; typescript of meeting at Cooper Junior High, December 12, 1968, in Yanta "confidential file," Gonzalez Collection, Box SRH, Scrapbook, 1966–1969, Center for American History, University of Texas at Austin.

4. See Supplementary Report, SAPD Intelligence, January 3, 1969, Gonzalez Collection, Box SRH, Scrapbook, 1966–1969. Among the "intel" reports in Gonzalez's scapbook were a copy of José Ángel Gutiérrez's master's thesis on "La Raza and Revolution" and a Pentagon report on Gutiérrez's military status.

5. U.S. Congress, House, Congressman Gonzalez speaking on "Foundation Responsibility," April 16, 1969, *Congressional Record*, H 2734.

6. See, for example, Henry B. Gonzalez, "Hope and Promise: Americans of Spanish Surname," *AFL-CIO American Federationist,* June 1967, 13–16

7. The *Texas Observer,* as cited in *Southern Patriot* (New Orleans), Vol. 15, No. 5 (May 1957); Chris Anglim, "Remembering San Antonio's Champion of Equality—Henry B. Gonzalez (1916–2000)," *The Scholar: St. Mary's Law Review on Minority Issues,* Vol. 3, No. 1 (Fall 2000): 2–40.

8. García, *Rise of the Mexican American Middle Class,* 312.

9. Paul Thompson, "Top of News," *San Antonio Express & News,* April 27, 1969, 1A; included in the *Congressional Record-House,* E 3937.

10. The honorary cochairs were Congressman Gonzalez and Mayor McAllister. See the HemisFair 1968 World's Fair Archives, Institute of Texas Cultures, University of Texas at San Antonio. Also see Hufford, "The Forces Shaping San Antonio," 24–27.

11. Interview with George Velásquez, February 24, 2002.

12. Indeed Willie had once dated Gonzalez's daughter, Rosemary. Sepúlveda, *The Life and Times of Willie Velásquez,* 55–56, 82–83; Dugger, "Henry B. Gonzalez: Conversations with a Congressman, Part V," 6.

13. Dugger, "Henry B. Gonzalez: Conversations with a Congressman, Part V," 6.

14. Ibid., 7.

15. Gonzalez felt that the CBS special was deliberate sabotage. Later, in May 1969, when the House Appropriations Committee concluded in its investigation that CBS had used "sensational-type material" and "contrived drama" to "inflame the nation," Gonzalez raised the possibility of legal action against CBS to recover damages caused to HemisFair. See U.S. Congress, House, July 31, 1968, "Hunger in America?" *Congressional Record-House,* H 7951–7954; also May 27, 1969, "Fraud in America," *Congressional Record-House,* H 4228–4229.

16. At the San Antonio hearings of the U.S. Commission on Civil Rights, Father Ralph Ruiz of Guadalupe Church provided compelling testimony about FBI interrogations of poor families in his parish. Peña decried the interrogations as "police state tactics." In response, Gonzalez accused the commission of hiring key witnesses. See U.S. Commission on Civil Rights, *Hearings,* 801–802, 1118; U.S. Congress, House, "Questions for the Commission on Civil Rights," May 26, 1970, *Congressional Record-House,* H 4807.

17. "Gonzalez Militants' Target," *San Antonio Express,* March 31, 1969, 1.

18. Interview with George Velásquez, February 24, 2002.

19. Cardenas, "The Impatient New Breed," 1A, 12A. Journalist Cardenas concluded his series of articles about "Chicano 1969" by saying that the siesta was over as far as the Chicano was concerned. Also see Rodolfo Acuña, *Occupied America: A History of the Chicanos* (New York: Longman, 2002), 351; Dugger, "Henry B. Gonzalez: Conversations with a Congressman, Part V," 8.

20. "Protest Taped on County Door," "Cactus Curtain Up at Del Rio," *San Antonio Express,* March 31, 1969, 1A.

21. "Protest Taped on County Door," *San Antonio Express*, March 31, 1969, 1A; Hayes was with the Harris County Council of the United Organizations of Houston.

22. Leo Cardenas, *Chicano 1969: Viva La Raza* (San Antonio: Holy Cross Office of Public Affairs, 1969). Del Rio councilman Ruben Flores summed up the feelings of many in Del Rio when he stated that after the marchers leave, "We still will have poverty . . . and it still will be up to us to try to correct the local situation." "Average Del Rioan Stays Home," *San Antonio Express*, March 31, 1969, 14A.

23. In Leo Cardenas, "La Raza Stirs Pride," *San Antonio Express*, April 13, 1969, 1A. For the full plan, see Navarro, *Mexican American Youth Organization*, 253–256.

24. "Protest Taped on County Door," *San Antonio Express*, March 31, 1969, 1A; "Gonzalez Militants' Target," *San Antonio Express*, March 31, 1969, 1A.

25. Bernal's comment could be taken as a reference to Dr. Alfredo Gutiérrez, the mayor of Del Rio, or Congressman Gonzalez, as well as a general reference to class. "Bernal Supports MAYO, Raps Hate," *San Antonio Express*, April 6, 1969, 2A; "Gonzalez Militants' Target," *San Antonio Express*, March 31, 1969, 1A.

26. "Gonzalez Militants' Target," *San Antonio Express*, March 31, 1969, 1A.

27. Gonzalez did not say that any Texas MAYOs had gone to Cuba, "just that they had been influenced by those who had." "HBG Answers Peña," *San Antonio Express*, April 1, 1969, 10A.

28. Ibid. State representative Guy Floyd of San Antonio also blasted Senator Bernal and Commissioner Peña for their role in the Del Rio demonstration. Floyd said that MAYO "preaches brown power instead of American power through understanding." Bernal dismissed Floyd's comments as "puerile." "Floyd Blasts Bernal," *San Antonio Express*, April 1, 1969, 1B.

29. "Peña Says Not After HBG's Seat," *San Antonio Express*, April 3, 1969, 8G.

30. "VISTA Ldr Denies 'Hate' Lit," *San Antonio Express*, April 2, 1969, 1B; "VISTA Supervisor, Bernal Called Liars by HBG," *San Antonio Express*, April 3, 1969, 1A, 16A. Ironically, the FBI had been keeping a dossier on Gonzalez since his days as a state senator. Upon his election to Congress, the local agent in charge notified FBI director J. Edgar Hoover that Gonzalez had been elected with Communist help. Anglim, "San Antonio's Champion of Equality," 16.

31. These letters and reports came from all parts of Texas and the southwestern states. See also Yanta's "confidential file," Gonzalez Collection, Box SRH, Scrapbook, 1966–1969. On Fritz, see Paul Thompson, "Top of News," *San Antonio Express*, June 21, 1970, 1A.

32. There were notable exceptions among the Catholic clergy. Fathers Henry Casso, Antonio Barragan, Edmundo Rodríguez, and the "Mexican-ized" Sherrill Smith risked violating the vow of obedience to the Church for their participation in the Chicano movement. Basically, the movement exposed the absence of

. "indigenous" clergy in barrio parishes and in the Church hierarchy. The hierarchy responded by assigning the first Mexican American bishop, auxiliary bishop Patricio Flores, to the San Antonio diocese. See Sepúlveda, *The Life and Times of Willie Velásquez*, 66–67; Skerry, *Mexican Americans*, 118, 191–193. Also see Martin McMurthy, *Mariachi Bishop: The Life Story of Patrick Flores* (San Antonio, Texas: Corona, 1987).

33. "How S.A. Voted," *San Antonio Express*, April 3, 1969; "City Council Vote by Precinct," *San Antonio Light*, April 2, 1969, 14–15. Also see Navarro, *Mexican American Youth Organization*, 189–190; Rosales, *Illusion of Inclusion*, 120.

34. The other two CBB candidates, small businessman "Candy" Alejos and math teacher Darío Chapa, also bested the Good Government League incumbents in the West Side precincts and drew even stronger support than that given to Compean. In the Place 3 contest, Chapa received 17,877 votes; in Place 2, Alejos received 13,783 votes; and in Place 1, Compean received 11,838 votes. "City Council Vote by Precinct," *San Antonio Light*, April 2, 1969, 14–15; "How S.A. Voted," *San Antonio Express*, April 3, 1969, 1A.

35. "GGL Film to be Previewed," *San Antonio Light*, March 18, 1969, 2; "GGL Film Previewed," *San Antonio Light*, March 20, 1969, 6; "League of Women Voters Poses Questions: The Ladies and What They Want to Know," *San Antonio Light*, March 30, 1969, 6F; also see "GGL Sees Peril of 'Radical Racism, Brown Power,'" *San Antonio Express*, April 9, 1969, 8D.

36. U.S. Congress, House, Congressman Gonzalez speaking on "Race Hate," April 3, 1969, *Congressional Record-House*, H 2531–2532.

37. U.S. Congress, House, Congressman Gonzalez speaking on "Race Hate," April 3 1969, *Congressional Record-House*, H 2531; *San Antonio Express*, April 5, 1969, 6A.

38. "Hate Peddlers Lack Following But They Sow Destructive Seeds," *San Antonio Express*, April 4, 1969, 8F.

39. Ibid.

40. Paul Thompson, "Top of News," *San Antonio Express*, April 5, 1969, 1.

41. "Bernal Supports MAYO, Raps Hate," *San Antonio Express*, April 6, 1969, 2A.

42. Ibid.

43. "Gonzalez to Take 'Hate' Info to Ford Probers," *San Antonio Express*, April 8, 1969, 8D; James McCrory, "MAYO Jefe Raps 'Gringo' Policies," *San Antonio Express*, April 11, 1969, 8F.

44. "Gonzalez to Take 'Hate' Info to Ford Probers," *San Antonio Express*, April 8, 1969, 8D; U.S. Congress, House, Congressman Gonzalez speaking on "Foundation Responsibility," April 16, 1969, *Congressional Record-House*, H 2734–2735.

45. See Sepúlveda, *The Life and Times of Willie Velásquez*, 95.

46. Gonzalez Collection, Box SRH, Scrapbook, 1966–1969.

CHAPTER 5

1. James McCrory, "MAYO Jefe Raps 'Gringo' Policies," *San Antonio Express & News*, April 11, 1969, 8F. Also see Kemper Diehl, "MAYO Leader Warns of Violence, Rioting," *San Antonio News*, April 11, 1969, 3A; Ed Castillo, "'Most Texans Gringos,' Says MAYO Chieftain," *San Antonio Light*, April 11, 1969.

2. McCrory, "MAYO Jefe Raps 'Gringo' Policies," 8F; Sepúlveda, *The Life and Times of Willie Velásquez*, 85–87.

3. Ibid.

4. McCrory, "MAYO Jefe Raps 'Gringo' Policies," 8F; Cardenas, "The Young Activists," 1A.

5. MAYO was committed to effecting meaningful social change that would "enable La Raza to become masters of their destiny, owners of their resources, both human and natural, and a culturally and spiritually separate people from the 'gringo.'" Sepúlveda, *The Life and Times of Willie Velásquez*, 85–87.

6. See Sepúlveda, *The Life and Times of Willie Velásquez*, 77, 80–81, 85–87. As *San Antonio Express & News* commentator Paul Thompson put it, Gutiérrez had "let the cat out of the bag. He came right out and gave 100 per cent confirmation to everything Congressman Henry B. Gonzalez has been saying about MAYO." Thompson, "Top of News," *San Antonio Express & News*, April 12, 1969, 1A.

7. Thompson, "Top of News," *San Antonio Express & News*, April 12, 1969, 1A.

8. Ibid.

9. Ibid.; emphasis in original.

10. Congressman Gonzalez was studying state statutes for a possible request for a grand jury probe into the matter. District judge Archie Brown was of the opinion that a court of inquiry would be "a superior method of airing such a problem." "Anti-Hate Drive Backed," *San Antonio Express*, April 10, 1969, 6E.

11. "Gonzalez Reveals Threats," *San Antonio Express*, April 12, 1969, 10G.

12. At the April 11, 1969, meeting of the Bexar County Commissioners' Court, Com. A. J. Ploch and José Ángel Gutiérrez were involved in "a ferocious verbal clash that nearly resulted in their getting engaged in fisticuffs." Ploch, who had introduced a resolution commending Congressmen Gonzalez and O. C. Fisher for their anti-hate position, exchanged words with Gutiérrez, who was present to speak against the resolution. Ploch, sixty-four years old, then challenged twenty-four-year-old Gutiérrez to a fight. According to the news account, some twenty-five Mexican Americans supporting Gutiérrez chanted, "Sit down, old man, sit down." "DA Turns Down Charges Against Commissioner," *San Antonio Express*, April 12, 1969, 16A.

13. Other West Side leaders speaking at the meeting were Pete Salas of the Laredo Street Community Council, Bessie Flores of the Welfare Rights Organization of Mirasol Homes, and Darío Chapa of the Cassiano Park Resident Coun-

cil. "Gonzalez is Chastised," *San Antonio Light,* April 13, 1969, 12A, in Gonzalez Collection, Box SRH, Scrapbook, 1966–1969.

14. Ibid. A week later LULAC Council No. 2 invited Gonzalez, Bernal, Peña, city council members, to a community meeting to "halt polarization" growing out of charges and countercharges of hatred and racism via the newspapers. Apparently the meeting never took place. See "LULAC calls for End to Charges," *San Antonio Express,* April 20, 1969, 13A.

15. Calderón said he had been "hurt" that Gonzalez, "a personal friend," had made serious Communist allegations about the Del Rio demonstration. He asked "out of fairness to our relationship" to know what people were involved. He added that he would be glad to provide a list of those who had registered for the march—numbering more than 1,000. "Calderon Raps Gutierrez's 'Irresponsible Statements,'" *San Antonio Express,* April 12, 1969, 10G.

16. "HBG Offers VISTA Data," *San Antonio Express,* April 24, 1969, 10C.

17. Navarro notes that Gutiérrez's statement "proved to be the straw that broke the camel's back" as far as financial and organizational support for MAYO was concerned. Navarro, *Mexican American Youth Organization,* 174. Also see Dugger, "Henry B. Gonzalez: Conversations with a Congressman, Part V," 8.

18. "'Kill Gringos' Said Not Death Threat," *San Antonio Express,* April 21, 1969, 1A, 12A.

19. "The Cockpit," *San Antonio Express,* April 13, 1969, 8C. MAUC's Ford Foundation monies were actually a subgrant from the Southwest Council of La Raza, which had received $600,000.

20. To clinch the argument about how militant MAYO was, "The Cockpit" writers noted that one of the goals of *El Deguello,* the MAYO newsletter, was "an end to white 'supremacy,'" with the City Council serving as an example." *San Antonio Express,* April 13, 1969, 8C.

21. For Gonzalez's speeches, see the following *Congressional Record* entries for the House of Representatives: April 3, 1969, "Race Hate," H 2531–2532; April 15, 1969, "Cause for Concern," H 2640–2642; April 16, 1969, "Foundation Responsibility," H 2734–2735; April 22, 1969, "The Hate Issue," H 2928–2930; April 28, 1969, "Racism in Southwest Texas," H 3149–3154; April 29, 1969, "Foundation Responsibility," H 3205–3206; May 1, 1969, "Ford Foundation Plus San Antonio Equals Murder," H 3328.

22. "Cause for Concern," April 15, 1969, *Congressional Record-House,* H 2640–2642; "Gonzalez Charges 'Brown Bilboism,'" *San Antonio Express,* April 16, 1969, 8D. "Bilboism" was a reference to Sen. Theodore Bilbo of Mississippi, whose name became synonymous with Anglo racism in the late 1940s.

23. "Foundation Responsibility," April 16, 1969, *Congressional Record-House,* H 2734–2735; see also "The Hate Issue," April 22, 1969, *Congressional Record-House,* H 2928–2930.

24. Ibid.

25. "Foundation Responsibility," April 16, 1969, *Congressional Record-House,* H 2734–2735.

26. "HBG Questions Bernal Statement," *San Antonio Express*, April 17, 1969, 5A.

27. "Bernal Raps HBG Charges," *San Antonio Express*, April 18, 1969, 5A.

28. "Gonzalez Image 'Plot' Seen," *San Antonio Express*, April 22, 1969, 12D. By 1969, according to Paul Thompson, Gonzalez had "such all-pervading community support that not even his worst political enemies would dream of running against him." "Top of News," *San Antonio Express & News*, April 27, 1969, 1A, included in the *Congressional Record-House*, E3937. Gonzalez had won re-election in 1968 with a great majority, and in 1970 he had no opponent.

29. On April 28, the Texas congressional delegation held a lengthy exchange on the House floor about MAYO and affiliated groups. Joining Congressman Gonzalez were Fisher, from San Angelo; Kazen, from Laredo, who said that no one can speak for the Latin American people, and that this was a great country; de la Garza, from the lower Rio Grande Valley, who commented that the militants were instilling hate and Communism among young people and driving them away from religion; and finally Congressman Pickle, from Austin, who praised Gonzalez for his courageous stance, and called for a review of the Ford Foundation. See U.S. Congress, House, "Racism in Southwest Texas," April 28, 1969, *Congressional Record-House*, H 3149–3154.

30. "HBG Plans Report on 'Insidious Forces,'" *San Antonio Express*, April 26, 1969.

31. The zealot the congressman was talking about was his ex-protégé, Willie Velásquez. April 28, 1969, "Racism in Southwest Texas," *Congressional Record-House*, H 3152. The following day, April 29, Gonzalez highlighted the role of Ford Foundation monies in paying for the "purveyors of hate." See U.S. Congress, House, April 29, 1969, "Foundation Responsibility," *Congressional Record-House*, H 3205–3206.

32. Although Gonzalez frequently alluded to Communist infiltration in the Chicano movement in his public comments, he never produced any evidence. See memo to Gonzalez from "krm" concerning subversives and connections to the Cuban government, April 16, 1969, Box SRH, Scrapbook, 1966–1969, Gonzalez Collection. "HBG Hits Ford Foundation-Backed 'Hate Campaign,'" *San Antonio Express*, April 29, 1969; U.S. Congress, House, April 28, 1969, "Racism in Southwest Texas," *Congressional Record-House*, H 3149–3154. Cardenas, "The Young Activists," 1A; Dugger, "Henry B. Gonzalez: Conversations with a Congressman, Part V," 6.

33. Mills immediately promised to undertake a full investigation of militant groups in San Antonio funded by the Ford Foundation. Gonzalez's request of the U.S. comptroller general was sufficient to secure the assurances of the national head of VISTA to investigate and curtail the "malpractices" in the Minority Mo-

bilization program in San Antonio and South Texas. "Foundation Backed Groups Attacked," *San Antonio Express*, April 17, 1969, 5A; "Gonzalez Wants Probes of Poverty War, Foundations," *San Antonio Express*, April 22, 1969, 12D; "HBG Offers VISTA Data," *San Antonio Express*, April 24, 1969; "The Hate Issue," April 22, 1969, *Congressional Record-House*, H 2928–2930; see also Sepúlveda, *The Life and Times of Willie Velásquez*, 90–98.

34. Paul Thompson, "Top of News," *San Antonio Express*, March 1, 1970, 1; Sepúlveda, *The Life and Times of Willie Velásquez*, 104–108.

35. Gonzalez wrote on the margins of his speech outline: "I did not select the speech topic ["The Chicano in Texas"]—This is the general theme selected by the speakers' committee—To paraphrase [House speaker] Sam Rayburn, I am an American without prefix, suffix or apology." See text of speech, "The Political Position of a Minority," February 26, 1970, Box 127/321—Speeches, Henry B. Gonzalez Collection, University of Texas at Austin.

36. Interview with George Velásquez, February 24, 2002; "Man Threatens HBG," *San Antonio Express*, February 28, 1970, 1A, 16A; "HBG Says Walkout Planned," *San Antonio Express*, March 1, 1970, 6S.

37. "St. Mary's U. May Cancel Speeches by MAYO Friday," *San Antonio Express & News*, March 3, 1970, 2C; "MAYO Leaders Tell Goals to Big St. Mary's Crowd," *San Antonio Express & News*, March 7, 1970, 11A. Also Thompson, "Top of News," *San Antonio Express & News*, March 7, 1970, 1; "Telegram From St. Mary's Fails to Soothe Gonzalez," *San Antonio Express & News*, March 5, 1970, 12F; "Ledesma Sentenced to 2 Years," *San Antonio Express & News*, March 6, 1970, 1A, 16A.

38. Interview with George Velásquez, February 24, 2002. Among the SAPD reports in Gonzalez's possession was an "intel" report on Ramiro Ledesma dated January 3, 1969, and Ledesma's complete police record as of March 1970. See Gonzalez Collection, Box SRH, Scrapbook, 1966–1969, Center for American History, University of Texas at Austin.

39. "Miss Castro Sets Meeting on 'Attacks,'" *San Antonio Express & News*, March 12, 1970, 8B; "Velasquez Says He'll Prove Gonzalez Wrong," *San Antonio Express & News*, March 13, 1970, 20D; Sepúlveda, *The Life and Times of Willie Velásquez*, 108.

40. "The Political Position of a Minority," text of speech, February 26, 1970, Box 127/321—Speeches, Henry B. Gonzalez Collection. A couple of weeks after the St. Mary's brouhaha, Gonzalez presented his prepared remarks at St. Philip's College. But in obvious reaction to being labeled a "vendido," he honed his speech to attack the true and "modern vendidos"—the militants creating the Raza Unida Party—who were simply seeking to become political brokers. These modern vendidos, Gonzalez warned, might "succeed in polarizing this city and even this state into competing racist camps." "Leadership and Politics Among the Mexican-American," St. Philip's College, San Antonio, March 13, 1970, Box

127/321—Speeches, Henry B. Gonzalez Collection; "'Vendido' Always a Loser—Gonzalez," *San Antonio Express & News*, March 14, 1970, 2C

41. "Civil Rights Report Blasted by Gonzalez," *San Antonio Express & News*, March 10, 1970, 8D. The thirty-five-member Advisory Committee also had as members state senator Joe Bernal, José Uriegas of VISTA, and Rev. Henry Casso, coauthor of the Del Rio Manifesto. The report called for reforms in education, the administration of justice, and employment practices. See *Civil Rights in Texas: A Report of the Texas Advisory Committee to the U.S. Commission on Civil Rights*, (Washington, D.C.: U.S. Government Printing Office, February 1970); also U.S. Commission on Civil Rights, *Mexican Americans and the Administration of Justice in the Southwest* (Washington, D.C.: U.S. Government Printing Office, March 1970).

42. "The Angry Chicanos: Deepening Frustration of Mexican-Americans Stirs Fears of Violence," *Wall Street Journal*, June 11, 1970, 1, 18.

43. Ibid.; Navarro, *Mexican American Youth Organization*, 61.

44. In April 1972, the Committee to Re-elect the President (or CREEP) commissioned a confidential "Spanish Speaking Study" in Los Angeles, San Antonio, Chicago, and New York to assess receptivity to Nixon campaign overtures. The Spanish-speaking community of San Antonio was found to be a "much better natural territory for the President" because of its stability, confidence and "belief in government and the system." However, Alex Armendáriz, author of the findings, also found that three "militant" organizations—the United Farm Workers, the fledging Raza Unida Party, and LULAC—had high visibility and approval. The Brown Berets were "not highly visible and fewer than 45% approve of them." Memorandum (June 16, 1972) from Alex Armendáriz of the Committee to Re-elect the President.

45. Cardenas, "More Militancy from Mexican-Americans Seen," *San Antonio Express*, April 19, 1969, 1A, 9A.

46. Ibid.

47. Paul Thompson, "Top of News," *San Antonio News*, November 13, 1969, 1A.

48. Ibid.

49. Anonymous, "¿Porqué MAYO?" *La Nueva Raza*, Vol. 2, No. 4 (September 1969), 7.

50. Ibid.

51. Cardenas, "More Militancy," 1A, 9A.

52. Armando Cavada, "Raza Unida Party and the Chicano Middle Class," *Caracol* (San Antonio) (September 1974): 19.

53. Ibid., 18–19.

54. Ibid., 21.

55. Interview with George Velásquez, February 24, 2002; Navarro, *Mexican American Youth Organization*, 227–228; Sepúlveda, *The Life and Times of Willie Velásquez*, 57, 66, 73–78, 101–102.

56. Sepúlveda, *The Life and Times of Willie Velásquez*, 98, 102; also see Navarro, *Mexican American Youth Organization*, 168–171.

57. The Raza Unida Party, which Bernal had defended vigorously, fielded a candidate against him, thus ironically causing his loss. Dugger, "Henry B. Gonzalez: Conversations with a Congressman, Part V," 6. See also Sepúlveda, *The Life and Times of Willie Velásquez*, 57, 66, 73–78, 101–102; Navarro, *Mexican American Youth Organization*, 168–171.

58. "Pete Tijerina Firing Requested by Ford," *San Antonio Express & News*, March 21, 1970.

CHAPTER 6

1. García, *United We Win*; Navarro, *Mexican American Youth Organization*.

2. "La Universidad de los Barrios: Economic Opportunity for Mexican American Youth," grant proposal, February 1970; see also the U.S. Catholic Conference newsletter, *Task Force on Urban Problems*, Vol. II, No. 3 (November 1970); Tom Cutting, "University of the Streets: Chicano Youth Master Economics," *Texas Presbyterian* (September 1970).

3. LUB grant proposal, typescript, circa 1971. "Oro del barrio" was a reference to Tomás Atencio and La Nueva Academia.

4. The Teatro de los Barrios was based on the skits of Luís Valdez's Teatro Campesino, but adapted to San Antonio content. They used the neighborhood networks—the housing projects, in particular—to present skits on pressing social issues. "Teatro de los Barrios," *Caracol* (January 1975): 2, 14–16; interview with George Velásquez, February 24, 2002.

5. "Universidad de los Barrios Restaurant: A Step Towards 'Self Determination,'" *San Antonio Express & News*, circa July 1970, LUB scrapbook. The minutes discuss how to request $6,000 from the Episcopalian Church for funding their Chaleco restaurant. The approach to be used was to say: "The Universidad is doing this, not MAYO." LUB minutes, June 24, 1969.

6. Cutting, "University of the Streets." The example given in the article was that of Carlos Flores, a high school dropout on San Antonio's West Side. Flores considered himself neither fully American nor fully Mexican, but Chicano, "a brand new people." The Universidad de los Barrios had given him "a band of men with whom he has discovered himself and his purpose." In Carlos's words: "I finally found out who I am, man. I finally found out who my people are. I'm no damn animal, man. I'm a human being."

7. Ibid., 5.

8. LUB minutes, December 30, 1970.

9. LUB grant proposal, February 1970.

10. We know quite a bit about Ledesma because Congressman Gonzalez had his police record among his papers, as well as a SAPD "intel" report about Ledesma and La Universidad dating back to early 1969—long before the walk-

out at St. Mary's. See Gonzalez Scrapbook, Center for American History, University of Texas at Austin.

11. Ledesma's arrest record as of March 1970 was a disturbing resumé: a charge of aggravated assault (May 1968) that should have been a murder charge; two more charges of aggravated assault (slapping, December 14, 1969; stabbing in arm, December 19, 1969), and an auto theft charge (January 17, 1970). Ramiro Ledesma folder, Box 2004-127/394, Gonzalez Collection. Also see Supplementary Report, SAPD Intelligence, January 3, 1969, in Box SRH, Scrapbook, 1966–69, Gonzalez Collection, University of Texas at Austin.

12. The letter was dated September 9, 1969. LUB scrapbook, George Velásquez Papers.

13. A March 3, 1970, memo to Gonzalez by "km" indicates that Kelsay Meek, Gonzalez's longtime aide, was "obtaining an FBI rap sheet on this man." Box SRH, Gonzalez Collection. Also see Dugger, "Henry B. Gonzalez: Conversations with a Congressman, Part V," 10; Sepúlveda, The Life and Times of Willie Velásquez, 107; "Ledesma Sentenced to 2 Years," San Antonio Express, March 6, 1970, 1A.

14. When I interviewed Juan Guajardo on April 7, 1975, he said the West Side Berets had stopped meeting the year before.

15. Ibid.

16. Ibid.

17. Tomás Atencio, Luis Jaramillo, and other activists had created the "education-action-research institute" called La Academia de La Nueva Raza in Dixon, New Mexico, in 1969. That year Atencio and Jaramillo "hooked up" with sociologists Theodore Abel, who had retired in New Mexico; Kai Erikson, who was spending a year there; and Pedro David, chair of sociology at the University of New Mexico. The sociologists said that Atencio and Jaramillo were practicing the teachings of Heidegger, a phenomenologist who believed that one could only uncover social phenomena through logos, or diálogos, which is what the guys at La Academia were doing. Atencio had never heard of Heidegger; he just knew that they were doing right. Interview with Tomás Atencio, March 29, 2002. For an argument for a new kind of social work based on education-action, see Tomás Atencio, "The Survival of La Raza Despite Social Services," Social Casework (May 1971): 262–268.

18. Interview with Juan Guajardo, April 7, 1975.

19. Semana de la Raza Souvenir Program (pvt. printing, San Antonio, 1971), 13.

20. Ibid.

21. Ibid.

22. Ibid.

23. Lalo joined the Berets in 1972 and stayed until the West Side chapter dissolved in 1973–1974. Interview with Lalo Martínez, April 1, 1975.

24. Sancudo traced his joining the movement to an experience in a small Texas town where he was refused a haircut. That opened his eyes! Then in his senior year in high school, he attended an AFL-CIO conference where "they started talking about these kinds of things." Interview with David "Sancudo" Martínez, August 11, 1974.

25. Interviews with David "Sancudo" Martínez, August 11, 1974, and Lalo Martínez, April 1, 1975.

26. Ernie said that the police didn't like *Chicano Times* "porque 'tabamos exposing, tú sabes, mucho de lo que de verás 'taba pasando y no querían la gente que supiera . . . en las escuelas, venían los policías y nos quitaban el papel y nos querían encerrar, este" (because we were exposing, you know, much of what was really going on and they didn't want the people to know. . . at the schools, the police would come and take away the paper and they wanted to arrest us, este). Interview with Ernie García, November 15, 1974.

27. Interviews with Ernie García, November 15, 1974, and David "Sancudo" Martínez, August 11, 1974.

28. Interview with José Morales, April 10, 1975.

29. Interviews with Lalo Martínez, April 1–2, 1975, and Carlos Garza, April 1 and 6, 1975.

30. Interviews with Juan Guajardo, April 7, 1975, and José Morales, April 10, 1975.

31. "Gang Warfare: S.A. Brown Berets Succeed," *San Antonio Light*, circa February 1971; the LUB scrapbook contains a photo of chavalitos from El Detroit raising clenched fists in the air. George Velásquez Papers.

32. Interview with José Morales, April 10, 1975.

33. "Brutality Charged," *El Portavoz* (San Antonio) Vol. 1, No. 8 (1971). The same issue of *Portavoz* carried an article about the police shooting of a sixteen-year-old Chicano in Austin who had been stealing a loaf of bread and a can of lunch meat.

34. Ibid.

35. "Brown Berets Picket City Hall and Police Headquarters," *San Antonio Express*, July 30, 1971, 11A; "Brown Berets March at City Hall," *San Antonio Light*, July 30, 1971, Brown Beret scrapbook. The *Light* article has an accompanying photo of nine women, some wearing berets, carrying picket signs.

36. "COPP Group to Keep Close Tabs on Police," news clipping, circa August 1971, in Brown Beret scrapbook, private collection; "Police Review Board Disputed," *San Antonio Light*, August 22, 1971, 11E.

37. Morales said the local organization had 150 members; "Police Capture Policy Attacked," *San Antonio Light*, October 12, 1971, 9A.

38. The police estimated 500; the Berets estimated 100 Berets plus 850 Chicanos. "500 Peacefully Protest Alleged Police Misconduct," *San Antonio News*,

November 21, 1971, 2A; also "Protest March Held," *San Antonio Light*, November 21, 1971, 19A. In the Brown Beret scrapbook, a handwritten comment on a copy of a *San Antonio News* article reads: "Brown Berets from Houston, Dallas, Austin, San Antonio, Los Angeles, marched against the perros." An accompanying photo shows Brown Berets with the "clenched fist salute" leading the march.

39. Interview with José Morales, April 10, 1975.

40. Interview with Juan Guajardo, April 7, 1975.

41. Among the news clippings in the Brown Beret scrapbook: "Gang Warfare: S.A. Brown Berets Succeed," *San Antonio Light*, circa February 1971; "Houston school boycott planned," Associated Press, August 15, 1971; Villa Coronado article by Frank Trejo in *San Antonio Light*, September 8, 1971.

42. SAPD Juvenile Bureau Annual Reports, 1959–1972. Of the most serious offenses, those involving physical violence, aggravated assault, simple assault, and affrays, taken together, comprise the best indicator of possible group conflict over time.

43. "Juveniles Start with Petty Crimes," *San Antonio Light*, December 12, 1978, 1B.

44. The probation program was headed by a director and six assistant probation officers, who were "within easy and ready accessibility of the children and families whom they serve." *1973 Annual Report of the Bexar County Juvenile Probation Department*, 6–7.

45. The Youth Service Project was essentially a preventive program. Besides providing some attention to these children, the program was able to "divert these cases from the official Juvenile Justice System, thus avoiding the stigma attached to such a referral and preventing possible labeling of the child as a delinquent." The project was first launched in 1971–1972 in the Model City Area, and thereafter expanded to other sides of town. *1973 Annual Report of the Bexar County Juvenile Probation Department*, 6–7.

46. Interview with José Morales, March 26, 2008.

47. *1974 Annual Report of the Bexar County Juvenile Probation Department*, 1.

48. "Juveniles Start With Petty Crimes," *San Antonio Light*, December 12, 1978, 3A; also "Hooligan Menace Spreading—Eureste," *San Antonio News*, May 20, 1980, 3A.

49. Interview with Frank García, December 7, 1974.

50. In an interview with Ronnie Dugger in 1980, Gonzalez denied "going for the jugular" in trying to take funding away from the Southwest Council of La Raza and MALDEF. Gonzalez said that his target was a related Ford-funded West Side project, La Universidad de los Barrios. With respect to the other projects, he only asked the Ford Foundation for "closer oversight of the programs they funded." Dugger, "Henry B. Gonzalez: Conversations with a Congressman, Part V," 8.

PART TWO: INTRODUCTION

1. Semana de la Raza Souvenir Program. Full-page ads were bought by the distributors of five beer companies. These, along with the full-page ads bought by MAUC, Mario's Restaurant, and Centeno Super Markets, underwrote much of the festivities. Another six pages of half- or quarter-page ads were bought by small businesses, various labor organizations, and Spanish-language radio and television.

2. Semana de la Raza Souvenir Program, 5.

3. The centerfold of the program featured the honorary chairmen of La Semana—state senator Joe Bernal; county commissioner Albert Peña; Edgewood School superintendent José Cardenas; Gilbert Pompa, associate director of the Community Relations Service of the Department of Justice; auxiliary bishop Patrick Flores; supermarket owner Eloy Centeno; former councilman Pete Torres, Jr.; Richard Avena, director of the Southwestern Field Office of the U.S. Commission on Civil Rights; and Américo Paredes, professor at the University of Texas at Austin.

4. Semana de la Raza Souvenir Program, 11.

5. "MAYO—La Raza Unida," Semana de la Raza Souvenir Program, 4.

6. Semana de la Raza Souvenir Program, 14–15.

7. Ibid., 13.

8. For an assessment of Mexican American leadership, see Grebler et al., *Mexican American People*, 551–554; also see Skerry, *Mexican Americans*, 342–346.

9. A broad spectrum of the Mexican American organizational field was represented. In addition to those already mentioned, the following each had a page or so of commentary and description: Chicano III, a South Side organization; Movimiento Estudiantil Chicano de Aztlán (MECHA), a college student organization; the National Farm Workers Association boycott organization; the Commission for Mexican American Affairs; La Universidad de los Barrios and its Teatro de los Barrios; the GI Forum; the Bilingual Bicultural Coalition on Mass Media; and the Mexican-American Betterment Organization.

10. Such reverberations, or "chain effects," presupposed organizational capacity and community readiness. Thus one MAYO leader could claim that the San Antonio high school walkouts of late spring 1968 were not influenced by the East Los Angeles "blowouts" of that March because "MAYO was far ahead of everyone else in the use of the boycott." See Navarro, *Mexican American Youth Organization*, 118; also see Gutiérrez, *The Making of a Chicano Militant*, 142–176.

11. According to Mario Compean, the idea behind the Committee for Barrio Betterment did not initially include the Raza Unida Party, but that idea emerged shortly after their campaign began. The other project designated as a priority by the delegates at the national MAYO conference was the establishment of an all-

Chicano college. This project, Colegio Jacinto Treviño, had a tumultuous five-year existence and never really got off the ground. Interview with Compean, April 20, 1974; see also Rosales, *Illusion of Inclusion*, 120; Navarro, *Mexican American Youth Organization*, 102, 190.

12. See Navarro, *Mexican American Youth Organization*, 227–228; Sepúlveda, *The Life and Times of Willie Velásquez*, 73–74, 101–102.

13. Interview with Compean, April 20, 1974. The distinction between "college guy" and "street bato"—basically a class-cultural distinction—should not be overdrawn. Many of the leaders of the movimiento were both college students and barrio residents. A key cohort was the first-generation, college-bound guys from the West Side barrios. They were the key to politicizing los batos.

CHAPTER 7

1. Marta P. Cotera, *Diosa y Hembra: The History and Heritage of Chicanas in the U.S.* (Austin, TX: Statehouse Printing, 1976).

2. For a discussion, see Sonia A. López, "The Role of the Chicana within the Student Movement," from *Essays on La Mujer* (Los Angeles: UCLA Chicano Studies Center, 1977), 16–29, reprinted in Alma M. García, ed., *Chicana Feminist Thought: The Basic Historical Writings* (New York: Routledge, 1997), 100–106. Also see Beatriz M. Pesquera and Denise A. Segura, "There Is No Going Back: Chicanas and Feminism," in *Mujeres Activas en Letras y Cambio Social, Chicana Critical Issues* (Berkeley: Third Woman Press, 1993), 97–98.

3. Ibid. See also Kuumba, *Gender and Social Movements* (New York: Altamira Press, 2001), 1–18, 38–39, 80.

4. Enriqueta Longeaux y Vásquez recalls that the Chicana caucus report to the full conference was "quite a blow. I could have cried. Surely we could at least have come up with something to add to that statement." The workshop statement actually read: "We resolve not to separate but to strengthen and free our nation of Aztlán, women, men, and children." See "Resolutions from the Chicana Workshop," from *La Verdad* (June 1970); Longeaux y Vásquez, "The Woman of La Raza," from *Magazín*, Vol. 1, No. 4 (1972). These have been reprinted in García, *Chicana Feminist Thought*, 146–147, 29–31, respectively.

5. Ignacio García, *United We Win*, 80; Marta P. Cotera, "Raza Unida Women: Ideology and Strategies on Race and Gender Issues," unpublished paper (May 1991), 3–4; Vicki Ruiz, *From Out of the Shadows* (New York: Oxford University Press, 1998), 116, 198–199.

6. Raza Unida activist Cynthia Orozco called El Plan de Santa Barbara, which did not make a single reference to women, a "man-ifesto." Orozco, "Sexism in Chicano Studies and the Community," in National Association for Chicano Studies, *Chicana Voices: Intersections of Class, Race, and Gender* (Austin: CMAS Publications, 1986), 13. For gender tensions within teatros and other cultural organizations, see Yolanda Broyles, "Women in El Teatro Campesino,"

in National Association for Chicano Studies, *Chicana Voices*, 162–187. Also see Mirta Vidal, "New Voice of La Raza: Chicanas Speak Out," *International Socialist Review* (October 1971), reprinted in García, *Chicana Feminist Thought*, 21–24.

7. See Lori Flores, "An Unladylike Strike Fashionably Clothed: Mexican American and Anglo Women Garment Workers Against Tex-Son, 1959–1963," senior thesis, Yale University, 2005, 4, 29–31, 43; Toni Nelson-Herrera, "Constructed and Contested Meanings of the Tex-Son Garment Strike in San Antonio, Texas, 1959: Representing Mexican Women Workers," master's thesis, University of Texas at Austin, 1997, 56, 90.

8. Rosie Castro provides an important historical reminder: "Women have always been there. Emma Tenayuca was not totally unique. Manuelita [Sanger] was there, there were others who were there. We know only about those few who we have focused on." Rosales interview with Castro, August 19, 1992.

9. Ibid.

10. See Navarro, *Mexican American Youth Organization*, 110–112.

11. Carlos Vásquez, "Women in the Chicano Movement," in Magdalena Mora and Adelaida R. del Castillo, eds., *Mexican Women in the United States: Struggles Past and Present* (New York: Palgrave Macmillan, 2007), 27.

12. Ibid.

13. Cotera, "Raza Unida Women," 20–21.

14. Rosales interview with Rosie Castro, August 19, 1992.

15. Inés Hernández, "Testimonio de memoria," in Charles M. Tatum, ed., *New Chicana/Chicano Writing 2* (Tucson: University of Arizona Press, 1992), 15.

16. Cotera, "Raza Unida Women," 8.

17. Ibid., 2.

18. Rosales interview with Mariano Aguilar, March 12, 1993.

19. Among the members of El Rebozo were Sylvia González, Andrea Velásquez, Carmen Aguilar, Licha Compean, Rosie Castro, Gloria Cabrera, and occasionally Mary Alice Pérez (later Cisneros). Rosales interview with Mariano Aguilar, March 12, 1993.

20. *El Rebozo* (San Antonio) (November 1969): 1.

21. Ibid., 4.

22. Police disrupted the August 29th protest of the National Chicano Moratorium against the Vietnam War, leaving three dead (including journalist Ruben Salazar), many injured, scores arrested, and millions of dollars' of damage done to the business section where the march had taken place. See Oropeza, *Raza Si! Guerra No!*, 145–182.

23. News columnist Paul Thompson accused Martínez of being "the mastermind" and of having run everything out of the House of Neighborly Service settlement house. Rosales interview with Alicia Martínez, September 21, 1992.

24. "29 Arrested at Picket Line," *San Antonio Express*, September 10, 1970, 1; "10 Arrested After Melee at Frost National Bank," *San Antonio Express*, September 11, 1970, 1. Congressman Gonzalez had copies of the SAPD arrest records

of all twenty-nine arrested on "Business and Professional Men's Day." Next to Albert Peña's mug shot was a handwritten note asking for six duplicates. See SASA Boycott folder, Box 2004-127/394, Henry B. Gonzalez Collection.

25. Rosales interview with Rosie Castro, August 19, 1992.

26. Ibid.

27. Rosales interviews with Mario Compean, January 23, 1993, and Mariano Aguilar, March 12, 1993.

28. Rosales interview with Rosie Castro, August 19, 1992.

29. Ibid.; see also Navarro, *Mexican American Youth Organization*, 110–112.

30. By the time Cabrera ran for city council, she was working with MALDEF and exploring the issues of redistricting and single-member districts. Rosales interview with Gloria Cabrera, August 31, 1992; see also José Ángel Gutiérrez, Michelle Meléndez, and Sonia Adriana Noyola, *Chicanas in Charge: Texas Women in the Public Arena* (Lanham, MD: Altamira Press, 2007), 111–112.

31. Although women were active in various committees of Ciudadanos Unidos, they would never be part of its leadership during Raza Unida's five years of community control. See Navarro, *The Cristal Experiment*, 76, 310. For other incidents, see Emilio Zamora, "Raza Unida Party Women in Texas, 1960–2004: An Exercise in Pedagogy, Research and Historical Interpretation," paper presented at SIGLO XXI: Research into the 21st Century, IUPLR Triennial Conference, Austin, Texas, Spring 2005. Zamora and his associates interviewed nine Raza Unida women: three elected officials, two campaign managers, and four rank-and-file members.

32. Cotera, "Raza Unida Women," 9.

33. Francisca Flores, "Conference of Mexican Women in Houston—Un Remolino," in García, *Chicana Feminist Thought*, 159–161.

34. See López, "The Role of the Chicana," 100–106; Marta Cotera, "La Conferencia de Mujeres por la Raza: Houston, Texas, 1971," in García, *Chicana Feminist Thought*, 155–157; and Flores, "Conference of Mexican Women in Houston," 157–161.

35. Vidal, "New Voice of La Raza," 21.

36. Flores, "Conference of Mexican Women in Houston," 157–158.

37. Rosales interview with Rosie Castro, August 19, 1992.

38. Flores, "Conference of Mexican Women in Houston," 157–158; see also Vidal, "New Voice of La Raza," 22.

39. Anna Nieto Gómez and Elma Barrera, "Chicana Encounter," *Regeneración*, Vol. 2, No. 4 (1975): 49–51, reprinted in García, *Chicana Feminist Thought*, 162.

40. Ibid., 164.

41. Jennie V. Chávez, "Women of the Mexican American Movement," in García, *Chicana Feminist Thought*, 36–37.

42. Flores, "Conference of Mexican Women in Houston," 159–161.

43. Cotera, "La Conferencia de Mujeres por la Raza," 155–156.

44. Vidal, "New Voice of La Raza," 22.

45. See García, *United We Win*, 71–73.

46. La Raza Unida Party of Texas, "Party Platform on Chicanas, 1972," in Alma García, *Chicana Feminist Thought*, 167–169; see also Evey Chapa, "Mujeres por la Raza Unida," *Caracol* (October 1974): 3–5, reprinted in García, *Chicana Feminist Thought*, 178–181. Also see Zamora, "Raza Unida Party Women in Texas, 1960–2004."

47. "Party Platform on Chicanas, 1972," in García, *Chicana Feminist Thought*, 167–169, emphasis added.

48. Chapa, "Mujeres Por la Raza Unida," 178–181; also see Zamora, "Raza Unida Party Women in Texas, 1960–2004."

49. Cotera, "La Mujer Mexicana," *Magazín*, Vol. 1, No. 9 (September 1973): 30–32.

50. *New York Times*, June 20, 1972, 31; "Echeverría," por "María," *Magazín*, Vol. 1, No. 7 (October 1972): 27–29.

51. "Echeverría," 27–29.

52. Cotera, "Chicana Conferences and Seminars, 1970–1975," in García, *Chicana Feminist Thought*, 142–144.

53. Among those in the women's caucus were Rosie Castro, Alicia Salinas, Bambi Cardenas, Yolanda Santos, Choco Meza, María Elena Martínez, Alma Canales, and Irma Mireles. Rosales interview with Mario Compean, January 23, 1993; Evey Chapa, "Mujeres por la Raza Unida," 178–181.

54. Cotera, "La Mujer Mexicana," 30–32.

55. Ibid., 30.

56. Ibid., 32; also see Zamora, "Raza Unida Party Women in Texas, 1960–2004."

57. Cotera, "Raza Unida Women," 7–8, 16, and "Chicana Conferences and Seminars"; Chapa, "Mujeres por la Raza Unida," 178–181.

58. López, "The Role of the Chicana," 89.

CHAPTER 8

1. Interview with Lalo Martínez, April 1–2, 10, 1975. This complicates Haney López's argument that the Chicano movement signaled a switch from ethnic to race consciousness. Generally the street youths had no qualms about their race identity. See Ian Haney López, *Racism on Trial* (Cambridge, MA: Belknap Press, 2003, 187.

2. Author's field notes, November 1974.

3. The batos from the Valley stayed with Mario Compean, who put them in touch with Juan Guajardo. Even some Raza Unida activists became Berets. The paths to political consciousness and involvement were many and varied. Interview with Compean, April 20, 1974.

4. Luisa: "Hijo, me sentía de aquella. Aquí estaba mi chanza de deveras, voy hacer algo, voy a desarrollar la onda del carnalismo y educar la gente. Ya había llegado a un punto en que estaba lista a dar mi vida si se llegaba a eso." (Wow, I felt great. Here was my real chance to do something, to spread the spirit of brotherhood and educate the people. I had already reached the point where I was ready to give my life if it came to that.) Interview with Luisa, November 14, 1974.

5. Ibid. For an account of the gender tensions and divisions within the Brown Berets of Los Angeles, see Dionne Espinoza, "'Revolutionary Sisters': Women's Solidarity and Collective Identification among Chicana Brown Berets in East Los Angeles, 1967–1970," *Aztlán* 26 (1) (Spring 2001): 17–58.

6. Interview with Susana Almanza, Austin Brown Beret, March 20, 2007.

7. Interview with Luisa, November 14, 1974.

8. Interview with Juan Guajardo, April 7, 1975.

9. Manipulating bureaucracy was an interesting application of Gideon Sjoberg's theory of conflict between middle-class bureaucracies and the lower classes. See Sjoberg, Brymer, and Farris, "Bureaucracy and the Lower Class," 325–337.

10. Luisa: "Nunca la dabas, nunca la prestabas. Traíbas la beret contigo todo el tiempo. Wear it as much as possible." (You never gave it up, you never loaned it out. You had the beret with you at all times. Wear it as much as possible.) Interview on November 14, 1974.

11. Ibid.

12. Ibid.

13. Juan Guajardo: "It would be good to get rid of pushers in the barrios, only that many of our camaradas are tecatos, so you're hurting them too." Interview with Juan Guajardo, April 7, 1975.

14. Paul Thompson, "Top of News," *San Antonio Express & News*, July 31, 1971.

15. "Parting Shot," *San Antonio Express*, July 31, 1971; "Fair Enough," *San Antonio Express*, August 1, 1971.

16. "New Ballgame," *San Antonio Express*, August 16, 1971; "Three Stages," *San Antonio Express*, August 20, 1971.

17. Ibid.

18. "Good Samaritan Cited," *San Antonio Light*, 1971; "Brown Beret Aids Victim," *San Antonio Express & News*, undated, 1971. In Brown Beret scrapbook.

19. "The Rumor Mill," *San Antonio Light*, circa November 1971.

20. The story came up because Lalo was showing me his telescopic 30-30 rifle, which made the Berets pick him to be the sniper. He spent the night on the roof. They really believed that the police were going to come down on them. Interview with Lalo Martínez, April 1, 1975.

21. Interviews with Lalo Martínez, April 1, 1975; David "Sancudo" Martínez, August 11, 1974; and Juan Guajardo, April 7, 1975.

22. Interview with Luisa, November 14, 1974.

23. Frank and Victor San Miguel recalled being rebuffed by Raza Unida gubernatorial candidate Ramsey Muñiz. The Berets had volunteered to protect him, but Muñiz apparently reacted negatively to these unsolicited bodyguards. Field notes, September 25, 1974.

24. Velásquez mimicked "the walk" of a bodyguard for me. Victor's mannerisms, facial expressions, and language were usually seen as menacing to the unaccustomed observer or target, but I came to see such mannerisms and rhetoric as a performance or demonstration of personal power. Interview with Pancho González, January 8, 1975; field notes on "The Bodyguard Walk," October 2, 16, and 17, 1974.

25. Interview with Luisa, November 14, 1974.

26. After the incident, they returned and tried to torch the door of the bar, but since it was raining, the door never caught fire. Interview with Big John, November 2, 1974.

27. After four years at MAUC, Morales lost his job because of tecata (heroin). Interview with José Morales, April 10, 1975.

28. This is apparently what Chale meant when he said that professionalization killed the Berets. Interviews with Juan Guajardo, April 7, 1975, and "Chale," April 6, 1975.

29. Interview with Patlán, April 8, 1975.

30. Under the directorship of Patlán, MAUC was transformed from a "crusading" militant organization into one of Texas's most successful economic development agencies, with ties to the medical school, the city government, and various federal agencies. In 1975, it had a budget of $3.5 million. Rodolfo Rosales, "A Case Study of the Mexican American Unity Council," 21–22; Navarro, *Mexican American Youth Organization*, 157.

31. Interview with "Chale," April 6, 1975.

32. Chale and the others from the Detroit area thought that the officers used the soldiers for personal "jale" because the soldiers didn't know better. Later they heard that the movida against MANCO also involved a personal jale over a woman. Interview with "Chale," April 6, 1975.

33. Ibid.

34. Interview with José Morales, April 10, 1975.

35. Interview with Juan Guajardo, April 7, 1975.

36. Big John recalled that when he was minister of discipline, he tried to enforce Juan Guajardo's order not to drink on the road, "Frank a fuerzas quería," and he took out his cuete (handgun) and pointed it at him. Frank and Victor agreed that the South Side batos were crazier than the batos from the West Side because "in the South Side that's the way things were." They were kicked out of the Chicano Three organization, a Chicano pinto organization involved in social action and social services. Interviews with Big John, November 2, 1974; Victor San Miguel, September 19, 1974.

37. Interview with Luisa, November 14, 1974.

38. Big John mentioned that Victor would cuss Clara and Luisa, and that he would get on Luisa's case at meetings just to put her down. Interviews with Victor San Miguel, September 19, 1974, and Big John, November 2, 1974.

39. Interviews with Luisa, November 14, 1974, and Juan Guajardo, April 7, 1975.

40. Interview with Juan Guajardo, April 7, 1975.

41. Interview with Luisa, November 14, 1974.

42. Beret founder Sánchez had been fired on October 21, 1972, by the National Brown Beret Central Committee for exceeding his authority, among other serious allegations. Sánchez responded by calling a press conference and announcing that he was disbanding the organization. Haney López, *Racism on Trial*, 203; Chávez, "¡Mi Raza Primero!," 57. See Dale Torgenson, "Brown Beret Leader Quits, Dissolves Units," *Los Angeles Times*, November 2, 1972, 9A; also Roberto Hernández, "Silencing the Voices of Working-Class Homeboys and Homegirls in the Chicana/o Movement: The Brown Berets and the 1972 Occupation of Catalina Island," unpublished paper (Spring 2003).

43. Memo to FBI Director, March 27, 1972, in José Ángel Gutiérrez Papers, Box 5-5, University of Texas at San Antonio Archives.

CHAPTER 9

1. Colegio Jacinto Treviño class discussion, October 31, 1974; García, *United We Win*, 110.

2. Ernesto B. Vigil, *The Crusade for Justice: Chicano Militancy and the Government's War on Dissent* (Madison: University of Wisconsin Press, 1999), 195–197; García, *United We Win*, 223–224.

3. On the factional politics of "self-destruction," see García, *United We Win*, 197–218; Navarro, *The Cristal Experiment*, 325–332; Juan Gómez-Quiñones, *Chicano Politics: Reality and Promise, 1940–1990* (Albuquerque: University of New Mexico Press, 1990), 142–146. For a discussion of police and FBI repression, see Gutiérrez, *The Making of a Chicano Militant*, 269–271; Carlos Muñoz, Jr., *Youth, Identity, Power: The Chicano Movement* (Verso, 1989), 171–174; Ernesto B. Vigil, *The Crusade for Justice*, 338–345; and Edward J. Escobar, "The Dialectics of Repression: The Los Angeles Police Department and the Chicano Movement, 1968–1971," *Journal of American History* (March 1993): 1483–1514.

4. García, *United We Win*, 71–72; also "Handbook of Texas Online," s. v. "Raza Unida Party," www.utexas.edu/handbook/online/articles/RR/war1.html.

5. Gutiérrez, *The Making of a Chicano Militant*, 218.

6. Ibid., 219.

7. Ibid., 218–222; García, *United We Win*, 71–73. Gómez-Quiñones concluded that this "electoral stress" led to a view of the two-party system as "the source of domination and elevated the question of electoral participation and party

loyalty to the level of principle rather than that of a conditional strategy or of tactics." Gómez-Quiñones, *Chicano Politics*, 131.

8. Rodríguez, "Look Back in Anger, Part I," 10.

9. García, *United We Win*, 128.

10. Cavada, "Raza Unida Party," 17–19.

11. Ibid. As for educated Chicanos, the poor people were often suspicious of them "because they act and talk as if they were white instead of brown."

12. See the marginal handwritten notes on the "Report of Texas Voting Results, 1972" in the Raza Unida Party Collection, 1969–1979, Box 3, Folder 4.

13. This confidential report would later surface during the Watergate hearings. Memorandum from Alex Armendáriz of the Committee to Re-elect the Present, June 16, 1972.

14. "Señor Nixon Makes a Pitch for the Votes of Mexican-Americans," *Wall Street Journal*, April 11, 1972, 1.

15. In 1972 Nixon carried Zavala County 1,288 to 1,122 for McGovern, while 1,490 chose not to vote. Gutiérrez didn't apologize for the deal. "The Democrats and Republicans are just two fingers on the same hand," he noted. "Raza Unida Leadership Criticized at Conference," *San Antonio Express*, August 30, 1973, 18E.

16. "Se Aclara el Oportunismo del Partido Raza Unida en Texas," *Sin Fronteras: El Periódico de la Raza de Bronce*, Vol. 1, No. 5 (May 1974): 10.

17. "Raza Unida Head Pleads for New Spirit," *San Antonio Light*, May 12, 1974, 2A.

18. Interview with George Velásquez, February 24, 2002.

19. "Buscan en EU a jefe de la AIT," *El Norte* (Monterrey), October 10, 1975; also "Caen agentes de AIT aquí y en Venezuela," *El Norte*, November 20, 1975, in Mario Cantú Papers, Benson Latin American Collection, University of Texas at Austin.

20. "Chicano Leader 'No Gunrunner,'" *San Antonio Light*, October 12, 1975, in Mario Cantú Papers.

21. See "Smuggling of U.S. Guns Into Mexico Said Rising," *The Monitor* (McAllen, Texas), October 26, 1975, in Mario Cantú Papers, Benson Latin American Collection, University of Texas at Austin. A couple of years later, Cantú gained still more notoriety when he led freelance journalist Dick Reavis on a trip to interview the peasant rebel leader Güero Medrano in the mountain jungles of Michoacán. Medrano was the successor to Lucio Cabañas, who been captured and executed years earlier. Dick Reavis, "At War in the Mexican Jungle," *Mother Jones* (May 1978): 23–33.

22. Interview with Compean, April 20, 1974; Muñoz, *Youth, Identity, Power*, 171–174; Haney López, *Racism on Trial*, 149–150, 197.

23. U.S. Government Memorandum to Director, FBI, from SAC, San Antonio, February 1, 1972, in José Angel Gutiérrez Papers, University of Texas at San Antonio Library Archives; SAPD Intelligence Report, August 16, 1972, in José

Angel Gutiérrez Papers, University of Texas at San Antonio Library Archives. For the photo of the Berets in front of the Alamo, see David Sánchez, *Expedition Through Aztlán* (La Puente, CA: Perspective Publications, 1978), 171.

24. U.S. Government Memorandum to Director, FBI, from SAC, San Antonio, February 1, 1972, in José Angel Gutiérrez Papers, University of Texas at San Antonio Library Archives.

25. Memorandum on "Los Mascarones," U.S. Department of Justice, FBI, San Antonio, Texas, September 24, 1971. Mario Cantú Papers, Box 1, Folder 5, FBI, 1971–1982, Benson Latin American Collection, University of Texas at Austin.

26. "The Nixon Tapes," June 15, 1972, 10:31 a.m.–12:10 p.m., Oval Office. Conversation No. 735-1; Cassette Nos. 2246–2248, National Security Archive, as transcribed by Kate Doyle, "The Nixon Tapes: Secret Recordings from the Nixon White House on Luis Echeverría," electronic briefing book. Although both were apprehensive about Chicano activism, Texas congressman Henry B. Gonzalez did not meet with Echeverría during his visit to Washington and San Antonio. Having never forgiven Mexico for the dispossession of his family property during the Mexican Revolution, Gonzalez wasted no affection on the country's leaders. He considered Echeverría's entire family to be "definitely pro-Russian, pro-communist." Dugger, "Henry B. Gonzalez: Conversations with a Congressman, Part I," 9.

27. The Watergate burglary took place on June 17, 1972. *New York Times*, June 20, 1972, 31; María, "Echeverría," *Magazín* Vol.1, No.7 (October 1972): 27–29.

28. "Chicano Wants Probe: S.A. FBI Fascist?" *San Antonio Light*, December 13, 1977, 1, 12; also "FBI Surveillance Charged," *San Antonio Light*, December 14, 1977. Mario Cantú Papers, Benson Latin American Collection, University of Texas at Austin. The original story was carried by the *Washington Post*, "15 Years of Dirty Tricks Bared by FBI," November 22, 1977.

29. Letter from María Elena Martínez, State Chair, Raza Unida Party, to Clarence Kelley, Director, FBI, October 6, 1976, in Box 6, Folder 5, "Directives and Letters Issued by Chair María Elena Martínez, 1976–1979," La Raza Unida Papers; also Rick Casey, "Justice Undone: Crystal City 'Misconduct' Trial," *Texas Observer*, March 25, 1977, 3–5.

30. Sánchez, *Expedition Through Aztlán*, 173–192; also Hernández, "Silencing the Voices of Working-Class Homeboys and Homegirls."

31. Dionne Espinoza, "Revolutionary Sisters": Women's Solidarity and Collective Identification among Chicana Brown Berets in East Los Angeles, 1967–1970," *Aztlán* 26(1) (Spring 2001): 17.

32. Mario T. García, *Memories of Chicano History: The Life and Narrative of Bert Corona* (Berkeley: University of California Press, 1994), 309.

33. Ibid., 309–310.

34. Carlos Vásquez, "Women in the Chicano Movement," in Magdalena Mora and Adelaida R. del Castillo, eds., *Mexican Women in the United States: Struggles*

Past and Present (Chicano Studies Research Center Publications, University of California, Los Angeles, 1980), 27; Laura Pulido, *Black, Brown, Yellow and Left: Radical Activism in Los Angeles* (Berkeley: University of California Press), 181. Also see Kuumba, *Gender and Social Movements*, 1–18, 80.

35. Vásquez, "Women in the Chicano Movement," 28.

36. Elizabeth Martinez, "Chingón Politics Die Hard: Reflections on the First Chicano Activist Reunion," *Z Magazine* (April 1990).

37. Ibid., 49.

38. "Meeting to define Centro Ruben Salazar," October 7, 1973, minutes, George Velásquez Papers; Holley, "The Texas Farmworkers' Split," *Texas Observer*, April 17, 1981, 4–8; Curtis, "Raza Desunida: José Angel Gutiérrez' Dream Turned Out to Be a Nightmare," *Texas Monthly* (February 1977).

39. Gómez-Quiñones, *Chicano Politics*, 138.

40. García, *United We Win*, 189–193; Holly, "The Texas Farmworkers' Split," 4–8; Curtis, "Raza Desunida."

41. "Brown Berets March On," *Nuestro* (June/July 1980): 63.

42. Cited by Curtis, "Raza Desunida," 132; *Texas Observer*, May 15, 1981. Martín Sánchez-Jankowski, in a ten-year follow-up of high school students who had identified with Chicano nationalism, found that *cultural* nationalists had switched to conventional political party affiliations, as opposed to the *political* nationalists, many of whom remained active in independent political causes. See Sánchez-Jankowski, "Where Have the Nationalists Gone?" in David Montejano, ed., *Chicano Politics and Society in the Late Twentieth Century* (Austin: University of Texas Press, 1999), 190–223.

43. See Gutiérrez, Meléndez, and Noyola, *Chicanas in Charge*.

44. Interviews with Lalo Martínez, April 2, 1975, and Juan Guajardo, April 7, 1975.

CHAPTER 10

1. As previously discussed, Congressman Gonzalez and the Raza Unida Party leadership had negative views of each other. Carrasco is reported to have issued a contract on Gonzalez, although the threat was dismissed as barroom bravado. McKinney, *Fred Carrasco*, 13–14.

2. The Carrasco saga inspired a number of books and a new genre of border ballads known as "narco-corridos." See B. V. Olguín, *La Pinta: Chicana/o Prisoner Literature, Culture, and Politics* (Austin: University of Texas Press, forthcoming).

3. Gutiérrez, *Making of a Chicano Militant*, 269–271; García, *United We Win*, 197–201.

4. See Dugger, "Henry B. Gonzalez—Conversations with a Congressman, Part I: A Depression, King Crime, Nuclear Crime, and Economic Crime."

5. A post-mortem article on the Carrasco operation warned that even though most of its leaders were either dead or imprisoned, the "Mexican Mafia" re-

mained potentially strong because "some of Carrasco's key women friends are still on the streets." "Carrasco Is Gone, But Dope Flowing," *San Antonio Express*, August 4, 1974, 1A, 2A. See Reed Holland and John Moore, "The Laredo–San Antonio Heroin Wars," *Texas Monthly*, August 1973 (www.texasmonthly.com /mag/issues/1973-08-01/).

6. Carrasco ran an international narcotics operation through Texas, with cocaine coming from Peru and heroin from Tampico, but there is disagreement over how big his operation was. One investigator said that Carrasco's organization stretched from Canada to South America and crossed over to Europe. Another called it only one of the largest organizations in southwest Texas, but added that it dealt in "multikilos of heroin and cocaine." See "Carrasco's Story: Violence and Dope," *San Antonio Express & News*, July 28, 1974, 1A, 5A; also McKinney, *Fred Carrasco*, 13–20.

7. Gregg Barrios, ed. and trans., *Fred Gómez Carrasco: Memories of My Life* (Los Angeles: Posada Press, 1979), 13.

8. Ibid., 14.

9. Ibid., 13.

10. Los Dons bragged that they were more vicious than the Mafia. Holland and Moore, "The Laredo–San Antonio Heroin Wars"; see also "Violence Built Carrasco Legend," *San Antonio Express & News*, July 28, 1975, 6A; "Carrasco Is Gone But Dope Flowing," *San Antonio Express & News*, August 4, 1975, 2A, 3A.

11. At the time of his capture, police authorities wanted Carrasco for parole violations and for questioning in the deaths of five of his "narcotics henchmen." As a result of the shootout, Carrasco pled guilty on January 8 to a charge of assault to murder of San Antonio Police lieutenant Dave Flores and received a life term. "Carrasco Demands Weapons," *San Antonio Express & News*, July 25, 1973, 2A; "Violence Built Carrasco Legend," *San Antonio Express & News*, July 28, 1973, 6A.

12. "Hostages Blast Briscoe Inaction," *San Antonio Express*, July 28, 1974, 1A. The House Judiciary Committee voted for the second and third articles of impeachment of President Nixon on days six and seven of the takeover.

13. Carrasco and two accomplices had taken sixteen hostages, including four inmates. Two hostages were released the first day, and another two over the following ten days. One escaped. Prison chaplain Rev. Joseph O'Brien "joined" the hostages on the second day. At the end of the ordeal, Carrasco had twelve hostages. "Who Was Carrasco? Nobody Remembers," *San Antonio Express*, August 4, 1974, 3A.

14. "No Hostage Release Yet," *San Antonio Express*, July 26, 1974, 1A, 2A; "Hostages Blast Briscoe 'Inaction,'" *San Antonio Express*, July 28, 1974, 1A, 4A.

15. "Carrasco Talkative on Phone," *San Antonio Express*, July 26, 1974, 1A, 2A; "Carrasco Refuses Offers," *San Antonio Express*, July 27, 1974, 1A, 2A.

16. *Chicano Times* (San Antonio), 3.

17. "No Hostage Release Yet," *San Antonio Express*, July 26, 1974, 2A; "Carrasco Refuses Offers," *San Antonio Express & News*, July 27, 1974, 1A; "Carrasco's Story: Violence and Dope," *San Antonio Express & News*, July 28, 1974, 5A.

18. "Carrasco, 2 Women, Con Die in Hail of Bullets," *San Antonio Express & News*, August 4, 1974, 1A; see McKinney, *Fred Carrasco*, 283–290.

19. "Federico Gómez Carrasco—A Hero or a Criminal?" *Chicano Times* (San Antonio), August 2–16, 1974, 2, 3, 5, 10; "Does Federico Carrasco Have Rights?" *Chicano Times*, August 2–16, 1974, 6–7; "Ignacio Cuevas Relata Su Historia," *Chicano Times*, August 2–16, 1974, 10.

20. *Chicano Times*, August 2–16, 2. In a provocative piece defending Carrasco and his rights, the iconoclastic commentator Mrs. Saldivar said that the grand jury had discounted testimony favorable to Carrasco because the witness was a "dope peddler." Mrs. Saldivar then asked: "You good people know that being a dope peddler and a liar are not synonymous." See "Does Federico Carrasco Have Rights?" 6–7.

21. Olguín, *La Pinta*.

22. Ricardo Sánchez quoted in Olguín, *La Pinta;* interviews with Big John, October 6, 1974, and Victor San Miguel, October 29, 1974; October field notes. I find San Miguel's comment hard to believe, but he has a different "database" than I do, so I can't dismiss his comment.

23. John F. Galliher and Allynn Walker, "The Puzzle of the Social Origins of the Marihuana Tax Act of 1937," *Social Problems*, Vol. 24, No. 3 (February 1977), 367–376.

24. García, *United We Win*, 74.

25. Ibid., 77–78.

26. Ibid., 78–80; also Navarro, *Mexican American Youth Organization*, 234.

27. Miguel Berry, "Ramsey: Esfuerzo Político del Movimiento," *Magazín* (October 1972), Vol. 1, No. 7: 2–6.

28. Ibid., 6.

29. Berry, "Sueño/Realidad—Las Elecciones," *Magazín* (January 1973): 27.

30. García, *United We Win*, 83.

31. "Evaluating Voter Education Through Political Participation: General Election Results, Texas 1972," typescript, 3 pages, Box 3, Folder 5, Raza Unida Party Papers, 1969–1979, Benson Latin American Collection, University of Texas at Austin.

32. García, *United We Win*, 189.

33. Letter from Carlos Guerra, Campaign Manager, to Evey Chapa, 31 May 1974, "Muñiz File, 1974," Box 5, Folder 5, Raza Unida Party Papers; see also García, *United We Win*, 195.

34. Press release of Ramsey Muñiz campaign, no month/day, 1974, "Muñiz File, 1974," Box 5, Folder 5, Raza Unida Party Papers.

35. Ibid. Carrasco was killed August 3, 1974.

36. For a discussion of these obvious political trials, see Rick Casey, "Justice Undone: Crystal City 'Misconduct' Trial," *Texas Observer*, March 25, 1977, 3–5; see also "Parting Shot," *Texas Observer*, June 3, 1977, 15.

37. García, *United We Win*, 197.

38. Ibid., 197–198; *San Antonio Express*, March 19, 1977, 3A.

39. García, *United We Win*, 197–198.

40. Javier Rodriguez, "Look Back in Anger, Part III," *San Antonio Current*, July 9, 1987, 10; "Muñiz Pleads Guilty," *San Antonio Express*, February 3, 1977, 1.

41. Judge Wood sentenced Muñiz to the maximum penalty of five years, plus a ten-year special parole term. At the second trial, held in Corpus Christi, Muñiz was sentenced to an additional five years. "Muñiz Sentenced," *San Antonio Express*, March 3, 1977, 3A; also "Five More Years for Muñiz," *San Antonio Express*, March 19, 1977, 3A.

42. Gutiérrez, Meléndez, and Noyola, *Chicanas in Charge*, 82–83; García, *United We Win*, 202; Gutiérrez, *The Making of a Chicano Militant*, 269–270, 300. Attorney General Hill lost the gubernatorial contest to Republican Clemens in an extremely close race. Although he received only about 15,000 votes, Mario Compean claimed to have made the difference. García, *United We Win*, 219, 255n2.

43. Gutiérrez, *The Making of a Chicano Militant*, 270; "Muñiz's Magical Rise Bottoms Out: Former Gubernatorial Candidate Sentenced to Life for Drug Trafficking," *San Antonio Express & News*, December 17, 1994, 13D.

44. In 1987 Muñiz was interviewed by freelance reporter Javier Rodriguez, and in 1996 he corresponded with graduate student Geeta Mohan Gurnaney. See Javier Rodriguez, "Look Back in Anger, Part III," *San Antonio Current*, July 9, 1987, 8–9; Geeta Mohan Gurnaney, "One Candidate, Two Approaches: The Ramsey Muñiz Gubernatorial Campaigns of 1972 and 1974," master's report, University of Texas at Austin, 1996, 99–116.

45. Letter from Muñiz to Gurnaney, April 22, 1996, in Gurnaney, "One Candidate," 112.

46. Rodriguez, "Look Back in Anger, Part III," 8.

47. Letter from Muñiz to Gurnaney, April 22, 1996, in Gurnaney, "One Candidate," 110.

48. Letter from Muñiz to Gurnaney, April 22, 1996, in Gurnaney, "One Candidate," 116; also see letter from Muñiz to Gurnaney, March 9, 1996, 101.

49. See letter from Muñiz to Gurnaney, April 22, 1996, in Gurnaney, "One Candidate," 115.

50. See Michael King, "The Legacy of Henry B.," *Austin Chronicle*, December 8, 2000, 42; Molly Ivins, "Listening to Henry B.," *Texas Observer*, September 26, 1997, 20–21; also Dave Harmon, "Texans Lose Their Crusading Congressman, Henry B.," *Austin American Statesman*, November 29, 2000, A1, A9.

51. Dugger, "Henry B. Gonzalez: Conversations with a Congressman, Part II," 10.

52. Dugger, "Henry B. Gonzalez: Conversations with a Congressman, Part V," 20–21.

53. Ibid., 22.

54. Gonzalez noted: "Americans of Spanish surname are called Mexicans, Mexicanos, Latins, Latinos, Latin Americans, Mexican Americans and Hispanic Americans; not one of these labels is accepted everywhere. A name accepted in one place is enough to produce violence elsewhere." "Hope and Promise: Americans of Spanish Surname," *AFL-CIO American Federationist* (June 1967): 13–16.

55. U.S. Congress, House. Congressman Henry B. Gonzalez speaking on "The Hate Issue," 91st Congress, 1st sess., April 22, 1969, *Congressional Record-H* 2929; also U.S. Congress, House. Congressman Henry B. Gonzalez speaking on "Racism in Southwest Texas," 91st Congress, 1st sess., April 28, 1969, *Congressional Record-House*, H 3150.

56. For Gonzalez 's philosophical position, see U.S. Congress, House. Speech of Hon. Henry B. Gonzalez, "The Politics of Race," 90th Congress, 2nd sess., May 23, 1968, *Congressional Record*, Extensions of Remarks, 14852–14854. The speech was originally given to the Catholic Interracial Council of Dallas–Fort Worth, May 17, 1968.

57. Letter from Gonzalez to Clay, May 22, 1971, "Miscellaneous Correspondence, 1966–1994," Box 2004-127/93, Gonzalez Collection, Center for American History, University of Texas at Austin.

58. Ibid.

59. See "Montoya, Texas lawmaker split over Mexican American Committee," *Albuquerque Tribune*, December 10, 1969; Dugger, "Henry B. Gonzalez: Conversations with a Congressman, Part I, 9, 17.

60. Ivins, "Listening to Henry B.," 20–21; "HBG Says Walkout Planned," *San Antonio Express & News*, March 1, 1970, 6S.

61. Dugger, "Henry B. Gonzalez: Conversations with a Congressman, Part V: The Politics of Fratricide," 17–18.

62. The University Regents, the American GI Forum, and others were quick to condemn the "cowardly mob attack on a person totally undeserving of such action." See letter to the editor, "Forum Condemns Mob," *San Antonio Express*, October 2, 1973; also see letter to the editor, "Rep. Gonzalez's Texas Constituents," *Denver Post*, September 1, 1973. See Gonzalez's letter to Eureste, May 21, 1974, "Miscellaneous Correspondence, 1966–1994," Box 2004-127/93, Gonzalez Collection.

63. Letter from Albert Peña to Charles Kilpatrick, publisher, *San Antonio Express & News*, June 10, 1971, on improving race relations.

64. Dugger, "Henry B. Gonzalez: Conversations with a Congressman, Part V," 15.

65. Ibid., 16.

66. Rodriguez, "Look Back in Anger, Part II," *San Antonio Current*, July 2, 1987, 10.

67. Dugger, "Henry B. Gonzalez: Conversations with a Congressman, Part V," 15. Roel Rodriguez, the La Salle County commissioner elected under the Raza Unida banner, said this about Congressman Gonzalez:

> Él dice que es mejicano [He says he is Mexican], but at the same time he has completely turned his back to us. This man has done more harm to us, politically, en el movimiento in the past 2 or 3 years than any gabacho que vive en Tejas [Anglo who lives in Texas] . . . he gets all the attention when it comes to matters of el movimiento. He has control of the media, and no matter what he does, he gets all the publicity.

Interview with Roel Rodriguez, *Magazín*, Vol. 1, No. 5 (May 1972): 7.

68. Dugger, "Henry B. Gonzalez: Conversations with a Congressman, Part V," 15; King, "The Legacy of Henry B.," 42.

69. E-mail sent to historia-l@mail.cas.unt.edu, August 31, 2005.

70. Gonzalez's public acknowledgment came in 1995, seven years after Velásquez's death. Maria Durand, "HBG Praises Past Rival Velásquez," *San Antonio Express & News*, September 29, 1995, 1A, 9A; Sepúlveda, *The Life and Times of Willie Velásquez*, 390–392.

71. King, "The Legacy of Henry B.," 42.

CHAPTER 11

1. Frank del Olmo, "1972 Marked Zenith, Nadir for Chicanos," *Austin American Statesman*, July 5, 1997, 3A.

2. Ibid.

3. Sepúlveda, *The Life and Times of Willie Velásquez*, 233–236; Skerry, *Mexican Americans*, 116, 118, 176–179; Diehl and Jarboe, *Henry Cisneros*, 57–58.

4. John A. Booth, "Political Change in San Antonio, 1970–82: Toward Decay or Democracy?" in Johnson, Booth, and Harris, *The Politics of San Antonio*, 195.

5. Skerry, *Mexican Americans*, 178.

6. Booth, "Political Change in San Antonio," 193.

7. Thomas A. Baylis, "Leadership Change in Contemporary San Antonio," in Johnson, Booth, and Harris, *The Politics of San Antonio*, 112; see also Booth, "Political Change in San Antonio," 200.

8. See John A. Booth and David R. Johnson, "Power and Progress in San Antonio Politics, 1836–1970," in Johnson, Booth, and Harris, *The Politics of San Antonio*, 27.

9. Hufford, "The Forces Shaping San Antonio," 24–27; see also Booth and Johnson, "Power and Progress," 25.

10. Diehl and Jarboe, *Henry Cisneros*, 55.

11. As paraphrased by Mary Beth Rogers, *Cold Anger: A Story of Faith and Power Politics* (Denton: University of North Texas Press, 1990), 101.

12. Diehl and Jarboe, *Henry Cisneros*, 52.

13. Rogers, *Cold Anger*, 76; Diehl and Jarboe, *Henry Cisneros*, 52–56; Booth and Johnson, "Power and Progress"; Rosales, *The Illusion of Inclusion*.

14. Robert Brischetto, Charles L. Cotrell, and R. Michael Stevens, "Conflict and Change in the Political Culture of San Antonio in the 1970s," in Johnson, Booth, and Harris, *Politics of San Antonio*, 85; Diehl and Jarboe, *Henry Cisneros*, 52.

15. Diehl and Jarboe, *Henry Cisneros*, 55–56; see Brischetto, Cotrell, and Stevens, "Conflict and Change," 83.

16. Booth, "Political Change in San Antonio," 197.

17. Ibid., 201–202.

18. The referendum passed with 31,530 votes in favor and 29,857 against, for a margin of 1,673 votes. See Booth and Johnson, "Power and Progress," 24–25.

19. The council's five Mexicanos were "inflammatorily dubbed the 'Crystal City Coalition'" by their detractors. Booth, "Political Change in San Antonio," 201. See, for example, Diehl and Jarboe, *Henry Cisneros*, 64–65; Skerry, *Mexican Americans*, 49–52, 131–174; Brischetto, Cotrell, and Stevens, "Conflict and Change," 90.

20. Booth and Johnson, "Power and Progress," 27.

21. Italics in original. Skerry, *Mexican Americans*, 120.

22. Rosales, *Illusion of Inclusion*, 147–152, 213n24.

23. Booth, "Political Change in San Antonio," 201–202.

24. Ibid., 201.

25. See Skerry, *Mexican Americans*, 49–52, 131–174.

26. See Montejano, *Anglos and Mexicans*, 290; Rosales, *Illusion of Inclusion*, 111; Gutiérrez, *The Making of a Chicano Militant*, 268–269. The state Democratic Party, responding to local and national pressures under the so-called "McGovern rule," had opened up its ranks to "minorities" and women. This breakup of conservative Anglo rule in Texas reflected the party realignment taking place throughout the South.

27. Italics in original, Rogers, *Cold Anger*, 27. Cortés was speaking at a training session for the Texas Interfaith Network in San Antonio, February 15, 1986.

28. Willie Velásquez, "Why Hispanics Didn't Vote in the Past and Are Beginning to Vote Now," paper, December 1983.

29. Ibid.

30. Ibid.; Mariana Scuros, "Profile: The Southwest Voter Registration Education Project," *Citizen Participation* (Medford, MA), Vol. 4, No. 1 (October 1982): 8.

31. Scuros, "Profile," 8.

32. Olga Peña signed a contract with SVREP to chair a four-week registration drive with a modest $1,000 start-up grant. Sepúlveda, *The Life and Times of Willie Velásquez*, 146, 161.

33. Ibid., 161.

34. Ibid., 160–161.

35. Ibid., 156. "Woman-ing" the central office at various points were Choco Meza, Annette Aviña, Liz Salazar, Rosie Martínez, and Mariana Scuros.

36. Before a campaign could begin, the formation of a local coalition of minority group organizations was "an absolute requirement." The coalition created a representative steering committee, which recruited volunteers and hired a coordinator. SVREP provided the training and funds to actualize a four- to six-week registration campaign. Scuros, "Profile," 9.

37. Ibid., 8; Frank del Olmo, "Activist Sets Sights on Making Latinos the 'Swing Vote,'" Los Angeles Times, July 29, 1983, J3.

38. William C. Velásquez, Report on Litigation Department, Memorandum to Board of Directors, SVREP, San Antonio, TX, January 23, 1981.

39. Scuros, "Profile," 10; Velásquez, Report on Litigation Department; Montejano, Anglos and Mexicans, 293–297.

40. Sepúlveda, The Life and Times of Willie Velásquez, 156.

41. Scuros, "Profile," 8.

42. Ibid., 28.

43. Joseph D. Sekul, "Communities Organized for Public Service: Citizen Power and Public Policy in San Antonio," in Johnson, Booth, and Harris, Politics of San Antonio, 176; Rogers, Cold Anger, 107–108.

44. Rogers, Cold Anger, 109; Skerry, Mexican Americans, 178; Curtis, "Raza Desunida," 106.

45. Skerry, Mexican Americans, 144–165; Richard A. Buitrón, Jr., The Quest for Tejano Identity in San Antonio, Texas, 1913–2000 (New York: Routledge, 2004), 87–88.

46. Skerry, Mexican Americans, 177; Diehl and Jarboe, Henry Cisneros, 57; Hufford, "The Forces Shaping San Antonio," 24–27.

47. For example, to pressure the business community into supporting badly needed drainage projects on the West Side, 200 COPS members descended on Frost Bank and tied up bank tellers for hours by forcing them to change pennies for dollars until Tom Frost, the bank's board chairman, finally agreed to meet with them and listen to their complaints. See William Greider, Who Will Tell the People: The Betrayal of American Democracy (New York: Simon and Schuster, 1997), 229; Rogers, Cold Anger, 114–115; Diehl and Jarboe, Henry Cisneros, 58.

48. Greider, Who Will Tell the People, 224.

49. Diehl and Jarboe, Henry Cisneros, 58; Rogers, Cold Anger, 38, 121.

50. Rogers, Cold Anger, 25, 111–113; Skerry, Mexican Americans, 178–179.

51. As described by journalists Kemper Diehl and Jan Jarboe, "The era of defiant confrontation was past. COPS had won and lost enough fights to realize it was time to compromise. So had the business community. Cisneros was ready to make his move to become mayor." Diehl and Jarboe, Henry Cisneros, 66.

52. Booth, "Political Change in San Antonio," 199.

53. Diehl and Jarboe, *Henry Cisneros*, 85–87; Brischetto, Cotrell, and Stevens, "Conflict and Change," 93.

54. Diehl and Jarboe, *Henry Cisneros*, 73.

55. Brischetto, Cotrell, and Stevens, "Conflict and Change," 93.

56. "Hispanic Voter Registration and Civic Participation in the U.S.: A Report and Analysis," unpublished report prepared by Geto & DeMilly, Inc., for the Minority Civic Association, October 1981. See also Greider, *Who Will Tell the People*, 229.

57. George Cisneros as quoted in "Hispanic Voter Registration and Civic Participation," 33–36.

58. Sepúlveda, *The Life and Times of Willie Velásquez*, 235–236.

59. Diehl and Jarboe, *Henry Cisneros*, 86–87.

60. Ibid., 81. Sepúlveda described Cisneros's commanding victory as "an amazing feat, given the torrid history of racial and ethnic relations in and around San Antonio." On the other hand, Booth warned that "Despite the decline of ethnic tension in 1981–82, the danger of polarization still lurks among the city's possible political futures. But this danger resides far less in the new Chicano activism than in *potential recourse by Anglo political figures to ethnic fear-mongering.*" See Sepúlveda, *Life and Times of Willie Velásquez*, 235; Booth, "Political Change in San Antonio," 202, emphasis added.

61. "Interfaith Is Riding Waves of Success," *San Antonio Light*, September 9, 1984, 5B; "More than 100,000 Registered in Drive," *San Antonio Light*, October 10, 1984, 13A; see also Rogers, *Cold Anger*, 8; Skerry, *Mexican Americans*, 176.

62. Del Olmo, "Two Latino Activists Travel Separate Paths," *Los Angeles Times*, July 29, 1983, J1, J3.

63. Skerry, *Mexican Americans*, 179.

64. Rosales, *Illusion of Inclusion*, especially 178–189.

65. Rodolfo Acuña, "La Generación de '68: Unfulfilled Dreams," *Corazón de Aztlán*, Vol. 1, No. 1 (January–February 1982).

66. Farris and Brymer, "Types of Families in Poverty Areas." Only in the mid-eighties, after a decade of successful operation, did COPS even attempt to organize the poorest Mexican Americans in various West Side public housing projects. "Alinsky efforts among such populations have generally not been very successful." Skerry, *Mexican Americans*, 177.

67. Rogers, *Cold Anger*, iii.

68. Ibid., 122.

69. Ibid., 123.

70. Ibid.

71. *Directory of Community Service*, San Antonio and Bexar County, Texas, May 1974.

72. "Juveniles Start With Petty Crimes," *San Antonio Light*, December 12, 1978, 3A.

73. Bill Hendricks, "Hooligan Menace Spreading—Eureste," *San Antonio News*, May 20, 1980, 3A.

74. West, "An American Family," 176.

75. Such generational ties, Valdez argues, were weakened by the increasing marginalization of low-income Chicano communities. In the 1980s and 1990s, youth gangs were more involved in criminal activity associated with dealing drugs, weapons, and stolen property than in defending "turf." Avelardo Valdez, *Mexican American Girls and Gang Violence: Beyond Risk* (New York: Palgrave Macmillan, 2007), 12, 22–23, 43.

76. "Kid Berets Recruit for Crime Fight," *San Antonio Light*, March 23, 1985, 1.

77. Ibid.

78. "Youth Patrol Wants City Funds," *San Antonio Light*, June 2, 1985, 7C.

79. Throughout the Southwest, new youth groups with no relation to the original Berets emerge every now and then, seemingly spontaneously, to protect the community. In Watsonville, California, for example, some youths studied the history and "linked up with the founders and OGs [old guys] of the past and re-birthed the Berets after the tragic killing of a young Latina" in 2006. They remain "in the forefront of helping elevate the mind state of troubled youth." They are also "knee deep" in the immigration debate. Davey D., "Fighting the Power—Meet the Brown Berets," April 17, 2006, www.odeo.com/audio/1039627/view.

80. Antonio González, "President's Report for 2000," memorandum to board members, Southwest Voter Registration Education Project, Los Angeles, February 22, 2001.

81. See website for Industrial Areas Foundation: www.industrialareasfoundation.org.

APPENDIX

1. Much work on class, race-ethnic, and gender identity has pointed to their social construction. This follows the classic argument of E. P. Thompson, that classes have to be made, that the consciousness of a commonality of interests has to be actively maintained. See E. P. Thompson, *The Making of the English Working Class* (New York: Vintage Books, 1966). For race-ethnicity, see Michael Omi and Howard Winant, *Racial Formation in the United States: From the 1960s to the 1990s*, 2nd ed. (New York: Routledge, 1994).

2. Muñoz, *Youth, Identity, Power*, 7.

3. See Mariscal, *Brown-Eyed Children of the Sun*, 63.

4. Pesquera and Segura, "There is No Going Back," 99, 101. The women in the Black civil rights movement faced a similar dilemma. As Bahati Kuumba notes, women remained in relative obscurity. They were invisible leaders, organizing from below, linking movement organizations together, and galvanizing mass support. Kuumba, *Gender and Social Movements*, 1–18, 38–39, 80.

5. Muñoz, *Youth, Identity, Power*, 8–12; Haney López, *Racism on Trial*, 157–229; Oropeza, *Raza Si! Guerra No!*, 83. Also see Edward J. Escobar, *Race, Police, and the Making of a Political Identity: Mexican Americans and the Los Angeles Police Department, 1900–1945* (Berkeley: University of California Press, 1999).

6. Haney López, *Racism on Trial*, 164.

7. Ibid., 178–204.

8. Ibid., 182.

9. Ibid., 187.

10. Interview with José Morales, April 10, 1975.

11. For a discussion of segregation of Mexican Americans, see Montejano, *Anglos and Mexicans*, 158–254. For a discussion of "common-sense" racism, see Haney López, *Racism on Trial*, 6–8, 239–241, 244–245.

12. See, for example, Marable, *Race, Reform and Rebellion*; Carson, *In Struggle*.

13. Reginald Major, noting that Charles Garry, Huey Newton's lawyer, had become chief counsel for Los Siete in Los Angeles, commented: "thus, by some historical coincidence, a rally called to comment on Huey Newton's treatment in the courts became the springboard for a Panther-like organization among Mexican-Americans." Major, *A Panther Is a Black Cat*, 59–60; also see Haney López, *Racism on Trial*, 184–189; Mariscal, *Brown-Eyed Children*, 174–178.

GLOSSARY

ORGANIZATIONS

Barrios Unidos—United Neighborhoods, an organization of settlement house social workers, a precursor to MANCO

CASA—Centro de Acción Social Autónoma, an immigrant rights organization

CBB—Committee for Barrio Betterment, a slate of city council candidates

COPS—Communities Organized for Public Service, a Catholic parish-based citizens' group

GGL—Good Government League, the political arm of San Antonio's business elite

LUB—La Universidad de los Barrios, a "freedom school" for barrio youths established by MAYO

LULAC—League of United Latin American Citizens, a civic organization founded in the 1920s

MALDEF—Mexican American Legal Defense and Educational Fund, a legal organization focusing on civil rights

MANCO—Mexican American Neighborhood Civic Organization, a social services and advocacy organization

MAUC—Mexican American Unity Council, a nonprofit economic development and advocacy organization

MAYO—Mexican American Youth Organization, an organization dedicated to challenging "gringo rule"

RUP—Raza Unida Party (El Partido de la Raza Unida), the political party organized by MAYO

SAPD—San Antonio (Texas) Police Department

SVREP—Southwest Voter Registration Education Project, a nonprofit organization established to register and educate underrepresented communities

VISTA—Volunteers in Service to America, a domestic organization modeled after the Peace Corps

FREQUENTLY USED SPANISH TERMS

Barrio—Mexican American neighborhood
Bato, bato loco—slang for "guy," "crazy guy" (also spelled "vato")
Cabrón—slang for "mean person" (literally an "old goat")
Camarada—friend
Carnal, carnala—someone considered as close as a brother or sister
Carnalismo—brotherhood, sisterhood
Causa—cause
Chicano, Chicana—person of Mexican American descent, particularly one involved in the Chicano movement
Gabacho, gringo—pejorative terms for an Anglo
Jale—activity, job
Onda—idea, spirit
Pachuco—barrio youth with distinctive argot and dress style
Pedo—slang for "trouble" (literally a "fart")
Pendejo, pendejada—slang for "stupid person" and "stupidity"
Perro—pejorative term for police officer (literally a "dog")
Raza unida—united people
Ruca—slang for "woman"
Vendido—sellout

BIBLIOGRAPHY

MANUSCRIPTS AND PAPERS

Cantú, Mario. Papers. Benson Latin American Collection, University of Texas at Austin.

Gonzalez, Henry B. Papers. Henry B. Gonzalez Collection, Center for American History, University of Texas at Austin.

Gutiérrez, José Ángel. Papers. University of Texas at San Antonio Library Archives.

Muñiz, Ramsey, and Albina Piña Muñiz. Papers. Benson Latin American Collection, University of Texas at Austin.

La Raza Unida. Papers. Benson Latin American Collection, University of Texas at Austin.

San Antonio Brown Berets. Scrapbook. Private collection.

Semana de la Raza Souvenir Program. 48 pp. Pvt. printing, San Antonio, TX, 1971. Private collection.

La Universidad de los Barrios. Meeting minutes, October 1968–December 1970. Private collection of George Velásquez.

INTERVIEWS BY AUTHOR

Almanza, Susana, Brown Beret (Austin), March 20, 2007.

Arispe, Jerry, Brown Beret, November 2, 1974.

Atencio, Tomás, social worker, March 29, 2002.

"Big John," Brown Beret, November 2, 1974.

Bustamante, Mike, social worker, January 6, 1975.

Castro, Rosie, MAYO–Raza Unida activist, March 19, 2007.

"Chale," Brown Beret, April 6, 1975.

"Colorado," Brown Beret (South Side), November 30, 1974.

Compean, Mario, MAYO–Raza Unida activist, April 20, 1974.

Delgado, Arturo, Brown Beret, November 16, 1974.

García, Ernie, Brown Beret, November 15, 1974.

García, Frank, Brown Beret, December 7, 1974.

Garza, Carlos, Brown Beret, April 1, 6, 1975.

Gómez, Ernesto, social worker, November 12, 1974.

Guajardo, Ben, Brown Beret, April 30, 2004.

Guajardo, Juan, Brown Beret, November 2, 1974; April 7, 1975.

"Javalina," Brown Beret (South Side), October 3, 31, November 14, 1974.

"Luisa," Brown Beret, November 14, 1974.

Maldonado, Juan, MAYO–Raza Unida activist, November 20, 1999.

Martínez, David "Sancudo," Brown Beret, August 11, 1974.

Martínez, Lalo, Brown Beret, August 11, December 28, 1974; April 1–2, 10, 1975.

Montejano, Diana, Brown Beret, September 26, 1974; November 14, 1975.

Morales, José, Brown Beret, April 10, 1975; March 26, 2008.

Olivares, Manuel, Brown Beret, December 29, 1974.

Patlán, Juan, MAYO–Raza Unida activist, April 8, 1975.

Rivas, Paul, Brown Beret, December 30, 1974.

San Miguel, Victor, Brown Beret (South Side), September 19, October 29, 31, 1974; March 28, 29, 2008.

Sauceda, Jesse, social worker, May 25, 1974.

Vasques, Gene, Brown Beret, October 29, 1974.

Velásquez, George, MAYO–Raza Unida activist, April 5, 1975; February 24, 2002.

Velásquez, Pancho, Raza Unida activist, January 8, 1975.

Villarreal, Eduardo, social worker, January 7, 1975.

INTERVIEWS BY RODOLFO ROSALES

Aguilar, Mariano, social worker, March 13, 1993.

Cabrera, Gloria, MAYO activist, August 31, 1992.

Castro, Rosie, MAYO–Raza Unida activist, August 19, 1992.

Compean, Mario, MAYO–Raza Unida activist, January 23, 1993.

Cotrell, Charles, professor, March 30, 1993.

Martínez, Alicia, community organizer, September 21, 1992.

NEWSPAPERS AND PERIODICALS

Caracol (San Antonio)

Chicano Times (San Antonio)

El Deguello (San Antonio)

Magazín (San Antonio)
La Nueva Raza (San Antonio)
El Portavoz (San Antonio)
El Rebozo (San Antonio)
San Antonio Express
San Antonio Express & News
San Antonio Light
San Antonio News
San Antonio Sun
Sin Fronteras (Los Angeles, CA)
Texas Observer (Austin)

GOVERNMENT DOCUMENTS

Armendáriz, Alex. Memorandum for the Honorable Frederic Malek, Committee to Re-elect the President, June 16, 1972.
Bexar County Juvenile Probation Department Annual Reports, 1959–1961, 1963–1966, 1973–1974, 1976.
Civil Rights in Texas: A Report of the Texas Advisory Committee to the U.S. Commission on Civil Rights, (Washington, D.C.: U.S. Government Printing Office, February 1970), 51 pp.
San Antonio (Texas) Police Department, Juvenile Bureau, Annual Reports, 1959–1974.
U.S. Commission on Civil Rights. *Hearings Held in San Antonio, Texas, December 9–14, 1968* (Washington, D.C.: U.S. Government Printing Office, 1969).
———. *Mexican Americans and the Administration of Justice in the Southwest* (Washington, D.C.: U.S. Government Printing Office, March 1970).
U.S. Congress, House. Speech of Hon. Henry B. Gonzalez, "The Hope and the Promise—Poverty and Progress in the Southwest," 89th Cong., 2nd sess., May 12, 1966, *Congressional Record*, reprint.
———. Speech of Hon. Henry B. Gonzalez, "The Politics of Race," 90th Cong., 2nd sess., May 23, 1968, *Congressional Record*-Extensions of Remarks, 14852–14854.
———. Congressman Henry B. Gonzalez speaking on "Hunger in America?" 90th Cong., 2nd sess., July 31, 1968, *Congressional Record*-H 7951–7954.
———. Congressman Henry B. Gonzalez speaking on "Race Hate," 91st Cong., 1st sess., April 3, 1969, *Congressional Record*-H 2531–2532.
———. Congressman Henry B. Gonzalez speaking on "Cause for Concern," 91st Cong., 1st sess., April 15, 1969, *Congressional Record*-H 2640–2642.
———. Congressman Henry B. Gonzalez speaking on "Foundation Responsibility," 91st Cong., 1st sess., April 16, 1969, *Congressional Record*-H 2734–2735.
———. Congressman Henry B. Gonzalez speaking on "The Hate Issue," 91st Cong., 1st sess., April 22, 1969, *Congressional Record*-H 2928–2930.

————. Congressman Henry B. Gonzalez speaking on "Racism in Southwest Texas," 91st Cong., 1st sess., April 28, 1969, *Congressional Record*-H 3149–3154.

————. Congressman Henry B. Gonzalez speaking on "Foundation Responsibility," 91st Cong., 1st sess., April 29, 1969, *Congressional Record*-H 3205–3206.

————. Congressman Henry B. Gonzalez speaking on "Ford Foundation Plus San Antonio Equals Murder," 91st Cong., 1st sess., May 1, 1969, *Congressional Record*-H 3328.

————. Congressman Henry B. Gonzalez speaking on "Fraud in America," 91st Cong., 1st sess., May 27, 1969, *Congressional Record*-H 4228–4229.

————. Congressman Henry B. Gonzalez speaking on "Questions for the Commission on Civil Rights," 91st Cong., 2nd sess., May 26, 1970, *Congressional Record*-H 4806–4807.

U.S. Equal Employment Opportunity Commission. "Spanish-Surnamed American Employment in the Southwest." Washington, D.C.: U.S. Government Printing Office, 1970.

U.S. National Security Council. "The Nixon Tapes: Secret Recordings from the Nixon White House on Luis Echeverría." Transcribed by Kate Doyle. Electronic briefing book.

Woods, Sister Frances Jerome, C.D.P. *The Model Cities Program in Perspective: The San Antonio, Texas, Experience.* U.S. Congress, Subcommittee on Housing and Community Development of the Committee on Banking, Finance and Urban Affairs, House of Representatives, 97th Cong., 1st sess., January 1982, 317 pp. Washington, D.C.: U.S. Government Printing Office, 1982.

NEWSPAPER AND MAGAZINE ARTICLES

Acuña, Rodolfo. "La Generación de '68: Unfulfilled Dreams." *Corazón de Aztlán,* Vol. 1, No. 1 (January–February, 1982).

Barnes, Peter. "Chicano Power: Liberating a County." *New Republic* (December 1, 1973): 10–12.

Berry, Miguel. "Ramsey: Esfuerzo Político del Movimiento." *Magazín* Vol. 1, No. 7 (October 1972): 6.

————. "Sueño/Realidad—Las Elecciones." *Magazín* Vol. 1, No. 8 (January 1973): 27.

————. "Universidad de los Barrios Restaurant: A Step Towards Self Determination." *San Antonio Light,* ca. June 1970. Clipping in LUB scrapbook.

Calderón, Herbert. "Not Needed: Mr. Peña." Letter to the editor, *Texas Observer,* May 13, 1966, p. 16.

Cardenas, Leo. "The Impatient New Breed Wants a Change—Now." *San Antonio Express,* April 13, 1969, pp. 1A, 12A.

————. "La Raza Stirs Pride." *San Antonio Express,* April 13, 1969, p. 1A.

————. "More Militancy from Mexican-Americans Seen." *San Antonio Express,* April 19, 1969, pp. 1A, 9A.

———. "The Young Activists Lean Heavily on Grants." *San Antonio Express*, April 15, 1969, pp. 1A, 18A.

Casey, Rick. "Justice Undone: Crystal City 'Misconduct' Trial." *Texas Observer*, March 25, 1977, pp. 3–5

———. "Parting Shot." *Texas Observer*, June 3, 1977, p. 15.

Castillo, Ed. "'Most Texas Gringos,' Says MAYO Chieftain." *San Antonio Light*, April 11, 1969.

Cavada, Armando. "Raza Unida Party and the Chicano Middle Class." *Caracol* (September 1974): 17–21.

Chapa, Evey. "Mujeres por la Raza Unida." *Caracol*, Vol. 1, No. 2 (1974): 3–5, reprinted in Alma García, *Chicana Feminist Thought*, pp. 178–181.

Cotera, Marta. "Chicana Caucus." *Magazín*, Vol. 1, No. 6 (August 1972): 24–26.

———. "La Mujer Mexicana." *Magazín*, Vol. 1, No. 9 (September 1973): 30–32.

Curtis, Tom. "Raza Desunida: José Ángel Gutiérrez's Dream Turned Out to be a Nightmare." *Texas Monthly* (February 1977): 102–107, 132, 160.

Cutting, Tom. "University of the Streets: Chicano Youth Master Economics." *Texas Presbyterian* (September 1970): 5.

del Olmo, Frank. "Activist Sets Sights on Making Latinos the 'Swing Vote.'" *Los Angeles Times*, July 29, 1983, p. J3.

———. "1972 Marked Zenith, Nadir for Chicanos." *Austin American Statesman*, July 5, 1997, p. 3A.

———. "2 Latino Activists Travel Separate Paths." *Los Angeles Times*, July 29, 1983, pp. J1, J3.

"The Del Rio Manifesto, 1969." *Magazín*, Vol. 1, No. 8 (January 1973): 44.

Diehl, Kemper. "MAYO Leader Warns of Violence, Rioting." *San Antonio Express*, April 11, 1969.

Dugger, Ronnie. "Henry B. Gonzalez—Conversations with a Congressman, Part I: A Depression, King Crime, Nuclear Crime, and Economic Crime." *Texas Observer*, March 28, 1980.

———. "Henry B. Gonzalez: Conversations with a Congressman, Part II: From Revolution to the Capitol." *Texas Observer*, April 11, 1980.

———. "Henry B. Gonzalez—Conversations with a Congressman, Part III: The South Texas Cauldron." *Texas Observer*, May 9, 1980.

———. "Henry B. Gonzalez—Conversations with a Congressman, Part IV: The Establishment." *Texas Observer*, October 17, 1980.

———. "Henry B. Gonzalez—Conversations with a Congressman, Part V: The Politics of Fratricide." *Texas Observer*, December 12, 1980.

Durand, Maria. "HBG Praises Past Rival Velásquez." *San Antonio Express & News*, September 29, 1995, pp. 1A, 9A.

Gonzalez, Henry B. "Hope and Promise: Americans of Spanish Surname." *AFL-CIO American Federationist* (June 1967): 13–16.

Gutiérrez, José Ángel. "Under Surveillance." *Texas Observer*, January 9, 1985, pp. 8–13.

Harmon, Dave. "Texans Lose Their Crusading Congressman, Henry B." *Austin American Statesman*, November 29, 2000, pp. A1, A9.

"Hayes Case Won't Die." *Texas Observer*, September 3, 1976, pp. 12–14.

Hendricks, Bill. "Hooligan Menace Spreading—Eureste." *San Antonio Express*, May 20, 1980, p. 3A.

"Henry B.: 30 Years." Special issue of *Texas Observer*, December 13, 1991.

Holland, Reed, and John Moore. "The Laredo-San Antonio Heroin Wars: Drug Rings in Texas Say They're Tougher than the Mafia and They Kill to Prove It." *Texas Monthly* (August 1973).

Holley, Joe. "The Texas Farmworkers' Split." *Texas Observer*, April 17, 1981, pp. 4–8.

Hufford, Larry. "The Forces Shaping San Antonio." *Texas Observer*, April 20, 1984, pp. 24–27.

"Interview with Roel Rodriguez, RUP County Commissioner." *Magazín*, Vol. 1, No. 5 (May 1972): 1–13.

Ivins, Molly. "Listening to Henry B." *Texas Observer*, September 26, 1997, p. 20.

King, Michael. "The Legacy of Henry B." *Austin Chronicle*, December 8, 2000, p. 42.

"Little People's Day." *Texas Observer*, July 21, 1967, pp. 3–10 (re: Capt. Allee and Rangers and hearings of Senate Labor Subcommittee that included Senator Edward Kennedy).

María (pseud.), "Echeverría," *Magazín* Vol.1, No.7 (October 1972): 27–29.

Martinez, Elizabeth. "'Chingón Politics' Die Hard: Reflections on the First Chicano Activist Reunion." *Z Magazine* (April 1990): 46–50.

McCrory, James. "Gringos Gotta Go," *San Antonio Express*, April 11, 1969, p. 8F.

———. "MAYO Jefe Raps 'Gringo' Policies." *San Antonio Express*, April 11, 1969, p. 8F.

"Mexican-American Leaders Hold a Summit Conference." *Texas Observer*, January 20, 1967, pp. 11–12.

"Mexican Americans in Texas." Special issue of *Texas Observer*, December 9, 1966.

"Muniz's Magical Rise Bottoms Out: Former Gubernatorial Candidate Sentenced to Life for Drug Trafficking." *San Antonio Express*, December 17, 1994.

Peña, Albert. "Needed: A Marshall Plan for Mexican-Americans." *Texas Observer*, April 15, 1966, pp. 1, 4.

Reavis, Dick. "At War in the Mexican Jungle." *Mother Jones* (May 1978): 23–33.

Rodriguez, Javier. "Look Back in Anger." 3 parts. *San Antonio Current*, June 25, July 2, and July 9, 1987.

Ruiz Ibáñez, M. "Gang Members Tell 'Their' Story." *San Antonio Sun*, May 19, 1966.

Shaffer, Richard A. "The Angry Chicanos: Deepening Frustration of Mexican-Americans Stirs Fears of Violence: San Antonio Deemed Likely to Have

Trouble: Poverty, Bad Housing Cause Unrest." *Wall Street Journal*, June 11, 1970, pp. 1, 18.

"Texas' Sleeping Giant—Really Awake This Time?" Special issue of *Texas Observer*, April 11, 1969.

Torgenson, Dale. "Brown Beret Leader Quits, Dissolves Units." *Los Angeles Times*, November 2, 1972, p. 9A.

"Walkout in Crystal City." *Texas Observer*, January 2, 1970, pp. 5–7.

West, Richard. "An American Family." *Texas Monthly* (March 1980): 109–119, 166–181.

THESES, REPORTS, AND UNPUBLISHED PAPERS

Bruckman, Idel R. "Psychological Problems Involved for the Mexican-American in His Choice of Occupation." Preliminary report to Southwest Educational Laboratories, Austin, TX, February 24, 1968.

Cotera, Marta P. "Raza Unida Women: Ideology and Strategies on Race and Gender Issues." Unpublished paper, May 1991.

Farris, Buford. "A Comparison of Anglo and Mexican-American Stratification Systems in San Antonio, Texas, and Their Effects on Mobility and Inter-group Relations." Ph.D. dissertation, University of Texas at Austin, 1972.

Farris, Buford E., Jr., and Richard Brymer. "A Five Year Encounter with a Mexican-American Gang: Its Implications for Delinquency Theory." Paper read at the April 16, 1965, meeting of the Southwestern Sociological Association, Dallas.

———. "Types of Families in Poverty Areas." Typescript. Wesley Community Centers Youth Research Project, San Antonio, TX, May 1967.

Farris, Buford E., Jr., and William M. Hale. "Responsible Wardheelers: Neighborhood Workers as Mediators." Unpublished paper presented at the National Conference of Social Welfare, May 1966, Chicago.

Farris, Buford E., Jr., William M. Hale, and Gilbert Murillo. "The Settlement House: Caretakers, Revolutionists, or Reluctant Social Reformers?" Paper presented at the National Conference of Social Welfare, Dallas, May 1967.

Farris, Janie Salinas. "A Study of Socio-Cultural Factors in 573 Case Records of Juvenile Delinquents in Bexar County, Texas." Master's thesis, Worden School of Social Service, Our Lady of the Lake College, San Antonio, TX, 1962.

Flores, Lori. "An Unladylike Strike Fashionably Clothed: Mexican American and Anglo Women Garment Workers Against Tex-Son, 1959–1963." Senior thesis, Yale University, New Haven, CT, 2005.

Gonzalez, Antonio. "President's Report for 2000." Memorandum to board members, Southwest Voter Registration and Education Project, Los Angeles, CA, February 22, 2001.

Gonzalez, Henry B. "The Political Position of a Minority." Text of speech, St.

Mary's University, February 27, 1970. Henry B. Gonzalez Collection, Center for American History, University of Texas at Austin.

Good Samaritan Center. "Outline for In-service Training Seminar." Typescript, 5 pp., ca. 1967.

Gurnaney, Geeta Mohan. "One Candidate, Two Approaches: The Ramsey Muñiz Gubernatorial Campaigns of 1972 and 1974." Master's report, University of Texas at Austin, 1996.

Hernández, Roberto. "Silencing the Voices of Working-Class Homeboys and Homegirls in the Chicana/o Movement: The Brown Berets and the 1972 Occupation of Catalina Island." Unpublished paper, Spring 2003.

"Hispanic Voter Registration and Civic Participation in the U.S.: A Report and Analysis." Unpublished report prepared by Geto and DeMilly, Inc., for Minority Civic Association, Inc., October 1981, 200 pp.

Iscoe, Ira. "The Ethnic Preferences of Anglo, Latin-American, and Latin-American Juvenile Delinquents as Determined by Choice of Proper Names." Unpublished paper, ca. 1968.

Mexican American Neighborhood Civic Organization. "A MANCO Proposal to Model Cities Project." Typescript, 2 pp. San Antonio, TX, ca. 1968.

Nelson-Herrera, Toni. "Constructed and Contested Meanings of the Tex-Son Garment Strike in San Antonio, Texas, 1959: Representing Mexican Women Workers." M.A. thesis, University of Texas at Austin, 1997.

Olguín, Ben V. "Culture, History, and Power in South Texas: Fred Gómez Carrasco as a Floating Signifier of Nation and Identity." Latinos 2000 Conference, Hanover, NH, February 5, 2000.

Rosales, Rodolfo. "A Case Study of the Mexican American Unity Council." Master's thesis, Trinity University, San Antonio, Texas, 1972.

La Universidad de los Barrios. Grant proposal, typescript, ca. 1971.

La Universidad de los Barrios. "Economic Opportunity for Mexican American Youth." Typescript, 12 pp., February 1970.

Valdez, Raúl. "The Writing on the Wall." Unpublished report, Good Samaritan Center, 1968.

Velásquez, William C. "Report on Litigation Department." Memorandum to Board of Directors, SVREP, San Antonio, TX, January 23, 1981.

———. "Why Hispanics Didn't Vote in the Past and Are Beginning to Vote Now." Draft paper, December 1983.

Villarreal, Eduardo. "A Study of Group Processes in Two Small Natural Groups of Latin-American Adolescents." Master's thesis, Worden School of Social Service, Our Lady of the Lake College, San Antonio, TX, 1962.

Wesley Community Centers. "Multi-Service Neighborhood Center." Typescript, 2 pp., ca. 1965.

Wesley Youth Project, Wesley Community Centers. "Meaning of Mediator Role and Implications for Total Agency." Typescript, ca. 1966.

———. "Notes on Poverty." Typescript, ca. 1966.

Zamora, Emilio. "Raza Unida Party Women in Texas, 1960–2004: An Exercise in Pedagogy, Research and Historical Interpretation." Paper presented at SIGLO XXI: Research into the 21st Century, IUPLR Triennial Conference, Austin, Texas, Spring 2005.

BOOKS AND JOURNAL ARTICLES

Acuña, Rodolfo. *Occupied America: A History of the Chicanos.* 5th ed. New York: Longman, 2002.

Alinksy, Saul David. *Reveille for Radicals.* New York: Vintage Books, 1946.

———. *Rules for Radicals: A Practical Primer for Realistic Radicals.* New York: Vintage Books, 1971.

Alvarez, Rodolfo. "The Psycho-Historical and Socioeconomic Development of the Chicano Community in the United States." *Social Science Quarterly* 53 (4): 920–943.

Anglim, Chris. "Remembering San Antonio's Champion of Equality—Henry B. Gonzalez (1916–2000)." *The Scholar: St. Mary's Law Review on Minority Issues,* Vol. 3, No. 1 (Fall 2000): 2–40.

Atencio, Tomás. "La Academia de la Nueva Raza, Su Historia." *El Cuaderno,* Vol. I (1971).

———. "The Survival of La Raza Despite Social Services." *Social Casework,* Vol. 52, No. 5 (May 1971): 262–268.

Barrios, Gregg, ed. and trans. *Fred Gómez Carrasco: Memories of My Life.* Los Angeles: Posada Press, 1979.

Baylis, Thomas A. "Leadership Change in Contemporary San Antonio." In Johnson, Booth, and Harris, *The Politics of San Antonio,* pp. 95–113.

Booth, John A. "Political Change in San Antonio, 1970–82: Toward Decay or Democracy?" In Johnson, Booth, and Harris, *The Politics of San Antonio,* pp. 193–211.

Booth, John A., and David R. Johnson. "Power and Progress in San Antonio Politics, 1836–1970." In Johnson, Booth, and Harris, *The Politics of San Antonio,* pp. 3–27.

Brischetto, Robert, Charles L. Cotrell, and R. Michael Stevens. "Conflict and Change in the Political Culture of San Antonio in the 1970s." In Johnson, Booth, and Harris, *The Politics of San Antonio,* pp. 75–94.

Broyles, Yolanda. "Women in El Teatro Campesino." In National Association for Chicano Studies, *Chicana Voices: Intersections of Class, Race, and Gender.* Austin: CMAS Publications, 1986, pp. 162–187.

Buitrón, Richard A., Jr. *The Quest for Tejano Identity in San Antonio, Texas, 1913–2000.* New York: Routledge, 2004.

Cardenas, Leo. *Chicano 1969: Viva La Raza.* San Antonio, TX: Holy Cross High School, Office of Public Relations, 1969.

Carson, Clayborne. *In Struggle: SNCC and the Black Awakening of the 1960s.* Cambridge: Harvard University Press, 1981.

Chávez, Ernesto. *"¡Mi Raza Primero!" Nationalism, Identity and Insurgency in the Chicano Movement in Los Angeles, 1966–1978.* Berkeley: University of California Press, 2002.

Cotera, Marta P. "Chicana Conferences and Seminars, 1970–1975." In Alma García, ed., *Chicana Feminist Thought*, pp. 142–144.

———. "La Conferencia de Mujeres por La Raza: Houston, Texas, 1971." In Alma García, ed., *Chicana Feminist Thought*, pp. 155–157.

———. *Diosa y Hembra: The History and Heritage of Chicanas in the U.S.* Austin, TX: Statehouse Printing, 1976.

Cotrell, Charles L. *Municipal Services Equalization in San Antonio, Texas: Explorations in "Chinatown."* Southwest Urban Studies Series, Vol. 2. San Antonio, TX: St. Mary's University, 1976.

del Castillo, Adelaida. "Mexican Women in Organization." In Mora and del Castillo, *Mexican Women in the United States*, pp. 7–16.

Diehl, Kemper, and Jan Jarboe. *Henry Cisneros: Portrait of a New American.* San Antonio, TX: Corona Publishing Co., 1985.

Escobar, Edward J. "The Dialectics of Repression: The Los Angeles Police Department and the Chicano Movement, 1968–1971." *Journal of American History* (March 1993): 1483–1514.

———. *Race, Police, and the Making of a Political Identity: Mexican Americans and the Los Angeles Police Department, 1900–1945.* Berkeley: University of California Press, 1999.

Espinoza, Dionne. "'Revolutionary Sisters': Women's Solidarity and Collective Identification among Chicana Brown Berets in East Los Angeles, 1967–1970." *Aztlán* 26 (1) (Spring 2001): 17–58.

Fetzer, Philip L. *The Ethnic Moment: The Search for Equality in the American Experience.* Armonk, NY: M. E. Sharpe, 1997.

Galliher, John F., and Allynn Walker. "The Puzzle of the Social Origins of the Marihuana Tax Act of 1937." *Social Problems*, Vol. 24, No. 3 (February 1977): 367–376.

García, Alma M., ed. *Chicana Feminist Thought: The Basic Historical Writings.* New York: Routledge, 1997.

García, Ignacio M. *Chicanismo: The Forging of a Militant Ethos Among Mexican Americans.* Tucson: University of Arizona Press, 1997.

———. *United We Win: The Rise and Fall of La Raza Unida Party.* Tucson: MASRC, University of Arizona, 1989.

García, Mario T. *Memories of Chicano History: The Life and Narrative of Bert Corona.* Berkeley: University of California Press, 1994.

García, Richard A. *Rise of the Mexican American Middle Class: San Antonio, 1929–1941.* College Station: Texas A&M University Press, 1991.

Gerlach, Luther, and Virginia Hine. *People, Power, Change: Movements of Social Transformation*. New York: Bobbs-Merrill, 1970.

Gómez, Ernesto. "The Barrio Professor: An Emerging Concept in Social Work Education." In *Chicano Faculty Development Program*. New York: Council on Social Work Education, 1972.

Gómez-Quiñones, Juan. *Chicano Politics: Reality and Promise, 1940–1990*. Albuquerque: University of New Mexico Press, 1990.

———. *Mexican Students por la Raza*. Austin, TX: Relampago Books, 1978.

Gonzalez, Henry. "From Participation to Equality." In Philip L. Fetzer, ed., *The Ethnic Moment: The Search for Equality in the American Experience*. New York: M. E. Sharpe, 1997, pp. 153–173.

Graham, Henry J. *History of Texas Cavaliers, 1926–1976*. San Antonio, TX: Pvt. printing, ca. 1976.

Grebler, Leo, Joan W. Moore, and Ralph C. Guzman. *The Mexican American People: The Nation's Second Largest Minority*. New York: Free Press, 1970.

Greenberg, Stanley B. *Politics and Poverty*. New York: John Wiley and Sons, 1974.

———. *Race and State in Capitalist Development: Comparative Perspectives*. New Haven: Yale University Press, 1980.

Greider, William. *Who Will Tell the People: The Betrayal of American Democracy*. New York: Simon and Schuster, 1997.

Gutiérrez, José Ángel. *The Making of a Chicano Militant*. Madison: University of Wisconsin Press, 1998.

Gutiérrez, José Ángel, Michelle Meléndez, and Sonia Adriana Noyola. *Chicanas in Charge: Texas Women in the Public Arena*. Lanham, MD: Altamira Press, 2007.

Haney López, Ian F. *Racism on Trial: The Chicano Fight for Justice*. Cambridge, MA: Belknap Press, 2003.

Heller, Celia S. *Mexican American Youth: Forgotten Youth at the Crossroads*. New York: Random House, 1966.

Hernández, Guillermo. *Chicano Satire: A Study in Literary Culture*. Austin: University of Texas Press, 1971.

Hernández, Inés. "Testimonio de memoria." In Charles M. Tatum, ed., *New Chicana/Chicano Writing 2*. Tucson: University of Arizona Press, 1992, pp. 9–17.

Hernández, Patricia. "Lives of Chicana Activists." In Mora and del Castillo, *Mexican Women in the United States*, pp. 17–26.

Hernández-Avila, Inés. "In Praise of Insubordination, or, What Makes a Good Woman Go Bad?" In Emile Buchwald, Pamela R. Fletcher, and Marta Roth, eds., *Transforming a Rape Culture*. Minneapolis: Milkweed Editions, 1993.

Horowitz, Ruth. *Honor and the American Dream: Culture and Identity in a Chicano Community*. New Brunswick, NJ: Rutgers University Press, 1983.

Johnson, David R., John A. Booth, and Richard J. Harris, eds. *The Politics of San Antonio: Community, Progress and Power*. Lincoln: University of Nebraska Press, 1983.

Kuumba, M. Bahati. *Gender and Social Movements*. New York: Altamira Press, 2001.

López, Sonia A. "The Role of the Chicana within the Student Movement." From *Essays on La Mujer*, Los Angeles: UCLA Chicano Studies Center, 1977, pp. 16–29, reprinted in Alma García, *Chicana Feminist Thought*, pp. 100–106.

Madrid-Barela, Arturo. "In Search of the Authentic Pachuco: An Interpretive Essay." *Aztlán* 4 (1) (Spring 1973): 31–60.

Madsen, William. *Mexican-Americans of South Texas*. New York: Holt, Rinehart and Winston, 1973.

Major, Reginald. *A Panther Is a Black Cat*. New York: William Morrow and Co., 1971.

Marable, Manning. *Race, Reform and Rebellion: The Second Reconstruction in Black America, 1945–1990*. Jackson: University Press of Mississippi, 1990.

Mariscal, George. *Brown-Eyed Children of the Sun: Lessons from the Chicano Movement, 1965–1975*. Albuquerque: University of New Mexico Press, 2005.

McKinney, Wilson. *Fred Carrasco: The Heroin Merchant*. Austin, TX: Heidelberg Publishers, 1975.

McMurthy, Martin. *Mariachi Bishop: The Life Story of Patrick Flores*. San Antonio, TX: Corona, ca. 1987.

Mendoza, Louis Gerard. *Historia: The Literary Making of Chicana and Chicano History*. College Station: Texas A&M University Press, 2001.

Montejano, David. *Anglos and Mexicans in the Making of Texas, 1836–1986*. Austin: University of Texas Press, 1987.

———, ed. Chicano Politics and Society in the Late Twentieth Century. Austin: University of Texas Press, 1999.

Moore, Joan W., with Robert Garcia, Carlos Garcia, Luis Cerda, and Frank Valencia. *Homeboys: Gangs, Drugs, and Prisons in the Barrios of Los Angeles*. Philadelphia: Temple University Press, 1978.

Moore, Joan W., and Raquel Pinderhughes, eds. *In the Barrios: Latinos and the Underclass Debate*. New York: Russell Sage Foundation, 1993.

Mora, Magdalena, and Adelaida R. del Castillo, eds. *Mexican Women in the United States: Struggles Past and Present*. Occasional Paper No. 2, Chicano Studies Research Center Publications, University of California, Los Angeles, 1980.

Morales, Armando. *Ando Sangrando (I Am Bleeding): A Study of Mexican American-Police Conflict*. La Puente, CA: Perspectiva Publications, 1972.

Mujeres Activas en Letras y Cambio Social. *Chicana Critical Issues*. Berkeley, CA: Third Woman Press, 1993.

Muñoz, Carlos, Jr. *Youth, Identity, Power: The Chicano Movement*. New York: Verso Press, 1989.

National Association for Chicano Studies. *Chicana Voices: Intersections of Class, Race, and Gender*. Austin, TX: CMAS Publications, 1986.

Navarro, Armando. *The Cristal Experiment: A Chicano Struggle for Community Control*. Madison: University of Wisconsin Press, 1998.

———. *Mexican American Youth Organization: Avant-Garde of the Chicano Movement in Texas*. Austin: University of Texas Press, 1995.

Nieto Gómez, Anna, and Elma Barrera. "Chicana Encounter." *Regeneración*, Vol. 2, No. 4 (1975): 49–51.

Olguín, B. V. *La Pinta: Chicana/o Prisoner Literature, Culture, and Politics*. Austin: University of Texas Press, 2009.

Omi, Michael, and Howard Winant. *Racial Formation in the United States: From the 1960s to the 1990s*. 2nd ed. New York: Routledge, 1994.

Oropeza, Lorena. *Raza Si! Guerra No! Chicano Protest and Patriotism During the Vietnam War Era*. Berkeley: University of California Press, 2005.

Orozco, Cynthia. "Sexism in Chicano Studies and the Community." In National Association for Chicano Studies, *Chicana Voices: Intersections of Class, Race, and Gender*. Austin, TX: CMAS Publications, 1986.

Paz, Octavio. *The Labyrinth of Solitude*. New York: Grove Press, 1961.

Pesquera, Beatriz M., and Denise A. Segura. "There Is No Going Back: Chicanas and Feminism." In *Mujeres Activas en Letras y Cambio Social, Chicana Critical Issues*. Berkeley, CA: Third Woman Press, 1993, pp. 95–115.

Pulido, Laura. *Black, Brown, Yellow and Left: Radical Activism in Los Angeles*. Berkeley: University of California Press, 2006.

Rendón, Armando. *The Chicano Manifesto: The History and Aspirations of the Second Largest Minority*. New York: Collier Books, 1971.

Rogers, Mary Beth. *Cold Anger: A Story of Faith and Power Politics*. Denton: University of North Texas Press, 1990.

Romano, Octavio I. "The Historical and Intellectual Presence of Mexican-Americans." *El Grito*, Vol. II, No. 2 (Winter 1969): 32–46.

———. "Minorities, History and the Cultural Mystique." *El Grito*, Vol. I, No. 1 (Fall 1967): 5–11.

Rosales, Rodolfo. *The Illusion of Inclusion: The Untold Story of San Antonio*. Austin: University of Texas Press, 2000.

Rubel, Arthur. *Across the Tracks: Mexican-Americans in a Texas City*. Austin, TX: Hogg Foundation for Mental Health, 1966.

Ruiz, Vicki L. *From Out of the Shadows: Mexican Women in Twentieth-Century America*. New York: Oxford University Press, 1998.

Samora, Julian, Joe Bernal, and Albert Peña. *Gunpowder Justice: A Reassessment of the Texas Rangers*. Notre Dame, IN: University of Notre Dame Press, 1979.

Sánchez, David. *Expedition Through Aztlán*. La Puente, CA: Perspectiva Publications, 1978.

Sánchez-Jankowski, Martín. "Gangs and Social Change." *Theoretical Criminology* 7 (2) (2003).

———. *Islands in the Street: Gangs and American Urban Society.* Berkeley: University of California Press, 1991.

———. "Where Have the Nationalists Gone?" In David Montejano, ed., *Chicano Politics and Society in the Late Twentieth Century.* Austin: University of Texas Press, 1999.

Scuros, Mariana. "Profile: The Southwest Voter Registration Education Project." *Citizen Participation* (Medford, MA), Vol. 4, No. 1 (October 1982): 8–10, 28.

Sekul, Joseph D. "Communities Organized for Public Service: Citizen Power and Public Policy in San Antonio." In Johnson, Booth, and Harris, *The Politics of San Antonio*, pp. 175–190.

Sepúlveda, Juan A., Jr. *The Life and Times of Willie Velásquez: Su Voto Es Su Voz.* Houston: Arte Público Press, 2003.

Sherif, Carolyn W. "Self Radius and Goals of Youth in Different Urban Areas." *Social Science Quarterly*, Vol. 42, No. 3 (December 1961): 259–270.

Sherif, Muzfer, and Carolyn W. Sherif. *Reference Groups: Exploration into Conformity and Deviation of Adolescents.* New York: Harper and Row, 1964.

Sjoberg, Gideon, Richard A. Brymer, and Buford Farris. "Bureaucracy and the Lower Class." *Sociology and Social Research*, Vol. 50, No. 3 (April 1966): 325–337.

Skerry, Peter. *Mexican Americans: The Ambivalent Minority.* New York: Free Press, 1993.

Telles, Edward E., and Vilma Ortiz. *Generations of Exclusion: Mexican Americans, Assimilation, and Race.* New York: Russell Sage Foundation, 2008.

Thompson, E. P. *The Making of the English Working Class.* New York: Vintage Books, 1966.

Valdez, Avelardo. *Mexican American Girls and Gang Violence: Beyond Risk.* New York: Palgrave Macmillan, 2007.

Vásquez, Carlos. "Women in the Chicano Movement." In Mora and del Castillo, *Mexican Women in the United States.*

Vidal, Mirta. "New Voice of La Raza: Chicanas Speak Out." *International Socialist Review* (October 1971): 7–9, 31–33, reprinted in Alma García, *Chicana Feminist Thought*, pp. 21–24.

Vigil, Ernesto B. *The Crusade for Justice: Chicano Militancy and the Government's War on Dissent.* Madison: University of Wisconsin Press, 1999.

Vigil, James Diego. *Barrio Gangs: Street Life and Identity in Southern California.* Austin: University of Texas Press, 1988.

INDEX

Page numbers in *italics* indicate illustrations.